The Rise of the
Irish Linen
Industry

BANBRIDGE LINEN MARKET IN 1783

The Rise of the

Irish Linen

Industry

BY

CONRAD GILL

M.A. Cantab., Litt.D. Leeds

*Reader in Constitutional History in the University of
Birmingham ; formerly Lecturer in Economic
History in Queen's University, Belfast*

TEXTILE BOOK SERVICE
266 LAKE AVE. • P. O. BOX 178
METUCHEN, NEW JERSEY 08840

Oxford University Press, Amen House, London E.C.4

GLASGOW   NEW YORK   TORONTO   MELBOURNE   WELLINGTON
BOMBAY   CALCUTTA   MADRAS   KARACHI   LAHORE   DACCA
CAPE TOWN   SALISBURY   NAIROBI   IBADAN   ACCRA
KUALA LUMPUR   HONG KONG

FIRST PUBLISHED 1925
REPRINTED LITHOGRAPHICALLY AT THE UNIVERSITY PRESS, OXFORD
FROM SHEETS OF THE FIRST EDITION
1964

PRINTED IN GREAT BRITAIN

PREFACE

THIS study was begun at the time when I was teaching Economic History in Queen's University, Belfast; but most of the actual writing has been done in England. I have been very conscious of the difficulty of working at a distance of several hundred miles from the chief sources of information. Moreover, the best of those sources suddenly failed in the catastrophe of the Dublin Record Office. I was fortunate enough to find some valuable material in the Record Office only a few days before the use of the building was diverted from civil administration to civil war; but much more material has gone beyond recovery.

My purpose in approaching the subject was not to write a technical history—a task to which my knowledge is quite inadequate. I have kept in view three objects: in the first place, to show why the north of Ireland became the chief centre of linen manufacture in the world; secondly, to discover the part played by successive governments in this process; thirdly, to trace the change from domestic to factory production. This last object has been my main interest, for it bears the most closely on general Economic History. It includes not only the advance in methods of manufacture, but also the development of markets and credit, improvements in transport, the accumulation of capital, and the gradual emergence of new classes and new social relationships. It includes, in fact, so much of the Industrial Revolution as concerned the linen trade. And as linen was the most important Irish manufacture, the treatment of this topic must at least suggest something of the contribution made by Ireland as a whole towards that great transformation of industry and society.[1]

---

[1] Taken by itself, the history of the linen trade may perhaps suggest too much; for the population of Ireland, like that of many Continental countries, through all the changes of the last two centuries has always remained largely agricultural.

If opportunity had served I should have liked to give the inquiry a wider cast, so as to include a survey of all the chief industries in Ireland. But it has not been possible to do more than offer a brief sketch of the cotton manufacture and its influence on the linen industry. On the other hand, since Irish history cannot be properly studied in isolation, comparisons are given with the trade and policy of several foreign countries ; and a good deal of attention is paid to the economic relations of Ireland with Great Britain, the continent of Europe, and America.

I hope that this work may help to induce some other students to carry further the investigation that is begun here—to present more fully the recent history of the linen trade, and to follow the development of Irish commerce and industry in general. They will find a foundation well laid for them in the treatment of modern industry by Mr. Riordan and Mr. A. S. Moore, and in the historical works of Dr. D. A. Chart and Dr. G. O'Brien. They will find, too, much useful guidance in the studies of textile and metal trades by Professors Unwin and Daniels, Dr. H. Heaton, and Mr. T. S. Ashton, which have done so much to expand and clarify our views on the growth of the present economic system.

It is a pleasure to acknowledge the great help that has been given me by the officials of the various libraries that I have used, especially by Mr. J. Salmon, of Queen's University, Belfast, Messrs. Burgoyne and Maxwell, of the Linen Hall Library, Belfast, and several members of the staff of the National Library, Dublin. Guidance has also been willingly given to me, as it is to all students, by the officials of the Public Record Offices in Dublin and London. Messrs. Richardson, Sons & Owden, of Belfast, were kind enough to give me leave to use their early ledgers and cash book, and to allow me every facility for working with them. They have also allowed the reproduction of the plan in their possession, showing bleachgreens by the River Lagan in 1760. For leave to publish the drawing of the Belfast Linen Hall I am indebted to the

Governors of the Linen Hall Library. The late Mr. John Horner gave me valuable advice in the early stages of this work, lent me several of the eighteenth-century pamphlets and reports to which frequent reference is made below, and showed me parts of the manuscript of his book, *The Linen Trade of Europe*. Less direct, but none the less real, is my debt to Dr. J. H. Clapham, of King's College, Cambridge, whose lectures first aroused my interest in the period of the Industrial Revolution, and to Professor G. Unwin, of Manchester, whose guidance and suggestion, given in letters and conversation as well as through his published work, have been of the greatest value in my later study of the period. Those who find pleasure in good printing will appreciate, as I have done, the part played by the officials of the Clarendon Press in the preparation of this book. Finally, I wish to express my thanks to the Research Committee of the University of Birmingham for their grant towards the cost of publication.

CONRAD GILL.

The University, Birmingham,
December 1924.

CONTENTS

LIST OF ILLUSTRATIONS

The illustrations are all reproduced from photographs taken by Mr. W. A. Green, of Antrim.

I

DOMESTIC INDUSTRY

Linen and Cotton. The Irish linen trade grew up rapidly during the eighteenth century, and in common with many other trades in the British Isles it made remarkable progress after 1780. Thus its growth covered the period of the industrial revolution, and was contemporary with that of the Lancashire cotton industry. We might, therefore, expect its history to be characteristic of the time. We might expect to find enterprise in the linen and cotton industries working on similar lines, quickly adopting successive devices for mechanical spinning and weaving, applying steam power to manufacture, raising factories, concentrating production in fast-growing towns, and forming an elaborate system of commerce and credit. The expectation would be increased by the knowledge that both industries sprang up in new centres, where enterprise was free from the trammels imposed in most ancient towns by law or custom. But in fact there was a striking contrast between the two. Cotton manufacturers were pioneers of large-scale production and modern town industry, whereas linen remained until far into the nineteenth century a domestic and rural manufacture, in a sense a by-product of agriculture.

Survival of the Domestic System. Even at the present day a little cambric is woven on hand looms, and the domestic manufacture of damask is a flourishing industry, which is not unlikely to increase in the near future. I had recently an opportunity of seeing damask weavers at work in co. Armagh, under conditions which were typical of the domestic system. There were five looms in a workshop belonging to the employer. The weavers working these looms were paid by the piece, and chose their own hours of labour. Subsidiary processes, such as warp-dressing and card-punching, were done on the same premises, and there were store-rooms for raw material and finished goods. Most of the cloth was made, however, by weavers working in their own homes, who took ' chains ' of warp from the warehouse and returned two or three weeks later to deliver the webs and receive their wages.

Such domestic production is now, of course, exceptional, but it was by no means so within the memory of very many persons still living. As recently as 1877 the wages paid to hand-loom weavers of cambric in this same district were said to amount to £10,000 weekly,[1] and the receivers of these wages must have numbered many thousands. The fact is that power-loom weaving was only beginning to affect the coarse branches of manufacture a little before 1850, and at that time spinning mills driven by steam power were still a recent growth : the earliest had been in existence no more than twenty years.

But in this long period of domestic production, from the seventeenth century to the middle of the nineteenth, there was no fixity either in the volume or in the method of trade. The linen industry was only conservative in comparison with the most progressive industries in Great Britain : its conservatism was never stagnation.

In this respect its history was in keeping with that of all the chief trades in Europe ; for domestic manufacture, although its development has been very varied and irregular, has seldom implied a rigid, unchanging organization. The essence of the domestic system was production by small craftsmen, who sold either part or the whole of their goods to merchants, for disposal in distant markets—too distant to be reached directly by the craftsman himself. The system began with a movement which broke down the local economy of the medieval gild. The process of expansion continued for centuries, from a local to a national scale, from a national to an international ; and although the great majority of craftsmen still worked in their own homes, the increase of trade brought far-reaching changes in organization and social classes. Craftsmen came to depend on merchants, not only for the sale of their goods, but also for

---

[1] ' The trade of this neighbourhood is chiefly cambric, in which about 95 per cent. of the hand-loom weaving population is engaged, and the wages paid amount to about £10,000 weekly.' Letter from Dr. John Hancock, of Lurgan, to Sir Michael Hicks Beach, January, 1877. A copy of this letter was kindly lent to me by Mr. James Thomson, of Newcastle-on-Tyne, a near relative of Dr. Hancock, and of another eminent Ulsterman, Lord Kelvin.

the supply of raw material, and often for the provision of implements as well. In this way, their remuneration was gradually changed into the payment of regular wages for their labour.

Again, with the expansion of trade, the larger merchants found it increasingly useful to secure their goods in bulk, without troubling either to distribute raw material or to collect manufactures from a multitude of scattered craftsmen. Therefore the work of organizing production and collecting goods for the supply of merchants came to be undertaken by a new class, the class of industrial employers. Already, quite early in the seventeenth century, an employing class was firmly established in several trades in England, and it had a counterpart in the class of employees, permanent journeymen, who soon joined together in informal associations, the precursors of the modern trade union. Thus, in the West of England woollen trade, the industrial employer, known as a clothier, was an important and aggressive figure before 1700.[1] Even in Yorkshire, where capitalism developed more slowly, there were clothiers early in the eighteenth century, dealing, either directly or through factors, with wholesale merchants, and evidently acting as employers of the small farmers who still formed the bulk of the manufacturing class.[2]

The development, moreover, affected commerce quite as much as manufacture. The expansion of markets involved both an organization of credit and the growth of complex groups of middlemen with varying, and often overlapping, functions.[3]

Thus it is clear that great and fundamental changes took place under the cover of the domestic system ; and the further advance from domestic to factory production was really no more than a step, though an important step, in a long progress, which began far back in history and still continues.

It has often been supposed that the great textile inventions,

---

[1] The position of the clothier is clearly shown in many of the documents collected in Smith's *Memoirs of Wool*. In Professor G. Unwin's *Industrial Organization* (chap. vii) there is a suggestive account of the development of an employing class in several industries during the seventeenth century.

[2] *Letters of Joseph Holroyd and Sam Hill*, edited by Dr. H. Heaton. See also the same writer's *Yorkshire Woollen and Worsted Industries*, pp. 295–301.

[3] Useful information on this point is given in Dr. R. B. Westerfield's *Middlemen in English Business*.

together with the use of steam power, suddenly opened a flood-gate of social change, and in half a century replaced a population of independent craftsmen with a proletariat of ill-paid factory workers. But recent investigation has done much to modify this view. It has shown that the movement was by no means a sudden revolution. Most of the great inventions came about in response to an urgent demand. Most of them could never have been exploited at all if there had not been ready to hand an organization of national and international markets, an elaborate provision of credit, an accumulation of capital, and a system of employment on a large scale for wages. Indeed, the very rapidity of the changes was only made possible by a long and thorough preparation.

All these aspects of domestic production, and of the transition to the factory system, are well illustrated by the history of the Irish linen trade ; and the main purpose of this study is to trace the development, during the eighteenth and nineteenth centuries, from a simple form of domestic industry to the modern system of steam power, joint-stock enterprise, and world-wide commerce. But the changes were in general the result of an increase of trade, and in order to gain a clear idea of the course of development, we need to know something of the conditions of growth as well as the methods of organization. In the first place we must inquire why Ireland should suddenly become, in the eighteenth century, the seat of a flourishing linen manufacture, which grew so rapidly that within the century the volume of its exports increased a hundredfold. Some explanation must also be given of the fact that a large proportion of this increase took place in the northern counties. Further, in considering the causes of growth, we must examine the effect of governmental policy. The history of economic policy during the eighteenth century is to a considerable extent a record of mistakes and failures—and measures relating to the linen trade were no exception to the rule. Nevertheless this subject is interesting and instructive, because at a time when several Irish trades were undoubtedly crushed down by English colonial policy, the linen trade was specially exempted, and even encouraged, by the British Government, and throughout the eighteenth century was treated with peculiar favour by the

Irish Parliament. Hence the efforts, both legislative and administrative, to promote the linen manufacture offer an excellent illustration of the commercial policy of the time.

The discussion of these topics will carry the history down to about the year 1825. In conclusion a short survey will be given of developments during the next thirty or forty years, when the domestic system, after a long continuance, was swept away by the combined force of steam power, steam transport, and a reorganization of credit.

II

GROWTH AND LOCALIZATION

Early Trade. As the Irish linen trade was largely a growth of the eighteenth century we need not pay much attention to its earlier history, beyond noticing that there was before 1700 some foundation upon which enterprise could build. Flax-growing and linen manufacture were ancient occupations of the Irish people ; but the manufacture must have been almost entirely that of the narrow cloth, twelve or fourteen inches in width, known as ' bandle ' linen, for which there was very little sale outside of Ireland,[1] and the chief export trade was undoubtedly in yarn. In a statute of 1542 it is mentioned, in regard to the trade of Manchester, that ' many strangers, as well of Ireland as of other places within the realm, have resorted to it with linen yarn, wool and necessary wares for making of cloth, and have used to trust the poor inhabitants which had not ready money to pay, until they might make cloth and sell the same to pay their creditors '.[2] Three years later Leland described Liverpool as a centre of this trade, although at that time a good deal of it must have passed through Chester. ' Yrisch merchants ', he said, ' cum much thither, and moch yrisch yarn that Manchester men do by there.'[3] Most of the Irish traders who brought yarn to Lancashire and advanced it as capital for small manufacturers came probably from Drogheda and Dublin. Drogheda was a staple town in the fourteenth century and would therefore be likely to have some substantial merchants.[4] It could draw supplies from the ' yarn counties ' of the middle and west of Ireland. But flax grown in Ulster—always a considerable amount—would come from the northern districts by Derry,

---

[1] For the widespread manufacture of bandle cloth and its unsuitability for export, see R. Stephenson, *Journal, passim.* It was laid down in the regulating Act of 1705 that all cloth sold for export should be at least 22½ inches wide. According to Stephenson (*Inquiry*, p. 65) the minimum width in demand abroad was 25 inches. Sir Richard Cox (*Letter to T. Prior*, p. 18) said that the bandle was originally a measure of two feet : if he was right the cloth was curiously misnamed.

[2] 33 Henry VIII, c. 16. [3] *Itinerary*, quoted by Warden, p. 389
[4] Gross, *Gild Merchant*, vol. i, pp. 141, 147.

Carrickfergus or other ports, and by Carlingford and Dundalk from the southern.[1]

This export of yarn continued throughout the eighteenth century, and continues, in fact, to the present day. But before 1700 it was accompanied by only a very small trade in linen cloth.[2] Some of the yarn sent from Ireland to Manchester was returned in the form of woven linen.[3] If there was any appreciable export of cloth before 1640 the connexion was lost in the troubles of the next two decades. In 1665 the export of linen was valued at £590.[4] However, in the more settled period which followed there was a general increase of trade, which was not seriously or permanently set back by the campaign of 1689–91. Within four years the export of linen was nearly doubled, and by the beginning of the next century the trade was well established, with an annual export amounting to three or four hundred thousand yards, and valued at about £20,000.[5]

Strafford's Policy. Two statesmen, Strafford and Ormondé, have generally been given the chief credit for this advance. Strafford is held to have founded the industry,[6] and Ormonde to have set it on the road to prosperity. But this belief, although

---

[1] Carrickfergus was the administrative centre of co. Antrim and the chief port on the Antrim coast ; but as it was not very conveniently situated with regard to the flax-growing districts, the traffic would probably be shared with other ports such as Larne and Donaghadee. Dundalk was an old staple town (Gross, vol. i, p. 19). Carlingford, as its monastery, castle and fortified warehouses show, was a place of considerable trading importance in the Middle Ages, though it had no staple. In the second half of the eighteenth century it suffered, as did Carrickfergus, from the growth of a rival port farther inland—in this case the port of Newry.

[2] Cf. Sir Wm. Temple's evidence, ' Linen yarn is a commodity very proper for this country but made in no great quantities in any parts beside the north nor anywhere into linen in any great degree or sorts fit for the better uses at home or exportation abroad.' (*Essay upon the Advancement of Trade in Ireland*, pp. 113–14, a letter written in 1673 from Brussels in answer to an inquiry from Essex, the Lord Lieutenant.)

[3] Roberts, *The Treasure of Traffike*, 1641, p. 32. The manufacturers of Manchester ' buy yarne of the Irish in great quantity, and weaving it returne the same againe in Linen into Ireland to sell '.

[4] Scott, *Joint-Stock Companies*, iii. 98.

[5] In 1701, a comparatively bad year, the estimated value was only a little over £14,000 (Dobbs, p. 353 ; Murray, p. 115) ; but by 1705 it had risen to £24,000, and the quantity had risen in the same years from 188,000 yards to 520,000 (McCall, p. 13).

[6] e.g. Gardiner, vol. viii, p. 126 : ' The humble beginnings of the great flax culture of the North of Ireland owed their origin to him.' Lewis (*Topographical Dictionary*, i. 534) states that the linen trade ' owes its extension chiefly to the Earl of Strafford '.

it reflects their objects, is not in keeping with their real achievements. Strafford, in a fashion characteristic of seventeenth-
century bureaucracy, decided that a linen industry should be
developed in Ireland and the export trade in woollen cloth
prevented. As a means of promoting the growth of linen
manufacture he imported some spinning-wheels and half a dozen
looms from abroad, brought some workers also from France and
Belgium, and bought Dutch flax-seed—perhaps a ton of it
altogether. In these undertakings he himself invested and lost
£30,000. To raise the standard of work he gave orders that
implements of the type which he had imported should be used
universally, i. e. that all weavers should forsake their bandle
looms and buy looms of twice the width ; and that all women
who span should use Dutch wheels instead of distaffs. His
policy was conceived in exactly the same spirit as James I's
distribution of mulberry trees or his attempt to destroy the
Adventurers' trade in unfinished woollen cloth ; and Strafford's
measures, like James's, were bound from the outset to fail.
There is no evidence that they had any permanent effect at all
on Irish industry.[1]

Ormonde's Enterprise. Ormonde, a generation later, set to
work in a more reasonable manner, and without any attempt at
coercion. Through the agency of his friend Sir William Temple
he too brought workers from the Netherlands and formed colonies
of them at Chapelizod, near Dublin, and at his own town of
Carrick-on-Suir. By an Act of 1662 special privileges were
allowed to Protestant immigrants. In 1666 protective duties
were established for the benefit of the linen trade, and prizes
offered for flax-cultivation and weaving. Ormonde also introduced spinning-wheels from Holland.[2]

But he could hardly lay claim to much greater success than
Strafford's. There was ' a general neglect in the execution '
of his measures. The regulations were not enforced, because
' common guilt had made the penalties impracticable '. For
lack of candidates few prizes were awarded : in some counties

---

[1] His most important service to Irish trade was probably the suppression
of piracy.

[2] Carte, *Life of Ormonde,* ii. 85, 342 ; McCall, p. 3 ; Horner, pp. 18–22 ;
Wakefield, *Account of Ireland,* i. 681 ; Murray, p. 114.

there was only one candidate, in others none.[1] In the parts of the country to which his efforts—like those of most other statesmen concerned with industry—were chiefly directed, the linen trade never flourished.[2] On the other hand it grew unexpectedly and without special encouragement in the north—a fact of cardinal importance, which will engage our attention at a later stage. If the work of the seventeenth-century administrators had any permanent result it was in developing the use of spinning-wheels, and so increasing the output of yarn. But even this matter is by no means certain. It is not known to what extent spinning-wheels were used in Ireland before the middle of the seventeenth century. It is known that their introduction was a gradual process which was still continuing a hundred years later.[3] And although the ' low Irish wheel ' was almost certainly copied from the Dutch, another type, the ' castle wheel ', a very efficient implement still used in the woollen industry, was widely adopted, without any help or favour from the Government.[4]

We must not, then, take the will for the deed, and assume that because Strafford and Ormonde wished to promote the linen industry, and made some slight efforts in that direction, the advance which actually took place was due to their initiative. There were factors of far greater importance : constant enterprise on the part of manufacturers and traders, and conditions, both of industry and of trade, which allowed this enterprise to prosper.

[1] Temple, *Essay*, p. 115.

[2] I have been unable to find any sign of manufacturing activity in Chapelizod or Carrick in the early years of the eighteenth century. There is, however, an interesting record of a concern in Chapelizod which probably owed its origin to Ormonde's favour, and certainly owed its collapse to the disturbance of 1690. Alderman Christopher Lovett, of Dublin, had been granted by the Government, in 1677, the lease of a bleachyard for twenty-one years, together with stock, valued at £1,200, including twenty looms for linen and others for tapestry. The equivalent of this stock was to be returned at the end of the lease. After Lovett's death the bleachworks were managed by his wife. But she suffered severely in 1690 because, as a supporter of William III, she refused to supply the Irish and French armies. She claimed that her goods had been seized and sold to these armies by one Broomfield, a Quaker. It is to be hoped that this unquakerly action was punished, or that the accusation was untrue. But the Government, at any rate, admitted her claim, and she was released by letters patent from her contract (*State Papers, Domestic*, 1691-2, pp. 321-2).

[3] The fact is clearly shown by the constant efforts of the Linen Board to extend the use of wheels.

[4] Horner, p. 18, and illustrations with notes on pp. 19, 20.

Expansion of Trade. Before we examine the causes it will be well to have in mind a few figures which give a rough idea of the result—the growth of trade between 1700 and 1750. The following table shows the number of yards of plain linen cloth exported from Ireland in every fifth year : [1]

1705	.	.	520,000	1730	.	.	4,136,203
1710	.	.	1,688,574	1735	.	.	6,821,439
1715	.	.	2,153,120	1740	.	.	6,627,771
1720	.	.	2,437,984	1745	.	.	7,171,963
1725	.	.	3,864,987	1750	.	.	11,200,460

These figures indicate a healthy trade, growing steadily for about forty years and increasing fast towards the middle of the century, when technical processes were much improved, workers had become skilled in making a variety of cloths suitable for consumption abroad, and markets were well organized. The figures suggest, too, that Irish traders found from the beginning a ready sale in England for their cloth. What, then, were the circumstances which favoured the growth of this trade ?

Favouring Circumstances. In the first place Ireland is well fitted in the matters of soil and climate for flax production and linen manufacture. Flax grows well in many parts of the country. The moist atmosphere undoubtedly helps spinning, weaving, and bleaching alike, and the abundance of rivers was an important asset in the days when water power was used to drive machinery in the bleachworks.[2]

Secondly, flax crops can be grown remuneratively on very small holdings ; and flax was grown, both for home manufacture and for the sale of yarn, before the export trade in cloth developed. Thus, linen could readily be made in Ireland, and it will be shown later that early in the eighteenth century there were many people in the country competent to produce good cloth. An export trade would be likely to spring up if there were a reasonably strong demand for linen goods in England and abroad. The demand was forthcoming. Before cotton manu-

---

[1] The figure for 1705 is from McCall (p. 13) ; that for 1710 is from Miss Murray (p. 129). For details of exports after 1710 see the table given below, Appendix II.

[2] Cf. Charley, p. 104 : ' Ireland possesses the best climate in the world for bleaching, and it is this advantage—this gift of nature—that has gradually given to her, and secured to her still, so high a position in this branch of commercial industry.'

facture became abundant, linen was much more necessary than it has been since ; and as the wealth of England steadily grew and trade with Europe and the colonies increased, there was a growing demand in England for linen, both for home consumption and for export.[1] The market was supplied partly by imports from the Continent, especially of fine cloths (in times of peace) from France and the Netherlands, and cloths of medium or coarse quality from Silesia and Westphalia.[2] A considerable amount— perhaps a third of the total quantity sold in the English markets— was made in England : the rest in Scotland and Ireland.

English Manufacture. If it had been found worth while to pay so much attention to linen manufacture, there was no inherent reason why almost the whole English market should not have been supplied at home. Flax could be grown well in most parts of the country ; and experience showed that manufacture as well could be carried on efficiently in many districts—notably in Durham, Yorkshire, Lancashire, and Somerset. Indeed, although the linen industry was never prominent in England, it was actually greater than either the Scottish or Irish during at least the first half of the eighteenth century. In a parliamentary report of 1756 it was stated that about 30,000,000 yards were annually imported into England from the Continent ; 12,200,000 yards from Ireland ; and 12,000,000 yards from Scotland. At the same time about 25,800,000 yards were manufactured in England.[3] The home consumption in Ireland may have been about equal to the export. Thus it appears that in 1756 the total production in England was still rather greater than that of Ireland.

However, there was a steadily growing market for Scottish and Irish linen, because the competition was never as serious as it would have been if the manufacture had been fully exploited in England. There are obvious reasons for this comparative slackness. Although flax would grow well in England there

---

[1] The following figures (from a table in Horner's *Linen Trade of Europe,* pp. 231, 232) give some idea of the growth of export. They show the export from England of both English and Irish cloth :—1743, 93,700 yds. ; 1750, 1,330,900 yds. ; 1760, 3,766,200 yds. ; 1770, 5,924,000 yds.

[2] A large part of the imports from Germany consisted of the ' Germany narrow ' cloths. See Report of H. of C. Committee, 1751, *Reports*, vol. ii, p. 301.   [3] Quoted by Horner, p. 233.

were other more urgent uses for the land, to meet the ever-growing demand for foodstuffs. Moreover the flax-crop, as we have already noted, was specially suited to small, enclosed holdings. Such holdings were common all over Ireland, but their number in England was small and grew still smaller as the century advanced. For this reason a great proportion of the flax and yarn used in English manufacture had to be imported.[1]

Further, capital and enterprise found a readier outlet, first in the woollen industry, and later in cotton manufacture, which soon replaced much of the production of linen in Lancashire. Even though merchants were prepared to buy English linen, workers could not readily be found, for both wool and cotton offered them a better income. Therefore in the linen trade Scotland and Ireland had a relatively open field which they exploited with success.

Foreign Competition. There was still competition from the Continent to be reckoned with ; but this rivalry too had limits. It was restricted, in the first place, by tariffs which gave a strong preference to Irish trade ; for, as a part of the famous bargain of 1698, plain linen from Ireland was admitted free of duty into England. Again, in the early years of the eighteenth century, when the Irish trade was struggling to gain a foothold, France and Belgium were cut off by war from the English market.[2] The French trade had also lost heavily by the departure of Huguenot manufacturers and merchants. Belgium had had since at least the sixteenth century a substantial trade in fine linens.[3] But its growth had also been checked by policy. The closing of the Scheldt was a serious blow, for Antwerp had been the central market for linen, and the Scheldt had been the chief outlet. Moreover, the Hapsburg rule had been no more fortunate for the Austrian Netherlands than for Spain. The local jealousies, which had ruined the old urban manufacture of wool, still

---

[1] A large amount came from Russia. See tables given by Horner, op. cit., pp. 495–504.

[2] The difficulty of trade with cloth finishers in Holland, the delays due to the convoy system, and the actual losses from privateering, are vividly shown in Joseph Holroyd's letters, written in 1707–8. (Heaton, *Letter Books of J. Holroyd and S. Hill.*)

[3] Some well-known makes of cloth took their names from Flemish towns, e.g. kentings from Ghent, and diapers from Ypres.

expressed themselves in a clumsy system of *octrois*, from which Belgium suffered at least as severely as many parts of Germany. Goods passing, for instance, from Ostend to Charleroi paid duty ten times.[1] Therefore, in spite of the high quality of the cloth and Belgium's excellent position for trade, the linen manufacture never developed during the eighteenth century as it would have done under a freer system. In 1800 the output of linen from Flanders appears to have been only about 10,000,000 yards—certainly not more than a quarter of the output of Ulster.[2]

Holland has been mentioned as the chief centre in Europe for bleaching and finishing, and as a source of the finest flax-seed. But although Dutch farmers and manufacturers grew flax and finished the cloth produced in other lands, they were not much concerned with the intermediate processes. There was a great variety of industries in Holland, and there, as in England, a profitable woollen industry, the main occupation of Leyden, stood in the way of a large development of the linen trade. As the Dutch people had a wide freedom of choice they naturally chose the best-paying parts of the linen industry, and left to others the comparatively ill-paid work of weaving.[3]

Dutch enterprise, indeed, was rather an advantage than a handicap to Ireland. Just as manufacturers in England, potters and iron founders for example, improved their methods by copying Dutch models, so Irish flax-growers, wheelwrights, loom-makers, and bleachers learnt part, at any rate, of the arcana of their craft from Holland. Moreover, Dutch merchants probably did much more than either Strafford or Ormonde to lay the foundations of the Irish export trade. Even in the early part of the seventeenth century, while the Eighty Years' War was still in progress, many of them came to trade in Ireland. For the most part they brought manufactures and took back raw material ; but it is quite likely that they supplied both flax-seed and implements for linen manufacture. It would be to their interest to encourage manufacture, and to give good credit, in order to secure cheap Irish cloth for bleaching in Holland.[4]

[1] Lewinski, p. 22.   [2] ibid., p. 27.
[3] Goldberg, *Nederlandsche Textielindustrie*, pp. 91–3, 138, 139.
[4] Hill, *Plantation in Ulster*, pp. 182–3, 363. Hill gives several interesting notes on Dutch enterprise. Maximilian van der Lever, ' who, like most of his nation, was diligent and industrious to improve the commodities of this

Some of the north German states, such as Silesia, Saxony, and Brunswick, were more serious competitors. Their ' Germany narrow ' cloths and creas (or crash) were similar to some of the coarse cloth produced in Antrim, Derry, and Tyrone ; Saxony and Ireland were rivals in the manufacture of damask and diapers.[1] Moreover, both Germany and Ireland developed during the eighteenth century a linen trade with Spain and America ; and as London was the focus of this export trade from both countries, there was often keen competition in the London markets.[2] However, it was not a case of a new Irish manufacture struggling against a well established trade from the German states. The German export trade, like the Irish, was very small in 1700, and it was hampered by both natural and artificial difficulties of transport. Goods going, for instance, from Silesia to western Europe by way of the Baltic had to pay almost prohibitive tolls before they reached the sea, and land carriage to Hamburg was very expensive.[3] At the end of the century the export of linen from all Prussian lands, including Silesia,

kingdom ', proposed to Sir John Davis, the Attorney-General, to establish a colony on the shores of Lough Erne. Davis answered : ' A plantation of the Dutch in this place will be a great encouragement to the undertakers (i. e. the English and Scottish colonists) ; for by their industry all the commodities will be wrought and vented and the lake will be so full of boats and barks that they will be a great strength to all the civil inhabitants round about.' In 1604 there had been a similar project to plant Dutchmen by Lough Foyle, ' whose trades and example may draw the people to grow civil '. When the Livery Companies of London were considering the plantation of co. Derry, Sir Thomas Phillips, who had charge of the negotiations in Ireland, wrote in his *Motives and Reasons*, addressed to the City merchants, that the traffic from London to Ireland would soon decay, unless a closer connexion were formed, ' by reason of the Dutchmen's trade thither, who, by reason of their small charge in shipping, are able to afford their wares cheaper than those who bring it from London '. He mentioned that the Dutch sold in Ireland ' wines, brandy, &c., salt, kersies, broadcloth, starch, grocery, tobacco, gunpowder, hops, fowling-pieces, paper, knives, gloves, tape, hard and soft wax, felts, glasses, earthenware, pewter, pins, points, laces, ribbons, combs, nails, drugs, holland, cambric, lawn, thread, madder, indigo, brass and iron pots and other vessels, playing and working cards '. They took in return hides, cattle, tallow, and fish. ' These the merchants of Ireland do mostly give in truck, for there are little monies stirring.' They also dealt in timber, and Phillips, who had a large interest in deforestation, was anxious to drive them out of competition.

[1] Young (*Tour*, p. 114) said that the Germans were competitors in dowlas and diapers, but that they could not rival the Irish fine linens.

[2] Stephenson, *Inquiry*, p. 28.

[3] Oddy, *European Commerce*, p. 413. The greater part of Silesian linens destined for western Europe went, apparently, to Hamburg and thence to London.

was less than the export from Ireland ; and a considerable part
of the Prussian trade would go to districts with which Ireland
had little or no traffic.[1] Brunswick and Westphalia had comparatively easy access, through Hamburg, to foreign markets, but
they had no great volume of trade.[2]

Russia, the only other country with a large interest in the
linen industry, was not so much a competitor as an invaluable
source of raw material, both seed and flax. Apparently the only
competition of any importance from Russia was in sheetings.[3]

Therefore, in the early years of the eighteenth century, there
was great scope for the growth of the Irish linen manufacture.
The country was closely connected with England and Holland,
the two great distributing centres ; it was not troubled with local
restrictions on trade ; the climate was suited to manufacture ;
there was a good water-supply for bleaching ; the peasantry could
supply themselves with a certain amount of flax, and could carry
on spinning and weaving as subsidiary occupations at a very
small cost. The conditions of success were satisfied by Scotland
and Ireland, better perhaps than by any other country ; and in
both Scotland and Ireland the linen trade became firmly established during the first quarter of the eighteenth century.

Scottish Pioneers. But favourable conditions could not cause
the industry to grow unless enterprise were forthcoming to take
advantage of them. The peasantry could hardly be expected on
their own account to prepare goods for markets overseas. However, there were in Ireland certain merchants who could both
guide the manufacture and supply the necessary capital. It has
been suggested that the Dutch may have had a share in this
work.[4] A larger share was in the hands of Scottish settlers,

---

[1] Warden, p. 268. The value of linen exported from Prussia in 1799 is
given by Warden as about £2,000,000. The exports from Ireland in the same
year were worth about £2,500,000.   [2] Oddy, p. 423.

[3] Young, *Tour*, u.s. There was very little export of linen cloth from Russia
during the eighteenth century. According to Mavor (*Econ. Hist. of Russia*,
vol. i, p. 545) the peasants made cloth for local consumption, and the factories
worked for the Government.

[4] Some Irish manufacture during the seventeenth century may have been
promoted from Lancashire. Just as Flemish manufacturers settled at various
times in England, so linen workers from Lancashire may have carried their
enterprise back to the districts from which raw material was supplied. In the
eighteenth century there was certainly some migration of this kind, but I have
found no evidence of it before 1780.

especially in Antrim and Down. A great number of Scotsmen had come to these counties during the sixteenth and seventeenth centuries, not as landowners enjoying the profits of confiscated estates, but as peaceful colonists, bringing with them capital, and a knowledge of agriculture, trade, or handicraft. Many of them ' entered into [the linen trade] with spirit, and manufactured cloth themselves '.[1] Although it may not be strictly true that the linen manufacture—i. e. the export trade— ' began among the Scots in the north of Ireland ',[2] they were at least among the pioneers of the industry.

Huguenot Settlements. One circumstance which certainly favoured the growth of trade, above all of the linen trade, in Ireland was the settlement of Huguenots there. Some of them came slightly before 1700,[3] others during the next ten or twenty years ; and their presence must have given strength to the industry at a critical time when the all-important overseas trade was just beginning to develop. They brought with them both personal and material wealth. They knew the best methods of flax-culture. They could teach fine spinning. They had the most efficient looms, adapted to the weaving of cambric, damask, and the finest broadcloths. They had had experience of bleaching, partly gained at Haarlem. They were acquainted with the methods of trade in highly organized markets, and the kinds of cloth most in demand in other countries. Many of them were men of substance who were able to invest capital, and thus to supply to some extent the greatest of all the economic needs of Ireland.

Louis Crommelin and the Royal Corporation. Their leader, Louis Crommelin, belonged to a family which had been connected with the linen trade for several generations and had prospered in it.[4] He himself had a flourishing business and owned a large amount of land. He was fortunate and shrewd enough to anticipate the Revocation of the Edict of Nantes, and so had time to sell his property and remove in comfort to Holland before the storm broke. Holland, however, was not a very satisfactory home for Huguenot linen manufacturers, because

---

[1] Warden, p. 390.   [2] Macpherson, *Annals*, vol. ii, p. 559.
[3] McCall, p. 4. McCall, probably by a misprint, gives the date of Crommelin's arrival as 1690 ; it was really 1698.
[4] Smiles, *Huguenots*, p. 296.

weavers were hard to find, and spinners, as Crommelin himself pointed out, could not produce so fine yarns as those of France and Belgium. Therefore several of the Huguenots were glad to move to the British Isles, where there was promise of a free and rapid growth of trade. Many had preceded them, some to carry on industries, such as silk-weaving or hatting, in England; others to settle among Scottish Calvinists; others again had gone to Ireland, where the law gave them special protection, to make a living as silk-weavers in Dublin, as merchants or professional men in various southern towns, or, if they could afford it, to acquire land and mix with the gentry.[1]

But most of the linen dealers went to the north of Ireland, where they found already the nucleus of an export trade, and a congenial atmosphere of Puritanism. Louis Crommelin, though not the first in point of time, was the most prominent member of their circle. His contract with the Government is famous—perhaps too famous; for although he did much more for the linen trade than either Strafford or Ormonde, he too has been credited with more than his real achievement.[2] As part of the bargain between the English and Irish Governments in 1698, for the discouragement of woollen manufacture and the promotion of the linen industry in Ireland, Crommelin was invited to form a Society, or Royal Corporation, for carrying on the linen trade. His concern was a curious mixture of public patronage and private enterprise, rather like the structure of a Stuart monopoly without the monopolist's patent. Crommelin undertook to supply, on behalf of himself and his friends, capital to the amount of £10,000 in the form of machinery and raw material. He also promised to spread technical knowledge among the Irish people. In return he was to receive interest from the Government at the rate of eight per cent., a salary of £300 a year for himself, and grants for the salaries of three assistants and for a minister to serve the Huguenot community.[3] This contract, first made by William III in 1700, was renewed in the following year by Anne, in more general terms. Interest at eight per cent. was offered

---

[1] Smiles, op. cit., chap. xvii.

[2] e.g. McCall (p. 4) says that Crommelin introduced the spinning-wheel into Ireland. What he actually did is explained below, p. 19.

[3] Scott, *Joint-Stock Companies*, iii, 102; McCall, p. 11, Smiles, p. 297.

for ten years to any one who brought looms into Ireland, but in practice this offer meant a continuance of Crommelin's grant.[1]

There had previously been several projects of joint-stock trading in Irish linen. But they had all failed, and Crommelin, who had seen similar schemes on the Continent come to grief, wisely refused an ordinary joint-stock venture. The Corporation consisted of a number of partners who undertook to bring machinery to Ireland, practise manufacture themselves, and teach the processes to others. The so-called interest paid to them was in effect a bounty, or an insurance against risk. The Huguenots were free to make whatever profit they could by their own trading, but they were expected to give up some time to technical instruction as well. The funds for distribution were entrusted to a committee of twenty,[2] which continued to serve until 1711, when it was replaced by the Board of Trustees. Crommelin's salary was continued until his death in 1727.[3]

Crommelin seems to have taken seriously his position as Overseer of the Royal Linen Manufacture and to have done his work well. He himself wrote a small book, giving clearly and concisely and with the help of good illustrations, particulars of all the processes from flax-growing to bleaching.[4] His assistants had similar work to that of the ' itinerant men ' employed later by the Linen Board, or of instructors under the Department of Agriculture at the present day. It is not known how much of this work was done by Crommelin himself. He had his own bleachgreen, and his teaching would probably consist largely of the training of apprentices.[5] The Linen Board, in recommending

[1] Horner, p. 29. A good reason for this change is shown in the statement, made in 1702, that Crommelin's investment had fallen far short of £10,000 (*State Papers, Domestic*, 1702–3, p. 331). But as he had introduced several looms the Government agreed to pay him interest for them. Some of the looms were valued at £30 each, others at £50. These figures were, of course, much higher than the market price of the looms : allowance was probably made for the cost of other machinery, of buildings, and of trading capital, necessary to set and keep the looms at work.

[2] ibid., p. 332. The committee included the Lord Lieutenant, the Primate, the Chancellor and Chief Justices, and several Members of Parliament.

[3] Smiles, *Huguenots*, p. 297.

[4] *Essay on the Improving of the Hempen and Flaxen Manufactures in the Kingdom of Ireland*, 1705.

[5] His bleachgreen was at Hilden, near Lisburn (McCall, p. 9). Cf. grants made to James Quin of Carlow in 1711 and 1712, of eight per cent. on capital and a salary of £20 a year for teaching eight persons to weave damask (*Precedents and Abstracts*, p. 2).

the continuance of his grant after 1712, made this statement :
' The said Crommelin and colony have been very serviceable and
greatly instrumental in the improving and propagating the flaxen
manufacture in the north part of this kingdom ; and . . . the
perfection to which the same is brought in that part of the
country is very much owing to the skill and industry of the said
Crommelin.' [1]

We may accept this testimony as a fair statement of Crommelin's services ; but it is difficult to estimate the work of the
Huguenots as a whole. From their mere numbers it is clear that
they must have had great influence. Crommelin brought seventy
companions with him, and fifty others came later.[2] The total
strength of the Huguenot colony in Ulster was estimated at five
hundred families.[3] This accession of highly skilled workers and
experienced traders, in a district in which only a few thousand
weavers (working moreover for only a part of their time) were
making cloth suitable for export, could not fail to give a great
impulse to the industry.[4]

Their influence was not wholly good. Crommelin, for example,
tried, fortunately in vain, to compel the Irish people to use
a French spinning-wheel, driven by hand instead of a treadle,
and therefore intermittent in its action.[5] The Huguenots in
general had by no means a single eye to the public good ; in
fact they tried to secure by law a partial monopoly for themselves. Their influence is seen in the regulations of 1705 and
1709, prescribing a five years' apprenticeship, followed by two
years' service as a journeyman, for every master weaver, but
exempting foreign Protestants from any such restriction.[6] As
the trade could be learnt thoroughly in far less than seven years,
these measures were plainly meant to limit the number of workers
and prevent Irishmen from setting up as independent craftsmen
until they had served an apprenticeship to Huguenot employers.

---

[1] *Precedents and Abstracts*, p. 4.
[2] ibid., p. 3.   [3] McCall, p. 26.
[4] The annual export of linen from the whole of Ireland at the beginning of
the century was only three or four hundred thousand yards. In 1701, a bad
year, it fell to 188,000 yards (Dobbs, *Essay*, p. 353). Such quantities only
implied the work of a few thousand weavers in the whole country.
[5] Crommelin, *Essay*, pp. 26, 27, Horner, pp. 30–4. The more efficient
' low Irish ' and ' castle ' wheels were already widely used.
[6] 4 Anne, c. 3 ; 8 Anne, c. 12.

The acts could only have been enforced if most weavers had
lived in towns, as the government expected them to do ; but
there is evidence that they caused some trouble.[1]

Against this disservice we must set the work done by the
Huguenots in teaching advanced methods of manufacture and
improving the reputation of Irish linen, although we cannot
measure the extent of this work.   There is no question that the
general quality of Irish cloth improved as its volume increased.
We may take as evidence the statement made in 1737 by Huey,
a London merchant, that Irish linen was at that time much better
in quality than it had been when he began to deal in it twenty-
five years before.[2]   The Joncourts, who were Huguenots, were
among the earliest manufacturers of cambric in Ireland ; [3] and
if other Huguenots did not actually found the damask trade they
certainly helped to promote it, and to encourage the spinning of
yarns suitable for the higher branches of manufacture.   For the
rest, they probably had a large share in setting up the brown
linen markets and the specialized trades of bleachers and weavers,
which were organized round about the year 1720.   Either as
working weavers or as drapers most of the Huguenots had been
used to attending markets on the Continent, and they could
appreciate the advantage of a good system of marketing.   Many
of them were drapers or bleachers, and it was probably as
organizers of trade and manufacture, rather than actual makers
of linen cloth, that they chiefly affected the industry of Ulster.

Localization of Manufacture.   Although small groups of
Huguenots were settled sparsely in other parts of the country,

[1] In 1722 a number of northern weavers sent a complaint through the
agency of the Bishop of Dromore, to the Linen Board, against the irksome
apprenticeship regulations (*Precedents and Abstracts*, p. 59).   In the following
year Parliament reduced the apprenticeship to four years (10 Geo. I, c. 2).
But the spread of country manufacture made any strict apprenticeship
difficult to enforce.   In a statute of 1727 it was stated that apprentices spent
much of their time in farm work ' by means whereof, such apprentices, when
they have served their time, are in great measure ignorant of their trade, and
incapable of carrying on the business thereof in a workman-like manner '.
The statute prescribed vaguely that no apprentice should be employed in
farming for ' unreasonable ' hours (1 Geo. II, c. 11).

[2] *H. of C. Reports*, vol. ii, p. 68.

[3] *Precedents and Abstracts*, 146, 150, 151.   With help from the Linen Board
they set up works on ten acres of land, and brought weavers, spinners, and
hacklers from France.   Other Huguenots started the manufacture of cambric
near Lurgan, which became the chief centre of this branch of the industry
(McCall, p. 76).

none of the other groups could compare in size and importance with the colony in the north, and their presence there was closely bound up with a development which has been, from the beginning, one of the most striking features of the linen industry in Ireland, its localization in the north-eastern counties.

Already in the seventeenth century the manufacture of broad linens was growing in Ulster, but was hardly to be found else-where.[1] In the eighteenth century the tendency to localization was still clearer. It is significant that in 1710, when names were prescribed by Act of Parliament for cloths of various dimensions, they were all, with only one exception, those of places in the north of Ireland. The widest webs were to be named Ulsters, the narrowest Munsters, and the intermediate webs were called Lurgans, Lisburns, Coleraines, Antrims, and Dungannons.[2] At one of their earliest meetings, in 1711, the Linen Board mentioned the increase of trade *in the northern part of the country*.[3] A parliamentary committee reported in 1725 that Ulster ' had universally run into the manufacture '.[4] The committee added that a foundation had been laid in Leinster, Munster, and Connaught ; and both the Irish Parliament and the Linen Board cherished a constant hope of improvement in the south. But although the southern industry did show promise of growth at times, there was never a really great or permanent increase. Dobbs, the economist, wrote in 1727 : ' When I say there are not above five counties employed and fully embarked in making linens, viz. Antrim, Down, Armagh, Tyrone, and Derry, I am, I believe, near the truth.'[5] A genera-tion later Robert Stephenson said more emphatically that the whole of the linen made in the rest of Ireland did not equal the output of a single north-eastern county ;[6] and Arthur Young, after travelling through the whole country, formed the opinion that the industries of Ireland, apart from the linen manufacture of Ulster, were 'too insignificant to merit a particular attention'.[7]

In England, linen was woven and bleached in many different districts ; in Scotland every county shared in the industry to

---

[1] Cf. Temple's statement quoted above p. 7, n. 2.
[2] 9 Anne, c. 3. The names never came into general use, but that fact does not affect the argument.
[3] *Precedents and Abstracts*, p. 4. [4] *Commons Journals* (Irish), viii, 975.
[5] *Essay upon the Trade and Improvement of Ireland* (in *Thom's Tracts*, vol. ii, pp. 355–6). [6] *Journal* (1755), p. 196. [7] *Tour*, p. 121.

some extent;[1] on the Continent it was very widely diffused. We might well expect a similar extension of industry in Ireland, particularly at a time when manufacture everywhere tended to spread over the whole countryside. In respect of climate, soil, and water-supply most parts of Ireland were as suitable as the north for flax-growing, weaving, and bleaching. There was everywhere a population of small farmers and labourers, who might add manufacture to agriculture as the northern farmers did. Many districts had better communications with Bristol, Dublin, and London than had any part of Ulster.

The position seems even more striking and anomalous if we remember that Parliament, the Linen Board, and many private persons were doing their utmost to increase production in the other provinces, in fact, more attention was paid to them than to Ulster.

Scots and Huguenots. One reason was obviously the immigration of Scots and Huguenots into Ulster. The settlers came from lands more highly industrialized than Ireland; they had capital, which was sorely lacking in Ireland as a whole; they were used to the manufacture of broadcloths for export; and the Huguenots in particular had skill in the finer branches of the industry. Their presence in large numbers in the north-east of Ireland could hardly fail to give a preponderance of manufacture to that district.

Moreover, when once an industry is well established in any district it generally shows a strong disposition to stay there. Raw material and specialized machinery are at hand; markets are organized for the sale of finished goods; skilled labour is readily available, and all the population has grown up in an atmosphere and tradition of the industry.

Yet this explanation is only partial. If there had been no stronger cause at work than the settlement of Huguenots and Scots the industry would almost certainly have spread in course of time beyond Ulster. It has just been pointed out that natural conditions were favourable in all parts of the country.

---

[1] Bremner, *Industries of Scotland*, p. 224. Linen manufacture never spread far through the Highlands, and in the latter part of the eighteenth century it was superseded in the south-west by cotton; but Bremner states that in 1727 twenty-five counties supplied linen to the central market in Edinburgh.

Raw material was produced in many counties of the south and west. For more than a century the chief market for export was in Dublin. Through the agency of the Linen Board machinery could be had, either free of cost or at a very low price, anywhere in Ireland, and skilled workers were often sent to teach the processes of manufacture. It is clear that the southern provinces were hindered by deeper and more serious disadvantages.

Operation of penal laws. An obstacle which lasted through a great part of the eighteenth century was the existence of penal laws against Roman Catholics. Without doubt the restrictions on land tenure and on the possession of property in general by Catholics, together with the exclusiveness of gilds in the towns, made it very difficult for Catholics to acquire capital, and so hindered them from taking up manufacture. But it is easy to attach too great importance to this handicap, for on the one hand many Catholics shared in the linen trade in Ulster, and on the other, Protestants who attempted the trade in the south did not fare conspicuously better than Catholics.

Land Tenure. The worst feature of the penal laws, from an economic point of view, was that they encouraged a bad system of land tenure, and there can be little doubt that the growth of industry in Ulster and its comparative failure elsewhere were due to the difference in land systems more than to any other cause. The Ulster Custom was certainly a condition of success in the north. The faulty and unfair methods in use over most of the rest of Ireland were a constant bar to progress, the main obstacle alike to private enterprise and public policy.

Land tenure was, then, a very important factor in the development of the linen trade. But although there is a large literature on the Irish land system from the Plantations to the Act of 1870, and much detailed study has been devoted both to the Ulster system of tenant right and to the abuses which appeared elsewhere, the influence of land tenure on the course of manufacture has seldom been realized by historical writers, and apparently it was not appreciated by any one in the eighteenth century. Therefore we ought to examine the subject with some care.

The land system of Ireland, both northern and southern, was an outcome of the Plantations and the Cromwellian settlement.

A large part of the agricultural land had escheated to the Crown, and was handed over in fee-simple to the chief landowners, in return for a small annual rent-charge. Many owners, in turn, disposed of their land, often on very long leases, to large tenants, who sub-let parcels on such leases as twenty-one or thirty-one years, or a term of years and a life, or several lives. The authors of the plantation policy intended that such long leases should be universal. If their wish had been carried out, the country would have been far more prosperous and peaceful during the last two centuries. But in practice land was constantly sub-let in very small holdings and for absurdly short periods ; and an act of 1702—one of the most important and disastrous of the penal laws—forbade Catholics to hold land for long terms of years or for lives.[1] This law must have given fresh strength to the custom of short leases. At any rate the custom gained so much hold that by far the commonest lease in Ireland during the eighteenth century was for one year, with six months' grace.[2]

The result of this system was a frequent auction of peasants' holdings. No tenant, even if he had paid rent regularly, and worked his land well, was secure in his holding ; for in any year the land might be offered to a higher bidder, and the tenant would be driven away without compensation. If he would escape eviction he must pay, or at least promise, a higher rent than any competitor. Thus short leases meant rack-renting ; and rack-renting meant that it was never worth while for a tenant to improve his land, because all the benefit would go to the landlord or the agent. The depressing effect of rack-rents was all the greater, since the peasants were very often tempted to promise more than they could pay. Their rents were always in arrears, and if they made any additional wealth it would simply go to reduce slightly a burden of debt from which they could never wholly escape. Consequently it was to the interest of the peasantry to starve the soil, and to draw from it no more than would keep themselves and their families at the subsistence level, with only so much surplus as would just satisfy the most urgent claims of the rent-agent.

[1] 1 Anne, c. 26.

[2] The system of yearly tenancy, or ' conacre ', is still common in Ireland ; but it is now a matter of agreement between farmers for sub-letting one or two fields for a single season.

PULLING FLAX

RIPPLING, OR REMOVING THE SEED

Such a system was as fatal to manufacture as to agriculture. Few tenants had enough capital to set themselves up as weavers. Even if they did begin weaving they would work under a continual threat of eviction. Above all, any income made from weaving would often have to go in increased rent, or in payment of arrears.

There was, it is true, a certain amount of weaving, though chiefly for home consumption, in the southern provinces, and in some parts, especially Connaught, much flax-growing and spinning. Very short leases were not universal, and wherever longer leases existed there was more inducement for manufacture. In some counties, Sligo and Leitrim for example, there was a sporadic appearance of tenant-right.[1] Many landlords and agents were public-spirited and far-sighted enough to allow fair rents and security of tenure, and many took great pains to encourage manufacture among their tenants. Therefore we should expect to find some industry, based on a rather uncertain foundation, among the more fortunate of the southern peasantry.

When particular undertakings did succeed for a time it was nearly always the case—I doubt whether there were any exceptions—that the workers held their land on unusually good terms, with reasonably long leases. But as there was no guarantee in law or custom that the conditions would be permanent, these undertakings were always in an unsafe position. Most of them collapsed after a few years.[2]

Flax-culture and spinning were fairly widespread because they were comparatively cheap and simple, and they would often serve, like corn crops, to eke out the minimum of rent which would satisfy the landlord. Weaving was a more serious matter, needing an apprenticeship and some capital. Moreover yarn could be sold to jobbers or 'grey merchants', who carried it to the northern and eastern markets ; but there was no such easy way of selling linen. The web had to be sold, after a good deal of waiting and expense, at a fair or market ; and in the southern provinces there was no such organization of markets as was found in Ulster early in the eighteenth century. This point can be readily understood if we notice the methods of farming

[1] Montgomery, op. cit., p. 95 ; Marmion, *Maritime Ports*, p. 155.
[2] For examples of manufacturing enterprise in the south see below, chapter v.

carried on in the southern provinces. A great part of the land was used for grazing. In the Plain of Dublin there was much grazing of fat cattle, in the western counties of lean cattle and sheep, and a wide area in the south was occupied with dairy farming.[1] Large farmers owned most of the stock and were chiefly concerned in the marketing. The peasantry, as employees of these graziers and dairy farmers, would seldom have stock of their own to sell. There was more tillage in the central counties, and we might expect to find more organization of markets there. But the peasants, even when their land was largely arable, carried on subsistence farming. Their holdings were so small that they would supply little more than potatoes for the family and grazing for a goat or cow. If there was any surplus produce it would commonly go, not to market, but to the agent, to pay rent in kind.

The position of the small farmer in Ulster was very different. His environment should not be painted, indeed, in too bright colours. Tenant right was by no means universal ; the country-side was covered with thousands of minute and ill-kept holdings ; a great majority of the houses outside the most prosperous manufacturing districts were mud cabins ; and if economic conditions had been satisfactory there would hardly have been such persistent emigration from Ulster as there was in practice throughout the latter half of the eighteenth century. Neverthe-less the tenantry of the north lived normally under much better conditions than those of the south.

We need not discuss here the difficult question of the origin of tenant-right : [2] it is enough for our purpose to accept the fact of its existence during the eighteenth century ; and to note its three essential features, security of tenure, reasonable rent, and the right to sell the goodwill of a holding. The importance of tenant right can hardly be over-rated. There can be no doubt that the custom, although it had no legal sanction until 1870, was generally observed over a large part of Ulster. Seeing that it must have been in existence during the seventeenth century, and was still in full force about the middle of the nineteenth,[3]

---

[1] Bonn, *Die Englische Kolonisation in Irland*, ii, 148–9.
[2] A short note on tenant right is given at the end of this chapter.
[3] See evidence given in Ulster before Devon Commission, *passim*.

one can safely assume its prevalence in the intervening time ; and it is known that such attempts as were made during the eighteenth century to break down the custom were strongly resisted. One main cause of the rising of the Hearts of Steel was a flagrant breach of tenant right.[1]

The fact that the Ulster Custom was widely observed meant that great numbers of peasant farmers were secure in their holdings as long as their rent was paid regularly ; that the rent was fixed at a moderate level ; and that if they improved their land or put up fresh buildings, and afterwards left the farm, they would be compensated by the incoming tenant. Thus the system encouraged them to make the best of their holdings. Any additional wealth made either by intensive tillage or by manu-facture would remain with the farmer himself, and would not be absorbed by rack-rents. Therefore the Ulster tenant had a fair chance of saving a little capital, which could be invested in the linen industry when the opportunity arose, with the certain knowledge that he would keep the whole return from his manu-facture, at any rate during the period of a reasonably long lease. He would also be more likely than the southern tenant to have a surplus of farm produce which he could sell at a market or fair on his own account. It is highly probable that many of the farmer-weavers in Ulster were in the habit of regular attendance as sellers at fairs and markets before the linen trade had grown to importance, and that the formation of special markets for linen and yarn was much easier in consequence.

Northern Landlords. The linen trade in Ulster benefited not only by the custom of tenant right, but also by the tradition of goodwill between landlord and tenant which made that custom possible—a tradition dating at least from the Plantation, and possibly in Antrim and Down from a still earlier time.[2] Indivi-dual landowners in the north, including some who were absentees, certainly took an interest in the trade and gave favourable terms to weavers and bleachers. There is little doubt that Crommelin's

---

[1] Montgomery, *Land Tenure in Ireland*, p. 96.

[2] The rest of Ireland suffered correspondingly from the lack of any such tradition as those which held between landlords and tenants in Ulster and in England. When an Irish landowner did more for his tenants than the law demanded, it was a matter of individual benevolence, not a following of custom.

decision to settle in Lisburn, after a careful survey of the whole country, was particularly due to the cheapness of land there. The town had been burnt during the rising of 1641, and it had never been properly rebuilt. Lord Conway, the owner of the land, was an enterprising man, who would be fully alive to the advantage of attracting industry to the district. He supplied Crommelin with a bleachgreen at Hilden, close to Lisburn, and ' contributed liberally to every project set on foot '.[1] His successor, who was made Earl of Hertford and became Lord Lieutenant in 1762, followed the same policy ; and under these two proprietors Lisburn became one of the greatest centres of trade in Ireland.[2]

Lord Hillsborough, the owner of a beautiful town and demesne five miles from Lisburn, was also interested in the linen trade and gave long leases to weavers. Hillsborough acquired a flourishing market and gave its name to a heavy kind of cloth made in the district.

The chief market for the finest linens was at Lurgan. The town was owned by the Brownlow family, who encouraged weavers with secure leases, and ' made liberal covenants of land to manufacturers and drapers '.[3] The livery companies of London, which shared the ownership of co. Derry, encouraged manufactures in the same way. Landlords in co. Armagh commonly helped their tenants with presents of timber and other materials for carrying out improvements.[4] These few instances help to confirm the statement that ' the landlords of Ulster, as a class . . . liberally patronized the linen trade, and their doing so laid the foundations of that prevailing security in regard to rental agreements for which the north has long been justly celebrated '.[5] If most observers in the south failed to understand that a reform of the land system was the first essential to success in manufacture, the relation between tenure and manufacture

---

[1] McCall, p. 9.   [2] ibid., p. 12.
[3] ibid., p. 76.   [4] Coote, *Armagh*, p. 23.
[5] ibid., p. 25. On the other hand, the landlords in Ulster were ready to drive a hard bargain at times with tenants who could afford to pay. A Dublin factor, named Ogilvie, who took an estate in co. Derry about the year 1770 from the Skinners' Company, had to pay a fine of £25,000 for his lease. (Marmion, p. 409.) In 1819 J. and J. Richardson paid £384 11s. 7d. to ' Margaret Hertford ', i. e. the Countess of Hertford, for a renewal of the lease of their bleachgreen.

was appreciated in the north. In the words of the historian of co. Down, the prosperity of the linen industry was ' all owing to the encouragement of long tenures, and kind landlords, living on their estate among their tenants '.[1]

There were spirited landlords in the south who also made great efforts to promote linen manufacture on their own estates, sometimes with temporary success. But they were only a few individuals working against hostile forces and unsupported by tradition.

NOTE TO CHAPTER II

THE ORIGIN OF TENANT RIGHT

There is a general agreement among writers on this subject that the Ulster Custom arose in connexion with the colonization by Scots and English in the sixteenth and seventeenth centuries. Perhaps it is too freely assumed that tenant right was a condition offered by ' undertakers ' in the Plantation to attract colonists. As a matter of fact the colonists in the early days did suffer from high rents, e. g. the rents in co. Derry were trebled by a royal commission in the reign of Charles I. I am inclined to think that the origin is not to be sought so much in the formal plantation of the six counties (1608–10) as in the gradual settle-ment of Antrim and Down, which were never officially ' planted '. The Scottish settlers there would be used to ' kindly tenure ' ; and a tradition of fixed holdings and moderate rents would be more readily established during the piecemeal colonization than during the rapid reorganization of the other counties. But the tradition, once it was established in Antrim and Down, might spread over the whole province as a means, not of attracting, but of retaining tenants. The landlords depended very largely on settlers from Great Britain for the improvement of their estates. The early increases of rent were encouraging these settlers to sub-let at rack-rents to Irishmen who had not enough capital to make the best use of the soil ; and there was a serious danger that the value of the land would fall. Cf. Bonn, i, 346–7 : ' Hätte der Unternehmer die Häuser fur die Kolonisten erbauen und das Land mit eigenem Gelde entwässern mussen, so wäre

---

[1] Harris, *Ancient and Present State of the County of Down* (1744), p. 106.

die Kolonisation geradezu unmöglich geworden, da das Kapital der wenigsten hierzu ausgereicht hätte. Der Grundgedanke der Kolonisation war vielmehr, dass der anzusiedelnde Kolonist Meliorationen machen solle. So enstand von Anfang an die Möglichkeit eines Konfliktes indem der Kolonist den Wert des Landes durch seine Arbeit erhöhte und dann für denselben Rente zahlen musste ... Wenn der Kolonist trotz der erhöhten Rente einen Vertrag einging, so konnte er dessen Bedingungen nur erfüllen, wenn er Iren zu Afterpächtern nahm und selbst von der Rentdifferenz lebte.'

In order to avoid a serious fall in land values the owners might very well be willing to offer generous terms, on the lines of the Ulster custom, and eventually to extend them even to the descendants of those Irish peasants who had first been only tenants at will. The troubles of 1641 and later emigration may have helped this process. The long struggle for tenant-right suggests rather a claim that was gradually established than a principle admitted from the outset.

III

EARLY ORGANIZATION (1700–50)

Rural Industry. Throughout the eighteenth century, and far into the nineteenth, linen was made in country districts, and the workers were small farmers, or farm labourers, and their families. The growth of the linen trade meant, therefore, not a growth of towns, except as marketing centres, but the spread of manufacture over the whole countryside. This was a leading characteristic of the industry, not only in Ireland, but wherever it was established, in any part of Europe. The following account, written in 1819, describes the conditions both of that time and of the previous two or three centuries :

' In the countries where this manufacture is most firmly established, it does not consist of specialized concerns, large or small, but is rather to a great extent a side occupation of the farmer ; and the so-called manufacturer is only a trader, or perhaps a finisher. The farmer of Germany, Ireland, Flanders, and Hainault, using yarn which is mostly grown and prepared by himself, and spun by his wife, daughters, and servants, weaves enough linen during the time when agricultural work is slack to enable him to sell a certain proportion each year.' [1]

There is similar evidence from the North of France, the original home of Crommelin and other pioneers of the Irish Linen Industry :

' Un fabricant possédait au moins un arpent de terre ; sur lequel il avait son logis, son atelier, une écurie pour son cheval ou son mulet, des étables pour ses vaches, un jardin potager, et enfin

---

[1] ' In die landen, alwaar deze fabriek bij uitstek gevestigd is, bestaat dezelve niet zozeer in enkele min of meer grote ondemeemingen, welke op zich zelve zoude bestaan, maar dezelve is grotendeels een bijwerk van de landman, en de zcogenaamde fabrikeur is eigenlijk alleen koopman of ook wel bereider. De Duitsch, Irelandsche, Vlaamsche, en Henegcwsche boer weeft van het garen, door zijn vrouw, dochters en dienstmeiden meestal uit eigen-geteelde en bereidde vlas gesponnen, gedurende den tijd, welke het werk van de landbouw ledig staat, zoveel linnen, dat hij daarvan jaarlike eene parthij verkoopen kan.'—Goldberg, *Nederlandsche Textielindustrie,* reprinted in Economisch-Historisch Jaarboek (Ed. N. W. Posthumus), I, 91.

un espace assez grand pour en tirer une quantité de lin suffisante pour etre filée par une famille nombreuse, et ensuite répartie entre six à huit ouvriers tisserands. De sorte que, sans sortir de sa maison, un tel fabricant trouvait toute la quantité de matière première qui lui était nécessaire.'[1]

Another writer gives this account of the weaving of fine linens in Flanders :

' Les tisserands étaient des agriculteurs, qui, en hiver surtout et pendant les chômages, se consacraient au métier. Ils travaillaient pour leur propre compte, apportaient les produits de leur travail aux marchés de Gand, Courtrai, Ypres, &c.'[2]

But this growth of rural handicraft was not peculiar to the linen industry. The same expansion of trade which had led to the domestic system had also carried manufacture in general from old towns to new centres in the country. In England in the sixteenth century there was a great rivalry between town and country, which was really a struggle between ancient privilege and new enterprise. Rural industries gradually forced their way, until the West Riding of Yorkshire was filled with the homes of woollen weavers, Lancashire and the east Midlands were covered by a variety of textile manufacture, and the west Midlands by a still greater variety of metal crafts.[3]

In Flanders a similar movement had appeared still earlier, and the struggle between town and country, and old towns and new, was a serious trouble to the Burgundian princes in the fifteenth century. ' New draperies ' of wool and the ' belles étoiles ' of linen were some of the many manufactures that sprang up on the ruins of the old gild industries.[4] The penetra-tion of the country districts continued for generations, so that in the latter part of the eighteenth century, while half the inhabitants of Bruges were said to be in poverty, industry was thriving in the country—' la campagne était le centre de l'activité industrielle de cette époque '.[5] Schmoller has shown how the transition from ' town economy ' to ' territorial economy ' in Germany implied the same dispersal of manufacture ; and more

---

[1] Tarlé, *L'Industrie dans les Campagnes en France*, p. 44.
[2] Lewinski, *L'Evolution Industrielle de la Belgique*, p. 26.
[3] See Professor Unwin's *Industrial Organization*, chap. iii.
[4] Pirenne, *Belgian Democracy*, pp. 206–9, and *Histoire de Belgique*, iii, 212–43, especially p. 239.
[5] Lewinski, *L'Evolution Industrielle de la Belgique*, pp. 26, 92.

recently M. Tarlé, in his study of rural industries in France, has described the same process at work there in the eighteenth century :

'Si du Midi nous passons au Nord, nous y observons un état de choses de tout point identique à celui que nous venons de constater. En Picardie, en Flandre, dans le Hainaut, dans le Cambrésis, dans le Beauvaisais, même situation. La vaste activité industrielle de toute la région du Nord se déroule presque tout entière dans les campagnes et non dans villes.'[1]

This picture of rural industry will be constantly before us ; but it is well at the outset to realize that the growth of linen manufacture in Ireland was in keeping with the spread of manufacture over the whole of Western Europe ; that it was, in fact, an integral part of that development of 'fabrique dispersée' which continued in full force until the use of steam power drove industry and the workers once more, and more than ever, into towns.

The purpose of the present chapter is to show how the linen industry was organized in Ireland about the second quarter of the eighteenth century, when the system had taken a fairly definite shape, but its form was still simple ; before the increase of trade had caused complexities in marketing and the growth of capitalism in manufacture. The outline can best be drawn by following the processes of production in order, from the cultivation of raw material to the output of bleached and finished cloth.

Local supply of raw material. The method of securing raw material tended strongly in itself to keep the linen manufacture both rustic and simply organized. A certain proportion of the raw flax—and in the early days a great proportion—was grown at home by the weaver himself : consequently he was not dependent on a merchant for his supplies. The webs that he produced were his own property, and in his dealings on the market he was a trader as well as a craftsman. Moreover, the business of flax-growing kept him on the farm and helped to prevent a migration to towns. Wherever the raw material of an industry has had to be imported from a distance there has been a tendency at all times for the workers to fall into depend-

---

[1] Tarlé, op. cit., pp. 12–13.

ence on the importer, who must have some command of capital, and for the industry to be managed on more or less capitalistic lines. The West of England woollen trade was dominated by merchants and clothiers chiefly because a large part of the wool was brought from Spain and Ireland; while the simpler and freer organization in Yorkshire in the early eighteenth century was largely due to home supplies from sheep belonging to the weavers or their neighbours. The cotton trade early developed a capitalistic organization, since all the raw material had to be imported, and in later years those who controlled the import became the ruling 'junta' of merchants and spinners, whose power aroused the indignation of William Radcliffe.[1] There was, it is true, a similar tendency in the linen trade, but it was constantly hindered by the home-production of yarn.

Flax-seed. Flax-seed, the fundamental raw material, was indeed largely imported; but as it was the raw material of agriculture rather than of manufacture, the traffic in flax-seed had little effect on the organization of industry. Most of the seed came from the Baltic provinces, Holland, and later America. Dutch seed was found to serve best for heavy soils, American for light soils.[2] This importation was due to the habit of growth of the flax plant. When the stalk is ready for pulling, the seed is still unripe, and if the seed is to be ripened and 'saved' for sowing in the next season, the stalk must be sacrificed. Irish farmers were anxious to grow as much flax as possible, and had more interest in the stalk than in the seed—in any case the seed could be sold to be crushed for the extraction of linseed oil.[3] It was doubtless cheaper to buy seed and produce flax at home than to save seed and buy a corresponding amount of imported flax. In the countries which exported seed there was less demand for yarn, and it was worth while for the farmers to allow a considerable part of their crops to ripen.

There is little evidence as to the regular import and distribution

---

[1] Similarly in the parts of France in which Spanish wool or imported flax or cotton were used there was a capitalistic system, controlled by the entrepreneurs who supplied and owned the raw material. (Tarlé, op. cit., pp. 48 sqq.) [2] Young, *Tour*, p. 107.

[3] The removal or 'rippling' of seed is still observed as a family festival, as sheep-shearing is in various parts of England. The seed is removed by hand, by means of a combing process, and it is collected in sheets stretched on the ground.

of seed in the early eighteenth century. No doubt a large part of the supply was brought to London in ships which had taken out English and Irish linen, and was carried in the main stream of Anglo-Irish traffic to Dublin. Thence it would be dispersed to all parts of the country—for flax-growing was widely distributed in the eighteenth century—and probably sold at markets and fairs by corn chandlers or other dealers in agricultural goods.

Towards the middle of the century there were several different agencies for the sale of seed. Advertisements in the Belfast newspapers show that it was supplied by merchants in Dublin and Belfast who dealt in seeds of all kinds. A pamphleteer who wrote in 1763 hinted that the northern drapers were flax-seed merchants as well, and accused them of importing condemned seed from Scotland.[1] Early in the nineteenth century, merchants who exported linen from Belfast—most of them bleachers—were also importers of seed.[2] These men would either sell seed privately in their bleachworks or warehouses, or would offer it in the open markets which were regularly held for the sale of flax, yarn, and linen.

Frequently, though not regularly, between 1711 and 1763, the Linen Board also imported flax-seed from Holland and Riga, and distributed it at less than cost price. For considerable periods (e. g. from 1720 to 1730) about a third of the Board's revenue was spent in this way. But the official importation was only meant to be a special stimulus : the regular trade remained in private hands, although, as one of the inspectors pointed out, it was seriously upset by the subsidized trade of the Board.[3]

Flax-growing. The flax crop is a difficult, laborious and uncertain crop to grow, and at a first glance it seems rather strange that peasants with minute holdings, and scarcely any capital, should care to risk their livelihood in such an enterprise. Good judgement is needed in deciding when the crop is ready to be gathered. The stalks must be carefully pulled by hand and laid in neat rows. Next, the outer part of the stalks must be allowed to decay in order that it may be easily separated

---

[1] *Observations on Materials*, pp. 8, 9.   [2] Corry, *Report*, 1816, p. 36.
[3] Stephenson, *Inquiry*, p. 8. For the Board's efforts to encourage flax growing see below, chap. iv, pp. 72–4.

from the fibre. This 'retting' process, again, which is carried
out partly by exposure on the damp grass and partly by steeping
for about ten days in pools, requires delicate judgement : even
a small mistake may mean a serious loss in the value of the flax.
In bad seasons, or at times when foreign yarn was exceptionally
cheap, the Irish peasant actually lost money on his flax crop.[1]
Nevertheless much flax was grown in Ireland, not only by Ulster
weavers but by peasants in other districts, particularly in
Connaught. The peasants wove little cloth themselves, but sold
flax and yarn to jobbers, who disposed of it in Ulster or sent
it to Great Britain. The explanation was, in the first place,.
that a flax crop yielded on the whole a larger return from a given
area of land than any other crop which a peasant could grow ;
and, secondly, that the careful hand-labour needed in its harvest-
ing made it particularly suitable for very small holdings.[2]
Further, the preparation of yarn, although it was ill-paid labour,
brought at any rate some increase to the trifling income of the
cotter's household. In certain parts of the country flax crops
were the more attractive because they were exempted by custom
from tithe.[3] Moreover, it was found that flax could be grown
satisfactorily after potatoes—which were also exempted from
tithe—and thus a small farmer who knew nothing of the Norfolk
course could at least use a flax-crop in establishing a simple
rotation.[4]

[1] Cf. Murphy, *Ireland, Industrial, Political and Social*, p. 41 : ' Flax is the
most costly, troublesome and precarious of all crops.' Dubourdieu, *Survey
of Down*, p. 233, states that weavers sometimes doubled their profits by
supplying their own yarn, but were ' often great sufferers ' from the fluctuation
of prices in the flax market.

[2] Statistics given in the *Proceedings* of the Linen Board, 1810, App. I and
XX, show that an area of 76,700 Irish acres under flax was cultivated by
101,700 farmers—an average of three-quarters of an acre (or in English
measure an acre and a quarter) of flax to each holding.

[3] Montgomery, *Land Tenure in Ireland*, p. 95.

[4] Young, *Tour*, ii, 113. But Young said that it was a common practice
to exhaust the soil with several crops of oats before sowing flax. Cf. Robert
Stephenson, *Journal*, p. 163 : ' Every potato garden in the kingdom is fitter to
produce flax than any other ground whatever.' Ctr. Miss Murray (p. 118),
who was wrongly informed on this point : ' The culture of flax . . . was
unprofitable and no farmer would undertake the work solely on his own
initiative. . . . In the woollen trade Ireland worked up the raw material she
possessed : in the linen she had to depend for her material on foreign countries.'
In point of fact much home-grown flax has always been used in Ireland ; and
if the woollen industry had developed far, and a variety of cloths had been
produced, there would have been large imports of wool and yarn, as in England

STEEPING FLAX

The stones are used to keep the flax under water

Preparation of Flax. When it had been retted, the flax was dried—sometimes in the open air, sometimes in ovens, often by the less desirable and more risky method of toasting on hurdles over a fire. Then came the scutching process, performed by hanging the flax over an upright board, and beating the straw with a wooden knife, in order to remove the outer layers (which were already softened by retting), and to leave the fibre ready for further treatment. After the scutching it was usual to hammer, or beetle, the fibre in order to break it up into finer strands. The last process of preparation was hackling, an operation similar to the combing of worsted, by which the flax was cleaned, broken still finer, and drawn out into even ' sticks ', each strick consisting of a handful of parallel strands of fibre, ready to be tied to the distaff as part of the ' rock ' for spinning.

There is a great deal of interest in the study of these processes, in the comparison of methods in different countries, and the contrast of the domestic methods with those in use to-day.[1] But as we are not concerned here with technical history, and as these processes had no great effect on the organization of industry, there is no need to describe them in further detail. As a rule they were carried out by the grower, although a weaver might buy rough flax and hackle it himself.[2]

It was impossible for each weaver to grow exactly the quality

and as in the Irish linen trade, in order to provide the required mixtures. Murphy (op. cit., p. 39) said that as a general rule a flax crop should be grown on a given piece of land once in nine years. But this was a counsel of perfection.

[1] The Dutch system of preparing flax, which was the best in Europe at that time, is described by R. Hall in *Observations in Dutch Methods.* See also Horner, *Linen Trade of Europe,* chap. xlv for the treatment of flax in Holland and Ireland ; chap. xxxiii for methods in Scotland. At the present day the ' ruffing ' process, which combines combing and sorting, is still done by hand, and is highly skilled work. The subsequent hackling is done by a beautiful and elaborate machine, which combs several dozen sticks together, screws the sticks into position and unscrews them again automatically. The methods of cultivation and preparation of flax in use before the introduction of machinery are well described in Kane's *Industrial Resources of Ireland* (1844), pp. 308–20.

[2] The Linen Board employed professional hacklers for a short time ; their business, however, was not primarily to hackle large quantities themselves, but to teach the farmers how to prepare flax. Young (*Tour,* p. 195) mentions travelling hacklers, who were paid 7s. for working up a cwt. of flax. It is not likely, however, that there were many of these specialized workers before the middle of the eighteenth century.

and quantity of flax that he needed for his own loom. On the other hand many farmers had more flax than they needed, especially those in the southern provinces, or the non-manufacturing districts of Ulster. Thus there was scope for traffic in flax between growers and weavers. The trade was carried on, no doubt, by the class of jobbers who also brought yarn to the manufacturing centres ; and it led to the growth of flax markets over the whole of Ulster, some in the chief towns, for sale to the weavers, others in small, remote towns and villages, for collection from the growers.[1]

Spinners, and Sale of Yarn. As a rule, however, the growers would prefer to sell their flax in the form of yarn, in order that their womenfolk might gain the price of spinning. Women in Ireland, as in other countries, were almost universally trained to spin either wool or linen, and gradually during the eighteenth century they learnt the use of spinning-wheels. The first census returns made in Ireland described a very large proportion of the women as spinners.

Some writers of the eighteenth and early nineteenth centuries mention a class of itinerant spinners, who would settle in a weaver's house for some weeks or months and would spin his stock of flax in return for board and lodging and a trifling money payment.[2] But this class must have been comparatively small. As manufacture spread the number of professional spinners would tend to increase ; yet the census returns show that as late as 1821 the spinner was as a rule a member of the weaver's family. In certain parts of the country, which were technically called the ' yarn counties ', much flax was grown and spun, but little was made into cloth.[3] Therefore these counties had a large

---

[1] There were more than seventy flax markets in Ulster, and about fifty for yarn and linen (Horner, chaps. xvii, xxii ; Corry, *Report*, 1816). The flax markets were more numerous because flax was grown in districts (e.g. in co. Donegal) outside the area of manufacture.

[2] See Young, *Tour*, p. 116 ; Wakefield, ii, 685 ; Dubourdieu, *Down*, p. 233.

[3] The chief yarn counties were : Meath, Westmeath, Longford, Tipperary, Galway, Leitrim, Sligo, Mayo, and Roscommon. (See Besnard's *Report*, 1817, *passim*.) It is curious that so much flax-growing should take place in Connaught, far away from the centres of weaving and from the Dublin market. In all probability the peasants of Connaught turned to flax cultivation because they found it more difficult to supply either cereals or dairy produce, which were staple goods in the midland and southern counties. (Cf. Bonn, *Die Englische Kolonisation*, ii, 248–9.)

surplus of yarn, of which they were relieved by the jobbers,
' itinerant merchants ', or ' grey merchants ', who have just been
mentioned as dealers in flax.

Yarn Jobbers. The jobber obtained his yarn in various ways,
sometimes buying it at fairs, sometimes collecting it from door
to door, or even, for convenience, receiving it at church.[1] In
any case he would pay cash to the spinner. He would then carry
the yarn, by pack-horse or cart, to the linen markets of Ulster,
and there dispose of it to weavers—or later to drapers and
manufacturers. The jobbers' business led to the organization
of yarn markets, which—like those for flax—seem to have been
adjuncts of the weekly or fortnightly markets for brown linen.
When these markets were established is not clear, but the
jobbers were certainly at work in 1727, for they are mentioned
in a statute of that year.[2] Seeing that there had been no legislation for them before, although the government regarded them
with no friendly eye, their trade was probably a new institution
at that time. Ten years later they had become so unpopular
with the dealers in regular markets that they were described,
with more spleen than reason, as ' the vermin of the trade . . .
that buy from the industrious housewife, and run about from
fair to fair, and market to market, enhancing the price till the
commodity comes out so dear to the manufacturer and exporter
that they frequently lose by it '.[3]

Yarn was sold not only to weavers in Ulster but also to
merchants in the Eastern ports, especially Dublin and Drogheda,
for export to England.[4] In the minutes of the Linen Board there
is evidence of an active yarn trade in Drogheda, for the Board
often complained to the merchants—even to the Mayor and
Corporation—of the sale of yarn which was not made up in the
manner prescribed by Parliament. The Board's labour was in
vain, because the customers in Lancashire showed an obstinate
preference for ' unstatutable ' yarn, which was probably cheaper,
and certainly far more abundant, than yarn of the official type.[5]

---

[1] This was the custom in Sligo (Besnard, op. cit., p. 53).   [2] Geo. II, c. 2.
[3] *Thoughts on the Importance of the Linen Manufacture* (1737), pp. 23-4.
[4] Young (*Tour*, p. 144) mentioned that yarn from Donegal was also sent to
Manchester by way of Derry.
[5] *Precedents and Abstracts*, passim. The buyers in Drogheda ordered their
agents to pay no attention to the statutes (p. 38).

There was a fairly steady demand for linen yarn in England—especially in Lancashire, where it was used chiefly as warp, to be mixed with a cotton weft.[1] The early export trade in yarn, during the sixteenth and seventeenth centuries, had probably been very small. In 1711–12, the first year for which figures are available, the amount was less than 8,000 cwts. By 1720 the export had grown to 15,722 cwts., which would be nearly equal in value to the cloth sent out in the same year.[2] But during the rest of the century, while the linen trade grew rapidly, there was only a slow increase in the export of yarn. The amount crept up gradually until 1780, when it reached 42,000 cwts. Then the demand for linen yarn in England began to fall, because of the growing production of pure cotton goods. A few years later, the introduction of machine-spinning into the English and Scottish linen trade drove down the demand for coarse Irish yarn still further, and caused unspun flax to be exported instead.

Import of Yarn. While some kinds of yarn, for the most part of medium quality, were being exported, others were imported for the Irish manufacture. There is no such detailed record of the amount imported as there is of exports ; but we may be sure that at first the imports were very small, and that they increased rapidly after the middle of the century. A report made to the Irish Parliament in 1758 showed this increase in a striking way. The returns for the previous seventeen years gave the following averages :

Average annual import of yarn 1741–50 . . 5,400 cwts.
Average annual import of yarn 1751–57 . . 20,000 cwts.[3]

Thus, soon after 1750 imports of yarn were nearly equal to exports, for the average export for the years 1751–57 was only 25,500 cwts. Seeing that the finest branches of manufacture were beginning to make progress at that time, a large part of the imports probably consisted of the high counts of yarn spun

[1] Cf. Daniels, *Early English Cotton Industry*, pp. 8, 58. There was also a considerable manufacture of pure linen in Lancashire ; but the statement in a petition of 1703 that 60,000 persons were employed in the manufacture in that one county is certainly an exaggeration, even if the number were meant to include spinners and finishers as well as weavers (ibid., p. 39).

[2] See table of exports given below, Appendix II.

[3] *Commons Journals*, 1757–60, p. cxxii.

in the Netherlands. Some coarser yarns were brought from the Baltic states, but they were used much more in Scotland than in Ireland.[1]

The import of yarn into Ulster, whether from other parts of the country or from abroad, would naturally tend to bring the weavers under the power of merchants, who could afford to buy yarn in large quantities. This movement belongs, however, to a later period, and it must be left for discussion elsewhere.

Moreover, the fact remains that much of the raw material was provided by the weavers themselves—in Ireland as on the Continent—enough to produce a marked effect on the organization of industry and to delay the advance towards capitalism. In co. Antrim there was actually too much fondness for local supplies : sheetings were made from hard northern yarns, although the yarns of Connaught would have served the purpose better.[2]

Farmer Weavers. Of the domestic weaver himself, although he was the mainstay of the industry, no detailed account need be given, for his figure is familiar in the economic history of nearly every country in the world. The descriptions already quoted of weaving in France and the Netherlands serve equally well for Ireland. The craftsman was primarily a farmer or farm-labourer, and manufacture was a *bijwerk*. Or if there were several male members of a family the father might work on the land while one or two of his sons, who had learnt their trade from him, would spend most of their time at the loom.[3]

In Yorkshire and Lancashire the weavers' houses generally had loom shops on an upper floor, lit by very wide, stone-mullioned windows. In Ireland, where cottages were seldom built with more than one story, the kitchen, bedroom, dairy and loomshop were all on the ground floor.[4] Because of the window tax there was less light than was really needed, but the

---

[1] Horner, pp. 294, 502, 503. Baltic yarns were also used for coarse cloths, such as sheetings, in Lancashire (Daniels, op. cit., p. 58).

[2] Horner, p. 46. Kane (*Industrial Resources*, pp. 323, 324) mentions that ' the quality of the fibre ' in certain parts of the south ' was of a delicacy but seldom met with in the ordinary flax of Ulster '.

[3] This division of labour is shown in very many instances in the 1821 census returns. Cf. Dubourdieu, *Survey of Antrim*, ii, 400 : ' Many of them (the weavers) are the sons of farmers, who assist in the work of the land and then return to the loom.'　　[4] Coote, *Survey of Armagh*, pp. 132, 134.

loom was always placed close to a window. A further reason for setting up looms on the ground level (or rather, in the ground) was the advantage of having an earthen floor ; the moisture rising from the earth helped to keep the yarn in a good condition for weaving.[1]

There is not enough evidence of the weavers' standard of life in the earlier half of the eighteenth century to enable us to form any definite judgement. This subject must be left for discussion when we are dealing with a later period, for which the evidence is more abundant.

Markets for Cloth. At first, when a web was finished, it was sold in a fair ; but as trade increased it became worth while to hold weekly or fortnightly markets for brown or unbleached cloths. The weavers then most commonly tied up the webs in packs, and carried them on their backs to a neighbouring market. We shall inquire later in this chapter into the origin of these markets, but it will help to give us a clearer idea of the system of production if we notice here how the sales were normally carried out when the markets were fully established.

Arthur Young in 1776 visited one of the chief markets for fine linen, and gave the following account of it, which will serve equally well for the earlier periods :

' This being market day at Lurgan, Mr. Brownlow walked to it with me, that I might see the way in which the linens were sold. The cambricks are sold early, and through the whole morning ; but when the clock strikes eleven, the drapers jump upon stone standings, and the weavers instantly flock about them with their pieces ; the bargains are not struck at a word, but there is a little altercation whether the price shall be one halfpenny or a penny a yard more or less, which appeared to me useless. The draper's clerk stands by him, and writes his master's name on the pieces he buys, with the price ; and giving it back to the seller, he goes to the draper's quarters and awaits his coming. At twelve it ends : then there is an hour for measuring the pieces and paying the money, for nothing but ready money is taken : and this is the way the business is carried on at all the markets.' [2]

---

[1] All the handlooms that I have seen are set up on earthen floors. The main pillars are driven into the soil, and a small pit is dug to allow room for depression of the treadles.   [2] Young, *Tour in Ireland*, i, 112.

Twenty years later a French émigré named Latocnaye gave a similar description of another northern market :

' Londonderry has not the air of an Irish town. There is there an activity and an industry which are not generally to be found in other parts of the country. The principal trade consists in linens, of which there is a market once or twice a week. It is surprising to note the speed with which the linen merchants examine the cloth. They stand on a sort of platform, with a little desk before them, while the peasants carry their webs past and stop for just a moment. The merchant looks, and immediately mentions a price : if it is accepted, he marks it on the cloth, and the peasant goes to the office for payment. There is one merchant who, on every market day, buys in a single hour cloth to the value of three or four hundred pounds sterling.' [1]

There is much more evidence in regard to dealings in the brown linen markets, especially in the reports of inspectors, but these two accounts give us all the essential features. The sellers were weavers, who attended each market in large numbers to dispose of cloth woven by themselves or by other members of their households. The buyers were middlemen, known as drapers, who were much fewer in number. There were regular market hours, and the usual troubles with forestalling, engrossing and regrating. Sales were all for ready money, preferably gold. Bargains were struck with extraordinary speed, and with only the most cursory examination of the cloth—a fact which had an important bearing on the later attempts at regulation and inspection. The business was transacted on these lines as long as the markets continued—that is, until after the middle of the nineteenth century.

Projects of Joint Stock. Although the weavers were for so long independent or semi-independent dealers, it was not intended by the government or by early projectors of the industry that they should remain so. The ruling authorities clearly had in view a large-scale, capitalistic organization. In the first regulating statute of 1705,[2] it was provided that weavers should be freemen of their boroughs, and in 1709 [3] an apprenticeship of five years was prescribed before the weaver could become a master crafts-

---

[1] Latocnaye, *A Frenchman's Walk through Ireland*, p. 200.
[2] 4 Anne, c. 3.   [3] 8 Anne, c. 12.

man. These clauses assumed that the industry would be carried on by urban workers, who could be controlled by a class of employing merchants—especially by Huguenots, who inspired much of the legislation of this period. Moreover, the numerous schemes for exploiting the linen trade which were begun, and in most cases ended, between 1690 and 1700, all contemplated an industry centred in towns and organized on a large scale by means of joint-stock. The Drogheda Linen Co., Dupin's scheme, and the rival project—which were all amalgamated and soon collapsed—the ambitious Flax and Hemp Co. of Ireland, which aimed at a capital of £300,000 ; and finally Crommelin's Royal Corporation, were all undertakings of this type.[1] So, too, were several early projects in Scotland : the Newmills Cloth Co., Dupin's Scottish concern, and the society formed in 1725 among ' the most topping merchants in Glasgow '.[2]

But a contemporary observer wisely said, ' I have seen frequent attempts of this nature come to very little.'[3] In practice neither joint-stock companies nor even private enterprise on a large scale had any lasting success. Industry avoided the towns, and the weaver retained his independence.

He was in a very real sense the mainstay of the industry, for without him it could never have developed. Time after time attempts were made in all parts of the country to set up manufacture on capitalistic lines, and nearly always the attempts failed within a few years. It was the independent farmers of Ulster who formed the basis of success ; and industry throve in the north because it was founded on agriculture.

Young's Criticism. Arthur Young, when he visited Ulster in 1776, formed a contrary opinion ; and it is worth while to notice, in some detail, his well-known criticism of the rural manufacture ; for the whole system of *Doppelbeschäftigung*, of which the linen industry is an example, is of great importance in economic history. As an agricultural expert Young was much distressed by the low standard of farming that was universal

---

[1] Scott, *Joint-Stock Companies,* iii, 98–102.
[2] Warden, pp. 427, 429, 432.
[3] Woodrow, quoted by Warden, p. 432. It should be noted that the period from 1690 to 1720 was a time of abundant joint-stock enterprise, good and bad. The projectors of linen manufacturing companies were only following the fashion of their day.

among weavers. He was troubled in the same way by the
country workers of northern France.[1] In the diary of his tour
through Ulster he exclaimed from time to time against the ruin
of agriculture produced by country manufacture :

' It has been his (the Lord Chief Baron's) general observation
that where the linen manufacture spreads the tillage is very
bad.' [2] ' Crossed the mountains by the new road to Antrim and
found them to the summits to consist of exceeding good loam,
and such as would improve into good meadow. They make no
other use of it than turning their cows on. Pity they do not
improve ; a work more profitable than any they could undertake . . . The linen manufacture spreads over the whole country,
consequently the farms are very small, being nothing but patches
for the convenience of weavers.' [3]

In the notes and discussions which followed the diary he
returned to the attack with great vigour.

' I do not mean to find fault with the establishment of this
manufacture,' he wrote. ' It has grown to a great degree of
national importance ; but from some unfortunate circumstances
in the police of it (if I may use the expression) that importance
is not nearly equal to what it ought to be, from the extent of
country it absolutely fills . . . Ulster contains 2,836,837 plantation
acres : suppose that vast tract under sheep, and feeding no
more than two to an acre, their fleeces at five shillings each
would amount raw to £1,418,418 and spun into bay yarn,
without receiving any farther manufacture, the value would be
£2,127,622, reckoning the labour half the value of the wool.
That is to say the amount would be more than the whole value
of the linen manufacture both exported and consumed at home.'

Young then pointed out how Norfolk exported corn and
cattle from the country districts, and at the same time had a
great woollen manufacture in the towns ; and he continued :

' Change the scene and view the north of Ireland : you there
behold a whole province peopled by weavers. It is they who
cultivate, or rather beggar, the soil, as well as work the looms.
Agriculture is there in ruins ; annihilated ; the whole region is
the disgrace of the kingdom ; all the crops you see are contempt-
ible ; are nothing but filth and weeds. No other part of Ireland
can exhibit the soil in such a state of poverty and desolation.
A farming traveller, who goes through that country with attention, will be shocked at seeing wretchedness in the shape of a few

---

[1] *Travels in France*, p. 504.   [2] *Tour in Ireland*, p. 100.   [3] Ibid., p. 128.

beggarly oats on a variety of most fertile soils, which, were they in Norfolk, would soon rival the best in that county.'

' But the cause of all these evils, which are absolute exceptions to everything else on the face of the globe, is easily found— a most prosperous manufacture, so contrived as to be the destruction of agriculture, is certainly a spectacle for which we must go to Ireland. It is owing to the fabrick spreading over all the country instead of being confined to towns . . . But if instead of the manufacture having so diffused itself as absolutely to banish farming, it had been confined to towns, which it might very easily have been, the very contrary effect would have taken place, and all those vast advantages to agriculture would have flowed, which flourishing manufactures in other countries occasion . . . The manufacturers would have been confined to their own business and the farmers to theirs. That both trades would have flourished the better for this, the minutes of the journey very generally show.' [1]

The concentration of industry in towns, which Arthur Young desired, only began half a century after the time of his tour. It was far from being, as he maintained, an easy process and a matter of ' police '. It was a question of broad economic facts which no policy could alter. If it had been possible to coerce industry into towns, spinning and weaving would have become the sole means of livelihood for thousands of families, and wages would have been their total income instead of supplementary earnings.

Difficulty of Specialization. The problem of paying wages sufficient to keep these workers in the towns would have been extremely difficult : indeed it could only have been solved by the introduction of steam-spinning and the power-loom. In certain branches, such as the manufacture of cambric and damask, the product brought a high price, and the work required considerable skill, so that there was a great advantage in specialization. The weavers in these branches, therefore, could command a comparatively good wage, and at the time when Young wrote they were as a rule wholly employed in manufacture. But even these workers seldom lived in the market towns : they were found more often round about the homes of their employers, in the neighbourhood of bleachgreens. In the case of plain linens of medium or coarse quality the difficulty

[1] *Tour,* ii, 119, 120.

was greater. Prices were often kept down by the competition of woollen and cotton goods. At the same time raw material was expensive ; so that there was never a great margin available for wages—in fact the margin was generally too small to accommodate a subsistence wage. Moreover, there was no great advantage in specialization : the work of a full-time weaver would not be conspicuously better or more rapid than that of a farmer or farm labourer. These difficulties were recognized by Sir Richard Cox, one of the chief pioneers of linen manufacture in the south of Ireland. The weavers on his own estates were all farmers as well, and he attributed the ill success of weavers in most parts of the country to the fact that they worked for wages and had no supplementary income. ' The weavers are not fixed unless they be rich ; and rich they will never be by wages alone.' [1] The same considerations led another writer to say more crudely : ' Towards the prosperity of our linen manufacture there is a necessity that our poor continue poor.' It is ' a trade incompatible with a rich community '.[2]

On the other hand a farmer, especially if he used much home-grown flax, could gain enough profit from his own flax-growing, his wife's spinning, and the sale of his woven cloth, to make it worth while for him to carry on manufacture together with agriculture.[3]

It is impossible to judge exactly what would have followed if Young's recommendation could have been put into force, for no one can tell what economies might have been devised to meet the double problem of cheap production and adequate wages. But it was found so difficult, even in the nineteenth century, to apply steam power to linen manufacture that we can hardly imagine any great economies following a compulsory migration of industry to towns two or three generations earlier. The most likely consequence would seem to be a wholesale departure of weavers to America, leaving a small number of graziers and

---

[1] *Letter to T. Prior*, pp. 19–20.

[2] *Thoughts on the Importance of the Linen Manufacture*, pp. 14, 25. Apparently the writer lived in one of the southern provinces, where, as will be shown later, employment for wages was much commoner than it was in Ulster.

[3] In the same way rural industry in France undermined urban industry, because the farmer-weaver could underbid the town worker. Cf. Tarlé (p. 77) : ' Le travail industriel . . . n'était qu'une ressource supplémentaire, et l'ouvrier des campagnes pouvait accepter des prix inférieurs à ceux qu'était obligé de demander l'ouvrier des villes, qui, lui, ne pouvait compter sur aucun gain auxiliaire.'

shepherds as the inhabitants of Ulster. Such an emigration might have been an advantage in some ways. Many of the weavers would have made a better livelihood abroad, for in Ireland the linen trade afforded no more than a bare subsistence to the mass of workers ; but it would have deprived the country of its one staple manufacture and much of its trading organization, and so would have hampered any further development of commerce and industry.

Young's argument seems rational enough to-day because we are used to urban industry and know the value of specialization. But in the eighteenth century the actual course of events was all in the other direction. One reason we have seen already : the farmer-weaver could supplement his weaving with other sources of income. Another equally important reason was that this mixture of manufacture with farming gave to the industry in its early days a strength and flexibility which were essential to its success. Young himself remarked that during a slump in trade the weaver would become a farmer or labourer, and when trade recovered would go back to the loom.[1] If he had worked out all that was implied in this observation, he would have seen that the joint pursuit of agriculture and weaving was of great benefit at least to the manufacture, and in some respects to both industries. It meant an easy adjustment of labour and goods to changes in demand, and a smooth and rapid growth of manufacture as the scope for production increased. The small capital of a thrifty peasant could be used in acquiring a loom, building a weaving shed, or buying raw material. The profits of manufacture in turn could be invested in land, or in hiring additional workers. By such means a peasant could become in a few years' time both a substantial farmer and a substantial manufacturer. A great proportion of the employing class which appeared later in the linen trade seem actually to have raised their fortunes in this way.[2] Thus, the spread of manufacture over the province, although it may have helped to beggar the soil, was from another point of view a most important means of progress.[3]

[1] *Tour*, p. 118, 139.
[2] Coote, *Survey of Armagh*, p. 138. This statement is confirmed by the evidence of the 1821 census. Nearly every farmer in the area of linen weaving who held ten acres or more was described as a manufacturer.
[3] Although Young wrote at a later time the whole argument is equally applicable to the period with which we are dealing. By 1770, it is true, the

WARPING FRAME

CAMBRIC LOOM

Our interest in specialization is apt to obscure the fact that specialization is nearly always preceded by an opposite move-ment.   A new line of enterprise very often begins, not as a separate occupation, but as a branch of some established line of trade.   At the very time when Young was writing, this principle was being strikingly confirmed by the growth of banking as an offshoot from all manner of different trades ; and here, before his eyes, was another example of a trade growing and flourishing because it was grafted into a healthy stem.   When once the trade was well established, weaving could become a specialized occu-pation—at least the weaving of fine cloths, which brought higher wages—and there followed all the advantages of which Adam Smith was writing at this same time.   But as long as markets were only partially organized and employment was uncertain and at the best of times ill-paid, the industry could only exist by means of a system of joint-production.

We can realize now the full importance of this connexion. The linen manufacture was based on agriculture, and its localiza-tion in Ulster was largely due to the custom of land tenure. Thus the agrarian system both encouraged the growth of industry and determined its limits.   For the same reasons, we can see that the farmer-weaver was a vital factor in the rise of the linen trade.

Bleachers.   When the farmer had woven his cloth he generally disposed of it in the brown, unfinished state.   The bleaching and finishing processes were managed by men of greater substance. Before the eighteenth century, when linen was chiefly made for use at home, the cloth was often bleached by the farmer's wife, in Ireland as in Scotland.[1]   But the method was slow, primitive, and inefficient, and when a really good finish was desired the web was usually sent to Holland, to be bleached at Haarlem ; for at that time the Netherlanders were the best finishers in Europe, both of linen and of woollen cloth.[2]   Near the beginning

manufacture was well established, and specialization might be expected to follow. But as there had been no radical improvement in methods of pro-duction, conditions even then were not ripe for any specialization involving urban industry.

[1] McCall, *Staple Manufactures*, p. 85. Bremner, *Industries of Scotland*, p. 222.

[2] Cf. Goldberg, *Nederlandsche Textielindustrie*, p. 139 : ' De vreemde linnens, in een meer ruwe staat aangebracht, binnenslands en wel voornamelijk te Haarlem gebleekt en vol bereid worden, waardoor dus de waarde der linnens vermeerderd werd, hetgeen sedert aanmerkelijk veranderd is, doordat men zich

of the eighteenth century, however, and perhaps earlier, specialized bleachers had appeared in Ireland to meet the needs of the
expanding trade. Many of them were probably Huguenots, and
it is known that some of the Huguenot settlers brought Dutch
bleachers with them.[1] There is evidence that a fair number of
bleachworks had been set up by the year 1725. After 1719,
when public lappers, or aulnagers, were first appointed to inspect
white linen, seals were commonly given to owners of bleachyards ; and a few years later grants for the establishment of
bleachworks were regularly given by the Linen Board. Between
1722 and 1728 nearly £10,000 were spent in grants for the
purpose.[2] In 1723, for example, capital was advanced to
Richard Hall, an official of the Board, who had just returned
from a tour in Holland, to enable him to practice the methods
which he had learned in Haarlem.[3] And two years later an
Ulsterman, Hamilton Maxwell, received a grant for the salary
of his Dutch manager.[4]

Without doubt many other bleachgreens were opened in the
second quarter of the century, and bleaching became a very
important branch of the industry. It was not only that the
greater volume of trade made specialized bleaching a paying
concern. There was the further reason that in this period some
of the more advanced and delicate kinds of manufacture were
developing—the fine yard-wides of south Antrim, the cambric,
lawn, diaper, and damask of Armagh and south Down—which
demanded a high degree of skill in bleaching and finishing.

Even then the processes were by no means efficient, and
bleachgreens were as a rule quite small concerns. Buttermilk
was still commonly used for ' souring '. Washing was done in
the fields with water baled from trenches by means of wooden
scoops.[5] Machinery for finishing was only gradually coming

in andere landen meer bevlijtigd helf om in de kunst van bleken en bereiden
der linnens de Hollanders te evenaren.' See also Blok, *History of the Dutch
People*, v. 189.
  [1] McCall, u.s.   [2] *Precedents and Abstracts*, pp. 120, 121.
  [3] ibid., p. 64. Hall failed to carry out his promises—a common fault with
the beneficiaries of the Board—and his grant ceased in 1731 (ibid., p. 117).
  [4] McCall, p. 86.
  [5] Sampson, *Survey of co. Derry*, p. 356. Sampson says that these simple
methods were still in use about 1750. However, bleaching in co. Derry seems
to have been backward as compared with that of Antrim and Down : e. g.
there was no bleachgreen near Coleraine until 1734 (Lewis, *Top. Dict.*, i, 384).
Later in the century bleaching made great progress in co. Derry.

into use. The first beetling machine in Ireland was set up by Hamilton Maxwell in 1725.[1] It was not until the last decade of the century that bleaching attained to a really large scale, or made any approach to scientific method. Nevertheless, by 1725 it had already passed beyond the reach of the ordinary weaver.

Not only were weavers no longer able to bleach on their own account : in most cases they could not even afford to deal with bleachers. They would, of course, have been glad to gain an additional profit by selling finished cloth, but it was much more convenient to sell the webs unfinished. Bleaching was a long and tedious process—three months were a normal period— and until the last few years of the century it was only practised in the spring and summer months. In fact a law was passed in 1727 prescribing a close season, from the middle of August to the beginning of February, during which no webs might be laid down to bleach.[2] As the ordinary weavers could not wait for six or eight months before receiving the price of their cloth, the sale of white linen was necessarily undertaken by men who could command a certain amount of capital. Thus, as a result of the more advanced methods of bleaching, there arose a class of middlemen known as drapers.

Drapers. The normal business of a draper was to buy brown linen for cash from weavers ; to contract for the bleaching and finishing, when these processes were needed ; then, several months later, to dispose of the white cloth, usually to merchants and exporters in Dublin.

There is no definite evidence of the origin of the drapers' class or the date of their appearance. Drapers were not mentioned during the first forty years of the eighteenth century in statutes or in the proceedings of the Linen Board ; but that is not surprising, for the authorities were chiefly interested in flax-growing and the processes of manufacture, and concerned themselves very little with the commercial side of the trade. We may safely assume that drapers were becoming a distinct class about 1720, at the time when specialized bleaching was developing, for the presence of bleachers implied the existence of drapers. In all probability many of the early drapers were shopkeepers who had made a practice of buying linen at fairs.

---

[1] McCall, pp. 23, 86.   [2] 1 George II, c. 11.

They would keep part of the stock in their shops, and would sell some brown linen to larger merchants, who would export it to Holland for finishing. Their ordinary business would supply them with capital, and would enable them to build up a connexion from small beginnings as the linen trade increased.

The drapers had their heyday between 1740 and 1780. In the last few years of the century their position began to be assailed by wealthy merchants, who used more advanced methods, and could give longer credit. But in the meantime they were one of the chief connecting links between manufacturers and consumers. They must have done a great deal towards building up the prosperity of the trade, and the more successful among them gained a large share of the profits.

Origin of Brown Linen Markets. An important change in organization connected with the rise of drapers was the substitution of brown linen markets for fairs. We have noticed already the methods of trade in these markets, particularly the sale of cloth by a large body of weavers to a comparatively small number of drapers. The markets were, in fact, the new means of exchange suited to the new circumstances of manufacture. As long as bleaching was done at home, and the output of cloth from most households was small—the product of work done at odd times when labour in the fields was not needed—it was the custom for weavers to sell their cloth, either brown or bleached, in fairs. Each weaver would probably be able to dispose of all his webs by attending two or three fairs in a year. The webs were sold to local shopkeepers, or to the agents of Dublin merchants and wholesale houses in England. At Banbridge, for instance, great fairs for linen cloth were held five times a year, and were ' constantly attended by factors from England '.[1]

The following description of the fairs was given by a writer of the early nineteenth century :—' Each fair continued three days. The first was appropriated to yarn and linen cloth ; the second to cattle and toys ; the third to amusements. As patents were generally obtained for two fairs to be held in the year in the same town, they were then convenient for the manufacturer and the merchant.' [2]

[1] Harris, *Ancient and Present State of the County of Down*, p. 83.
[2] Stephenson, *Select Papers*, p. 28.

But when the demand for cloth increased, and many farmers began to devote more time to weaving than to agriculture, the old system gradually gave way. Weavers could no longer undertake bleaching. On the other hand, they had many more brown webs to sell. It was not now a question of selling a few cloths from time to time in order to gain some pocket-money. The seller was largely dependent on his weaving. He could not afford to wait and accumulate stock : he was obliged to sell his cloth at frequent intervals. Therefore weavers were very glad to support the markets—monthly, fortnightly, or weekly— which were organized in small towns all over the manufacturing districts of Ulster. The new system was also convenient to drapers. They lived close at hand, unlike the travelling merchants who bought at fairs, so that they could easily attend the markets with regularity. Moreover, when the trade was fully developed, it was as much as the drapers could do to transact all their business in the time available, even in weekly markets ; and it would have been impossible for them to rely on a small number of fairs. Thus weekly markets were to the interest of weavers and drapers alike. For this reason the system, when once it had been introduced, would be likely to spread quickly, the more so since the early markets were nothing more than meetings of buyers and sellers in the open street.

The detachment of linen markets was far from destroying the fairs ; in fact they continue to the present day as an important feature of Irish economy, although they have become virtually monthly markets for live stock and agricultural produce, which supplement the regular weekly markets of the larger towns. In the eighteenth century fairs were also used by the peasantry for the purchase of clothing and household goods, and outside Ulster they were still the chief means of disposing of such linen as was made for sale.

We may refer the origin of brown linen markets to the same period as that of the rise of the bleachers' and drapers' trades— from 1720 onwards—since these changes were all interdependent. The market in Belfast was organized in 1720;[1] those in some other towns, such as Lisburn and Armagh, may have

[1] Owen, *History of Belfast*, p. 142.

appeared a few years earlier.[1] But the movement continued steadily for at least thirty years. Even after 1760 markets were still being formed in the smaller towns. Thus in 1762 advertisements appeared in the press inviting attendance at a monthly market in Loughgall, co. Armagh, ' as many of the principal dealers in linen have declared against buying brown linens in any fairs ; ' and another at Seaford, co. Down, ' as markets are found by experience to be more convenient than fairs for buying or selling linen cloth with yarn.' [2]

The mention of yarn in the latter advertisement illustrates the fact that yarn was commonly sold in the markets together with linen. Flax was often sold as well. Sometimes there were special hours for different departments of trade. In Portadown, for instance, the yarn market opened at 8 a.m., the linen market two hours later.

Market Halls. When markets were well established, special halls were built in certain towns, chiefly in the most important centres of trade, such as Belfast, Londonderry, Ballymena, Banbridge, and Lisburn. The halls were often built by local landowners, a few by public subscriptions.[3] They were of the same type as the wool halls in Yorkshire, and many other market halls elsewhere : enclosures, partially or wholly roofed over, providing warehouse accommodation, and platforms, or ' stone standings ' for the buyers. But such buildings were exceptional :

---

[1] According to McCall (p. 13) bleached linen was still sold in fairs in 1720. Stephenson (*Select Papers*, p. 29) stated that the custom ended in 1728. But the context shows that he was alluding to the opening of the Linen Hall in Dublin in that year. His statement therefore has little value, because there had been a market for white linen in Dublin for many years before the hall was built.

[2] *Belfast News Letter*, 23 February, 26 March, 1762. On 6 April in the same year about sixty drapers announced that in future they would no longer attend fairs in Tyrone and Monaghan, but would confine their buying to markets. Owing to the large number of markets in Antrim, Down, and Armagh, fairs had become ' unnecessary and inconvenient '. This was a year of active trade, when drapers would be exceptionally busy, and they would prefer regular dealings in markets to the more casual and uncertain methods of the fairs. Further, at this time it was well known that Parliament was preparing a scheme for the inspection of all cloths sold in markets. The scheme was designed for the benefit of drapers and it would be a strong inducement to them to deal in goods that had been examined and sealed. For the outcome of the scheme see below, chaps. vi and viii.

[3] It is convenient to mention the market halls here, but as a matter of fact they were all built after the middle of the eighteenth century.

there were only about a dozen of them in Ulster, and the great majority of linen markets continued to be held in the open street. Indeed, there was a curious conservatism among both buyers and sellers. In Newry, although a hall was available, the market, one of the largest in Ulster, was always held in the open air, and in one of the most crowded streets, where dealers were constantly disturbed by the traffic.[1] The hall at Down-patrick was only used in bad weather. At Coleraine there was a hall on each side of the river. As the competition of the two halls was troublesome, the dealers decided to use neither. They returned to the street, and the buildings were turned to other uses.[2]

There is no record of the number of markets established between 1700 and 1750, or of the total volume of trade passing through them. But since the manufacture by 1750 was spread over a great part of Antrim, Down, Armagh, Londonderry, and Tyrone, there must have been some dozens of markets to meet the requirements of weavers. For each weaver would have to walk to market with a heavy pack, dispose of his goods and return home on the same day. Consequently he would need to be served by a market within a few miles of his home. If the weavers had all lived near the chief towns, a very few markets would have been enough; but the linen manufacture was a 'fabrique dispersée' carried on in farmsteads scattered over the whole province. In the latter half of the century there were usually forty or fifty markets. Seventy-six towns or villages had markets at one time or another between 1780 and 1820, but the number varied according to the state of trade; for in slack seasons some of the smaller markets were suspended, and at other times special enterprise on the part of a few persons would lead to the opening of a new market.

For about a century—roughly from 1730 to 1830—brown linen markets were one of the leading characteristics of the industry in Ulster. It was not so in the southern provinces. We have seen that the system of land tenure there did not lend itself to abundant markets and fairs for agricultural produce. Neither did the capitalistic methods of manufacture, which were

---

[1] Corry, *Report*, 1816, Appendix ; Coote, *Survey of Armagh*, p. 342.

[2] Corry, *Report*, u.s. For the curious case of the market in Enniskillen see below, chap. ix, p. 171, n.

common in the south, favour the growth of linen markets. There were never, I believe, more than two dozen such markets, and most of them were very small. The only one which really flourished was at Drogheda, and that market was of a peculiar type, supplied by manufacturing employers in place of small weavers. In 1816 (the only year for which there are figures to provide a comparison) the average weekly sales in the whole of the southern markets except Drogheda were estimated at £5,270.[1] The weekly average in Lisburn alone at that time was £5,000, and for the whole of Ulster it was £44,673. Thus the account of the industry which has been given in this chapter applies chiefly to Ulster. But seeing that Ulster soon gained a great preponderance in manufacture, it is true to say that most of the Irish linen trade in the period we have been describing (1725-50) passed through the local markets, and was organized by the three classes of farmer-weavers, drapers, and bleachers.

Commerce and Industry combined.   The classes of bleachers and drapers, however, seem always to have been more or less merged together. Even in the first half of the century drapers were often described as bleachers, and bleachers as merchants. This over-lapping is easily explained. The two classes both possessed some capital, and formed together a comparatively wealthy group at the head of the industry.[2]   Moreover, a draper who had enough capital to spare would find it to his advantage to bleach his own cloths and so gain a double profit. He could do so the more readily since the Linen Board, in its early enthusiasm, made rather lavish grants for the building of bleachworks. Similarly the bleacher could keep his works more steadily employed if he supplemented his customers' cloths with a stock of brown linen of his own. Thus bleachers and drapers joined in buying goods in the brown linen markets and selling them to exporting merchants.[3]

---

[1] Besnard, *Report.* For details of sales in Ulster see below, Appendix I. The figure for the important market in Drogheda was £3,500.

[2] They were only wealthy as compared with the weaver whose farm was from one to five acres in extent. Drapers often had from ten to twenty acres. Towards the end of the century, when bleaching was done on a much larger scale, a bleacher commonly had to make an initial outlay of two or three thousand pounds on machinery alone (Stephenson, *Select Papers*, p. 48).

[3] This is a further example of the advance of trade by the extension and branching of enterprise, which we have noted already in the case of the farmer-weavers.

The Dublin Market. Most of the bleached and some brown webs, whether for sale in the other provinces or for export, were taken by road to Dublin. It was natural that Dublin should be the great distributing centre. The main roads through Ireland converged on the capital ; so, too, did the most frequented shipping routes from English ports ; and the leading merchants were found there. Indeed it was expected for many years that Dublin would become the chief seat of industry as of trade.[1]

The drapers themselves travelled to Dublin, usually in companies for the sake of protection. There they sold to wholesale merchants the cloths that were needed for distribution in the southern provinces. Buyers from England also crossed to Dublin. They might meet the drapers there, and deal with them directly by cash payments. But purchasing would often be done for the English customers by Dublin merchants. In technical terms, the latter became factors for the buyers. On the other hand, drapers would sometimes find that, when they had sold as much as they could to merchants and factors, both Irish and English, some stock was still left on their hands. They would prefer not to take it home, but until the latter end of the century few of them had warehouse accommodation in Dublin.[2] Therefore it was the general practice for them to leave their unsold cloth with the factors, who would then act on their behalf, and dispose of the cloth at various times between the chief marketing seasons.[3] This system of dealing through factors was well established in 1728, when the Linen Hall was opened.

Export trade. The English buyers came chiefly from three ports, London, Bristol, and Chester. With the last two Dublin had an ancient connexion. In the thirteenth century colonists from Bristol played a large part in securing the first charter of

[1] This fact is illustrated by the freedom with which the Linen Board gave grants for bleachgreens and weaving factories in the neighbourhood of Dublin.

[2] Warehouse room was provided in the Linen Hall but most of it was leased to the Dublin factors. About the year 1800, when the Hall had been much enlarged, there were 131 rooms for drapers and 242 for factors. By 1825, however, for reasons which will be shown later, the drapers' rooms were hardly used at all, and it is doubtful whether they were ever in full use.

[3] Although some stock was held by drapers or Dublin factors, still more, at any rate in the earlier half of the eighteenth century, was held by merchants or factors in London, who could better afford to wait for payment.

the city ; [1] and ever since that time the trading connexion had been maintained. During the eighteenth century it even increased, for Bristol shared with Liverpool in the growing trade with the West Indies, and helped to develop the supply of linen to Spain and Portugal.[2] Much of the Portuguese coinage, which circulated freely in Ireland (and was, indeed, the best currency in the country),[3] probably came by way of Bristol. One of the chief articles of export from Dublin to Bristol had been wool, for use in the West of England manufacture—although, of course, the very fine wool which made the reputation of the western clothiers came chiefly from Spain. The wool-buyers from Bristol may well have developed a trade in Irish linens as a supplement to their main business.

In the fifteenth century the glovers of Chester bought raw leather from Ireland, and much of the linen yarn which was supplied to Manchester probably went by the same route.[4] During the whole of the eighteenth century the connexion of Dublin with these two towns was so important that the busiest times of the year in the Dublin linen market were regularly the periods preceding the Bristol and Chester fairs.[5] Among the officials and dealers in the Linen Hall these periods were appropriately known as the ' hurries '.[6]

There was no such periodic demand in the trade with London : wholesale merchants there could at all times distribute goods to retailers in the City and the provinces, or transport them to the Continent. We may imagine that the strongest demand would be in the spring, when cargoes were being collected for the East and West Indies ; and this special need may have been one reason for the early beginning of the bleaching season. It happened, too, that the supply was greatest at the same time. In the winter months farmers had leisure to weave, and in February there must have been a great accumulation of cloth ready for bleaching. As this cloth would normally be finished

[1] Gross, *Gild Merchant*, i, 19.

[2] Until, in the latter years of the century, direct trade began to develop between the northern Irish ports and the Continent and West Indies.

[3] Wakefield, *Account of Ireland*, ii, 156–9.

[4] Unwin, *Industrial Organization*, p. 72 ; Warden, p. 389.

[5] i. e. the first few days of February, June, and October. Stephenson, *Select Papers*, p. 29 ; Young, *Tour*, p. 107 ; O'Reilly, *The Dublin Linen Hall*, p. 6.

[6] This word is often used in the Board's Proceedings.

in April, the markets for white linen would in any case be very active in the spring.

Enough has been said already to show that the demand for linen in England had a great effect on the Irish markets. In this early period the trade with England was, both relatively and absolutely, less important than it became later, for exports certainly grew faster than home consumption, and nearly all exports went to England. It was estimated in 1802 that well over half the total output of linen in Ireland was exported ; [1] eighty years earlier the proportion was probably about a quarter.[2] Yet the true relation is hardly shown by these figures ; for, in the first place, the goods sent to England were of such a kind that there was scope for initiative and enterprise in their production—so that the demand from London was a constant force in the direction of technical progress ; secondly, the export trade would imply a more elaborate organization of marketing, and particularly of credit ; and thirdly, credit supplied from London was in effect an advance of capital which was used to develop industry in Ireland. The description of trading relations between Dublin and London must be deferred until we come to deal with a later period for which the evidence is more adequate. Indeed there is almost no evidence from the first half of the eighteenth century : we can only argue *a priori* that there must have been credit dealings similar to those of later years, for otherwise the export trade would never have grown as rapidly as it did. One of the very few definite examples is that of Patrick Adair, a linen merchant in London, who gave evidence before a parliamentary committee in 1744. He said that he had in his warehouse at that time more than £44,000 worth of Irish linens.[3] This amount was equal to several months' output of any one of the chief markets in Ulster : it was, in fact, about one-tenth of the total export from Ireland in 1744. The fact

---

[1] McCall, p. 69.

[2] In 1727, when the exports were valued at £238,000, Dobbs (*Essay upon the Trade . . . of Ireland*, p. 355) estimated the total consumption at ' not far short of £1,000,000 '. I think that Dobbs largely over-estimated the home consumption ; but the proportions which he assumed for 1727 would probably be about right for 1720, when the export was only £128,000. In 1738 the exports were estimated to be two-sevenths of the total production (Stephenson, *Inquiry*, p. 119, quoting *A Letter from a Merchant who has left off Trade*). At any rate it is clear that exports were growing faster than production for the home market.   [3] *H. of C. Reports* (Great Britain), ii, 69.

that their agents or customers overseas were bearing the cost of holding such large stocks was obviously of great importance to the producers in Ireland. If the capital had not been forthcoming in England, the burden would have fallen on drapers and bleachers in Ulster, and merchants in Dublin ; and as they had little capital of their own, and very limited powers of securing credit from banks, they would have had to be content with a much smaller volume of trade.

The system of trade and industry which has been outlined in this chapter was built up during the period of steady expansion, in the first half of the eighteenth century, and especially between 1720 and 1750. This system remained, with little outward change, for about a century. In 1820 there were still over forty brown linen markets in Ulster ; many thousands of independent weavers still supplied cloth to the markets ; drapers still took large quantities of this cloth to Dublin, for sale in the Linen Hall. Under the surface, however, there were considerable changes in organization between 1750 and 1820, which prepared the way for factory production and modern methods of trade. The development and its climax will be dealt with in the later chapters. But before discussing this question we must complete our survey of the earlier period by describing the work of the Irish Government and its chief agent, the Board of Trustees.

IV

PARLIAMENT AND THE BOARD OF TRUSTEES
(1700–50)

State Intervention. The success of the linen trade in Ulster is commonly attributed to three main causes. The foundations are said to have been laid by Strafford and Ormonde. Next a great impulse was given by the Huguenot settlement. Finally, the continued growth, through the eighteenth century and on into the nineteenth, was due to the fostering care of government, acting chiefly through the Board of Trustees. The woollen industry of Ireland was suppressed by the English Government, with help from the Irish. Other industries were hampered by navigation acts and prohibitive duties in Great Britain. The linen trade alone was encouraged by both governments ; and as this was the one flourishing manufacture in Ireland, it is an easy assumption that success in this case and failure in the others were alike due to deliberate policy. But a closer examination of the facts will make us cautious in accepting this view without a good deal of qualification. We have seen reason to believe that Strafford and Ormonde had no more than a trifling influence on the linen trade, and that the Huguenots, although their achievements were far greater, could have done little if they had not been helped by favouring circumstances, above all by a land system which encouraged the growth of country manufacture.

The fact is that the rise of a great industry is a very complicated and delicate process. It needs the co-operation and enterprise of craftsmen and traders, a steady improvement in methods of manufacture, the supply of capital, organization of markets and credit, development of transport, exploitation of sources of raw material, and a constant adaptation to demand. The growth of the Irish linen industry was a process of this kind, a movement far too wide and complex to be the work of any individual or any small group of patrons.

We shall be on our guard, therefore, against expecting very

much from the efforts of the Irish Government. Yet it is well
worth while to inquire with some care into the effects of their
policy and statesmanship. Even negative results are of value,
for it is almost as important to understand where and why
State intervention has miscarried as to learn of its success.
Moreover, in recent years, although private enterprise and
voluntary association have done an immense work in Ireland,
State activities, such as land purchase, the guarantee of tenant
right, and the undertakings of the Congested Districts Board
and the Board of Agriculture, have also been of very great
public service. The machinery of government in the eighteenth
century was much less efficient than it is to-day, but statesmen
at that time showed no lack of economic ambition. The Irish
Government was certainly interested in passing measures, both
constructive and regulative, for the benefit of trade, and of the
linen trade more than any other. In this chapter we shall
examine the measures passed before the middle of the eighteenth
century, during the period in which the foundations of the
industry were laid.

Linen Laws. Act of 1666. The series began in 1666, under
Ormonde's administration.[1] The chief feature of the Act passed
in that year was a clause instructing farmers to sow a certain
quantity of flax-seed every year, but there was, as we should
expect ' a general neglect in the execution ' of this clause.[2]
There was also a provision that £20 a year should be spent in
each county to encourage the making of ' Fine linen and broad '.
Even if this clause had been carried out, its effect would have
been inappreciable, but it was practically a dead letter—in some
counties there was not a single claimant for the prize. Sir Wm.
Temple, who criticized the Act, suggested two means of encouraging the linen manufacture. He held that increase of population
would be a natural stimulus : it would ' make things necessary
to life dear, and thereby force general industry from each member
of a family (women as well as men), and in as many sorts as they
can well turn to, which among others may in time come to run
in vein this way '.[3] The history of Ireland in the next two

---

[1] 18 Charles II, c. 9.　　　　　[2] Temple, *Essay*, p. 114.
[3] ibid. A Scotsman, writing in 1778, inverted Temple's argument in regard
to population and industry : ' The woollen manufacture is peculiarly favour-

centuries did not justify his hope. The rapidly growing population, instead of trying as many sorts of manufacture as they
could well turn to, were driven to rely almost entirely on the
land, until this one resource completely failed them, and left
them to emigrate or starve. Temple's second scheme was a wide
measure of State interference. He proposed that the Government should organize the whole manufacture ; ' or, should this
seem too great an undertaking for the present age,' that a public
department should buy linen cloth at ' common, moderate
prices ' in order to guarantee a stable market to the weaver.

Regulations of 1705. Fortunately no attempt was made to
carry out his project. Instead, charters were given to joint-
stock companies in Drogheda and Dundalk, and at length the
Royal Corporation was founded under Crommelin's management.
But Parliament did not leave the new enterprise to stand alone.
In 1705 the first regulating Act was passed, no doubt on the
initiative of the Huguenots. The existing export duties on linen
goods were removed ; flax-seed, machinery for linen manufacture, and potash for bleaching were admitted free of tax.[1]
For the first time, though by no means the last, the use of lime in
bleaching was forbidden. Throughout the eighteenth century
there was a strong prejudice against lime. The Government,
acting through the Linen Board, inspectors, and magistrates,
constantly strove to prevent its use, and bleachers as persistently
tried to use it without being caught. The minutes of the Linen
Board show frequent evidence of this struggle ; and defects in
white linen cloths were as a matter of course put down to lime.
It was only in the last decade of the century, when the research
of French chemists on chlorine had shown clearly the value of
chloride of lime as a bleaching agent, that the ' French method '
was countenanced by Government ; and even then it was only
half tolerated.

Another clause in the Act of 1705 forbade, with a few exceptions, the manufacture of cloth narrower than $22\frac{1}{2}$ inches.

---

able in promoting matrimony, and consequently, population. Children from
five years of age may begin to be useful, and are even employed in different
branches of it which are singularly adapted to their infant state.' (David Loch,
quoted by Bremner, op. cit., p. 152.)

[1] There was a duty of five per cent. on all exports from Ireland. Linen,
cloth, and yarn were now specially excepted.

This clause was probably put in to safeguard the position of the Huguenots. Its strict enforcement would have put an end to all the weaving of bandle linen in Ireland ; but if, as Stephenson suggested, the reference was only to cloth for export, the regu-lation was unnecessary, seeing that there was very little demand outside of Ireland for any webs narrower than 25 inches.[1] Another clause laid down standard lengths for reeling and making-up yarn. This Act also allowed to weavers the freedom of their boroughs and some minor privileges, on condition of a seven-years' apprenticeship—a clause of no great importance, since the industry in general avoided towns and flourished in the country.

Measures of Encouragement, 1707-9. The next statute, passed in 1707,[2] was designed to stimulate, rather than regulate, production. It prescribed, for the first time, bounties for pre-paring kelp to be used in bleaching ; for the import of hemp seed to increase the supply of raw material, and for the export of sail-cloth—the beginning of a long and unsuccessful struggle to promote the hempen manufacture. The other main effort suggested in this statute was the foundation of spinning schools in the chief towns, and in connexion with poor-houses.[3] This measure, again, was meant to benefit the Huguenots.[4] They were used to working with very fine yarn, and the object of teaching flax-dressing and spinning was to train workers in the finest branches of the trade. The Irish people already knew well how to grow and prepare flax of coarse or medium quality.

As these Acts were ' found by experience not to have fully and effectually answered the purposes for which they were intended ' a supplementary measure was passed two years later,[5] extending the bounties on imported seed to flax as well as hemp, increasing the bounties for exported sail-cloth, and offering grants to the masters of poor-houses of £2 for each apprentice to the linen in-dustry. The Act of 1705 had offered privileges to master weavers on condition of apprenticeship. Now an apprenticeship of five

---

[1] R. Stephenson, *Inquiry*, p. 65. This clause was repealed in 1739 (ibid., p. 152).   [2] 6 Anne, c. 9.
[3] Workhouses in Ireland were of course voluntary until 1838, and they only existed in Dublin, Cork, and a few other towns.
[4] Stephenson, *Inquiry*, u.s.   [5] 8 and 9 Anne, c. 12.

years for linen weaving and two years for sail-cloth was made
compulsory, together with two years' service as a journeyman,
before the weaver could become an independent master. This
was the clause already mentioned as aiming at a partial monopoly
for the Huguenots.[1] In the same year a prohibitive duty of
1s. 6d. a yard was laid on calico imported into Ireland, and
a heavy duty of 6d. a yard (roughly, forty to fifty per cent. *ad
valorem*) on imported linen.

These statutes were never put into force. Bounties were paid,
it is true, and customs duties were levied, although there was
much evasion by means of false stamps.[2] But the regulating
clauses were left to be administered by local justices, who as
a rule had no interest in them, or by informers who were not
forthcoming.[3] The only persons likely to be concerned, for
instance, with the reeling and measurement of yarn were wholesale merchants at the ports; but both they and their customers
in England actually preferred the 'unstatutable' yarns to
which they were accustomed.

Board of Trustees, 1711. While Parliament was passing these
inoperative laws the linen trade was growing rapidly on its own
account. The quantity of exports had at least quadrupled since
1700, and there was doubtless a large increase in the sales for
home consumption as well. Nevertheless the growth was almost
entirely in Ulster. Members from other districts probably
reported that they had seen no sign of activity, and there was
little progress in the neighbourhood of Dublin. It was fully
expected that the trade could be made to flourish in all parts
of the country. For this reason Parliament regarded its previous
acts as failures, held that manufacture was 'found to be in

---

[1] This clause was partially, though not strictly, enforced. Stephenson
realized that its true object was a monopoly for the French immigrants. He
attributed some of the early combinations among weavers to this regulation,
and he added the following just criticism: 'Gentlemen did not realise what
treasure the kingdom was possessed of in having many thousands of native
weavers, that had served little or no apprenticeship, that all must have been
suppressed, had this law taken effect.'

[2] For this reason the system of stamping was revoked by the Act of 1727
(1 Geo. II, c. 11).

[3] It was stated in the preamble to the Act of 1710: 'The several acts of
Parliament have not answered the said purpose for which they were intended
because the said encouragements so granted have not been put under just
regulation or management.'

a declining condition ',[1] and passed in 1710 a fresh measure,
' to enforce such acts as have been made for the improvement
of the linen manufacture and for a further regulation of the
same '.[2] The new Act continued the existing duties, and laid
down detailed rules for the measurement of linen webs. But
its chief outcome was the Board of Trustees. It was obviously
not enough to leave the enforcement of laws to the chance action
of individuals : some permanent authority was needed. Therefore the Lord-Lieutenant was instructed to appoint trustees who
should see to the administration of the Acts, distribute bounties
and prizes, and do everything in their power to promote the
trade. Parliament was to provide them with funds—in part
the proceeds of customs on calico and linen.

Eighty trustees were nominated, twenty from each province,
for it was still hoped that all the provinces would share about
equally in the manufacture. The Board first met at Dublin
Castle in 1711, and from that time until 1828 it held meetings
frequently, in active seasons as often as once a week. According
to its own description, the Board was ' composed of people of
the greatest rank in both Houses of Parliament '.[3]

Bargains with Great Britain, 1715–17. There was now a
definite organization for carrying out the law relating to the
linen trade, and before the middle of the century Parliament
enlarged this body of laws by nine or ten fresh statutes. In 1715
the import duties and bounties described above were renewed
for periods varying from seven to twenty-one years. At the
same time it was agreed that linen from Scotland should be
imported freely after the lapse of one year,[4] and in 1717 the same
freedom was extended to all linens made in England.[5] These
measures were the result of a bargain. Ormonde, in 1667, had
prohibited by order in council the import of linens and various
other goods from Scotland.[6] As a part of the agreement to
encourage the linen trade in Ireland, the English Parliament
had allowed free export of linen goods from Ireland to the
Colonies and had prohibited the export of Scottish linen to
Ireland. Moreover Irish linen, from 1696 onwards, was imported

---

[1] Cf. the opinion of the Linen Board : ' The linen trade here has languished
since 1707.' (Letter to Joshua Lee, 1713, *Precedents and Abstracts*, p. 8.)
[2] 9 Anne, c. 3.   [3] *Precedents and Abstracts*, p. 8.
[4] Geo. I, c. 13.   [5] 4 Geo. I, c. 6.   [6] Horner, p. 20.

free of duty into England, whereas English linen had to pay in Ireland a tax of twelve shillings for each hundred ells (or rather over five per cent. *ad valorem*). The Scottish prohibition was about to lapse, and quite naturally there was strong objection in Scotland, not only to its renewal but to the continuance of this one-sided bargain as a whole.[1] Therefore the British Government threatened to tax Irish linen unless the prohibition and import duty were removed in Ireland. The Irish government agreed, and passed the Acts of 1715 and 1717. The English Parliament responded by continuing the freedom of export from Ireland to Great Britain and the Colonies.[2]

Regulation of Bleached Linen and Yarn, 1719-23. Further regulations were enacted in 1719.[3] The most important change was the appointment by the Linen Board of lappers—officials who should do similar work to that of aulnagers of wool, the inspection and stamping of cloth in return for a fee of a penny or twopence for each piece. To make the lappers' work easier and more certain it was ordered that all linen and yarn should be sold in an open market or fair, and that no bleached webs should be sold without inspection and sealing. This clause could not be enforced: if it had been, it would have made 'customer weaving' impossible, and so would have checked any advance in organization. Bleachers or drapers were generally appointed to do this work of inspection:[4] they were supplied by the Board with seals, and were required to examine and stamp cloths either in the market or in their own works. The regulations applied only to white linen, which was ready for export or for retailing at home, and its object was to maintain the quality and uniformity of Irish goods.

[1] Preamble to Act of 1717. Irish woollen dealers had equal title to complain of their exclusion from the English market ; but that would not mend matters for the English and Scottish linen dealers.

[2] 3 Geo. I, c. (English). This statute was curiously entitled : ' Act for continuing the liberty of exporting Irish linen cloth to the British plantations in America duty free, and for the more effectual discovery of and prosecuting such as shall unlawfully export wool and woollen manufactures from Ireland, and for relief of John Fletcher in respect of duty by him paid for a quantity of salt lost in the exportation from Ireland.'

[3] Geo. I, c. 7. A similar measure had been passed in Scotland as early as 1613 (Bremner, pp. 215, 216).

[4] Lappers could charge an additional penny for each piece which they beetled. As beetling was part of the regular work of a bleacher, this regulation implied that bleachers would generally carry out the aulnage.

Detailed regulations for lappers were drawn up by the Board in January, 1720. But from the beginning, from this very year, the regulations were constantly broken. One lapper, for example, was found to be illiterate and therefore ignorant of the regulations, and unable to measure or mark the length of webs.[1] Another was in the habit of sending out his wife with seals to mark all webs without discrimination.[2] Complaints of this kind occupy a large space in the Board's minutes. Eventually, in 1735, a committee was appointed to inquire into the whole question. In the following year (its proceedings must have been leisurely) it recommended that no more persons who had linen of their own—i. e. drapers and bleachers—should be entrusted with seals.[3] This case illustrates very well the difficulty of regulating a widely diffused industry without a large staff of thoroughly reliable inspectors.

In 1723 [4] various duties were renewed, bounties continued or increased, and minor regulations added. In particular Parliament was troubled with the old question of 'unstatutable' yarn. On the ground that 'all methods hitherto used have proved ineffectual to oblige the people of this kingdom to reel and divide their own yarn in a regular and fair manner', it was made a punishable offence merely to possess unstatutable yarn. This clause was the result of a special visit paid by four inspectors to the unrepentant merchants in Drogheda.[5] If the clause had any effect its success was only temporary. In the next year, merchants in Manchester expressed their objection to yarn reeled according to law.[6] In 1727 the clause was repeated with slight additions,[7] and sixty years later the same question was still under discussion.[8]

Regulation of Brown Linen, 1733-45. The next step was taken in 1733, when provision was first made for the inspection of brown linen. Up to this time finished cloth alone had been liable to inspection and sealing. But bleachers who were accused of spoiling cloth had often blamed the weavers for supplying them

---

[1] *Precedents and Abstracts*, p. 43.   [2] ibid., p. 44.
[3] ibid., pp. 143, 149, 150. The recommendation, of course, was not adopted. If it had been, the whole system of sealing would have collapsed.
[4] 10 Geo. I, c. 21.   [5] *Precedents and Abstracts*, pp. 53, 58.
[6] ibid., p. 65.   [7] Geo. II, c. 11.
[8] Nevill, *Seasonable Remarks* (1783), Appendix.

with bad material. Therefore it was resolved that the weavers' work should be put under regulation. Since 1719, when the aulnage of white linen had begun, it had become possible to inspect brown webs, because they were now concentrated for sale in markets, as white linens were concentrated at the bleach-greens. Moreover, the methods of sale in the open markets made some scheme of inspection not only possible but very desirable ; for the draper seldom had a chance to examine the goods at all adequately before buying them. Standing on his stone or at his stall in the open market he was confronted with a crowd of weavers who passed quickly before him, allowing him time for only a glance at their webs. Each draper had to buy in this way, within one or two hours, some dozens of pieces from as many weavers. The pieces were nearly always rolled up tightly and tied at the ends, so that the buyers could see no more than the selvage and about a yard of cloth on the outside of the roll. It was regularly contrived that this exposed ' lap-yard ' should be the best part of the piece. The weaver, when his bargain was struck, would carry his cloth to the draper's warehouse, or more commonly to a room in an inn hired for the purpose, and there when the market was over the draper would measure the cloths, but necessarily with such haste that he could not thoroughly test the quality. Thus linen sold in the northern markets was never properly examined until it was opened out for bleaching, and often it was not inspected at all.

The statute of 1733 [1] allowed the Linen Board to appoint lappers for brown linen, and at the outset there were special officials charged with the duty of attending the markets as lappers. Weavers were expected to bring cloth to them for inspection and sealing before the opening of a market, and to pay them a penny for every twenty yards examined. It was hoped that this measure would serve as a permanent guarantee of the standard of Irish cloth. But two years later it was mentioned in another statute that the lappers were abusing their authority, stamping cloth without inspection and lending seals to their friends. [2] Complaints had probably come from bleachers and drapers that the new officials were as dishonest as any weaver ; for just after the passing of this second Act the

[1] 7 Geo. II, c. 10.   [2] 9 Geo. II, c. 4.

Trustees issued an order handing over the sealing of brown linens
to the owners of ' white seals '.[1] Seeing that most of the white
linen lappers had no time for this additional work, the work was
not done and the Act had no effect. More correctly, it had no
effect for a long time ; but it still remained in the statute book,
and thirty years later it leapt suddenly into importance, when
the system of sealing brown linen was revived.

From 1735, for nearly twenty years, both Parliament and the
Trustees seem to some extent to have lost interest in the linen
trade. The twelve statutes already passed since 1700 had
sanctioned practically all the known means of promoting trade,
and as hardly any fresh powers or duties were given to the
Trustees, their work became purely a matter of routine.

Only two measures of any note were passed in this period.
The first was a special attempt to increase trade in the southern
provinces. In 1735 Parliament made a grant of £2,000 to the
Linen Board, to be devoted in equal shares to Leinster, Munster,
and Connaught.[2] In 1737 it was evidently suggested to Parliament that the trade would have more scope in those provinces if
brown linen markets were organized there, similar to those in
Ulster. The northern markets had grown spontaneously, and
only when manufacture had struck a firm root. But Parliament
believed that the order could be reversed, and gave instructions
that public warehouses or market halls for brown linen should
be built in the capital towns of all counties. The cost was to be
defrayed by grand juries from the county rates.[3] Grand juries
were not as a rule very efficient bodies, but they seem to have had
enough common sense to leave the halls unbuilt. In the reports of
Stephenson's tours of inspection between 1750 and 1760 there is no
mention of any market hall except the linen hall in Dublin.

The other measure was an Act passed in 1745, which added a
few regulations for reed-making and lapping.[4] It was demanded,
very reasonably, that reeds should have even divisions, and
should be stamped with the maker's name.[5] The most important
clause provided that all brown linens should be ' crisped '—i. e.

---

[1] *Precedents and Abstracts*, pp. 140-41.
[2] ibid., p. 141.   [3] 11 Geo. II, c. 4.
[4] 19 Geo. II, c. 6. This measure was the work of Anthony Foster, who also
drafted the Act of 1764.
[5] A reed is the comblike part of a loom, consisting of a row of quills in
a frame. Warp threads pass between the quills, two through each ' split '.

made up in folds, so that they could easily be examined. It has been explained already that weavers as a general rule sold their cloth tied firmly in rolls, with only the best part of the web exposed to view. Selling in open folds would be a great help to lappers, and still more to the drapers who bought the cloth. Unfortunately ' these wise regulations were totally neglected '.[1] However, the clause relating to open folds, like the Act of 1733, after being in abeyance for several years, was revived in 1762, and figured prominently in the debates of that year and the next.

Bounties in Great Britain. To this account of legislation in Ireland we may add one measure of the British Parliament. Ever since 1696, when the import duty on Irish linen was removed, opinion and policy in England had been favourable to the linen trade in Ireland. Goodwill was shown, however, only by toleration, not by active support. But in 1743, when bounties were given for the export of linens from England, they were applied to Irish linens as well as to cloth made at home.[2] The bounties lapsed in 1753, but they were renewed from time to time, until 1830, when they were finally abandoned because of the growth of *laissez faire* principles. It has been generally believed that these bounties did much to promote the Irish export trade, and, further, that they had the effect of drawing trade to English ports, and so reducing the amount of direct export from Ireland to the colonies and foreign lands. But in the first place the cost of carriage to England would absorb at least half the bounty ; secondly, only about one-fifth of the linens sent from Ireland to England were re-exported, and therefore eligible for bounty ;[3] and thirdly, bounties were only paid after a personal application, so that Irish merchants had to travel to England whenever they wished to prefer a claim.[4] Obviously these bounties could have little influence on the course of Irish trade.

The evenness of the cloth depends on the even spacing of the splits. Reed-making, as a separate craft, is said to have been introduced into Ireland by Henri Dupré, one of Crommelin's companions.

[1] *Newry Magazine*, 1815, p. 269.

[2] The amounts, as amended in 1745, were : $\frac{1}{2}d.$ per yard for linen less than 5d. per yard in value ; 1d. per yard for linen from 5d. to 6d. per yard in value ; $1\frac{1}{2}d.$ per yard for linen 6d. to 1s. 6d. per yard in value. (Horner, p. 76 ; Miss Murray, *Commercial Revelations*, p. 120.)

[3] Miss Murray, op. cit., p. 127.

[4] *House of Commons Reports*, ii, 71. (Report of Committee on Linen Trade, 1744.)

Functions of the Trustees. In this brief survey of parliamentary efforts we have seen something incidentally of the Linen Board's activities, but a rather fuller statement is needed if we are to gain a clear idea of the government's work as a whole in support of the linen trade. The Board of Trustees was appointed in 1711, partly to see to the enforcement of regulations, partly to carry on the educational work begun by Crommelin, and in addition to give grants for new undertakings and prizes for meritorious work. Its duties can best be judged from a table showing the chief heads of expenditure during the first twenty-six years of the Board's existence.[1] The table is convenient for our purpose because it shows only the amount spent on the linen manufacture, and excludes the manufacture of sail cloth and other hempen goods.

The average annual expenditure in this period (1711–36) may be summarized as follows :

	£	per cent. of total
Salaries . . .	600	10·5
Flax and flax-seed .	3,300	58
Grants for manufacture .	1,400	24.5
Miscellaneous [2] . .	400	7

Total £5,700 [3]

The same volume contains a statement for the years 1722–8, including the expenditure on hemp and sail-cloth. The table shows that £4,300 a year were spent on the import of hemp and hemp-seed, and nearly £500 on the manufacture of hempen goods.[4]

Promotion of flax-growing. From these figures it is clear that the chief, or at any rate the most expensive, undertaking of the Trustees was the import and distribution of raw material, especially seed. Their object was twofold : to secure a supply of flax and hemp at home and to develop a new branch of agriculture.[5] We need not pay further attention to the dealings

---

[1] *Precedents and Abstracts*, Appendix. The table is reprinted in facsimile by Horner, op. cit., p. 36.

[2] Mainly incidental payments to workmen, and legal and clerical expenses.

[3] These figures are only approximate : the actual total was rather higher.

[4] *Precedents and Abstracts*, pp. 120–1. The table shows an average expenditure of £5,800 on flax, hemp, and seed. For the corresponding years the statement in the appendix gives an average for flax and flax-seed, in these seven years, of £1,500. The balance must therefore have been spent on hemp.

[5] Flax was already grown to a considerable extent in Ireland ; but anything on the scale intended by the Trustees would have been a new and important departure.

in hemp, beyond noticing the large amount spent in this direction and the fact that it produced almost no result.

From the very beginning of their operations the Trustees were much interested in the supply of flax-seed. Within a few weeks of their first meeting they had ordered a cargo of seed from Holland, which arrived in the spring of the following year (1712).[1] The seed was distributed from seven centres and was sold at much less than the cost price.[2] Payment was received by revenue collectors who, if they followed their usual practice, would allow themselves a generous commission.[3] This experiment proved so difficult and expensive, and gave rise to so much complaint from the private importers of seed, that it was not repeated during the next few years. But it was revived in 1716 and continued with slight interruption for a long time.[4] Seed from Holland had been used, no doubt, in the hope that it would produce flax as fine as that of the Netherlands, and so would minister to the favourite design of both Huguenots and Trustees, to promote the manufacture of cambrics and other fine linens. But, probably because it came to be realized that the highest counts of yarn could not be spun from flax grown in Ireland, the Board turned its attention to the coarser and cheaper seed from the Baltic provinces.[5] There is a detailed record of importation from the Baltic in 1735. On that occasion the seed was bought at Riga by a local agent who received credit for £6,000 from the Board, and the packing was supervised by an official from Ireland.[6]

In the absence of figures showing either the total import of seed into Ireland or the amount of flax produced, it is impossible

---

[1] *Precedents and Abstracts*, pp. 2, 3, 5.   [2] ibid., pp. 5, 6.
[3] There was frequently a leakage of seventeen per cent. in the collection of the Irish revenue. (Wakefield, vol. ii, p. 280.)
[4] *Precedents and Abstracts*, App. The practice continued until after the middle of the century, but I have not been able to discover when it was abandoned. Bounties for privately imported flax-seed continued until 1781. In that year the Irish Parliament reversed its policy : it decided to encourage the sowing of seed at home. Therefore bounties on imports were stopped, and replaced by bounties for home-grown seed. This new policy was abandoned ten years later, but no fresh encouragement was given to the importation of seed, and none was needed.
[5] e. g. Lord Limerick, shortly after 1750, tried to raise fine flax near Dundalk from Flemish seed ; but the outcome was a strong, coarse fibre, quite different from Flemish flax. (Stephenson, *Journal*, p. 162.)
[6] *Precedents and Abstracts*, p. 142.

to judge at all closely the result of the Board's efforts. But we have full statistics of the export of yarn from Ireland. They show, as we have already noticed, a gradual increase until 1780, when the export was 42,369 cwts. (the only occasion on which it exceeded 40,000 cwts.). From this time onwards, because of the competition of machine spinning in England and Scotland, the amount fell off much more rapidly than it had grown, until in 1830 it had fallen as low as 5,500 cwts.[1] These figures, even if allowance is made for the increased demand for yarn at home, do not suggest any great development of flax cultivation, certainly no more than we should expect to find without any artificial stimulus. There is good reason to believe Stephenson's statement that the Board's attempts to promote flax-growing had been ' very expensive and unsuccessful '.[2]

Flax Dressing. Next to the cultivation of flax came the preliminary processes of scutching, sorting, and hackling. To improve these processes the Board first appointed ' itinerant men ', two for each province, who should travel from farm to farm, giving instruction to the workers. Crommelin had already tried the experiment, and reported in 1711 that it had not then been of any use.[3] After nine more years the Trustees came to the same conclusion. Instead of itinerant men they decided to appoint a ' flax and hemp dresser ' in each county.[4] His duties were to maintain a model farm in which he should grow seed supplied by the Trustees ; to teach the preparation of flax and hemp to his neighbours and to two apprentices ; to scutch and hackle both his own flax and flax supplied by customers, and to sell his flax, together with a certain amount imported by the Board, in a shop in the chief market town.[5]

The project of flax shops was only partially carried out. According to the Board's accounts, between 1720 and 1737 there were never more than ten official flax dressers in the whole of Ireland, and usually only two or three. In the twelve years, 1720-31, £460 were spent on flax shops, and afterwards the grants were suspended altogether for many years.[6] Towards the middle of

---

[1] Table given by Horner, pp. 201-4.   [2] *Journal*, p. 196.
[3] *Precedents and Abstracts*, p. 3.
[4] ibid., p. 37. The word ' dresser ' was applied to a person who carried on the process of scutching. To-day the term includes sorters and hacklers.
[5] ibid., p. 41.   [6] ibid., table in Appendix.

HACKLING BY HAND

SCUTCHING STOCK, 'low Irish' SPINNING-WHEEL, and REEL,
showing the kinds of implements used in the eighteenth century

the century the shops were revived without success. In 1753 they cost the Board £4,400.[1] But in Ulster, where there were well organized yarn markets, the shops were not needed, and in other parts of the country, where manufacture refused to grow, they could do no good.

Spinning Schools. Thus the efforts of the Trustees to encourage both the growth and the preparation of flax were largely wasted. Their experiments with spinning were hardly more successful. Their main object was to promote the spinning of fine yarn, and their method was the foundation of schools all over the country, in which girls could be taught to spin.[2] As in the case of flax shops, the Board showed much interest in spinning schools between 1720 and 1730 ; interest and expenditure waned during the next decade and revived with great vigour about the middle of the century.[3] In 1751 grants amounting to £6,825 were paid for 182 schools.[4] Two years later a member of the Board stated that there were 199 schools, maintained at a cost of

[1] Stephenson, *Journal*, p. 196.

[2] Spinning schools were common on the Continent, especially in Silesia. Warden (pp. 364-5) quotes the following account of a German school from Andrew Yarranton's essay, *England's Improvement by Land and Sea*. The pupils were from six years of age upwards. Yarranton remarked that the wheels ' went easily with a delightful motion. Around a large room a number of benches were placed, on which sat, perhaps, two hundred children spinning. In the centre stood a pulpit, in which the mistress sat with a long white wand in her hand, watching the spinners. When any one was seen to idle she was tapped with the wand, but if that did not produce improvement in conduct a small bell was rung, which brought out a woman, to whom the offender was pointed out, and who took the idler into another room, where she was chastised. All this done without speaking a word ; and this training, the author thought, would do good in England, where the young women were too much given to chatting. In an adjoining room a woman prepared and put the flax on the distaffs, and when a maid had spun off the flax the bell was rung, the rod pointed to her, another distaff given and the bobbin with the threads was removed and put into a box, with others of the same size, to make cloth. As the children learned to spin finer they were raised to higher benches and great care was taken to sort the yarn and keep it uniform, and so to make regular cloth.' These methods were quite in keeping with the prevailing educational ideas of the time, but the discipline in this school must have been rather exceptional. Mr. Horner (quoting from Frahne's *Textile Industrie im Wirtschaftsleben Schlesiens*) said that the schools often ' served more as a source of fellowship and conversation than any real teaching ' (*Linen Trade of Europe*, p. 403). Many of them were only branches of ordinary village schools.

[3] According to the Board's accounts (which are by no means accurate), the average annual expenditure on spinning schools for the eight years 1721-8, was about £600 ; and for the following eight years only £50.

[4] Stephenson, *Journal*, p. 196.

£8,000.[1] Nearly all these schools were in the southern provinces, for the Board had decided in 1722 that no more teaching was needed in Ulster.[2] It cannot be said that all this expenditure produced much result. The great majority of the schools were in Leinster and Munster, the provinces which regularly produced the least yarn, and there is no sign that the output or quality of yarn was improved by the Board's policy.[3] In the ' yarn counties ' girls were universally taught by their mothers to spin the coarse or middling yarns, which were made from local flax. Parents were reluctant to send their children to be taught a kind of spinning which they could not practise at home. Moreover, in many cases, the schools existed only on paper, although grants and salaries continued to be paid for many years. Sometimes the mistress, in order to be quite sure of her salary, would bribe children to attend her school.[4]

Grants for Manufacture. With the remaining processes of weaving, bleaching and finishing, the Trustees were less directly concerned. They relied on private enterprise, and contented themselves with making grants, usually for a term of years, to ' undertakers ' or ' contractors '. Their design, as we have seen already, was from the outset to make weaving an urban industry. The contractor was an employer, who undertook to set up a certain number of looms, and to produce a certain amount of cloth ; or a bleacher, who similarly promised to use a given area of land and to install a prescribed amount of machinery.

In this case, as in the others, there was an outburst of activity between 1720 and 1730, then a slack period of about twenty years, and renewed activity, with very liberal grants, after the middle of the century.[5]

Most of the grants were spent in the southern provinces. Between 1722 and 1728, for instance, nearly £1,300 were divided among seven firms to encourage weaving. One of these firms was in Belfast, the rest were all in the south.[6] Manufacture in

---

[1] Letter by N. A., a member of the Board, quoted by Stephenson, *Journal*, p. 134.   [2] *Precedents and Abstracts*, p. 60.
[3] It might be argued that the need for schools was greatest in these provinces ; but to teach spinning, especially fine spinning, in districts where there was neither a supply of raw flax nor a demand for yarn, was a hopeless policy.
[4] Stephenson, *Inquiry*, p. 15.   [5] *Precedents and Abstracts*, App.
[6] ibid., p. 121.

the southern provinces, except that of bandle linen for local use, was nearly always worked on capitalistic lines, and it was this type of manufacture that the Board fostered. Organization of industry by large employers seemed, no doubt, to be the only means of making manufacture grow in the south ; and it would be more convenient to pay lump sums to a few contractors than to distribute help to thousands of peasant weavers.

As a rule the concerns founded in this way, with help from the Board, lasted for only a few years. Abundant evidence of this fact will be given in a later chapter, but a couple of typical instances may be quoted here. In 1723, Richard Hall, who had been sent by the Trustees to Haarlem to study bleaching, proposed to set up bleachworks similar to those in Holland, at Drumcondra, a northern suburb of Dublin. During the next seven years he received over £5,000 from the Board ; but in 1731 his grants ceased because he had not carried out a single one of his engagements.[1] In the same period a large concern for linen printing and other branches of manufacture was set up at Ballsbridge, another suburb of Dublin, by a contractor named Daniel Chappel. This business received great support from the Trustees, and its affairs have a large place in their minutes. Chappel began his work with high hopes and generous promises, which were never fulfilled, and eventually, in 1735, the Trustees dropped this experiment also. They wrote in their minutes : ' We do not think it for the service of the linen manufacture to be at any further expense for the encouragement or support of this undertaking.'[2]

There was nothing intrinsically wrong in the policy of giving grants for manufacture. ' Public bodies can often do a real service by advancing capital to individuals.'[3] Without doubt some of the Linen Board's grants were made for successful and lasting enterprises, but a large proportion went to concerns which collapsed after a short time or never came into existence at all. A condition was attached to the early grants that contractors

---

[1] *Precedents and Abstracts*, pp. 64, 117, and 121.

[2] ibid., p. 143. Two similar cases, of a bleachgreen and dowlas factory in co. Roscommon, and a bleachgreen and sail-cloth factory in co. Down, are quoted by Horner, pp. 41–43.

[3] e. g. the loans for land-purchase, mentioned at the beginning of this chapter.

must keep their machinery constantly employed. In most cases the contractor could not make any approach to carrying out such a demand. His employees would probably want to spend much of their time in farming, and the market for his cloth would be very uncertain. The Board learnt these difficulties to some extent by experience, and resolved in 1727 that in future no more than six looms should be granted to any contractor.[1]

Besides advancing capital in this way they distributed machines, chiefly spinning-wheels and reels, among the peasantry. Again there was no essential fault in this practice ; but as the machines were dealt out in a slip-shod, unorganized fashion there was great waste, and little good was done. In the middle of the century the Trustees were spending about £4,500 a year on utensils, and they were told by Stephenson that 'innumerable frauds' were committed by peasants who received these gifts.[2]

Inspectors. During the first half of the century a few inspectors were employed by the Board, some to see whether contractors were carrying out their obligations, others to attend yarn markets in order to see that the regulations for reeling yarn were enforced, or to visit bleachgreens in order to detect the use of lime. They were full-time officials, quite distinct from the lappers of cloth. It has been shown already that the regulations in regard to yarn were not observed by spinners or merchants ; and Stephenson, after examining the work of a number of yarn inspectors, wrote that there was 'no room to doubt of their insignificance to the publick'. In 1757 they were all dismissed, except one inspector who remained at the yarn market in Dublin.[3]

Text-books. The teaching given by flax dressers and in spinning schools was supplemented by books, such as Crommelin's essay and Richard Hall's account of flax cultivation in Holland.[4] In so far as these books were read they might help to raise the standard of production, although they contained advice that could not well be carried out in Ireland, and Hall himself was unable to put his own precepts into practice. But

---

[1] Horner, p. 43.
[2] *Journal*, p. 196. The fact that large sums were still spent on utensils in the slack period after 1730 suggests that the distribution went on automatically, without any check or supervision by the Board.
[3] *Journal*, pp. 154–5.
[4] *Observations on the Methods used in Holland, in Cultivating or Raising of Hemp or Flax.*

the value of any printed instructions would be limited by the fact that most Irish farmers were unable to read.

Premiums. From time to time the Trustees offered bounties and prizes for flax growing, fine spinning or weaving, and inventions. Such gifts could not do much to develop enterprise, but they would give some encouragement to those who had done good work : their effect would be similar to that of prizes at industrial exhibitions and agricultural shows. Their use might have been greater if they had been more honestly applied, but in this line, as in most of the Board's undertakings, there were many abuses. Prizes for spinning, for instance, were given by the grand jury of each county, and it was said that awards were often decided rather by the appearance of the competitors than by that of their yarn. Again, flax dressers who had not done enough work to earn a premium would hire flax from their neighbours for the occasion.[1] Sometimes, indeed, the fraud was too audacious, and defeated its own ends. A weaver from Larne, for example, gave to the Board in 1735 what purported to be ' a piece of extraordinary fine linen ', and the Board voted him in return a handsome present of fifty guineas, a superfine hackle, two barrels of flax-seed and a cambric loom, and decided to make a present of the cloth to the Prince of Wales. A month later it was found that the cloth was full of holes.[2] From 1734 to 1736 premiums of £3 a ton were offered for home-grown flax brought to Dublin. In the three years these premiums produced only thirty tons of flax—an amount which could be grown on fifty acres of land.[3]

Dublin Linen Hall. One other of the Board's undertakings must be mentioned—the building of the Linen Hall in Dublin. In 1721, when brown linen markets were being organized in Ulster and there was a steady and increasing traffic in bleached cloth to Dublin and across the Irish Sea, it was decided that a central market hall would be of advantage to the trade. The Board took as models the Cloth Hall of Hamburg and the great market of the Drapers' Company, Blackwell Hall, in London. Apparently the new market was copied mainly from Blackwell Hall, for detailed reports were received as to the design of the

---

[1] Cf. Stephenson, *Journal*, p. 164.
[2] *Precedents and Abstracts*, pp. 144–5. [3] *Inquiry*, p. 127.

building, the method of conducting sales, the equipment and staff.[1] Land was secured on the edge of the town, near to the river and to the streets in which carriers were in the habit of staying.[2] Two grants, of £1,500 each, were received from Parliament to pay for the land and building.[3] But the rate of progress was remarkably slow. A year passed between the first decision to build a hall and the first advertisement for land ; and although the building was begun in August 1722 it was not opened until November 1728.[4] Most of the interior of the Hall was occupied by a large exchange and by warehouse accommodation ; but later in the century there were added a coffee-room for traders and a council-room for the Trustees.[5] From the beginning the Hall seems to have been well used, and it was undoubtedly found convenient by drapers, exporters, and English buyers.

Trade in the Hall did not develop exactly on the lines designed by the Trustees. They intended that exchanges should be carried out by official factors, who should receive a commission of $1\frac{1}{4}$ per cent.[6] This system may have been copied either from Hamburg or from Veere in Holland, where official factors were employed by the Scottish merchants.[7] At the outset three factors were appointed in Dublin, but it is doubtful whether much trade ever passed through their hands. If they had had a large share of the trade they would hardly have found it necessary to ask for a doubling of their commission.[8] Drapers dealing in the Hall were always at liberty to sell on their own account or to employ private factors. Almost certainly the latter method was the most common. The private factor was

---

[1] *Precedents and Abstracts*, p. 46.   [2] ibid., p. 56.
[3] Stephenson, *Inquiry*, pp. 91, 93.
[4] Horner, p. 72 ; *Precedents and Abstracts*, p. 101. There was even more delay in paying for the building. In June 1731 the master carpenters who had fitted the interior were still unpaid and were threatened by their workmen with imprisonment for arrears of wages (ibid., p. 122).
[5] Cromwell, *Excursions through Ireland* (1815), vol. i, pp. 147-8.
[6] *Precedents and Abstracts*, p. 100.
[7] Davison and Gray, *Scottish Staple at Veere*, pp. 400-4.
[8] Linen exports from Ireland about 1730 amounted to 4,000,000 yards a year. Wholesale trade in Dublin would include a good deal of cloth for consumption in Ireland. In 1816 the volume of trade passing through the Linen Hall was equal to three-eighths of the total export from Ireland (Besnard, *Report*, 26 sqq.) ; but in 1730 direct export from the north had not developed, and the proportion of trade in the Hall would certainly be higher. Therefore it is not unreasonable to assume a trade of 1,500,000 to 2,000,000 yards in the Hall. The value of this cloth would be between £100,000 and £130,000 ; and a commission of $1\frac{1}{4}$ per cent. would yield to each of the factors an income of four or five hundred pounds.

a merchant, who could buy goods outright from drapers, or could advance cash to them, at the same time allowing credit to the English buyers. Such a method was flexible and offered a great advantage to drapers, who had to pay cash to the weavers, and would therefore need to receive prompt payment themselves, unless they were men of considerable wealth—as few of them were at that time.

Defects of the Board's policy. This account of the Board's work could be confirmed by many other examples, but enough evidence had been given to show that deliberate policy had little influence on the growth of industry in Ulster. That remarkable growth was mainly due to private enterprise, working against many difficulties. Even those undertakings of the Board which were desirable in themselves, such as technical instruction, advances of capital and machinery, and the granting of prizes, were carried out with a slackness and irregularity that neutralized much of their good effect. A great amount of energy and money was wasted in efforts to set up manufacture in the southern provinces. The first condition of success was a system of long leases with moderate rents, but no one recognized this need.[1] Instead, all hope was fixed in the enterprise of patrons and employers—a kind of enterprise which had little chance of success before the introduction of the power-loom, or at least, of machine-spinning.[2] Moreover, failure was made the more certain by constant attempts to develop fine spinning and weaving, although there was far more scope in the coarse branches.[3]

These mistakes were precisely what we should expect from such a body as the Linen Board. Its members were nearly all large landowners, quite ignorant of trade, and blind to the need of reform in the land system. Most of the eighty members seldom appeared at a meeting—the normal attendance was only five or six—and the few who did understand the work could take little part, because most of them lived in Ulster. Many of the officials knew nothing of the linen trade : the posts held by several of

---

[1] Stephenson (*Inquiry*, p. 15) did urge the importance of security of tenure, but only to induce ' men of substance.' to invest capital in weaving.

[2] I refer especially to whole-time employment. It will be shown later that in Ulster there was much domestic employment of weavers who were also farmers.

[3] Cf. Stephenson, *Inquiry*, p. 17. The southern provinces try to ' vie with the province of Ulster in the few branches the people of the north have by unwearied application become masters of '.

them were sinecures. The Board's accounts were in utter confusion, and their work went on from year to year with payments always far in arrears.[1]

Before leaving this subject it is worth while to quote two paragraphs from Robert Stephenson's detailed criticism of the Board's policy :

' During the last thirty years, notwithstanding they have distributed through the kingdom half a million, yet (except in 1755) there was not any person sent to inquire into the titles of the multitudes of claimants : some for spinning schools and flax shops never opened ; others for bleach yards or flax mills in ruins or never built ; some for flax dressers or yarn importers, where none such were to be found ; and multitudes for utensils never made or delivered. But where there was no check to their frauds, feigned or forged vouchers have scarce ever been wanting, so as to claim the premium and waste the fund.' [2]

' It is of most dangerous consequence to trust the sole management of a manufacture, on the prosperity of which the strength, wealth, honour, and very vitals of the inhabitants so much depend, entirely in unexperienced hands ; for had this not been the case it would have been impossible for the Trustees to have pursued measures for a long course of years at an immense expense, which to the experienced must have at first view appeared unnecessary, if not destructive, to the interest of the kingdom in general.' [3]

In Scotland the British Linen Company, after a few experiments in importing raw material, selling it on credit, and buying yarn and linen in order to maintain a steady demand, found that it could serve the industry best by simply providing credit for enterprise. Thus it became, and has remained ever since, purely a banking concern.[4] If the money supplied to the Irish Trustees had been put to a similar use, and as wisely administered, it would have done far more good than all the expenditure on bounties and prizes, spinning schools, import of seed, and the rest of the Board's undertakings.

[1] Stephenson, *Inquiry*, p. 138.   [2] ibid., p. 139.
[3] ibid., p. 109.   [4] Bremner, pp. 220-1.

V

SOUTHERN ENTERPRISE, 1740–60

ABOUT the middle of the eighteenth century there was a striking development of the linen trade in the southern provinces. Although they never came near to rivalling the north-eastern counties, there was for a time so much progress in them that great hopes were entertained of an extension of the industry over the whole of Ireland. One sign of the revival was a fresh activity in Parliament and among the Trustees, which will be described in the next chapter. But the first impulse did not apparently come from the Government: it was rather a matter of personal enterprise and sustained effort on the part of many individuals.

Enterprise of Landowners. There were two fairly distinct types of undertaking in the south. On the one hand, many concerns were started by progressive landowners with the object of developing their estates ; on the other, there was a still larger number of private firms, worked on ordinary commercial lines. The nature of these undertakings can best be judged from a few examples. Perhaps the most famous enterprise of the former class was the manufacture set up by Sir Richard Cox, at Dunmanway, co. Cork, which was said to be ' on the best plan of any out of Ulster '.[1] Cox, like the great English landowners, Lord Townsend and Coke of Holkham, had inherited an ' unimproved ' estate when he was a young man. But whereas Townsend and Coke undertook to improve agriculture, Cox was chiefly interested in manufacture. In 1735 he began, with the help of seed supplied by the Linen Board, to encourage his tenants to grow and prepare flax ; but linen manufacture was not fully established for another ten years. He had by that time persuaded his tenants to produce an abundant supply of flax, which was spun by the women and children on the estate. Wheels and reels, some provided by the Board, but most of them by Cox himself,

---

[1] Stephenson, *Journal*, p. 185.

were lent to the spinners, and every year at a festival held on 1st May the wheels were inspected. Next, he turned his attention to weaving, and brought in skilled workers from Ulster. His first experiment in this line was not a success, because the weavers worked with yarn supplied by the growers, and only received a small pittance of wages themselves. But the condition of the weavers quickly improved when a yarn market was set up. Weavers could then supply themselves with raw material, work on their own account, and sell their cloth in the fairs at Dunmanway. Every weaver with good credentials was given a house, at first rent free, with a lease for three lives, and the house was equipped with any required number of looms and wheels. Finally, a well-appointed bleachgreen was provided. Cox himself was not the owner of these concerns : all the profits went to the tenants. His functions were to furnish land and houses, to advance capital, and to encourage industry by means of prizes.[1] In this way, by standing aside and merely acting as a patron, he had on his estate ' the draper, manufacturer, weaver, spinner, and flax farmer, each dependent on the other and all independent of him '.[2] Within a few years Dunmanway was changed from a miserable poor village to a centre of manufacture, filled with prosperous and well-dressed people. Between 1747 and 1749 the number of houses increased from 87 to 117. In 1755, when Stephenson first visited Dunmanway, there were 70 looms at work on plain linen, cambric and diaper, and so much production of yarn that the looms could not cope with it all. Two new bleachworks were being built ; and there was ' neither a family nor loom unemployed '.[3]

Another concern of a similar kind, Lord Grandison's model village of Villierstown, co. Waterford, was also commended by Stephenson.

' This is a very good improvement,' he wrote, ' and there is no house, utensil or machine, necessary or in practice, but is provided in the greatest perfection here. . . . This place is a colony

<hr>

[1] Small weekly prizes were given for spinning ; annual prizes for flax-growing, weaving, and linen buying in the fairs, and for the greatest number of looms at work in one house. Special grants were also made to tenants who married Protestants.   [2] Stephenson, *Journal*, p. 186.

[3] Cox wrote a full and enthusiastic account of Dunmanway in his *Letter to Thomas Prior* (1749). Mr. Horner gives a summary of this pamphlet in *The Linen Trade of Europe*, chap. viii.

of Protestants formed into a village, at the expense and under the care of his Lordship, the houses neat and convenient, the people well chosen, and the linen manufacture in a healthful, flourishing condition. There is a careful, intelligent superintendent, by whose means the linens (which are generally low-priced yard-wides) are properly slea'd and made. The bleachyard is well conducted: their market for sale is chiefly the Hall in Dublin.'

Thomas Adderley, a neighbour of Sir Richard Cox, who lived at Ennis-Shannon, set up a factory which 'formed a town', and an excellent bleachyard, ' one of the best improvements of the sort in the kingdom'. His manager was 'a very ingenious and intelligent man'. In the weaving sheds a variety of cloths were made, including cambric and cotton; and the average output of his looms for six years before 1755 was about 45,000 yards.[1]

A slightly different enterprise was that of Marcus Lynch, of Galway, who divided a tract of 1,500 acres of unimproved land into over 120 small-holdings, which he let to Protestants on leases of three lives, and free of rent for 31 years. He advanced capital in the form of houses, seed, wheels and looms, and introduced a colony of twenty weavers.[2]

Stephenson mentioned many other landowners who adventured in manufacture, among them about a dozen titled persons; and he was much impressed with their 'noble patronage', the ' extraordinary care taken by the noblemen and gentlemen ' to promote industry, their ' extraordinary encouragements ' to workers, and the ' noble and extensive ' factories and bleach-greens which they founded.

Rural Development. If we ask the reason of all this enthusiasm on the part of the Irish gentry, we shall find the answer, I believe, in that movement of agricultural reform which in England accompanied and sustained the industrial revolution. The movement, however, proceeded on different lines in the two countries. The contrast between Sir Richard Cox's methods and those of Lord Townsend and Coke has already been pointed out. In England the ' improving' landowner paid attention to tillage and stock-breeding: in Ireland he was more interested

---

[1] *Journal*, p. 183.   [2] *Report*, 1763, p. 55.

in manufacture, because it was in that direction that he saw the greatest hope of advance. Some Irish landowners did, indeed, experiment in scientific methods, often with success. Young and Wakefield both paid tribute to their enterprise. Several of them, moreover, had estates in England, where they would be likely to practise 'horse-hoeing husbandry'. But the new ideas, which spread slowly enough in England, were still slower to extend over Ireland ; and those landlords who were absentees, although they might be keen agriculturists themselves, would find it hard to keep up the standard of farming in distant estates. Thus even those who had capital to invest in the land were seldom in the forefront of agricultural advance. The use of root crops, for instance, was so rare that when Arthur Young noticed four men in the Shane's Castle demesne sowing a field of turnips, he was as glad to see them as if they had been four emperors.[1]

There was a still greater point of contrast in regard to tenants. Much of the advance in England was due to enterprising and substantial tenant farmers ; but such men, although they were not unknown, were rare in Ireland. Too many of the large tenants were middlemen, who did no farming themselves, but merely sublet their land to peasants. The remainder were chiefly graziers, who had little concern with methods of tillage. The vast majority of tenants in Ireland were peasants, whose poverty was a byword. They could neither farm well themselves nor move into towns in order to make way for men with capital ; for no town industries were available—neither, for that matter, were the men with capital. On the contrary the peasant population grew rapidly, and clung to the land, because the land was its one means of livelihood. The great problem in rural Ireland was to find some means of improving the condition of the peasantry.

There were two sound methods of bringing about an improvement. The first was to increase manufacture, so as to provide additional work and income for the peasants and their families. The second, and the more important, was to reform the conditions of land tenure, and to reform them not merely here and there by the generosity of a few landowners, but universally and by

[1] *Tour*, p. 128.

statute. A radical change in the land laws, however, was one of the last measures that the Irish Parliament would think of passing. We have seen that the Trustees of the Linen Manu-facture, who might have been expected to realize the importance of land tenure to industry, were blind to the need : so, too, were patriots like Grattan and public-spirited men like Foster, the author of the famous corn law of 1784. Thus, as there was no question of agrarian reform, progressive landowners naturally turned to the other line of enterprise. When the example had once been set by Cox and a few others, the fashion soon spread, and there followed an outburst of interest in rural manufacture, which seemed to promise an era of thriving trade and general prosperity.

Enterprise of Large Manufacturers. Before inquiring into the results of this movement we will notice some examples of the other, and more usual, type of enterprise, that of middle-class merchants and employers. Robert Stephenson, who was himself a prosperous merchant in Dublin, gave many instances of this class of industry, and often wrote of the undertakings in terms of high praise. Some of the largest employers were settled in co. Louth. The most important firm in 1755 was probably that of William Bryan & Co., of Leixlip, who were both manufacturers and bleachers.[1] Their main interest was in cotton manufacture, but they produced as well some kenting, plain linen, and damask. The annual output from their bleachworks was over 100,000 yards of cloth, and from 10,000 to 20,000 lb. of yarn. Stephenson gave a full account of their equipment. They had four main buildings : two buck houses, a large drying house, and a water-mill. One buck house contained two pans, two wooden kiers,[2] and one brick kier for lees. The other buck house had a boiler, and two new brick kiers, ' of an extraordinary kind, plastered over with a cement ; and these, for continuance and preserving

---

[1] They bought the business about the year 1744, when they first received a grant from the Linen Board, and soon enlarged it considerably. Their extensions only cost £700, but this was quite a large sum for capital expendi-ture at that time. Cf. Professor Unwin's statement (*E. H. R.*, 1922, p. 211) that Samuel Oldknow, about 1784, doubled his warehouse accommodation at a cost of £90. ' That an eminent manufacturer, who claims to have estab-lished a new industry, should regard £90 as a considerable outlay shows how small a part fixed capital . . . as yet played in industrial enterprise.'

[2] Kier, a word borrowed from the Dutch, means a vat.

heat in bucking, are esteemed preferable to any other'. In the mill house there were a large water-wheel, two pairs of washing stocks, two rubbing boards, a mill for grinding ashes, two kiers for souring, a calendar, and a beetling engine.[1] This account shows that the finishing processes were done by water-power, but it also suggests that the largest bleachworks of this time were by no means on a level with those of normal size half a century later.

Another important bleachgreen in co. Louth, at Collon, had been bought by James Sidebotham, who had come to Ireland from Manchester. He had an excellent equipment, managed the works well, and did a very good trade. His bleaching of yarn was ' the best of any in the kingdom '. Sidebotham was also a manufacturer, and he supplied Stephenson with cloth. In Stephenson's later reports, for the years 1760-3, he is mentioned as still flourishing, and ' surpassing every one in whitening yarn '. Between 1755 and 1760 he added cotton bleaching to his other activities. His training in Manchester would be useful to him as a pioneer of the cotton industry in Ireland, and in the yarn trade he would benefit by his personal knowledge of manufacturers in Lancashire, who were the chief buyers of the yarn exported from Drogheda.[2]

The group to which these two firms belonged is noteworthy because it included nearly all the undertakings which had a lasting success. In Louth, King's County, and the neighbouring parts of Westmeath there were many large manufacturers. Production on a large scale seems to have been a tradition, at any rate in co. Louth, from the time of the Drogheda Linen Company, in the latter years of the seventeenth century. Between 1755 and 1763 Robert Stephenson alluded to several important firms in addition to the two which have been mentioned here ; and Besnard's report, written in 1817, showed that the same methods were still in use at that time. In his notes on King's County he gave the following description of the system of trade :

' The plan of carrying on the linen business in this county differs from that practised in most others, few weavers working on their own accounts, being for the most part employed by

[1] Stephenson, *Journal*, pp. 166-8.
[2] ibid., p. 165 ; *Reports*, 1760-1, p. 85 ; 1762, p. 23 ; 1763, p. 73.

masters, who purchase yarn in the counties of Roscommon, Longford, and Galway, which they bleach at home, and give out to be wove. The goods thus made are sold by the original manufacturer, either at his own house, or taken to a bleacher, and sometimes sent to the Dublin market.'[1]

Again, he wrote that the 'factory masters' of Westmeath, who were 'very respectable in their situation', made goods for stock as far as their capital, of £50 to £2,000, would allow, then sold in bulk to bleachers. He added that these methods had been common since the middle of the eighteenth century.[2]

In these counties production on a large scale was necessary because little flax was grown locally. But since the Drogheda market was the chief distributing centre for yarn from Connaught, a constant supply of raw material was available for wholesale dealers. The system was successful because the manufacturer, who was sometimes a yarn exporter as well, could obtain his yarn very cheaply and in considerable variety. Moreover, as he was near to the chief markets for both home and overseas trade, he had special facilities for selling his goods, and he could save largely in transport. These economies would enable him to sell at a reasonable price, and at the same time to pay a living wage to his workers.

At the time when Stephenson made his first tour there seemed to be a good prospect of flourishing trade in co. Waterford. Not only was Lord Grandison's scheme spreading manufacture over the northern districts, but in the city itself there was an interesting group of businesses, set up about 1750 by a family named Smith.[3] 'Those young ladies', Sarah Smith & Co., had a spinning concern for both yarn and thread, and a bleachgreen for yarn. Stephenson said of their thread works : 'This manufacture may equal all the rest of the kingdom in quantity and surpasses in quality.' Some of their yarn and thread went to Patrick and Arthur Smith, who made plain linens and sheetings—'the best ell-wide sheetings in the kingdom ' ; and to Samuel Smith, a tape manufacturer. The machines for tape and thread were made and managed by Dutch craftsmen.[4] A bleachgreen for the cloth, founded by Patrick Smith, jun., was at that time managed by his widow.

---

[1] Besnard, *Report*, p. 13.   [2] ibid., p. 22.   [3] *Journal*, pp. 172–3.
[4] The Dutch were still the chief manufacturers of tape, and pioneers of the inkle loom, which wove many tapes at the same time.

Two examples may serve to illustrate a more usual type of business. In Bessborough, co. Kilkenny, a man named Shaw set up bleachworks in 1740. He also undertook some weaving and flax-growing on his own account. The output of his bleach-green in 1754 was 960 pieces—probably about 50,000 yards—a good volume of trade for a concern so far from the chief centres of manufacture. Shaw was, moreover, a pioneer of the industry: he was ' one of the first that introduced anything better than bandle linen manufacture in this county ', and Stephenson added that ' since his settlement the linen trade had been daily increasing '.[1] Another typical southern manufacturer was William Rose, of Johnstown, co. Kildare, who had set up bleachworks and a weaving factory about the year 1744, and had built houses for his weavers. The annual output of his works for the few years preceding Stephenson's visit had been, on an average, 40,000 yards of linen and 8,000 hanks of yarn. His business was described by Stephenson as ' a very good improvement '.[2]

These manufacturing enterprises were not altogether a new growth. Attempts had been made, with varying success, ever since the seventeenth century to set up linen manufacture in the south of Ireland. Some of the Huguenots had carried on the tradition : Louis Crommelin himself had some thought of migrating to Kilkenny in order to industrialize the southern counties. But without doubt there was unusual activity in the middle years of the eighteenth century. Perhaps some of the projects were inspired by the example of the landowning class. In nearly all cases an important factor was the encouragement given by the Linen Board, in the form of grants for capital expenditure, gifts of machinery, payments for the salary of managers, and bounties for production.

Influence of Yarn Trade. A further cause was the increase of the yarn trade in southern Ireland. There was a rapidly growing demand for yarn in Ulster to meet expanding manufacture. Between 1730 and 1760, the export of linen cloth from Ireland was quadrupled, and there must have been at the same time a considerable increase of demand at home. Most of the cloth was manufactured in Ulster, but much of the yarn which fed the northern looms came from the southern counties. In

---

[1] *Journal*, p. 179.   [2] ibid., pp. 193-4.

addition to the domestic trade in yarn there was a growth in export, especially, of course, to Lancashire, for use in the manufacture of mixed linen and cotton goods. The development of this trade is shown in the following table :

AVERAGE ANNUAL EXPORT

1731–35	.	.	.	.	.	.	15,300 cwts.
1736–40	.	.	.	.	.	.	16,400 ,,
1741–45	.	.	.	.	.	.	18,400 ,,
1746–50	.	.	.	.	.	.	24,200 ,.
1751–55	.	.	.	.	.	.	24,200 ,.
1756–60	.	.	.	.	.	.	29,700 ,,

Such a substantial trade in yarn would account for much activity in the growth, preparation, and spinning of flax. As a matter of fact it gave a great stimulus to the bleaching industry as well. Seeing that cotton could be bleached in less than a week, at a time when linen bleaching occupied two or three months, it was much easier to finish mixed cloth if the linen warp were white, or nearly white, already. Therefore a large proportion of the yarn sent to Lancashire was bleached before it was put on the market ; and there was abundant scope for bleaching in the ' yarn counties ' of Ireland.

But the development did not stop there. If any weavers of bandle linen or wider cloths happened to live in the neighbourhood, they would naturally bring their webs to be finished at the bleachworks. And the bleacher himself, following a custom which was common in Ulster, would often employ weavers to work up a certain proportion of his yarn, in order to maintain a regular supply of cloth, and perhaps to make use of yarn which could not immediately be sold. Thus there was a tendency for a weaving industry to spring up round the bleachworks. In nearly all the cases mentioned by Stephenson a bleachgreen is the central feature of the manufacturing concern.

We have seen something of the industrial activities of southern Ireland about the middle of the eighteenth century : in a later chapter we shall have to examine the causes of their failure ; for the fact is that all this effort and enterprise had remarkable little result. But two other topics must be dealt with first : the policy of the government in this period of expansion, and the unexpected changes in Ulster during the same period.

¹ For details see table of exports given below, Appendix II. The sudden increase after 1755 was not to any great extent due to the Seven Years' War, for the output was well maintained after 1763.

VI

STIMULUS AND REGULATION (1750–64)

Effects of the Seven Years' War. About the year 1760, in most of the linen-producing countries of Europe, the governments showed an active interest in the trade. To some extent they were merely continuing efforts which had begun a generation or two earlier; but almost certainly an underlying motive, common to many countries, was supplied by the Seven Years' War. The war would naturally check international trade—for instance, the export of fine linens from Northern France and the trade from Silesia to western Europe. Silesian exports fell in value from nearly 4,000,000 thalers in 1751–6 to little more than 1,000,000 in 1761–2.[1] In the same period imports of continental linen into England were reduced from nearly 32,000,000 yards to less than 19,000,000.[2] Consumers were driven, as they are in all times of war, to look for larger supplies at home. The lack of foreign linens in England was evidently supplied to some extent, not only by home production, but also by greater purchases from Ireland and Scotland. The quantity of cloth stamped in Scotland increased from 8,500,000 yards in 1756 to 12,500,000 in 1763;[3] and exports from Ireland (nearly all to England) rose from twelve million to sixteen million yards.[4] This increased demand would lead to special efforts in certain branches of manufacture.[5] Thus in France from 1760 onwards attempts were made, exactly as they were in Ireland, to promote rural industries in places where they had not developed. Fifteen hundred spinning-wheels, for example, were distributed to 'fileuses pauvres'. The movement continued for at least

---

[1] Horner, p. 407.
[2] Report of Committee on the Linen Trade, 1773 (*H. of C. Reports*, iii. 296).
[3] Horner, p. 299. [4] ibid., pp. 202, 203.
[5] It is shown in the table and diagram 1, Appendix II, that the progress of exports from Ireland was slightly checked in the middle of the war, but recovered towards the end. The kinds of linen for which there would be a strong demand would probably be coarse cloth, three-quarters of a yard in width, similar to the 'Germany narrows'; damask, to replace the supply from Saxony; cambric and fine linen to take the place of cloth from France and Belgium.

fifteen years but produced no fruit.[1] A similar effort, beginning a few years before the war, was made to create a linen supply in the Highlands of Scotland, in order to rescue the people from idleness and savagery. The Board of Manufactures, a body resembling the Irish Linen Board, but concerned with several industries,[2] received from Parliament a special grant of £3,000 a year for nine years, ear-marked for this purpose. The grants were fruitless, for the Highlanders were as little responsive as the French peasantry.[3] Again, in Silesia, the Prussian government was very active in measures to stir the linen trade into more vigorous life. In Ireland, as we saw in the last chapter, the stimulus was chiefly a matter of private enterprise, and the function of government was merely to support the individual efforts.

But in all countries the efforts to promote manufacture were accompanied by measures of a different kind—attempts to order and control its growth. Suddenly increased production is apt to lead to irregular methods and disturbance of vested interests : consequently to fresh regulation in order to preserve those interests. During the recent war there was much legislation of this kind to protect organized and skilled labour against dilution. In France at the time of the Seven Years' War the main problem was the ' dilution ' of town. labour by rural industry. The Government was doing its best to promote rural industry, but recognized the claim for protection of old-established urban traders. In this dilemna the Conseil d'État passed the important Ordinance of 1762, putting country workers under the regulations which applied to the *métiers* of the towns.[4] Frederick the Great's efforts in Silesia were also accompanied by a strict system of regulation, notably a wide and detailed measure passed in 1765. Vested interests in Ireland were represented by bleachers and drapers, who secured, between

---

[1] Tarlé, op. cit., pp. 20-5.

[2] The methods of this Board were very similar to those of the Irish Linen Board, but the Scottish Trustees had the wisdom to realize the scope for coarse manufacture, and therefore pulled with the stream, while the Irish Trustees pulled constantly in the other direction. The Scottish Board also paid much attention to aulnage and inspection : a third of its income was spent in this way, and to no very good purpose. The Board began this work in 1727 and abandoned it in 1823.

[3] Bremner, *Industries of Scotland*, p. 218.   [4] Tarlé, op. cit., p. 4.

1757 and 1764, three statutes imposing fresh restrictions on the work of weavers.

In the present chapter we shall follow this dual policy of stimulus and regulation, chiefly as it appeared in Ireland, but with some reference to the parallel movements abroad.

Expenditure of the Linen Board. As far as the Irish Government was concerned, there was no change of policy between 1745 and 1757 ; there was only an increase in the scale of operations. Flax-growing had spread in response to the demand for raw material ; consequently larger sums were paid for importation of seed and in premiums to the growers. The increase of manufacture meant a much larger outlay on wheels, looms, hackles, and other implements, which were given or lent to the workers. The erection of new bleachworks meant in most cases a capital grant, or at least a contribution towards the manager's salary. For these reasons the annual expenditure of the Linen Board between 1738 and 1757 was more than three times as large as it had been in the period from 1711 to 1737. The following table (to which the figures already given for the earlier period are added for comparison) shows the main heads of expenditure : [1]

AVERAGE ANNUAL EXPENDITURE

	1738-57. £	Percentage of total.	(1711-37. £	Percentage.)
Flax and seed . .	8,100	44	(3,300	58)
Grants for manufacture . . .	7,700	42	(1,400	24·5)
Salaries, &c. . .	900	5	(600	10·5)
Miscellaneous . .	1,700	9	(400	7)
Total . .	18,400		(5,700)	

In the original table for the later period the figures are classified under eighteen headings, but they suggest no new activities— only a larger sum, especially for manufacture, the great bulk of which was probably spent after 1750. The chief expense was still on flax and seed (£4,525 a year in premiums and £2,260 for the cost of import) ; utensils accounted for £4,130 a year, and spinning schools—whether existing in fact or only on paper— for £2,150.[2] There was an important group of ' incidental '

[1] *H. of C. Journals*, vol. x, p. cxix.

[2] In the earlier period utensils had cost on an average less than £600 a year, and spinning schools about £300.

expenses, amounting to £1,050, which probably included a certain proportion of salaries, and those sums for which the clerks could not otherwise account.

But the larger expenditure was almost automatic. It did not necessarily imply greater keenness in Parliament or among the Trustees. We have seen already that the Board became very careless in its methods and wasted a considerable part of its income. As the accounts were never audited, they fell into confusion, and the Board fell into debt. For instance, the table given above shows an expenditure for the twenty years greater by £62,000 than that shown in another account for the same period. In 1757 the Secretary admitted that the Board was largely in debt : he believed that the debt was about £40,000, but he could only make a rough guess at the amount.[1]

Renewed Energy of the Board. Soon after 1750 the Trustees began to recover from this lethargy. They were almost certainly influenced by the growth of private enterprise in southern Ireland : some of the ' improving ' landlords, such as Sir Charles Bingham and Colonel Wynne, were among the small number of Trustees who attended the Board's meetings ; and it was precisely at this time that the fashion of improvement was gaining ground in Ireland.[2] Another factor was probably the removal, in 1753, of bounties for export of linen from England. Two years earlier a committee of the English House of Commons had considered the working of the bounty system, and had decided that it was unnecessary. The later course of trade in Ireland showed that the change of policy in no way affected the

---

[1] *H. of C. Journals*, u.s., Stephenson estimated the debt to be £38,666. According to another account presented to the parliamentary committee in 1758, the revenue for the previous twenty years had been approximately as follows :

From duties on imported linen . . .	£255,000
From annual parliamentary grants . .	£80,000
From special grants	£25,000
Total . .	£360,000

But if, as Stephenson held, the expenditure in the same period was no more than £368,000, it is difficult to see why there should be a debt of nearly £40,000 (unless there was a huge debt in 1737, and that is very unlikely). This discrepancy is a further proof that the accounts were in complete disorder.

[2] Cf. Arthur Young, *Tour*, p. 101 : ' The kingdom more improved in the last twenty years than in a century before. The great spirit began in 1749 and 1750.'

amount of Irish exports ; but the Trustees seem to have been
stirred to activity. They felt, no doubt, that as the English
Parliament had withdrawn its support, some special effort
was needed in Ireland. They immediately secured an additional grant of £2,000 a year, to be spent in the southern
provinces.[1]

, Perhaps it was the discussion on the use of these grants that
brought Robert Stephenson into touch with the Trustees. He
had come to Ireland in 1745, had evidently prospered, and was
now one of the leading figures in the linen trade. For more
than thirty years he had great influence among his fellow-
merchants and in the counsels of the Board. His first tour of
inspection was made in 1755 ; he made thirteen tours in later
years ;[2] he was sent to London in 1773 to represent the Board
before the parliamentary committee ; his last pamphlet was
printed in 1789. There can be no doubt that both Parliament
and the Trustees were largely guided by his opinion in the critical
years from 1753 to 1764. In the course of his regular business
Stephenson had probably seen the conditions and methods of
trade in all parts of the country, and had learnt how the Board
was allowing its funds to be wasted. He evidently gained the
ear of some one who had influence with the Trustees, and was
appointed in 1755 to report on the state of the linen industry
throughout the southern provinces, with the special object of
showing what use was being made of grants from the Board.
His *Journal of a Tour of Inspection* showed conclusively the
weakness of the Board's policy and the need for more care in the
distribution of its funds. The main points of his criticism have
been mentioned already, and they need not be repeated here ;
but we may notice that the very fact of his appointment as an
inspector was an important step in advance, for the Board could
no longer be ignorant of the state of manufacture in the country,
or of the inefficiency of their own work.

Stephenson was by no means content with this one report.
It was followed in 1757 by an historical and descriptive book,
*An Inquiry into the State and Progress of the Linen Manufacture
of Ireland.* This work was chiefly a review of earlier writings,
but it ended with a few pages of criticism. At the same time

---

[1] *H. of C. Journals,* vol. ix, p. 134.   [2] *H. of C. Reports,* iii. 107.

he was busy with a general audit of the Board's accounts for the past twenty years. In 1758 he was one of the chief witnesses interviewed by a committee of the Irish House of Commons.[1] The committee was formed on Stephenson's initiative, or at least it was largely an outcome of his efforts.[2] Its business was to examine into the Trustees' method of discharging their duties, and to review their finances : incidentally the committee dealt as well with the question of combination among weavers. These were all matters in which Stephenson was personally interested ; but the fact that his views were upheld before the committee by about a dozen other merchants shows that he was the spokesman of a considerable group.

As a result of this formidable attack the Trustees made some changes in their methods. They evidently decided to cut off all useless expenditure. The yarn inspectors had already been dismissed in 1757. Apparently spinning schools and flax shops were soon abandoned, for they do not figure in the later minutes of the Board. Further, it was resolved that although the more useful undertakings should be continued, they ought to be to some extent reorganized. There was to be a fresh system of bounties for flax-growing, and the advances of capital—in the form of grants to large employers, and implements to peasants and craftsmen—should be put under a regular supervision. Stephenson, whose first tour had yielded such important results, was appointed a special inspector for this purpose.[3]

Although Stephenson was such a severe critic of the Board's undertakings, he was by no means opposed to the system of bounties in general ; in fact he was convinced that by a properly contrived scheme of bounties and prizes the linen trade could

[1] *Commons Journals*, vol. x (1757–60), pp. 299 sqq.
[2] Stephenson himself said (*Observations*, 1784, p. vi) that his writings led to the appointment of the committee.
[3] It seems that he made no tour of inspection between 1755 and 1760-His reports show that he was on tour in 1760 and the three following years. In 1763 it was resolved that no further grants should be made to private firms for the salaries of their bleachers or flax dressers, until proof had been given to Stephenson ; and he was instructed to travel round twenty-five counties examining bleachgreens and workshops (*Proceedings*, 1763–4, pp. 292–3). In 1773 he told the parliamentary committee in London, that he had made fourteen such journeys : therefore his inspections must have been made annually from 1760 to 1773. They may have continued until 1781, when his system of bounties was abandoned, and he had a personal quarrel with the new Inspector-General.

be made to flourish in every district of Ireland. He proposed four kinds of prizes, and two of his suggestions were adopted.[1]

Prizes for Flax-growing. One was the new scheme for encouraging flax-growing, which has just been mentioned. In its final form, which was first tried in 1764, the plan was to grant prizes to those who grew the largest amount of flax and saved the largest amount of seed. In each county six prizes were offered, to the total value of £50, and they were to be administered by two persons (chosen presumably by the Board), who should inspect the work of all claimants and report to the grand jury or the county justices.[2] By this simple device, which differed only in details of administration from the scheme previously in force, Stephenson believed that Ireland could be made self-sufficing as regards both seed and flax. He knew, of course, that the finest flax could not be grown at home, but he insisted that Ireland ought to specialize in the making of coarse and medium cloth. The Trustees were evidently less sanguine, for they still paid bounties for imported seed. Indeed, in the previous year they had themselves imported 130 hogsheads of American seed, and distributed them evenly through the five counties of Connaught.[3] Stephenson's implicit belief in this plan shows that he had no more appreciation than any one else of the real obstacles to the growth of manufacture. He supposed that the main hindrance was carelessness on the part of the Board and its servants, and he consequently held that suitable bounties well administered would ensure a flourishing trade.

Premium Markets. His other proposal was a scheme for promoting brown linen markets in the southern provinces. We have noted already that open markets were a great convenience to weavers in Ulster, a convenience which was rarely to be found in the south. Stephenson realized this need and tried to meet

---

[1] *Journal*, pp. 199–201. The two proposals not carried out were : (i) prizes of £100, £60, and £40 each year to the merchants who should do the largest export trade to foreign countries ; (ii) £100 reward each year for the most useful invention : the Linen Hall merchants to act as judges.

[2] *Journal*, u.s. ; *Proceedings*, 1764, pp. 16, 39.

[3] *Proceedings*, 1762, p. 255 ; 1763, pp. 1–5, 31. The seed was imported for the Trustees by the Galway merchants, J. and D. French, who received £4 a hogshead.

it. From 1760 onwards, the Linen Board, acting on his advice, offered prizes in each of twenty-five counties to the merchants who should buy the largest amounts of linen in the open markets.[1] The full meaning of this scheme must be shown later. It is intimately connected with topics which will be discussed in the next two chapters—the differences of organization in northern and southern trade, and the causes of failure in the south. We may notice in passing that Stephenson doubted, with good reason, whether the large concerns started by landowners and others would have a permanent success ; and that he distrusted not only the concerns themselves, but still more the employees in them. Combination among workers was his *bête noir*. Acts against combination had already been passed, and others were under consideration at this time. Stephenson, though he entirely agreed with their aim, was by no means sure of their effect. In his view, as in that of the Philosophic Radicals sixty years later, the fruit of combination laws would be more combination. It was in this connexion that he wrote : ' The general dislike that seems to prevail against penal laws in this kingdom requires that some scheme should be proposed that may obviate this difficulty, and preserve the property of all concerned.' [2] His remedy was the scheme of ' premium markets ', which, instead of coercing the weavers, would relieve them of any need to combine by making them independent.

The system was first tried in 1760, and it was continued for eleven years.[3] Stephenson hoped to be able to give £100 in each county, but the Trustees only allowed him about a quarter of the sum that he wanted.[4] Perhaps it was partly because the state aid was so small that voluntary help was called in to complete the work. In several counties Linen Societies were formed among the landowning class, for the purpose of organizing markets and endowing them with prizes. It is doubtful how

[1] The scheme was to apply to all the counties outside Ulster, and to Donegal and Fermanagh, the two Ulster counties in which markets were the least developed. In practice, prizes were also given in Cavan, but the flourishing market at Cootehill was excluded from competition.

[2] *Journal*, p. 200.

[3] They were not renewed after 25 March 1771 (*Observations*, 1784, p. vii).

[4] *Journal*, u.s. ; *Proceedings*, 1762, pp. 249–51 ; 1763, pp. 260–1. The original grant in 1760 was £600 for twenty-five counties : in 1763 the actual expenditure was £710.

many of these societies actually came into existence, but they were at least projected in a dozen counties, and it was hoped that the system would spread all over the south and west of Ireland.[1] The scheme failed, of course, but to Stephenson and his contemporaries it might well seem likely to succeed, because at this time similar methods were being used, apparently with good results, to encourage new markets in Ulster.[2]

Other Grants. These two measures—premium markets, and county prizes for flax and flax-seed—were the new means of stimulating industry in the south. Older methods, such as the distribution of implements, and special grants in response to applications from individual firms, still occupied a large part of the Board's attention. Every year a schedule was drawn up showing the persons who were to receive utensils, and the number allotted to each person. The recipients were all Trustees, or other landowners, who were responsible for passing on the implements to the peasantry in their neighbourhood. We can easily understand how this method of distribution might lead to great waste ; for many of the landowners had little interest in manufacture, or in the peasantry, and they would simply get rid of the unwelcome gifts with the least possible trouble. A hurried visit once a year from a deferential inspector would not do much to set matters right. As for the special allowances to manufacturers, they were probably the most useful of all the Board's undertakings, seeing that most of them went to responsible firms, who would make good use of the grants. About 1760 there were several loans or gifts of expensive finishing machines to northern bleachers, and much help

---

[1] Stephenson's *Reports* for 1760–3. The counties were : Clare, Galway, Kerry, Kildare, Limerick, Louth, Mayo, Meath, Sligo, Tipperary, Wexford, Wicklow.

[2] Stephenson himself believed that the premiums had been a great success. Exports of linen had more than doubled during the period of the premiums : they had risen from 12,000,000 yards in the year ending 25 March 1761 to about 25,400,000 yards in the year 1770–1. This increase Stephenson attributed to his scheme (*Observations, u. s.*). If he had been more candid and observant he would have noticed that 1760–1 was a year of depression, and 1770–1 a year of great, in fact too great, activity. He would have seen moreover that the ' premium markets ' contributed only a small part of the exports : according to his own exaggerated estimate (*Observations*, p. 86) the sales in southern markets were less than a third of the sales in Ulster, where few premiums were paid.

was given with the growing manufactures of thread, cambric, and damask.[1]

In spite of the new bounties, the Board's total expenditure seems not to have risen appreciably after 1757. The average annual expenditure between 1737 and 1757 had been £18,500.[2] The measures of economy described above would save about £3,000 a year; but against this saving there must be set the additional £2,000 for the southern provinces.[3] Apparently this grant was earmarked for the new bounties, which would together amount to about £1,950. If this were the case, it would explain the Board's reluctance to give larger prizes for cloth buying in the markets : as the county prizes for flax and seed cost them £1,250 a year,[4] they would have only £750 left for the market prizes. There would be practically nothing left for Stephenson's two other schemes of prizes, and this fact would be sufficient reason for their rejection.

Expenditure in the South. We have noticed that the Board in its early days was mainly concerned with the southern provinces. The same thing is true of the period with which we are dealing. There is definite evidence in an account presented to the committee of 1758. This account gives the following as the sums spent in the previous twenty years : [5]

Expenditure in the Four Provinces, 1737-57

Leinster { Dublin	£57,563 }		
Leinster { Rest of Leinster	£98,775 }	.	£156,338
Munster	. . . .		£59,440
Connaught	. . . . . .		£49,477
Ulster .	. . . . . .		£40,380
		Total . .	£305,635

[1] Apparently the money saved by closing down spinning schools and flax shops was used partly to pay for the new bounties and partly to increase the number of utensils given away. The average cost of utensils from 1737-57 had been £4,130. In March 1763 the sum voted for the following year was £7,050 for wheels and reels, and £3,200 for looms and hackles. In the latter case £100 were to be spent in each county. This was a very uneven distribution, but it was probably argued that the counties which had the least manufacture stood most in need of help. [2] *Proceedings*, 1764, pp. 9–10.

[3] The balance of about £1,000 a year was probably spent on utensils ; but the account for 1762-3 is given in such a form that no comparison can be made with other years. Moreover, the amount voted for utensils varied greatly from year to year.

[4] i. e. £50 for each of twenty-five counties (*Proceedings*, 1764, pp. 16, 39).

[5] *Commons Journals*, 1757-60, p. cxxiii.

There is obviously something wrong either with this table or with the table quoted above showing a considerably larger expenditure for the same period [1]—perhaps with both. But although the figures may be inaccurate, they probably make some approach to the right proportions. It is likely that about half the total expenditure went to Leinster, and that less was spent in Ulster than in any other province. Although there are no such figures for the period from 1757 to 1763, we may be sure that the same state of affairs continued. All the industrial activity of the southern provinces at this time meant exceptionally large grants to individuals and firms ; and those provinces shared among them the additional annual grant of £2,000.

This brief review shows that private enterprise in the middle years of the eighteenth century was matched by renewed efforts on the part of the Linen Board, and that in both cases the chief efforts were aimed at the development of industry outside of Ulster. The measure of success achieved by these efforts will be discussed in the next chapter : it is enough to say here that the result was disappointing. The linen trade never grew to a satisfactory extent in the southern provinces—Stephenson had said that in 1755 the output of the rest of Ireland was not equal to that of a single county in Ulster. Sixty years later the same statement could have been made with literal truth. Moreover, the two special undertakings of the Linen Board do not seem to have had any appreciable effect. If the plan for raising flax and seed had been successful, it would hardly have been necessary to produce a fresh scheme, with the same object, in 1781. As for the ' premium markets ', although there were still in 1816 two dozen markets in the south, some of which may have been founded about 1760, they were for the most part small affairs. The average annual sales in each of them was less than a quarter of the average for each market in Ulster. Circumstances, such as the defective land system, and keen competition from the northern counties in both fine and coarse manufacture, were always strong enough to defeat even the best conceived plans of encouragement.

Ireland was, however, by no means alone in this respect. Many of the attempts to foster particular industries, so common

[1] See above, p. 95, n. 1.

and so widely advertised in the age of mercantilism, ended in failure. Those industries which prospered would as a rule have done so, and often actually did so, without any special help—the linen industry of Ulster is a case in point. On the other hand, when a trade depended almost entirely on patronage and governmental favour there was seldom more than a temporary success; sometimes none at all. At the beginning of this chapter it was mentioned that attempts made during the Seven Years' War to promote the linen manufacture in the Scottish Highlands and in France met with no response; and it is worth while to notice that Colbert himself had failed nearly a century before to exploit the industry in parts of France in which it had not already taken root.[1]

Policy of Frederick II in Silesia. The most famous mercantilist statesman after Colbert was Frederick the Great of Prussia; and his connexion with the linen trade of Silesia offers a particularly good comparison with the policy of the Irish government. There were, of course, some differences in method and conditions. Frederick's efforts were more strenuous; his failure was more complete; and he was trying, not to develop trade in new districts, but to force a new branch of industry where other branches were firmly established. The obstacles to success were also rather different in the two cases, but in both the central fact was the same. A government was making a frontal attack against very strong economic forces. It failed to realize either their nature or their strength, and it was beaten.

During the sixteenth and early seventeenth centuries there was a small export trade in linen from Silesia, organized chiefly by Dutch traders and Eastland merchants or interlopers from England, who shared, or rather disputed, among themselves and with Hanse merchants the trade from the Baltic to western Europe.[2] A minor campaign in the great struggle between English and Hanse interests was waged over Silesian linen; but it was soon overshadowed by the Thirty Years' War, which practically put a stop to export. There was a gradual recovery after 1648,

---

[1] P. Clément, *Colbert, Lettres, Instructions et Mémoires,* vol. ii, pp. 624, 851–2. Colbert tried to establish the linen trade in Burgundy with the help of workers from the north and north-east of France.

[2] Zimmerman: *Blüte und Verfall des Leingewerbes in Schlesien,* pp. 6–8, 62–70.

helped by settlements of Protestant refugees from Bohemia and France. In the eighteenth century the growth continued, although the Silesian trade never quite equalled the Irish in bulk. The growth was broken, however, by the War of the Austrian Succession, and with the outbreak of the Seven Years' War there came another great relapse, involving, as we have seen, a fall in exports to about a quarter of their former volume.

The Damask Industry. After the Peace of Paris, Frederick the Great sought to restore the linen trade and exploit its possibilities to the utmost extent. In 1765 he issued an important regulating act, which will be described later in this chapter. In the following year, while visiting the valleys of the Riesengebirge in which most of the weaving was carried on,[1] he was impressed with the fact that enterprise was almost confined to plain linens and lawn, although only a short distance away, in Saxony, there was a flourishing trade in damask. Therefore he determined that damask should be made in Silesia. The history of his efforts is full of interest, and deserves to be studied in detail ; but as our chief concern is with Ireland rather than Prussia, only a brief outline can be given.[2]

At first Frederick gave orders that damask weavers should be brought into Silesia, to the districts of Hirschberg and Schmiedeberg, that they should teach damask manufacture to those who had previously made only plain linen, and that Silesian merchants should buy this home-made damask. But the laws of Saxony forbade the emigration of weavers, and merchants in Silesia refused to buy the local damask. They urged the important fact that a very satisfactory exchange was already established, of good Silesian lawn for good foreign damask. If they tried to develop damask-weaving at home they would simply lose their lawn trade; and experiment showed that Silesian damask was both poor in quality and expensive, so that it could not be sold, even at home.

Frederick's minister, Schlabrendorff, answered these arguments with action and abuse. He put an embargo on the trade in lawn, set constables to watch the merchants houses, and even threatened compulsion by military force. The merchants still

---

[1] Zimmerman : *Blüte und Verfall des Leingewerbes in Schlesien,* p. 128. Bleaching was carried on, of course, along the line of the rivers, and usually near large towns.   [2] ibid., pp. 129-39.

refused to ruin themselves by obeying the royal mandate ; but an adventurer was found who undertook to organize the damask trade with help from the government. He received an advance of £900 a year, free of interest, and at his suggestion orders were given to merchants in the district to buy a certain quantity of his cloth. Those of another district were commanded to bring in 150 families of damask weavers and to find work for them. The adventurer in Schmiedeberg was in difficulties from the beginning : he had disputes with his weavers, and when they did produce cloth he was unable to sell it. The trouble with weavers was no doubt the same as that of the Irish ' contractors ' : if an adequate wage for full-time employment were paid to them the cost of production would be so high that no market could be found for the goods. The undertaker in this case, after demanding more help from the government, died opportunely when his contract was about to be cancelled. A Saxon merchant offered himself as a successor, but demanded such heavy grants, fees, and royalties, that negotiations with him ended abruptly.

In 1769, when affairs between the merchants and the Prussian minister had reached a deadlock, Frederick himself appeared again in Silesia ; but his advice was not very helpful. He suggested that another undertaker should be found, and encouragement given to the weavers. Two bad harvests, which caused serious famine, turned the government's attention to the more useful work of organizing relief. In the meantime trade in plain linens made satisfactory progress. Exports rose in value from rather less than 3,000,000 thalers in 1769 to 5,400,000 in 1774.

The increase probably brought many fresh weavers into the market, and the next step in policy may well have been made on the initiative of the old-established weavers, in order to restrain competition and keep the increase for themselves. An attempt was made in 1774 to form a general society of weavers (similar in some ways to the Stuart corporations of small masters) which should have a monopoly of manufacture. The scheme was approved by the government as a means to stricter regulation ; any weaver who broke the rules could be expelled from the union, and so deprived of his living. But the merchant class naturally offered a strong resistance, and the union never came into being.

Frederick's hope for the damask industry was not yet quite dead, but it expired a few years later. After 1774 two more undertakers were found.[1] One was soon dismissed. The other was put at the head of a joint-stock concern in which shares were held by the government and several municipalities. The company lost heavily, and at length the manager was allowed to take over its business as a private venture. He soon went bankrupt, and the project of damask manufacture came to an end in 1780. At that time only thirty weavers were more or less employed ; and in the annual statements of exports from Silesia damask never figured at all.

Frederick made very similar efforts to develop the weaving of the coarse, unbleached cloths known as ' creas '. These efforts were quite unsuccessful, and to recount them would be practically to repeat what has been said about the damask manufacture. The outcome may be judged from Oddy's statement that creas were made chiefly in Saxony and Bohemia and ' likewise attempted in Silesia '.[2]

The manufacture of damask and creas in Silesia played a very similar part to that of the southern linen industry in Ireland. In both cases the industry was promoted by the state and worked on a large scale ; in both it depended from first to last on patronage and never gave any promise or permanent success.

Fresh Legislation in Ireland. We will turn now from these efforts to promote new manufacture, and examine the other branch of industrial policy, the regulation of trades already established. Again, we will deal first with Ireland, and then glance at the contemporary measures in one or two other countries.

There had been so much legislation for the linen trade in Ireland early in the eighteenth century that it must have seemed in 1745 as if all the necessary rules had already been passed. But a few years later a new trouble appeared. The outburst of enterprise on the part of landlords and industrial employers, which began about 1750, caused the growth of a class of employees ; and these men, who were as a rule very badly paid, joined together to safeguard and improve their position. There

---

[1] Zimmerman, pp. 154–60.   [2] *European Commerce*, p. 404.

is no evidence as to the organization of their societies : they were probably local unions of a simple type. However, they were formidable enough to cause much complaint among the employers, to engage the attention of the parliamentary committee of 1758, and to call forth a couple of statutes. There were already two general combination Acts in Ireland, passed in 1729 and 1743, but they were evidently not observed. It was probably the failure of these measures that led Stephenson to think persuasion a better remedy than compulsion. But the sudden growth of trade unionism among the southern weavers seemed to call for something more rapid and drastic than persuasion. Stephenson himself urged stricter laws against combination, and Parliament was induced in 1757 to pass a fresh Act, providing specially for the linen trade.[1] According to this measure, any weaver, or other person engaged in the linen manufacture, who should be convicted of ' swearing or being sworn into a combination to raise the prices usually paid for weaving, or who should unlawfully raise mobs for that purpose, or (should) collect or pay money for any such purpose ', should be liable to imprisonment for any term up to six months.[2]

As unions still continued, a stronger law was passed in 1759.[3] Its terms were widened to include manufacture in general, although the linen, hempen, and cotton trades were specially named. Boycotting employers and refusing to finish contracts were added to the list of offences, and whipping was allowed as a penalty. This measure apparently had no more success than its precursors. It came into force in June, 1760 ; yet in that summer the Smiths, of Waterford, were hard hit by a strike among their workers.[4] In his report of 1763 Stephenson still spoke of ' this baneful check to the extension of manufactures ', and he added with truth that the laws ' ought to be made more effective against masters as well as men '.[5] In the general regulating Act of 1764 three clauses dealt with the question of combination. A generation later the Linen Board received complaints of an illegal combination among weavers in and about

---

[1] 31 Geo. II, c. 17. [2] ibid., c. 8. [3] 33 Geo. II, c. 5.
[4] Stephenson, *Report*, 1760, p. 26. He tried to act as a mediator, but without success. An employer, who was well known to have a strong prejudice against combination, was hardly the right man to undertake this task.
[5] *Report*, 1763, p. 24.

Drogheda, to support a ' bill of prices ' ;[1] and it is known that trade unions were flourishing in Dublin early in the nineteenth century, in spite of the English combination Acts, which now applied to Ireland.[2]

Inspection of Brown Linen. The laws of 1757 and 1759 were aimed against southern employers : it was next the turn of weavers in Ulster to come under regulation. The question with which Parliament was asked to deal was the examination of cloth sold in the open markets, before it was bought by drapers and sent to bleach. It will be remembered that this point had arisen in 1733, and that in the long run inspection of brown linen had been left to the lappers who stamped the white cloths. At the best this was a half-hearted measure, but now it had become quite useless. The boom in trade during the Seven Years' War would make the drapers and bleachers, who did the work of sealing, so busy that they would have no time to spare for examining any goods but their own. Three years after the war a draper, who acted as a lapper at three bleachgreens near Lisburn, wrote that he had been ' obliged to quit the manufactures ', because the work of inspecting, measuring, and lapping white linens filled his whole time.[3] Many of the lappers were probably no less occupied about the year 1760. Yet there was a general agreement that inspection of brown linens was much needed—all the more since drapers and bleachers could not do the work properly on their own account. Defects in weaving were sometimes only discovered when the cloth had been bleached and even exported. Shortly before 1760 one firm complained that they had just lost £1,000 through the return of cloth that had been badly woven.[4]

Linen Bill of 1762. The reforming movement in the south had been led by Stephenson : in Ulster the leader was John

---

[1] *Proceedings*, 1795, pp. 101–2.

[2] S. and B. Webb, *History of Trade Unionism*, p. 93 : ' The Dublin trades, then the best organized in the kingdom, ruthlessly enforced their bye-laws for the regulation of their respective industries, and formed a joint committee, the so-called " Board of Green Cloth ", whose dictates became the terror of the employers.'

[3] McCall, p. 22. The writer of the letter was Henry McCall, and the letter was addressed to John Williamson shortly after his removal to London. The three bleachgreens were those of Barclay (of Lambeg), McClure, and J. Fulton.

[4] ibid., p. 16.

Williamson, a bleacher of Lisburn. Under his guidance the
Linen Board was stirred to activity. A new Linen Bill was drawn
up, and brought before Parliament in the spring of 1762. The
first reading was on Wednesday, 14 April, the second reading on
the following day ; and on Monday, 19th, the Bill reached the
committee stage. It seemed likely to pass the remaining stages
within a few days. But in committee it was suddenly allowed
to lapse.[1] The reason was undoubtedly that rumours of impend-
ing trouble had just reached Dublin. The northern weavers
were closely following the actions of Parliament and the Trustees.
They would know from conversation with drapers and from the
gossip of the market what measures of regulation were proposed.
They would have official information when leave to bring in
the new bill was given in the House of Commons ; for at that
time the chief contents of the Bill would be stated in the House.
As leave was regularly given some weeks before the first reading,
there would be time for the weavers to organize a resistance,
and for word of their intention to reach Parliament when the
Bill was in its early stages. The text of the Bill has not been
preserved ; therefore we cannot tell precisely what clauses were
resisted by the weavers. But the main clauses certainly dealt
with the inspection of their work, and the weavers were convinced
that if the Bill were passed it would bring them more than ever
under the power of the drapers. It must have been felt in
Parliament that if the mass of weavers refused to obey the law, the
proposed reform would only injure the brown linen markets, which
Parliament was hoping to increase in numbers and in strength.

Determination of the Board. The sequel was curious, for the
Government's *volte face* meant very little in practice. Although
Parliament drew back, the Trustees went forward. The fact
was that under the Act of 1733 they had power already to
appoint special lappers, or ' sealmasters ', for brown linen, and
they must have decided to use their existing powers without
waiting for any further support from Parliament.[2] On 17 April,
the day after the second reading, they resolved ' that the laws

---

[1] *Commons Journals,* 1761–4, under these dates.
[2] As several of them were members of Parliament, they would know that
there was some doubt about the fate of the Bill. The Board met on 13, 14, 15,
17, and 19 April. These frequent meetings show that there were critical

relative to the sealing of brown linens before they are exposed
to sale, and also the laws relative to the exposing brown linens
to sale crisp'd, or in open folds, be put into execution as soon
as the nature of the trade will admit '.[1]

It is interesting to notice that the Board, by its own confession,
had never yet made any attempt to enforce the clauses passed
in 1745 and 1759, forbidding the sale of cloth in tight rolls.
At the same meeting they passed two other resolutions.
The first was that if any of the drapers or bleachers who held
' white seals ' should be found guilty of buying cloth tied in
rolls, they should be deprived of their seals—i. e. removed from
their office of lappers. The second was the momentous decision
to appoint sealmasters for brown linen. The persons appointed
were to be 'principal manufacturers', recommended by a Trustee
for their honesty and knowledge of the trade, and able to give
security of £20. They were to take up their office on 11 August
1762.[2]

On 19 April, the day on which the new Bill was abandoned
by Parliament, the Board drew up regulations for the appointment of sealmasters, and a schedule of instructions to accompany
each seal. The most important instructions were that no one
was to act as a lapper for both white and brown linen ; that
every web stamped must be of good and even quality ; that no
cloth might be sealed at the time of a market or fair ; and that
the sealmaster might charge 1d. for each piece that he sealed.[3]
It was decided on the same day to enforce the clauses of the
statute of 1745 which prescribed the length and breadth of
various sets and kinds of cloth, and laid down rules for the
making of reeds.[4]

Rising of Weavers. As these resolutions were published in
the form of proclamations, it was soon known that, in spite of
the failure of the new Bill, inspection of cloth would be enforced
by the Board.[5] Both drapers and weavers in Ulster took action

discussions, for I do not think that the Board met so often at any other period
in its career. By 19 April it had been decided that the new scheme should be
carried out.   [1] *Proceedings*, 1762, p. 15.
   [2] ibid., p. 16.   [3] ibid., pp. 26–31.   [4] ibid., p. 33.
   [5] The proclamations were sent to newspapers in Dublin, Belfast, and
Newry. They appeared in the *Belfast News Letter*, on 20 April and 4 May.
The instructions for sealmasters were not published until 25 May.

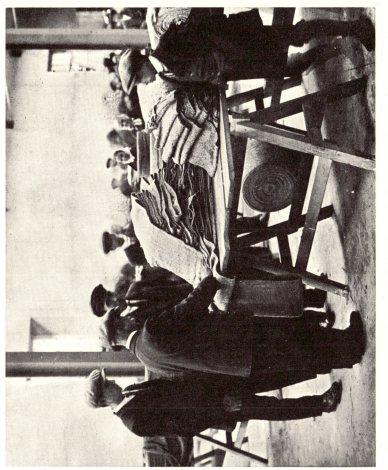

CLOTH IN ROLLS AND OPEN FOLDS

accordingly. A meeting of drapers was held at Lisburn, in the linen hall, on Tuesday, 4 May.[1] Tuesday was then, as it is now, the market day in Lisburn, and this meeting was evidently held after the close of the market. The drapers decided to form a permanent association with the object of enforcing the Board's regulations, especially those relating to the sale of cloth in open folds.[2] Further meetings were held, at Antrim on the 8th and Lisburn on the 10th. At these meetings it was resolved to put the regulations into force after the 11th.[3] In the Lisburn market, the most important in Ireland, this resolution would take effect on Tuesday, 18th.

In the meantime the weavers prepared to counter these measures. At a meeting held in Dromore, co. Down, on Wednesday, 12 May, they framed a strongly worded resolution :

' This is to give notice to all gentlemen manufacturers and weavers to meet in a body, like valiant and honest men, at Lisburn on Tuesday next, that we may oppose the imprudent and oppressive measures which are to be used against us by the merchants, and to bring them to reason by fair means, and if that will not do other means will be used ; and let us like Demetrius and his craftsmen stand valiantly up for our Diana, for our craft is in danger.' [4]

There was another meeting at Lisburn within the next few days : no further resolution was passed, but apparently there was a general agreement to adopt ' other means '. On the following Tuesday the law was to be enforced in Lisburn market for the first time. An unusually large crowd of weavers appeared in Lisburn on that day ; [5] but they came armed with black-thorns, and instead of attending the market in the usual way, they first formed a procession and paraded the streets. Their arch-enemy, Williamson, was in the linen hall. He was attacked

---

[1] *News Letter,* 4 and 7 May.

[2] Although the weavers afterwards used this society as a handle to justify their own union, it was certainly a legal body—at least it did not contravene the combination laws ; its professed object was to enforce the law, not to ' support a bill of prices '.

[3] ibid., 18 May. [4] McCall, p. 17.

[5] The number was said to be three or four hundred. In 1816 Corry gave from three to four hundred as the normal attendance ; but in 1762, when the volume of trade in Lisburn was probably only a third as great, this would be an exceptional number. Apart from the fact that they carried sticks instead of packs of cloth, it would be clear that most of the weavers had not come to trade.

by the mob, but escaped into a private house. The weavers nearly succeeded in capturing a more important person. Lord Hillsborough, a Trustee, who strongly supported the Board's recent decisions, had come to Lisburn, evidently to assist at the inauguration of the new régime. He escaped from the market with difficulty. Some of the drapers were less fortunate, for ten or twelve of them were caught, and forced to abjure the whole system of sealing. The weavers then marched to Lambeg, and were engaged in sacking Williamson's house when a force of soldiers arrived and dispersed them.[1]

The reasons of this remarkable outburst of feeling will be discussed later. We shall find that dislike of the linen laws was, with many of the weavers, no more than a proximate cause. The underlying source of trouble was a matter of social relationships, which could only be influenced indirectly by statutes or by decrees of the Linen Board. However, something had been gained by this firm stand. The Trustees saw that Parliament had been right in anticipating trouble, and they took measures to pacify their opponents. In the first place, to show their impartiality, they became very active in punishing lappers of white linen who misused their powers.[2] Secondly, they announced that the date on which sealmasters would take office was postponed from 11 August to 11 October.[3] Thirdly, they shelved for a time the question of enforcing the statutes of 1745 and 1759.

Beginning of Inspection. Many people believed that the system of sealing had been abandoned altogether; but the Board announced that sealing would actually begin in October. Lord Hillsborough himself was the first to act as sealmaster. He had voted against postponement because the delay and uncertainty would injure the markets,[4] and for the same reason

---

[1] This account of the ' turn out ' is based on an article in the *Newry Magazine* (vol. ii, p. 269). The article was reprinted by Corry (*Report*, 1822, App. V), and it was closely followed by McCall (op. cit., pp. 16–20). There is probably a report of the rising in the *Belfast News Letter* for 21 May 1762 ; but this number was unfortunately missing from the only file to which I have had access.

[2] Especially in 1763. Entries in the *Proceedings* for that year show that some dozens of ' white lappers ' were fined or dismissed.

[3] *Proceedings*, 1762, p. 109 (13 July).

[4] ibid., p. 111. On 2 August, Lord Hillsborough moved, and Lord Moira seconded, a proposal to revert from 11 October to 11 August, as the date of the first inspection.

he began, probably in August, to inspect brown linen on his own initiative. Although the Board had been ' fearful that complying with (his) proposals might be attended with dangerous consequences ', and although he must in fact have run some risk, he was not molested this time. The professional sealmasters, when they took up their duties, were also allowed to work in peace. Whether they actually began in October, 1762, is not clear. But they were certainly at work during the winter, for in February, 1763, the drapers were already complaining of frauds in the use of brown seals.[1] In the following October four sealmasters were fined for abusing their powers.[2]

Although there was so much difficulty and hesitation in starting the inspection of brown linen, the new system, when once it was established, proved to be permanent : it continued until 1828, when the Board itself was dissolved.

Act of 1764. With the inauguration of the sealing system the reformers had gained their main point. But this was not quite the end of their efforts. The Bill which had been abandoned in 1762 contained several fresh regulations, and the northern drapers were determined to carry them through Parliament. Early in 1763 they started a fresh agitation, and the weavers began a new movement of resistance. In March a document entitled *Materials for a new Linen Bill* was put before the Board by the drapers of Belfast and Lisburn.[3] Williamson was evidently still leading the agitation, for, in the company of another draper named Bell, he attended the Board's meeting to present this document.[4] In the following month—probably at Williamson's request—merchants in London, Liverpool, and Bristol sent letters pointing out the need for further regulations.[5] Fortunately this new aggression on the part of the drapers did not lead to violence. Battle was waged by means of a series of pamphlets stating the case for one side and the other without much lucidity, and with a good deal of personal abuse.[6]

The Trustees were more cautious than they had been in the previous year. They allowed the *Materials* to remain with

[1] *Proceedings*, 1762–3, p. 175.   [2] *Proceedings*, 1763–4, p. 126.
[3] *Proceedings*, 1762–3, p. 255.   [4] *Proceedings*, 1763–4, p. 44.
[5] ibid., pp. 34, 43.
[6] For a list of the pamphlets published at this time see the bibliographical note given in Appendix IV.

the Secretary for nine months. At last in December, 1763, encouraged no doubt by the peaceful state of Ulster, they began to consider the question of a new Bill. In January and February, 1764, they held five special meetings for the purpose.[1] By 24 February the measure was drafted and its heads were approved in Parliament. The Bill was read for the first time on 7 May. Its passage through both Houses was very smooth and rapid, for the royal assent was given five days later.[2]

The new Act[3] was a comprehensive measure. Besides confirming the system of sealing and the instructions to sealmasters, it laid down detailed regulations for all the processes of manufacture—for reeling and making up yarn, for reed-making and weaving, and for bleaching. The combination laws were renewed and slightly extended. To support Stephenson's scheme of ' premium markets ' a clause was inserted enabling grand juries to spend any sum not exceeding £300 for the building of a market hall in the chief towns of their county.[4]

In spite of its great length and wide scope the Act made no very striking changes. It was really a consolidating Act, which only modified and expanded the existing law in details. The great change of this time was the inspection of brown linen, but that was an accomplished fact before the Bill was drafted. The new measure, indeed, was received as quietly in the country as it had been in Parliament. Apparently the weavers made no complaint at all. That is hardly surprising, of course, seeing that the Act in itself made scarcely any difference to them. But the truly surprising point is that after all their rioting and pamphleteering they had settled down and ceased to grumble before the end of 1763. It was, as we have seen, for this very reason that the new Bill had been brought forward.

---

[1] *Proceedings*, 1763–4, pp. 224, 225, 240–8.
[2] *Commons Journals*, 1761–4, under the dates given.
[3] 3 Geo. III, c. 35.
[4] In 1737 grand juries had been commanded to build linen halls, but in this new Act the clause was only permissive. This Act, like that of 1745, was drawn up by Anthony Foster, Counsel to the Trustees, who afterwards became Lord Chief Baron of the Exchequer (Corry, *Report*, 1822, p. 10). Arthur Young was greatly impressed with Foster's personal character and his zeal for agricultural progress. He described the Lord Chief Baron as ' this prince of improvers' (*Tour*, pp. 98–101). Foster's estate was at Collon, co. Louth, where Sidebotham had a bleachgreen. Foster's son was an active member of the Linen Board, and the author of the most important regulating Act passed after 1764.

Results of Inspection. How are we to account for this change of mind on the part of the weavers ? In the first place it was gradually realized that sealing might prove a benefit instead of a danger. No honest weaver could complain if his cloth were examined before it was sold. On the other hand, if a piece of cloth were well made, it would be officially guaranteed, and therefore more marketable. Moreover, the drapers in future would not be able to follow their old custom of paying for less than the length of a web : they would have to pay for the full length marked by the sealmaster. Several weavers had seen these points from the beginning : others would learn them from newspapers, pamphlets, and discussions.

Further reasons were provided by the policy of the Linen Board. Their prosecution of drapers who misused their white seals would certainly make a good impression on the weavers. Again, they showed a disposition to remove any real grievances. For instance, it was pointed out to them that their regulation forbidding sealing on a market day would cause hardship. Some weavers would be obliged to waste much time by walking, perhaps several miles, to have their linen sealed, and would have to make the journey over again on another day to sell the cloth. The Trustees admitted the grievance and repealed the clause.[1]

Probably the strongest reason of all was their policy in the appointment of sealmasters. In their first set of instructions they said : ' We design hereafter to take no more sealmasters, or lappers, into the service than what appears absolutely necessary.' It was laid down at the same time in the regulations that no more than five hundred seals should be issued, to ' principal manufacturers '.[2] This decision was stated to be for the encouragement of the sealmaster. It meant that the five hundred would have among them a monopoly of the sealing, and that each of them would have a good income from fees. At the outset the weavers were convinced that these few sealmasters would simply be nominees and servants of the drapers. But the Board soon changed its mind, and the weavers changed their opinion. Within six weeks from the date of these resolutions nearly 1,300 sealmasters had been appointed.[3] Others

[1] *Proceedings*, 1762–3, p. 258 (22 March 1763).   [2] ibid., pp. 26 sqq.
[3] ibid., pp. 62, 66, 101–8.

were given seals in 1763, and afterwards more and more. It was said twenty years later that there was 'hardly a weaver in the north of Ireland but in time became a sealmaster '.[1] It is easy to see why complaints against sealing were so quickly silenced. The weavers who dealt in the open markets, instead of being crushed by the law, became themselves its chief administrators. This fact has an important bearing on the whole policy of regulation, as it was practised by the Linen Board and the Irish government. Immense pains had been taken to draft a code of industrial laws, and to find means of putting them into force. The efforts had produced a riot, great ferment of debate, organization and counter-organization. In the end the regulations were left to be enforced by those whom they were meant to restrict, and the weavers had, if anything, more liberty than they had had at the outset.

By a curious irony those who had most reason to complain of the Act of 1764 were its chief promoters. The London merchants who had asked for more regulations vainly protested against the rules which were laid down for the length and breadth of medium and coarse linen ;[2] and Williamson, the leader of the drapers' party, was the greatest sufferer of all. Within a year he had fallen foul of the regulations for bleaching, quarrelled violently with the Trustees, and gone into voluntary exile in London.[3]

Perhaps the person who benefited most by the Act was the Secretary to the Privy Council in London. For his services in securing the Council's assent to the statute he was presented with nearly £60 worth of fine linen.[4]

Results of Regulation in France. A similar result—the very opposite to the Government's intentions—followed the French ordinance of 1762. The ordinance was meant to bring country workers under rules like those of the town gilds : its actual outcome was to assimilate towns to the country, i.e. to do away with regulations in both. In France, as in Ireland and everywhere else, it was found impossible to control a *fabrique dispersée.* Even to-day it is difficult enough to enforce factory laws in multitudes of small workshops : in the eighteenth century, when communications were so much more difficult and the machinery

---

[1] Nevill, *Seasonable Remarks,* p. 32.   *Proceedings,* 1764–5, pp. 8, 12, 27.
[3] *Newry Magazine,* 1815, p. 271.   [4] ibid., pp. 27, 28, 55.

of government was so much less effective, strict control was out of the question. It was soon realized that the law of 1762 was inoperative. The town manufacturers, who had been forced to take their goods to a *bureau de visite* and to pay for inspection and stamping, began to demand a freedom similar to that of the country craftsmen. Merchants neglected the rules of their own gilds : they could buy unstamped goods freely in the country, and they began to deal in the same way in towns. If the law insisted that goods offered in the open market should be sealed beforehand, they were sold privately, and the markets disappeared. Even the inspectors themselves, before 1780, were giving up the effort to carry out the law.

In any case the advance of rural industry would soon have ruined the gilds ; but the regulations of 1762 hastened the process. The fact that rules newly imposed on the country were ignored made the old gild regulations all the more anomalous. Consequently when the gilds were swept away in the Revolution the reformers met with little resistance. Their work had been done for them thirty years before by the Conseil d'État.[1] M. Tarlé, in describing the effect of the ordinance on town gilds, says truly : ' " Ceci tuera cela," pouvait-on prédire dès ce moment-là.' [2]

Regulation in Silesia. The comparison between Silesia and Ireland is still closer, for in both countries there was much special legislation for the linen trade. In Silesia, under the old government, regulations had already been made very similar to those existing in Ireland at the same time—especially in 1724, when a consolidating Act was issued.[3] In 1765, three years after the French ordinance, and one year after the Irish consolidating Act, Frederick the Great produced a fresh code, evidently a part of his scheme for restoring trade after the war.[4] This code, like the Irish Act, contained rules for every branch of the industry. Farmers were to devote a certain proportion of their land to flax ; when it was retted they were to dry it, not in their own premises but in public ovens ; after drying it was to be

---

[1] The argument which is summarized above is the central theme, developed with much force and ability in M. Tarlé's work. The old system of inspection in France was abolished in September 1791 (op. cit., p. 76).
[2] Tarlé, op. cit., p. 53.   [3] Zimmerman, pp. 37-43.   [4] ibid., pp. 118-21.

officially inspected. A great system of spinning schools was to be established. In Ireland such schools were always voluntary, but in Silesia Frederick made it obligatory on every child— boy or girl—to learn spinning in a school at the age of eight. As further inducements, every male farm servant had to prove his ability to spin before he was allowed to marry, and every farmer's daughter who wished to marry had to qualify by owning a spinning wheel.[1] It is not clear whether this restriction was ever put into force ; but spinning schools were certainly founded in large numbers. In the district of Breslau alone there were 3,000 schools in 1783.[2] Jobbers who bought yarn were to be examined by public officials—who in most cases would know nothing of the trade—in order to test their fitness for the work.

There were careful regulations for weaving, very similar to those made by the Irish Parliament. In particular, the use of Bohemian reeds was forbidden, because the cloth made with them was not in accordance with the legal prescription. Bohemian reeds were cheaper than Silesian, and the cloth which they produced was evidently good, for it was preferred by the trade. The case is exactly parallel to those of the ' unstatutable ' Irish yarn for which there was a ready market in England, and the ' seven-eights ' and ' three-quarters ' cloths, which caused friction in 1764 between London merchants and the Linen Board. There was a clause, like that in the Irish Act of 1759, prescribing that all webs should be brought to market in open folds.

The rules for bleaching might have been designed to prevent any improvement in method. Every detail was prescribed by law ; the size of vats ; the amount of cloth to be put in each ; the chemicals to be used ; the length of time to be taken. Bleaching of cloth by foreigners was forbidden, so that local firms could not learn the superior methods of Dutch or British bleachers. As in Ireland, the use of lime was prohibited.

After 1780 there was a fresh access of industrial laws under Frederick William II. But as these laws give a useful clue to

---

[1] Spinning was always regarded in Silesia as work suitable for both men and women.

[2] Horner, p. 459. There were still over 2,700 in 1798 ; but most of them were probably very small affairs, no more than handicraft classes in ordinary schools.

later development in the organization of trade, we will leave them to be discussed when we have reached the same period in the history of the Irish linen industry.

These regulations seem to have been little better enforced than the Irish statutes. Those relating to yarn must have been carried out to some extent, for the inspectors of yarn were extremely unpopular. On the other hand, the fact that most of the regulations were repeated several times, with growing penalties, is a sure sign that they were not strictly observed. The storm of complaints against them shows that they would only be obeyed under strong compulsion ; and the constant disputes among the various branches of the industry, each branch blaming the others for violations of the law, show that the law was often broken. It is known that the injunction to sell cloths in open folds was no more regarded in Silesia than in Ireland. The attempt to compel the use of spinning wheels was also a failure, for even at the present day much of the spinning in Silesia is done by means of the ancient distaff and spindle ; [1] and all the efforts to teach spinning in schools did not prevent a serious fall in yarn production towards the end of the century.

Need for Inspection. To note the frequent failure of industrial regulation in the eighteenth century is not, of course, to condemn the whole system. In recent times regulation has been comparatively little needed because production is so largely in the hands of responsible firms, which would lose seriously by selling inferior goods. The firms are their own inspectors. The modern linen lapper, for instance, is not a public official, but the employee of a private firm. His duty is to examine all the finished cloth and to set aside every piece that is defective in weaving or bleaching. Even at the present day public inspection of certain foodstuffs is necessary in the interests of the consumer. There was the same need in many branches of manufacture at a time when manufacture depended chiefly on small independent craftsmen.

This was the position of the linen industry during the

---

[1] Horner, pp. 392, 417. Cf. Hager's description of hand-spinning in Switzerland in recent years, ' mittels der freien pendelden und am Boden rollenden Spille ' (*Flachs und Hanf*, p. 162).

eighteenth century, and there can be no doubt that regulation and inspection, with the object of standardizing the kinds of cloth and maintaining the quality, were really desirable. There is much truth in the view that domestic industry led the manufacturer to take pride in his work, and helped him to become an artist as well as a craftsman. But there are so many exceptions that it would be a great mistake to think of the artist-craftsman as the rule in any but the highest branches of manufacture. Among the makers of plain and coarse goods, whose life was spent in ' repetition work ' there must have been a strong inducement to sacrifice quality to speed. It is certain that many linen weavers could not be relied upon to make consistently good cloth. They used all manner of devices to cover up dishonest work, and drapers, buying in great haste, had no time to detect flaws. The practice, illegal but very common, of selling webs in tight rolls, made examination by drapers all the more difficult. Moreover, both weavers and small drapers sold for cash, and some of them, having themselves little credit or reputation, were quite satisfied to sell defective goods, provided only that the goods were taken off their hands before the faults were discovered.[1]

On the other hand it was a serious matter for a bleacher or a large merchant if his cloth proved defective, for he would lose money, credit and custom. We need not be surprised that bleachers led the movement for stricter regulation of weaving. It was important, moreover, for the whole trade that the reputation of its goods should be maintained. To this end honest work was essential ; and the only guarantee of honest work, where thousands of irresponsible weavers were concerned, was public inspection.

Difficulty of Regulation. There were three great drawbacks, however, to the system of inspection, as it was practised in the eighteenth century. In the first place it was nearly always accompanied by a narrow regulation of the methods of manufacture, which checked enterprise and aroused opposition to

---

[1] Cf. Nevill's statement : ' It is well known that if this man can answer the present purposes, he is regardless of any future consequence.' The whole passage is quoted below, chap. vii, p. 131. However, the standard of workmanship among Irish weavers as a whole seems to have been fairly high (*vide infra,* chap. xv, pp. 287-8).

control of any kind. Secondly, seeing that weavers could not spare time to come twice in a week to the same market, inspection had to be carried out on the market day, and was therefore quite as hurried in practice as examination by private drapers. Thirdly, lappers, sealmasters and inspectors of all kinds, especially those who were paid by the piece, were always tempted to over-look faults in manufacture. Thus there was a constant tendency for the inspection to become slack and perfunctory. These difficulties were never overcome before the days of large scale production. The character of the laws could only have been im-proved by a more liberal spirit and greater knowledge among the Trustees and members of Parliament. The administration could only have been made effective if the sealmasters had been replaced by some hundreds of competent inspectors, whose salaries would have absorbed the whole of the Board's revenue.

VII

FAILURE OF ENTERPRISE IN THE SOUTH

IN 1763, when Stephenson wrote his last published report, the southern linen industry seemed to give good promise of permanent success. Both landed proprietors and middle-class projectors were active in organizing work on a large scale; and if the authorities doubted the value of large undertakings, they felt their hope of healthy development justified by the growth of open markets. After the great ' turn out ' in Ulster, and lesser industrial troubles in the south, the Trustees may well have regarded the Act of 1764 as the introduction to an era of steady progress, in which domestic manufacture, for the supply of brown linen markets, should overspread the whole country.

But the experience of the next half-century—in fact, of the next decade—showed how little foundation there was for their hope. The evidence suggests, in the first place, that trade in the south was fairly active down to the prosperous years, 1770 and 1771 ; secondly, that many undertakings came to grief in the heavy depression of 1773 ; and thirdly, that there was never any satisfactory recovery after that time.

Trade in 1770. The comparative success of the first few years is shown in Stephenson's report to the parliamentary committee, which met in London in 1773.[1] His report included an estimate of sales in the open markets during the year 1770. His figures are certainly exaggerated ;[2] but when due allowance is made for his optimism and for his keen interest in brown

---

[1] *H. of C. Reports,* iii. 117. He reprinted the estimate in his *Observations on the Present State of the Linen Trade of Ireland* (1784), p. 86. It is also printed in the *Newry Magazine,* 1816, p. 267.

[2] e. g. he estimated the total annual sales in Ulster as £1,645,000 ; whereas Greer's estimate for 1784 was only £1,214,560. Seeing that the volume of exports in 1784 was five per cent. greater than in 1770, it is difficult to believe that the market sales were less by over twenty-five per cent. There is reason to believe that even Greer's estimate is too large ; and in that case there must be a great exaggeration in Stephenson's figures.

linen markets, we still find in ten of the southern counties an amount of trade which must have satisfied the hope of the Trustees. In five other counties the volume of trade might seem a fair nucleus for future progress : in the remaining eight the output was very small.[1] Stephenson believed that the sales in the southern provinces amounted to nearly a third of those in Ulster.[2] However little statistical value his statements may have they do at least suggest that the enterprise, which had been so conspicuous about the year 1760, was still alive ten years later. But in 1773 there came a disastrous slump in trade, which seems to have ruined a great part of the southern industry.

Crisis of 1773. This depression was common to the whole of the British Isles.[3] After the Seven Years' War there had been a set-back, followed by a too active recovery. The climax came in 1770 and 1771. In these years production went beyond the economic demand. The linen market in London was overstocked, and goods had to be sold at a loss. There was a reaction: buying became very slack, and many weavers were unemployed. Complaints reached the Government from the linen-producing districts in England, especially from Somerset and Darlington. In Scotland matters were still worse. Multitudes of weavers were out of work ; many who remained at work had their wages reduced below the level of subsistence. Riots were reported in Perth and Dundee, and great distress in Edinburgh and

[1] The following is a summary of the return :

Amount of Annual Sales. £	Counties.
100,000	Dublin, Louth.
20,000–60,000	Galway, Roscommon, Sligo, Meath, Westmeath, Longford, King's County, Kildare.
3,000–10,000	Mayo, Leitrim, Kilkenny, Waterford, Cork.
1,000 or less	Queen's County, Carlow, Wexford, Wicklow, Clare, Limerick, Tipperary, Kerry.

[2] His figures were :—sales in the southern provinces, £502,000 ; sales in Ulster, £1,645,000.

[3] The particulars given below are taken from the report of the parliamentary committee of 1773 (*H. of C. Reports*, vol. iii).

Glasgow.[1] It was probably the Scottish merchants and manufacturers, acting through the Convention of Burghs, who demanded higher protective duties and a renewal of bounties for export, and secured the appointment of a parliamentary committee to inquire into the matter.

The report of this committee shows that Ireland was also seriously injured by the check to trade ; so much so that in a letter quoted in the evidence it was said : ' If something is not done by Parliament this session, farewell to the linen trade of Ireland, for there will not be a weaver left that will not emigrate.' [2] This letter referred to the northern counties ; and it is true that many of the weavers in Ulster were driven about this time to emigrate to America. Arthur Young found that the number of emigrants, which for some time had been about 2,000 annually, rose in 1773 to 4,000.[3] The movement was due in part to religious and political causes, but undoubtedly the great increase in 1773 was the result of bad trade ; and it was so serious that if emigration had continued at this rate for another ten years there would have been in truth hardly a weaver left in Ulster.[4]

But the depression in trade was not really as heavy as people imagined at the time. Robert Stephenson, who was a witness at the inquiry, admitted that Antrim, Derry, Down, and Armagh were still ' considerably employed in the manufactory '.[5] The export of linen from Ireland in 1773 was only less by about 10 per cent. than the average of the previous decade. Moreover there was a complete recovery in the following year, and by 1775 emigration had stopped.[6]

Thus Ulster seems to have escaped lightly, but the rest of Ireland was probably harder hit. Most of the southern trade was in medium or coarse cloths ; and there is reason to believe that the falling off was chiefly in this branch of trade. In

[1] A Scottish linen merchant, who had been compelled to sell at less than cost price, wrote to his agent in London : ' I will certainly stop buying, and silently lament the approaching ruin of our country.' (Appendix to above Report, p. 115.) [2] ibid., p. 118. [3] *Tour*, p. 125.
[4] The output of linen in Ulster at the time when Young wrote was probably about 30,000,000 yards. This amount could easily be produced by 30,000 weavers. As a large proportion of the emigrants would be farmer-weavers, an emigration of 4,000 a year for ten years would seriously reduce the manufacturing population.
[5] *H. of C. Reports*, iii, 117. [6] Young, *Tour*, u.s.

Scotland, where the manufacture was largely coarse, the output in 1773 was 17 per cent. less than the decennial average.[1] On the other hand, the counties which Stephenson reported as flourishing were the centres of fine manufacture. Further, there were several complaints to the parliamentary committee of competition from Germany, and many of the German cloths were similar to those produced in southern Ireland. Statistics of export from Silesia show that German trade had recovered after the Seven Years' War, and was very active at this time.[2] On several grounds, therefore, it seems likely that a great strain was put upon Irish industry in 1773, and that the strain, which caused only a temporary lapse in Ulster, was fatal to many undertakings in the south.

Evidence of Failure. This view is confirmed by the striking fact that Arthur Young, who visited most parts of Ireland at various times between 1776 and 1779, had scarcely anything to say about linen manufacture in the southern provinces. There was, it is true, much more industry than his account would suggest, but his failure to mention it was not merely due to lack of observation. A diarist as keen and scrupulous as Young, if he had been travelling through Ireland sixteen years earlier, would certainly have made more than half a dozen allusions to the linen trade in the south. Many of his hosts would have been patrons of industry : in almost every county he would have been taken to see bleachgreens, or other ' improvements '; and everywhere he would have met with eagerness to promote manufacture. What he actually found led him to state, as we have noticed already, that the southern manufactures were ' too insignificant to merit a particular attention '. Young's evidence, therefore,

---

[1] Statistics of linen stamped in Scotland, see Horner, p. 299.

[2] Horner, p. 407. The following are the relevant figures :

			Talers.	Yards (approx.).
Export from Silesia in	1761–2		1,123,338	2,527,000
,,	,,	1766–7	2,857,799	6,430,000
,,	,,	1771–2	4,291,140	9,655,000
,,	,,	1773–4	4,408,763	9,918,000
,,	,,	1774–5	5,419,336	12,192,000

The fact that Silesian exports were still increasing in 1774, when Irish trade was recovering, suggests that foreign competition was by no means the only trouble. The disturbance seems to have been chiefly due to miscalculation of the markets.

strongly suggests that enterprise in the south had waned before the time of his tour.

After the collapse of 1773, and especially after 1780, when the increased freedom of overseas trade had aroused a fresh interest in the economic condition of Ireland, the Linen Board renewed its efforts to promote the southern linen manufacture. Moreover, the exports of linen from Ireland increased greatly in the last twenty years of the century, and we should expect the southern provinces to have some share in the increase. However, the slight information that is available shows that the revival did not go very far.

Negative evidence, of the kind that we gathered from Young's *Tour*, is to be found in Wakefield's *Account of Ireland*, published in 1812, and from the *County Surveys*, issued during the first quarter of the nineteenth century. The *Surveys* regularly gave particulars of manufacturing industry as well as agriculture ; and Wakefield dealt fully both with the cotton manufacture in all districts and with the linen industry in Ulster. Yet the Surveys speak of the linen manufacture in eight counties only— Meath, King's County, Cork, Clare, Kilkenny, Galway, Sligo, and Leitrim. Wakefield adds no more than Louth, Dublin, and Kerry to the list. Besnard, in his report to the Trustees, written in 1817, mentions Longford and Mayo also as possessing some manufacture ; but in the remaining ten counties there was practically none. Of the counties that have been named, Cork, Kerry, Meath, and Galway produced sail-cloth, sacking, and coarse sheetings. The sail-cloth industry was prosperous during the Napoleonic War, but collapsed in 1815, when the government contracts ceased. Weavers in Clare and Kilkenny worked entirely for local consumption. A considerable amount—perhaps a fifth or a quarter of the total output of the southern provinces— was in the hands of ' factory masters ' in Louth, King's County and Dublin, who sent their goods to the Dublin Linen Hall or to the large market in Drogheda.[1] The Linen Board particularly wished to encourage independent weavers, dealing in open markets, but Besnard mentioned that in the twenty-three counties which he visited the sellers in the markets numbered

---

[1] Besnard estimated the annual sales in Drogheda market as £100,000, so that this market alone, which appears to have been supplied almost entirely by large producers, accounted for nearly a sixth of the total output (£650,000).

only about 2,400. The cloth which they sold would represent the work of about 6,000 weavers. Thus there were on an average, in a whole county of the south and west, the same number of weavers as there were in a normal parish of the north-east.[1] In 1816 the twenty-five southern markets, including Drogheda, had on an average a weekly trade of £150 in each market, whereas the average turnover in the forty-five markets of Ulster was £993.

It is difficult to gain any accurate idea of the actual volume of trade, but we may estimate roughly that in the half-century after 1770, while the annual output of linen from Ireland as a whole doubled, or more than doubled, the increase in the southern provinces was no more than 30 per cent., perhaps less.[2] In 1816 their production was probably about a fifth of the amount produced in Ulster.

Evidence from Inspectors' Reports. These few examples may serve to substantiate the statement that southern industry never made real headway after 1773 ; but the extent of the failure can be most clearly grasped by a detailed comparison of Stephenson's reports, written in the period of high hopes and abounding enterprise, with the observations made by Besnard half a century later. Such a comparison is made in a summary form in the following table :

County.	Stephenson, 1762.	Stephenson, 1763.	Besnard, 1816.
LEINSTER.			
Meath . .	Much improved and increased.	Increasing beyond expectations.	Almost no manufacture.
Louth . .	Carried on with spirit and much increased.	Market in Drogheda growing. Hopes of others.	Large market in Drogheda. Another in Dundalk, used chiefly by jobbers.
King's Co. .	Considerable business, mostly on a large scale.	Industry spreading. Still on large scale.	Output £20,000 in 1816 (£50,000 in 1760).
Longford .	' A good spirit getting up in some parts ', but ' intolerably bad ' bleaching.	Fine trade increasing, coarse declined.	Thriving trade. Two good markets.

[1] e.g. in the parish of Ballintoy, on the North coast of County Antrim, there were 288 weavers in 1803 (Dubourdieu, *Survey of Antrim*, ii. 444).
[2] Stephenson's figure for sales in open markets in the south was about £500,000. If we were to accept this figure as representing the whole output (not market sales only), the increase between 1770 and 1816 would be just thirty per cent.

County.	Stephenson, 1762.	Stephenson, 1763.	Besnard, 1816.
LEINSTER.			
Kildare .	Promising.	Begins to get a footing.	' Entirely destitute of the linen trade '.
Wicklow .	Good prospect for coarse trade.	Still good promise.	No trade.
Queen's Co.	Little advance ; but hopes of a Linen Society.	Practically stationary.	No trade.
Kilkenny .	Nearly all bandle linen.	Manufacture greatly increased.	No trade.
Westmeath.	Great improvement. Large output of sheetings.	' Greatly surpassed every expectation '.	A little manufacture ; but chief output is yarn.
Carlow .	Increasing output.	Continued increase.	No trade.
Wexford .	Good sale for dowlas. Linen Society formed.	Linen Society at work.	No trade.
Dublin [1] .	—	—	Two large concerns, but no other manufacture.
MUNSTER.			
Cork, N. .	{ Business mostly by large manufacturers.	{ Scarcity of flax caused falling off in coarse trade. But some ' noble patronage ', e.g. by Lord Boyle.	{ Recent attempts by gentry, but little manufacture. Much manufacture of coarse linen : hard hit by lapsing of war contracts.
Cork, S. .	{ Lord Doneraile's prizes to weavers ' had a pretty good effect '.		
Clare . .	Flourishing Linen Society. Success ' exceeded all expectations '.	Improvement in quantity and quality. Gentry very active.	Little to report. Weavers in extreme poverty.
Limerick .	Very prosperous. Four markets.	No doubt of manufacture extending through the whole county.	Trifling manufacture : both yarn and cloth very bad.
Kerry . .	Some progress.	Great energy of patrons and employers.	A little manufacture of coarse cloth of poor quality.
Tipperary .	Only proposals of manufacture : nothing achieved.	Linen Society, but no markets yet, only flax-growing.	Hardly any manufacture, except for home use.
Waterford .	Less than in 1755.	Large concerns still flourishing.	Very little manufacture. Not more than 100 weavers in the county.

[1] Stephenson made no report on co. Dublin in these two years. In 1755 he mentioned ' a very extensive manufacture ' (*Journal*, p. 195). Again in 1760 he said that there were several factories in and around the city. But in the following year he reported that the output was declining. Most of the production in this county was evidently on a large scale.

County.	Stephenson, 1762.	Stephenson, 1763.	Besnard, 1816.
CONNAUGHT.			
Sligo . .	Great increase about the town.	Considerable increase. All on large scale.	Two markets.
Mayo . .	Weekly market at Castlebar.	Market doing well. Another proposed at Ballina.	Growing trade: 'spirit of industry '.
Galway [1] .	Successful efforts by Col. Trench and others.	Great energy of patrons.	Hardly any trade. Weavers enlisted in army and navy.
Leitrim .	Manufacture ' continued with attention and spirit '.	Keeps up pretty well.	Very little weaving.
Roscommon	' Great spirit.' Several ' new adventures '.	Manufacturers active : all working on a large scale.	Only a few weavers.

[1] In 1761 (Report, p. 55) Stephenson had written : ' This county is, in all parts, as it were, at once, electrified with a sort of fire, to excel in trade and industry.'

The main conclusion to be drawn from this survey is that whereas in 1763 there were only two or three counties in which trade did not appear to be making good progress, there were in 1816 only five or six counties which had more than a trifling trade. The large manufacturing concerns round about Drogheda showed real vitality, but elsewhere, even in the most flourishing districts, industry was in a precarious state. It was obviously struggling in Cork : in Mayo, Longford, and Sligo markets had recently been set up, and they depended for their success on patronage similar to that of the middle of the eighteenth century.[2]

[2] It is interesting to compare Besnard's estimates of market sales in 1816 with Stephenson's estimates, given on p. 2. The following is a summary of Besnard's figures :

Sales in 1816. £	Counties.
Over 100,000	Louth (£185,000).
80,000	Mayo.
20,000–60,000	King's County, Longford, Cork, Sligo.
10,000	Galway, Kerry.
1,000–5,000	Meath, Clare, Limerick, Leitrim.
Nil.	Kildare, Wicklow, Queen's County, Kilkenny, Westmeath, Carlow, Wexford, Dublin, Tipperary, Waterford, Roscommon.

Examples of Failure. As a final illustration we will follow the later history of some of those undertakings which have previously been described in the days of their early promise.

Sir Richard Cox's great enterprise had been highly praised by Stephenson in 1755. In 1760 he reported that the output was declining.[1] Cox was still receiving his annual grant from the Linen Board in 1764, but nine years later the grant had ceased. Young had nothing to say about Dunmanway, although he mentioned some recently established concerns in co. Cork ; and as no later writer spoke of Cox's work it is probable that the whole enterprise had been abandoned.[2] The factory of his neighbour, Adderley, lasted longer, perhaps because it was less ambitious ; but it was turned into a cotton mill, and was owned in 1815 by Mr. Orr.[3]

The two undertakings in co. Waterford, those of Lord Grandison and the Smith family, were still working in 1763.[4] We have seen that the Smiths in particular were most efficient and deserving manufacturers. But when Besnard visited Waterford in 1816, he found that there were no more than a hundred weavers in the whole county. The Smith's factory was ' long disused ' and their efforts were ' quite forgotten '.[5]

We noticed also the factory of William Rose, at Johnstown, co. Kildare, which was doing a good trade in 1755. Besnard mentioned that this factory had come to grief, and that others tried by branches of the Clibborn and Pim families had failed as well. The county in 1816 was ' entirely destitute of the linen trade '.[6]

Large Scale of Undertakings. What were the reasons of this widespread and persistent failure ? One cause was certainly the fact that nearly all the enterprises in the south were attempts to organize industry on a large scale. Whether the weaver worked in a factory or in his own home he was usually employed

---

[1] *Report*, 1760, p. 35.
[2] But a certain amount of industry survived. As late as 1823 a memorial from manufacturers and weavers in Dunmanway was sent to the Linen Board by J. H. Cox (*Proceedings*, 1823, p. 12). The Board's minutes do not show the nature of the memorial. In 1826 a grant was given to Henry Atkins for scutching machinery which he had set up in Dunmanway (P.R.O. London, A.O., 17, 428).   [3] Townsend, *Survey of Cork*, quoted by Horner, p. 112.
[4] Stephenson, *Report*, 1763, p. 45.   [5] Besnard, *Report*, 1817, p. 49.
[6] ibid., p. 17.

by a master who supplied the capital and sold the cloth. At a first glance such an organization seems a great advance on the system of independent weaving and open markets in Ulster. In other textile industries the whole drift was towards capitalistic production. In the English woollen trade, for example, there were factors in London and the provinces who took orders from wholesale buyers at home and abroad. They distributed the orders among manufacturers with whom they had regular dealings, and of whom, therefore, they had a personal knowledge. The manufacturer bought yarn, supervised the work of weavers and finishers, and examined the cloth before it went out. He used his judgement in making for stock and forecasting the course of markets, but he also worked to a large extent for orders. This system, in essentials very much like the modern organization, was flexible, yet it involved a minimum of waste ; it provided a means of sale which was perfectly suitable to factory production, and was in fact a great help to the introduction of steam power. In the cotton trade open markets never developed. There was almost from the beginning a class of manufacturers who organized the sale of cloth, and gave employment to weavers. Even in Ireland, when the cotton trade was fully established there, its organization was on capitalistic lines.

Small Scale in Ulster. The linen trade of Ulster was managed on a more elementary system ; and the fact was recognized by large dealers in Ulster who had knowledge of other trades and countries. John Nevill, a draper of Belfast, in a pamphlet written in 1783, pointed the contrast clearly :

' I presume there is no other trade in the world carried on in the same manner as the linen in the north of Ireland. In the silk, woollen and all other manufactures, a man of very considerable knowledge in the business, of a competent fortune, and with every convenience in readiness, employs a number of journeymen to work at his goods under his own immediate inspection, and they are finished under his own eye. Not so with the linen in the north of Ireland. Every weaver, as soon as he can muster up a few hanks of yarn, sets himself down to weave a piece of cloth which he takes to the market for brown linens, and there sells it to the highest bidder ; and it is well known that if this man can answer the present purposes he is regardless of any future consequences.' [1]

---

[1] *Seasonable Remarks on the Linen Trade of Ireland,* pp. 31, 32.

Under this system there was some flexibility, but there was also much risk of ill-balanced markets and consequent waste of effort and material. The English buyer, or the factor in Dublin, could not give orders to large manufacturers. He had to make his selection from such cloth as the drapers could offer on the spot. The drapers, in their turn, when they bought brown linen in the northern markets, had to anticipate as well as they could the state of demand a few months later in Dublin.[1] But their choice was not free, for they had to buy the goods offered by small weavers. Thus the final decision as to the kind and amount of cloth to be produced rested with a multitude of weavers who never travelled more than a few miles from home, who were often illiterate, and in general were in the worst possible position for judging the course of markets. In any case the weaver, although his reliance on agriculture would enable him to vary the *amount* of his output, could do little to alter the *kind*, for he was bound both by his own training and by the character of his loom. As the weavers and drapers were so numerous and so scattered, the supply of cloth was quite haphazard, and anticipation of markets was so much the more difficult. Hence there was a constant risk of dislocation and waste. The risk was partly borne by London merchants, who sometimes held a large stock of Irish cloth ; partly by factors in Dublin ; but it also fell upon bleachers, who had to make for stock in order to maintain an even supply of material ; upon drapers, who if they could not find a ready market for the particular cloths which they had carried to Dublin, would have to sell them at a loss or else store them until the demand improved ; and finally upon weavers, who might find that their cloth could not be sold at a remunerative price.

The capitalistic system, which had already appeared in other industries, and in the linen trade outside of Ulster, was a step towards the modern organization of certain textile markets, an organization which throws the main risk upon a small body of brokers, who can command abundant capital and credit, and have a large measure of control over prices.

---

[1] It is mentioned below (chap. ix, p. 176) that agents of English firms early in the nineteenth century often gave orders in advance to dealers in the Dublin Linen Hall. But it is doubtful whether such orders would be common half a century before, when there were few manufacturers who could carry out large contracts.

Failure of Capitalism in South. It would seem natural that the southern manufacture, designed for greater efficiency, elimination of waste, and better distribution of risk, should be more successful and more permanent than the ill-organized industry of Ulster. Yet the fact is that nearly all undertakings in the south came quickly to grief while trade in Ulster steadily increased. Employment by landowners, bleachers, or 'factory masters' was adopted not as an improvement on the northern system, but rather as a *pis aller*, the only means of enabling the peasants to work at all.[1]

When a class of manufacturing employers appeared in Ulster it came as a normal and healthy development, due to increasing trade. The manufacturer was a person who had so much sale for his linen that he could dispose of the output of several looms, and therefore found it worth while to employ several weavers. It was in this way, through a gradual expansion of markets, that the class of merchant employers had appeared during the later Middle Ages in the chief manufacturing centres of Europe, and that industrial employers—the clothiers and manufacturers of the eighteenth century—were rising to importance in other textile trades. But in the south of Ireland leaders of enterprise were trying to take a short cut to the modern organization without the preliminary process of building up a market. Moreover, most of them were far from having that 'very considerable knowledge in the business' which was essential to success. They were at the mercy of managers and workers, and were often defrauded. In their eagerness to serve as model employers and to be in every way up-to-date and efficient, they built expensive works without any guarantee of a sale for the output, and they were encouraged to lay out a large capital by the readiness,

[1] Besnard in his description of King's County (op. cit., p. 12) pointed out that enterprise on the part of landowners offered the only hope of increasing industry, 'the lower classes of its inhabitants, from their extreme poverty, were they ever so industriously inclined, being prevented from making any efforts to advance this, or indeed, any other business.' Young (*Tour*, pp. 193–4) was opposed to vertical combination of the southern type. But he supported this opinion with the more doubtful statement : ' A gentleman, for a shilling he will even make by manufactory, will profit a guinea by the improvement of land ; have rascals to deal with in one line and honest men in the other.' Moreover, he believed wrongly that there was no such enterprise in the north. ' I question ', he wrote, ' whether the most sagacious draper in Ireland would make considerably if he wove the cloth as well as bleached it.' The northern drapers themselves did not share this view.

indeed the recklessness, with which the Linen Board supplied them with grants. Stephenson wrote of one landowner near Waterford who had set up elaborate bleachworks : ' This gentleman very justly observes that he has gone to work at the wrong end, for he should first have been secure of a manufacture equal to his preparations for bleaching.'[1] The owner of a ' very fine bleachyard ' in co. Louth had been led into a needless expenditure of several hundred pounds owing to wrong advice from his employees. In describing his case Stephenson remarked : ' It is a great check to the extension of the linen manufacture that gentlemen disposed to promote it are so often deceived by workmen. . . . Whoever will view the North, where this manufacture is in the most flourishing state, will find that they seldom are liable to those extravagances . . . that gentlemen are but too often led into in the southern provinces.' [2]

There was a further difficulty, already explained, in regard to wages. Employers were left with the choice of paying higher wages than the industry would bear ; allowing weavers to spend part of their time in agriculture ; or paying low wages, having frequent disputes with their workers, and probably losing them altogether in a short time. Some chose to pay high wages. The Earl of Grandison, for instance, whose aim was ' to make the poor happy by their industry, and not to make a profit for himself ', gave a halfpenny a yard beyond the usual wage ; [3] but this was not the way to found a permanent industry. The second plan—manufacture and farming combined—was almost prohibited by the land system.[4] The third was often adopted, with disastrous results.

Another cause of failure, mentioned in the last chapter, was the attempt to carry on the finest branches of manufacture. Many of the peasantry already knew something of coarse spinning and weaving, but everywhere employers, with encouragement from the Linen Board, were urging them to make cambric and lawn—an enterprise for which there was very limited scope, even in Ulster.[5]

---

[1] *Journal*, p. 177.   [2] ibid., p. 165.   [3] ibid., p. 180.
[4] It was followed to some extent in Russia. e. g., at one factory the peasants were employed for only half the year, and spent the other half in agricultural work (Mavor, *Econ. Hist. of Russia*, vol. i, p. 515).
[5] *Journal*, p. 163 : cambric weaving was ' now diffused all over the kingdom '.

Sometimes, while grants from the Trustees continued, or a concern was under particularly able management, manufacture might flourish. But at the best its appearance was sporadic and short lived. If the Board withdrew its support, if workers demanded higher wages, or prices in Dublin fell, many southern enterprises would begin to show a loss and would soon be abandoned. Some continued as long as the founder lived, but came to an end after his death, because his successor was less capable or had no interest in manufacture.[1] Such lapses were inevitable when the whole industry of a district depended on the patronage of a few individuals. Manufacture in the south was too much the work of amateurs who were trying in vain to compete against skilled workers, expert dealers, and well-organized trade.[2]

It was for this reason that the Linen Board, acting on Stephenson's advice, tried to replace the capitalistic system by open markets, supplied by small craftsmen. Open markets had been the agencies of success in Ulster, and it was believed that production by independent weavers would avoid all the dangers and disadvantages of manufacture on a large scale. But the Trustees were inverting the proper order of events. Although they criticized private patrons for spending capital on factories and bleachworks before there was any certainty of a demand for the goods, the Trustees themselves were making a similar mistake. They were organizing and endowing markets in the hope that trade would follow ; and this attempt proved as difficult as any of the large undertakings of private patrons. The brown linen markets in Ulster had grown up gradually in the course of thirty or forty years, because they were found convenient both to buyers and to sellers. The trade was already in existence : the foundation of markets was merely a question of providing the best organization.

The attempt to increase the number of independent weavers failed because, in the first place, it was useless for the weavers to work unless there were buyers to pay them ; and a class of drapers, equipped with capital, experience and skill, could not be developed within a few months, or even a few years. The

---

[1] Cf. Besnard's allusion to ' the plan formerly adopted here of establishing large factories, dependent on one person, whose death or ill-success may be attended with the most fatal consequences.' *Report*, p. 15.

[2] This was no doubt a main cause of the collapse in 1773.

Trustees tried to hasten the appearance of drapers by their premiums for buying in the southern markets. But Stephenson wrote significantly in 1763 that it would be necessary ' to keep up the spirit of buyers ', and that 'something extraordinary' must be done ' towards raising a spirit among people of property . . . to become drapers and bleachers as they are in Ulster '.[1] Without doubt many artificially formed markets perished through lack of buyers.[2]

Secondly, the land system interposed a fatal barrier. If there had been in southern Ireland, as there was in Ulster, a custom of tenure which encouraged manufacture, trade would have flourished, and markets would have grown, without any special stimulus from the Linen Board. But the measures of reform which were essential as the basis of a sound and enduring industry never entered the mind of Parliament or of the Trustees ; consequently all their expensive tinkering and patching was in vain.

There is an amusing irony in the solemn persistence of the Government's constructive efforts in spite of their constant failure, but the results of this failure were altogether tragic. The evil lay not only in the waste of so much praiseworthy enterprise and public spirit, and in the disappointment of such high hopes : its worst feature was the suffering of millions of the peasantry, who for the lack of the means of industry were driven to emigrate, to starve, or else to lead such a stunted existence as scarcely deserved to be called a life. From the absence of other sources of livelihood there followed a sequence of misfortunes—the sole reliance on agriculture, the ' land hunger ' of the peasantry, the extreme subdivision of holdings—all leading up to the crowning miseries of famine and wholesale emigration. These are familiar facts of Irish history. We need not stop to elaborate them, or to picture what the state of Ireland might have been if the linen manufacture, and other rural industries as well, had been free to

---

[1] Stephenson, *Reports and Observations,* 1762–3, pp. 53, 64.

[2] Moreover, the growth of brown linen markets was hindered throughout the age of domestic industry by the lack of general markets for agricultural produce. This fact has been mentioned in connexion with the early localization in Ulster. As late as 1826 the same difficulty was mentioned by an English writer who had lived in Ireland : ' In the South there are few markets, and those at so far a distance that the corn is often carted twenty Irish miles.' As a result, there was little provision of markets ' for the proceeds of at best an imperfectly made up linen ' (W. Salisbury, Memorandum in P.R.O. London, H. O. 100, 216).

flourish in all parts of the country ; nor need we dwell on the responsibility of those rulers whose narrow policy sacrificed a nation to the interests of a class. But it is important to realize that under a more enlightened system of land tenure there would have been considerable scope for industry, and that the same statesmen and administrators who believed that they were building up the prosperity of Ireland were as a matter of fact ruining the country by maintaining an intolerably bad land system, which strangled enterprise and put a stop to manufacture.[1]

There is little more to be said of the southern linen trade. After the middle of the eighteenth century nearly all the interest is centred in Ulster, consequently the northern trade will occupy almost the whole of our attention in the following chapters.

[1] If the Irish peasantry had had more security of tenure, the large undertakings in the south might quite well have given rise to a widespread domestic industry. A development of this kind, from the trade of ' factory masters ' to that of independent weavers and small manufacturers, took place in Russia during the first half of the nineteenth century. Cf. Mavor (op. cit., pp. 545, 549) : ' The flax industry, which was, to begin with, concentrated in the hands of large merchants, afterwards was gradually transferred to the hands of peasants.' ' The factory did not grow out of the *Kustarny* (small workshop), but the *Kustarny* grew out of the factory.'

VIII

INDUSTRIAL CLASSES IN ULSTER, 1750–1800

Growth of Capitalism. The chief interest in the industrial history of Ulster after 1750 is the growth of new groups of producers and new social relationships. Although there are no figures to show the exact output from Ulster, it is certain that the linen trade was increasing fast in the middle years of the eighteenth century. A rapid extension of trade almost necessarily brings important changes in organization, and these changes in turn react on the social position and functions of the various classes of producers. The development often takes place so quietly that it leaves little trace in history, until some striking event suddenly reveals the forces that have been remoulding society. The ' turn out ' of 1762, and the battle of pamphlets which followed, serve this purpose in the history of Ulster. They show that the old system of domestic manufacture and sale in open markets was gradually yielding to new methods, and that a drift towards capitalism had begun.

This disclosure would be surprising if we had no source of information other than official documents, for the fact is that the governing authorities were themselves taken by surprise. The Trustees regarded the system of trade in Ulster as a mirror of perfection. Stephenson, their chief informant, had written in 1757 :

' In the province of Ulster, where the linen manufacture has become of such consequence as to counterbalance all the luxuries imported into this kingdom, it is conducted in the most convenient and easy method that can be prescribed, so as to promote industry and avoid disputes. There the draper, weaver and spinner meet in public markets : the draper to buy such linens as suit his purpose ; the weaver to dispose of such linen as he hath made of the yarn bought in market ; and the spinner to dispose of her yarn, and buy flax. By this means all are independent of each other, and only expect to be paid according to their merits.' [1]

---

[1] *Journal*, p. 203. Although Stephenson, in the course of his trade, must have come into contact with many dealers from Ulster, he seems to have

Stephenson contrasted the smooth course of trade in Ulster with the continual friction between masters and weavers in the south. We have seen that the Trustees promoted ' premium markets ' because they thought the northern system more stable than production on a large scale ; but in their view the great weakness and danger of large undertakings was the encouragement which they gave to combination among weavers and bleachyard workers. The Trustees must have had this faith seriously shaken when the craftsmen in Ulster, whom they had regarded as paragons of industrial virtue, suddenly rose in revolt, formed riotous mobs, destroyed property, and defied even the authority of Parliament.

Rising of 1762. However, when we inquire into the causes of the rising we shall find that there was some reason for the weavers' discontent, and that the state of industry in Ulster was not quite what it appeared to be on the surface. As the inspection of brown linen, proposed in the bill of 1762, led directly to the outbreak, it might seem at a first glance that the trouble was due to dishonest weavers, who were angry at the prospect of having their misdeeds made known and punished. But the movement included a great mass of weavers who could not all be dishonest, and the system of inspection was not their only ground of complaint. A subtler explanation was given by some of the bleachers, but this too hardly carries conviction. They said that certain drapers in the south of Ulster (in the district between Newry and Armagh) saw their own interests at stake. They had been in the habit of cheating weavers in the brown linen markets by various tricks : using a yard stick of more than a yard, clutching in a little extra cloth with each yard that they measured and demanding as perquisites an additional yard in each web, and a fee of 1*d*. to 3*d*. known as a ' measuring quart '.[1] Now,

known little of the actual conditions of work there. His reports only include very brief notes on the north-eastern counties, and in some of his tours of inspection Ulster was left out altogether.

[1] *Review of Evils*, p. 43. *Brief State of the Debate*, p. 15. Cf. *Reasons against the Brown Seals*, ll. 153–6 :

> ' They give but yard and inch, no more :
> We yard and fist oft took before,
> Or made behind the hand large slips,
> And slacks and folds and handful-grips.'

The measuring quart was originally the price of a drink paid to the draper

fearing that public inspection would deprive them of their ill-earned gains, they made catspaws of the ignorant weavers and urged them to rebel. These charges were admitted to be true ;[1] but the weavers, unless they had had some definite grievances and some interest of their own to maintain, would never have listened to advice from such a doubtful source.

The Weavers' Case. The real causes appear in the chief statement issued by the weavers' party, a pamphlet drawn up after a meeting of delegates held at Hillsborough in June 1763.[2] In the first place, they maintained their original idea that the new sealmasters would be nominees of the drapers, and having the force of law behind them would be able to bring the weavers completely under their power. Thus if they condemned a piece of cloth the weaver could only sell it for a nominal price, and if they chose to make an attack on any particular weaver, against whom some draper had a grudge, they could ruin him entirely. In Scotland, where a system of sealing had been in operation since 1727, sealmasters had been subservient in this way to drapers ; and the same result was naturally expected in Ireland.[3] This fear was soon removed ; but other and more serious grievances remained, and they show that the issue was no longer between buyers and sellers in the open market, but that the underlying cause of trouble was a change in the organization of industry.

The evidence on this point, given by the weavers' spokesman, is so important that it deserves to be quoted at some length :

' The greatest evil to the linen manufacture . . . is the wronging of the weavers of their prices.' This is the cause of bad craftsmanship, for a weaver who is underpaid must hurry and scamp his work in order to make a living, whereas ' the giving sufficient prices would have a manifest tendency to better the manufacture, for a sufficient price will generally secure sufficient workmanship, and whoever gives such prices generally gets the best workmen '.

for his service in measuring the cloth, and supposed to be spent at the draper's inn. Unless a draper had a warehouse of his own in the market town, he hired accommodation for market days at a public-house. (*Observations on Materials,* p. 23.)
  [1] *Observations,* pp. 22, 23.   [2] ibid., p. 1.   [3] ibid., p. 26.

So far there is nothing to show that the writer is dealing with anything but sales by a weaver to a draper in the open market. But his real meaning is disclosed in the next paragraph :

' In short, the manufacturing drapers have a great power over the weavers, whose very lives are in their hands, and therefore the obliging those manufacturers or drapers in all cases to give the full and proper prices would be the surest method that could be devised to have linens in all cases well and properly made.' [1]

The reference to ' manufacturing drapers ' and ' manufacturers ' gives the clue to the actual state of affairs. Twenty years later the manufacturer had become a familiar figure in Ulster. He was an industrial employer, working as a rule on a small scale, and holding a position very similar to that of the ' clothier ' in the English woollen industry. Manufacturers had ' great power ' over the weavers, not as buyers trying to keep down prices in a brown linen market, but as employers trying to keep down the level of wages. The word ' price ' was regularly used at this time in the sense of ' wage '.[2] Thus ' wronging the weavers of their prices ' meant the custom now known as nibbling wages, and described by the Ulster weavers as ' cribbing '. The remedy proposed was a legal minimum wage, a compulsion on all employers to pay ' such price as is voluntarily given by the wisest and best men amongst them '.

The weavers' apologist lays great stress on this point.

' I deny ', he says, ' that it is true that there can be no standard. This, I know, has often been altered at particular times and in particular places, but the idea of a standard has been still kept up. . . . Most of the drapers and manufacturers never attempt to make us take less than the price now usually given ; and some of them, moved by the sight of our distress, and the miseries we labour under, have not only themselves raised our prices but have endeavoured to get others also to raise them. If all of them were made to do what these have voluntarily done, this is all we would wish for.' [3]

A standard wage was not as a matter of fact the whole of the weavers' programme, although it was an important part. There

[1] ibid., p. 18.
[2] e. g., in the statutes of 1757, 1759 and 1764, and in the passage from Stephenson's *Inquiry*, quoted below.
[3] *Observations*, pp. 19, 20.

still remained the combination acts of 1757 and 1759, which they wished to see repealed.   They urged, quite truly, that although they were forbidden to combine for ' altering, fixing or raising the standards or price of labour ', their masters the drapers had combined freely to depress wages.[1]   In view of the acts against trade unionism, the rising of 1762, and the meetings which preceded it, appear as the organization of a strike in defiance of the law.   Indeed the word ' turn out ' which was several times applied to the rising, was simply the current name for a strike.

There was evidently in 1762 a fairly large class of permanent employees in Ulster.   They were already strong enough, and sufficiently class-conscious, to organize a series of meetings, to carry out a formidable strike, and to state their case with considerable ability in the public press.   These facts, together with the passing of laws against combination, might suggest that classes of employers and journeymen had existed for some time, and that the rising of 1762 was the outcome of a long agitation. But before this time there had been no sign of discontent : it was, indeed, the quietness and smoothness of northern trade that threw the authorities off their guard.   If trade unions had existed for long in the north there would certainly have been employers' societies as well ; and it is significant that the employers only began to organize themselves in 1762.   Moreover, we shall notice later some new developments in trade at this time which would lead naturally to a growth of capitalism.   Thus there is reason to believe that combination, and the system which produced it, were of recent growth in Ulster.   The very newness of the system—with the sense of subjection and loss of status that it would bring—was no doubt with many weavers the chief cause of discontent.   Fifty years later, cotton operatives in England and Scotland felt the same hostility against the new discipline imposed by factory production, and expressed their feeling in a very similar way.

Trade Unions in the South.   The existence of combination acts can readily be explained.   They were aimed against workers in the south, and at first had no reference to Ulster.   In the other

---

[1] *Observations* by Drapers of Belfast, p. 19.   It will be remembered that in May 1762 the drapers had formed a permanent society, which was virtually an employers' association.

provinces strikes and unions were already quite familiar, because the linen industry there had been organized from the beginning on capitalistic lines. Stephenson, a strong opponent of everything in the nature of trade unionism, was loud in his complaints against the southern weavers. ' If a manufacturer ', he said, ' wants to engage in any new branch of the linen manufacture, there must first be a consultation among the weavers to know if they will allow him to carry it into execution ; for in the southern provinces they are to a man sworn into a combination to support a bill of prices they have made ; and their method of rating the prices of workmanship is not according to the quality of the goods to be made, but to the demand or necessity there is for a quantity.' [1] In another essay he explained the lack of sheeting manufacture in Ireland as being chiefly due to ' combination of weavers who are mostly bound in an oath not to make anything of the kind without exorbitant prices '.[2]

Unions would be the more readily formed because many of the weavers were immigrants from other countries, in which there was already a tradition of organization among journeymen. Some, in fact a large number, were skilled workers from Ulster who had been used to comparative freedom. In the south they would be brought under the control of employers, and as they lived in compact settlements and had a strong common interest, they would naturally be led to organize themselves for mutual protection.

In most parts of the southern provinces the attempt at employment on a large scale only lasted a few years, and any societies of journeymen that might be formed could only be temporary. But in Louth, Dublin, King's County, and the neighbouring part of Westmeath, where the system of ' factory masters ' was permanently established, the workers could maintain regular unions ; and any unions that there might be in these districts, because of their nearness to the capital, would draw the attention of the Linen Board. Therefore the Trustees had

---

[1] *Inquiry*, p. 23. The last sentence implies that, owing to the system of employment in the south, labour had become in practice (though it was not recognized as such in theory) a commodity, the price of which was settled by supply and demand. As skilled labour was at a premium, a free market favoured the workers, and encouraged them to combine to keep up the level of wages. [2] *Letter to the Trustees* (1759), p. 19.

abundant grounds for proposing measures against combination, without having in view, or indeed in any way realizing, the new disposition of the northern weavers.

However, there was a new disposition, and it was due to the growing dependence of weavers on an employing class. The reasons for this change will be discussed later ; for the moment we must accept the fact that a class of permanent employees had appeared. Whereas in the earlier half of the century practically all apprentices and journeymen weavers could look forward to acquiring holdings, cottages, and looms, supplying themselves with flax, and weaving on their own account, many of them had no such prospect now.

Class of Journeymen in Ulster. It is impossible to gauge at all closely the strength of this class in 1760 and during the next two decades. But we should probably not be far wrong in estimating that in the year 1770 rather more than 35,000 weavers in Ulster were still independent and about 7,000 were employees.[1] We can say with more certainty that the employees were concerned only with the higher branches of manufacture, and consequently were limited to the districts in which the finest cloths were made, viz. south Antrim, west Down, and north Armagh. It is interesting to notice that these were the only districts affected by the troubles of 1762.[2] In the north and west of Ulster, where nearly all the weavers were undoubtedly their own masters, there was no disturbance at all ; and the statement that the regulations for cloth manufacture were not observed to the north of the town of Antrim suggests that the craftsmen were free from any sort of control.[3]

The class of journeymen included not only weavers, but some thousands of bleachyard workers as well—artisan bleachers, calender-men, and lappers. These men were, in fact, the earliest group of permanent employees in the north of Ireland ; and seeing that bleachyard workers in the southern provinces had

---

[1] The reasons for this statement are given at the end of the present chapter.

[2] The coincidence of the district of employees with the disturbed area in 1762 would lead us to suspect that the employees formed a large part of the discontented class. This idea is confirmed by the whole tenor of the weavers' arguments. Such questions as the level of wages, the power of employers, and the right to organize unions, clearly meant more to the writers than any details of the regulation of cloth.   [3] *Brief State of the Debate*, p. 9.

a large share in the trade union movement, it is highly probable that they were also among the pioneers of the movement in Ulster.[1] They were closely connected with the weavers : in fact, the same person often belonged to both classes ; for it was a common custom to work on a bleachgreen during the summer, and in the winter, when bleaching machinery was idle, to earn a livelihood by weaving.[2] Moreover, several master bleachers had taken to employing weavers, so that journeymen of both classes often served the same master. Thus the bleachers were doubly members of the employing class—a fact which helps to explain their unpopularity. Williamson himself, the chief enemy of the strikers in 1762, was both a bleacher and a manufacturer.[3]

Independent Weavers. A great majority of the weavers were still independent. But there was clearly a tendency for the system of working for wages to increase : consequently many free weavers would feel themselves in danger of falling into subjection, and would have a sense of common interest with the journeymen. We can actually see the transition from one class to another taking place, for some weavers worked partly on their own account and partly for employers, securing their own yarn when they could, but often being compelled to take yarn from a manufacturer. This semi-independent manufacture was common in co. Armagh at the time of Arthur Young's visit.[4]

We have noticed that the classes of journeymen and free craftsmen were unevenly distributed. In districts where much imported flax was used the old type of craftsman must have been comparatively rare. But elsewhere, especially in north Antrim, Londonderry and Tyrone, independent weavers remained, and even grew in numbers with the increase of trade. For more than a century after 1762 they continued to supply several brown linen markets in these districts.

Manufacturers. While a few weavers were sinking into the position of journeymen others were rising to a more comfortable position than that of the ordinary craftsman. Some weavers,

---

[1] Stephenson (*Inquiry*, pp. 22–3) mentioned that bleachyard workers were active in forming combinations. He added : ' From such lawgivers what terrible effects may not be apprehended.'

[2] Cf. *Observations on Materials*, p. 41 : ' Many of us work at the bleachyards in the summer season.'

[3] McCall, p. 17.　　　　　　　　　[4] *Tour*, p. 107.

who had been exceptionally fortunate or skilful, were able to increase the size of their holdings. From the profits of their farming and weaving they saved a little capital, with which they could buy a few looms and a stock of raw material, and set perhaps three or four weavers to work.[1] The weavers were often labourers, who worked sometimes on the land and sometimes at the loom, according to the wish of their employer.[2] A small employer of this type would still sell his cloth in the open market, in competition with ordinary craftsmen, and in official records he would himself be described as a weaver.

If he prospered and acquired a good connexion, he would spend so much time in attending markets and buying yarn that he would have to leave most of the actual weaving to his assistants, and devote such efforts as he could spare from his farming to the work of organization. He would then have entered unquestionably the class of 'manufacturers'. The following account of this class, although written early in the nineteenth century, applies equally well to the latter half of the eighteenth :

'Many of these farmers are master weavers, and are styled manufacturers ; though they do not work at the loom they employ many weavers : their time is occupied at market chiefly in procuring yarn and disposing of their webs. Where a man of this description settles, and is so fortunate as to get a few acres, he soon establishes a manufacturing village around him, with those families to which he gives employment.'[3]

Often the manufacturer's farm was only ten or twelve acres in extent ; but when it was possible he would rent enough land to sub-let small patches, with cottages, to his employees. These sub-tenants were not protected by the Ulster custom : they were tenants-at-will, and their cottages were held in part payment for their labour, according to the system of truck which was known in the south as ' dry cot '.[4] So long as their work satisfied the

---

[1] According to Charley (p. 96) the normal cost of a loom, fully equipped with headles and reeds, was £3. It would probably be rather less at this time.

[2] Coote, *Survey of Armagh*, p. 233.

[3] ibid., p. 138. It is shown below (p. 275) that this type of manufacturer was very common in south Armagh. Cf. Dr. Stephenson's description (*Select Papers*, p. 28) : ' He who was possessed of a larger capital established a small factory, or purchased and prepared the yarn for the loom, and employed the cottager to weave it. These are now called the manufacturers.'

[4] Or ' wet cot ' if grazing land was included.

manufacturer they would have secure tenure, but if they displeased him they could be evicted without notice. The weavers said truly that their employers had great power over them.

Double Motive of the Rising. It is interesting to notice that the three classes of journeymen, independent weavers, and small manufacturers were united, at the beginning of the crisis in 1762, in opposition to the system of sealing brown linens. The fact is that there was a twofold purpose in the rising. In the first place, weavers and small manufacturers who sold in the markets wished to work in their own way without being subject to an inspection, which, as they feared, might be used in the interests of the drapers. Already the drapers were in a strong position for bargaining, and they had recently added to their strength by forming a society which was not only an employers' association, but was also a combination of buyers in the brown linen markets. It was felt, no doubt, that the only effective answer to the drapers' policy was to set up a combination of sellers as well. From this point of view the ' turn out ' of 1762 was only one event in the age-long rivalry between commercial and industrial capital, in line with the Matins of Bruges, the Ciompi rising in Florence, and Evil May Day in London. The crisis, moreover, was soon past ; for the manufacturers and weavers learnt from experience that, so far from having anything to fear from the system of sealing, they gained more power and freedom than they had had before.

But, in the second place, the journeymen had joined in the contest with the object of securing a standard wage and the right to combine. They were not directly concerned with the question of sealing. That was a matter for their employers ; and unless the employer happened to sell in an open market, the cloth made by a journeyman would not be officially inspected or sealed until it was bleached and ready for export.

Evidently the wage-earners were only allied with the free-craftsmen because they had a common adversary. The merchants who dealt as buyers in the markets, and urged a closer regulation of manufacture, were often considerable employers of labour as well. Bleachers, in particular, not only employed bleachyard workers and weavers, but were usually buyers of brown linen in addition ; so that every class concerned in the rising had a grievance against them. But the manufacturers were soon appeased. Their alliance with the journeymen broke down; and in all probability the friendship of the former allies cooled very fast, for the manufacturers, as employers of labour, would have little liking for the journeymen's programme. The invitation to the first mass meeting at Dromore in 1762 was addressed to 'all gentlemen manufacturers and weavers'; but manufacturers were excluded from the meeting at Hillsborough in 1763, unless they themselves worked at the loom.

The rift between capital and labour was in fact deeper and more lasting than the misunderstanding between buyers and sellers in the market. Nevertheless it is remarkable, in view of the violence and importance of this dispute, that there is no record of any serious industrial trouble in the north of Ireland during the remainder of the eighteenth century.

The chief reason for this immunity is, I believe, that there was a strong demand for labour, so that the wage-earners were, on the whole, in a favourable position. The slump in the years 1772 and 1773 would not injure them as much as we should expect at a first glance. It affected mainly the coarse branches of manu-facture; and most of the coarse linen was still made by in-dependent weavers. A large proportion of the four thousand who emigrated in 1773 probably belonged to this class. On the other hand, when trade recovered, as it did in a very short time, the lack of these weavers would react on the whole industry and would almost certainly strengthen the demand for paid labour.[1] Further, in the last twenty years of the century the linen trade increased by leaps and bounds. Consequently, employment was more abundant than ever; and although the growth was checked by the Napoleonic War, two new factors served to prevent most of the suffering that might have resulted among the linen workers. The great demand for agricultural produce meant abundant scope for work on the land, and the rapid development of the cotton industry in Ireland offered a fresh field for labour at exceptionally good wages. There can be little doubt that flourishing trade was responsible for the smoothness of industrial

---

[1] The revival of trade might also reduce the supply, because some who had been wage-earners would find scope for independent work. In either case the employees would be in a stronger position.

relations in Ulster after 1762 : indeed it is highly probable that there would have been no serious friction even at that time but for the support given to the journeymen by independent weavers and manufacturers.

'Manufacturing' and *'Gentlemen'* *Drapers.* The three classes with which we have dealt thus far included all the proletariat of the linen trade. But of the manufacturers, only those who sold in the markets, and were not above making cloth themselves, should be grouped with the working weavers. The larger manufacturers belonged distinctly to the middle class. Many of them, in fact, had never been weavers : they were drapers who found it worth while to employ weavers directly, in order, perhaps, to supply themselves with kinds of cloth which they could not readily buy in the local markets. Thus the manufacturing class was recruited both from above and from below— from traders as well as craftsmen.

Drapers who engaged in manufacture were able to economize in several ways. By giving out their own yarn to be woven they secured brown linen at cost price ; they could buy comparatively large stocks of yarn when it was cheap—whereas the ordinary weaver could only afford to keep a small amount in stock ; and as holders of ' white ' seals they could avoid the sealmasters' fees by examining and stamping the webs themselves. We must not picture these drapers, however, as wealthy employers. They were only large dealers by comparison with working weavers, or with the small manufacturers who sold three or four webs weekly in the markets.[1] There was above them a class of substantial drapers who sometimes gave direct employment to weavers, but spent most of their time in travelling. They bought brown linen over a wide area, attended many markets, and made frequent journeys to Dublin. Thus they were really merchants rather than manufacturers. The difference between the two classes of drapers was well recognized by 1763, for in the pamphlets of that year a distinction is often drawn between ' manufacturing ' and ' gentlemen ' drapers. There was not, however, any sharp line of division. A manu-

---

[1] The clearest distinction that can be drawn between drapers and small manufacturers is that the draper was a buyer, and the manufacturer was a seller, in the brown linen markets.

facturing draper who acquired so much capital that he could make for stock might follow the example of the southern ' factory masters', and either sell goods in bulk to bleachers, or pay for the bleaching, and send the white cloth on his own account to the Dublin market. In this way he could rise to the position of a gentleman draper. Again the classes of drapers and bleachers overlapped, no less than they had done in the earlier half of the century. John Williamson's business is a case in point. He owned a bleachgreen, employed weavers, and was a buyer in the linen markets. At the time when he was attacked by the mob in Lisburn he had gone to the linen hall in order to buy brown cloth. In documents of the eighteenth century the same person is commonly described in one place as a draper, in another place as a bleacher, or perhaps as both together. Young mentioned that most of the drapers in north Armagh had bleachgreens. We shall find later that the overlapping gradually increased, until bleachers became the leading buyers in the brown linen markets, and the chief firms of bleachers were drawing as much profit from merchandise as from their original business.

Interlacing of Functions and Classes. This joining together of different functions is a point of special interest and importance. Critics of the southern trade had condemned vertical combination and pointed out the advantages of the system which they found in the north—the independent dealing of spinners, weavers, drapers and bleachers. But their criticism was only justified in so far as it applied to attempts to set up new and large concerns on an insecure foundation. In the north vertical combination, as it was practised by the bleachers, was successful, and indeed essential to progress ; for the branching out and interlacing of enterprise was one of the chief means by which the industry developed and grew. Every step—such as the organization of work by manufacturers or drapers, direct supply by private contract, and manufacture by bleachers in order to keep their greens steadily supplied—meant some gain in efficiency.

It was fortunate that there was enough freedom for enterprise to flow readily into fresh channels. We can easily imagine how much the trade would have been handicapped if there had been stricter regulation. If, for instance, manufacture had been confined to towns, as was first intended, the Linen Board would have been in a much stronger position for enforcing injurious rules, such as those for the reeling of yarn, the dimensions of cloth, and the time and method of bleaching. The laws in regard to apprenticeship would almost certainly have been used to secure a monopoly for certain groups of craftsmen, as they were in several other trades—for in the old-established towns, gilds and gild restrictions still flourished. It is highly probable that drapers, bleachers, and manufacturers would have followed the same policy : in fact, a ring of bleachers actually tried to set up a legal monopoly in 1782. Thus there was a distinct risk that the whole trade might be captured by exclusive groups of producers, whose restrictive spirit and internecine quarrels would have been a great hindrance to its growth. These dangers were avoided ; and one of the chief defences against them was the spread of rural industry, which prevented a too strict regulation, hindered the attempts at monopoly, and made the whole system of manu-facture both flexible and stable.[1]

A further characteristic, resulting from this freedom of enter-prise to expand and interlace, was a gradation of classes from one end of the trade to the other, implying a considerable ' upward and downward mobility '—an easy transition from group to group. We have noticed in one or two cases an overlapping of different branches of industry ; the same thing is true of the industry as a whole. The class of journeymen weavers merged into that of free craftsmen ; this group in turn merged into that of small manufacturers ; and so on, through the classes of manu-facturing drapers to the bleachers and large merchants. For con-venience of description we have treated these classes separately, but in practice there were no clear lines of distinction.

Scope of Employment for Wages. In view of later developments, the most important feature of the linen trade in this period was the growth of capitalism. One aspect of the growth was an increase in the size of individual firms, and accumulation of capital by the bleachers and large drapers—a subject with which

---

[1] A similar freedom in the English cotton trade produced similar results. The volume of trade increased remarkably, there was a rapid development in organization, and in particular there was the same interchange of functions that we have seen in the Irish linen industry. Weavers, such as Samuel Crompton, became machine-spinners ; spinners ' put out ' their yarn to weavers ; some machine-makers became both spinners and merchants.

we shall deal in later chapters ; but the aspect which concerns us here is the appearance of the modern classes of employers and employees. We have already seen something of this change, and Stephenson's estimates of trade in 1770 have enabled us to gain a rough idea of the proportion of wage-earners at that time. There is little evidence by which we can gauge the further advance of capitalism before 1800 : the only other estimate which bears on the question is Greer's statement of sales in the Ulster markets during the year 1784. The conclusion to be drawn from Greer's figures—the result of a necessarily rough calculation—is that out of a total production in Ulster of rather less than 40,000,000 yards of cloth, about 30,000,000 passed through the markets, and 10,000,000 were sold privately. Seeing that independent weavers would use the open market as far as possible—in order to benefit by the competition of buyers—we may assume that the whole of these 10,000,000 yards were produced by wage-earning weavers. But further, a certain amount of the cloth passing through the markets was sold by small manufacturers, and most of it would be made by their employees. It is impossible to estimate the amount of the manufacturers' sales ; but the indications are that about a third of the whole output was woven by employees. Thus if there were altogether 45,000 weavers in Ulster at that time, 15,000 of them might belong to the journeymen class. Although no accuracy can be claimed for these figures, we may at least be sure that the classes of employers and employees increased substantially between 1750 and 1800.

Import of Raw Material. How is this growth to be explained ? Some minor causes have been suggested already. Farmers gradually became manufacturers by finding work for their sons and their farm servants. Drapers who had some capital to spare used it to gain an additional profit by organizing the manufacture. Some weavers, who were uncertain of their success in marketing, might prefer regular employment under a master who took the risks of trade. But undoubtedly the main cause was a change in the supply of raw material. In the first chapter of this essay it was shown how the importer of raw material in many trades and in many periods of history came to dominate an industry, or at least how the import of material in bulk helped

forward capitalism in manufacture ; how, for instance, the class
of clothiers in the west of England woollen industry was supported by the trade in raw wool from Ireland and Spain.
Similarly we have seen that the large purchases of linen yarn
from Connaught led to the system of factory masters in some
of the eastern counties of Ireland. On the other hand the growth
of flax on their own farms helped to keep the weavers of Ulster
independent, and to preserve open markets and production on
a small scale.

But as trade increased, home supplies became less and less
adequate. The amount of flax which could be grown in Ulster
was limited by the social system. Every weaver needed land not
only for flax-growing but also for supplying his household with
food : plots for potatoes, oats and other foodstuffs, a certain
amount of grazing, and the hay crop. With the growth of trade,
the countryside was more and more overspread with weavers'
farmsteads, each consisting more of food-producing than of flax-
producing land. The return for weaving was so small that
weavers could not possibly have bought the whole of their food
supply : subsistence farming was essential to the linen industry.
In later years farming became only a secondary occupation, and
according to Sir Charles Coote many weavers would have been
glad to abandon it altogether if only food had been cheaper to
buy.[1] But in the actual state of affairs the weaver had to be a
farmer, and he could only devote a little land to flax-growing.
Hence as trade expanded there was a growing need for import
of raw material.

Some came from Donegal and the ' yarn counties ' of the west.
It was brought either as flax or as yarn by jobbers who were
prepared to sell in the open market, and consequently it was
available for any weaver who could afford to pay for it, though
the expense of much time and effort had often to be added to the

[1] *Survey of Armagh*, p. 261 : ' Agriculture is but a secondary motive : it is
merely pursued as a means of supply of provisions. . . . Land is sought for the
more easily and comfortably carrying on manufacture ; and notwithstanding
the supposed superior profit on rearing flax I believe that the people would
rather have nothing to do with agricultural pursuits, if the markets were
more numerous and constantly supplied with provisions.' Young, on the
other hand, held the more cynical view that if food were cheaper the people
would not even carry on manufacture : ' Meal and cloth never cheap together,
for when meal is cheap they will not work.' (*Tour*, p. 116.)

money cost. Other yarn came from abroad, and naturally was in the hands of wholesale merchants ; and the foreign yarns were increasing in importance. Irish yarn was only suitable for certain kinds of cloth. But new developments of industry, and the introduction or invention of fresh classes of goods, implied both the use of foreign yarns and a mixture of various kinds of yarn. In the middle of the century certain branches of manufacture—cambric and damask weaving, for instance—were just growing into importance. The drapers of Belfast, in the pamphlet of 1763, referred to the manufacture of cambric and lawn as ' those new branches lately established among us '.[1] Attempts had been made thirty years earlier to set up cambric weaving in Belfast and Dundalk, but evidently it made no great headway until after the middle of the century.[2] The best flax for cambric was imported from Holland by way of Bristol.[3] Therefore the growth of this branch of the industry would bring more employment for wages ; and we find that early in the nineteenth century manufacturers, in the technical sense, were very numerous in the districts of cambric weaving.[4]

Large Employers. Damask weaving not only needed a variety of yarns, but lent itself better than any other branch to the use of large capital. The machinery was elaborate and expensive : a damask loom might cost ten times as much as a loom for plain linen. Before he could begin weaving the worker would have to spend five or six weeks in warping and otherwise preparing the loom, and perhaps a fortnight in memorizing the pattern ; for until the introduction of the Jacquard loom with pattern cards, about the year 1825, it was necessary for the weaver to learn the pattern by heart, in order that he might know which threads to

[1] *Observations by Drapers*, p. 41.
[2] By Smith & Leath in Belfast (1730) and the Huguenot, Joncourt, in Dundalk (1736). See *Precedents and Abstracts*, pp. 108, 110, 146. For Nicholas d'Assaville's similar enterprise in Edinburgh cf. Bremner, p. 217. Young mentioned (*Tour*, p. 101) that the cambric undertaking in Dundalk had failed. But it was in operation in 1755, for Stephenson found a large factory at work there. He added that the weaving of cambric ' is now diffused all over the kingdom, and there is scarce a factory but there are some of the looms employed on thick or clear cambrics for the use of the neighbourhood ' (*Journal*, p. 163). There was probably a decline of cambric manufacture, as of other branches, in the southern provinces between 1760 and the date of Young's tour.
[3] Young, p. 106.   [4] McCall, p. 79.

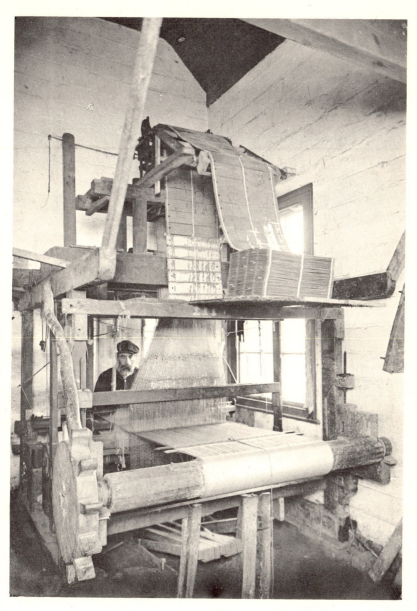

DAMASK LOOM, JACQUARD TYPE

raise for each stroke of the shuttle.[1] Further, because of its complexity, the process of weaving was very slow. For all these reasons it was difficult for any one to begin damask manufacture unless he had a fair amount of capital. As in the case of cambric, damask was made in Ireland to some extent about 1720, but it only advanced to importance in the latter half of the century. By far the most famous damask manufacturer in Ulster was William Coulson, a Scotsman, who settled in Lisburn, built a factory there in 1766, and soon developed a great business, the first really successful vertical combination in Ireland. He bought flax, much of it from Derry and the north of Antrim, supervised the spinning and dressing of yarn, employed designers and weavers trained by himself, and finished the cloths in his own bleachgreen.[2]

It was in these advanced lines of industry that there was the greatest scope for manufacture on a large scale. But even in the making of plain linens there was some economy in the new system. Different yarns were often needed for warp and weft, so that a weaver might have to spend many hours in an expedition in search of warp yarn, many more in buying weft, in addition to his day at market for the sale of his web.[3] Production could be carried on more cheaply if a draper or manufacturer bought the yarn, sorted it, supplied it made up into chains or wound on pirns, and received the cloth without waste of time when it was woven.

There can be no doubt, then, that the supply of flax or yarn in increasing quantities, in greater variety, and from a wider area, was one of the chief causes of change in the organization of manufacture.

Merchants and Weavers in Silesia. This conclusion is borne out by a comparison with the later history of the Silesian linen trade. In 1788, two years after the death of Frederick the Great, his successor, Frederick William II, issued a new series of regulations, drawn up by his officials after consultation with the chief

---

[1] See Bremner's account of damask weaving, *Industries of Scotland*, pp. 240-2.
[2] For accounts of Coulson's business, which still continues, see Dubourdieu, *Antrim*, vol. ii, p. 393 ; Stephenson, *Select Papers*, p. 33 ; McCall, pp. 38, 39, 41, 47 ; Wakefield, vol. i, p. 690.
[3] McCall, p. 72.

merchants and bleachers.[1]   Six years earlier the same class of
traders in Ireland had been responsible for the new linen law, and
in each case the regulations reflected the interests of their authors.
They suggest also that in both countries the same change had
occurred, a growth in the power and importance of the
merchants.

In some respects the new Silesian law resembled the Irish
statutes of 1759 and 1764.   There was a provision, for instance,
for a stricter inspection of markets ; and in Silesia enforcement
was delayed for some time—apparently, as in Ireland, until the
merchants pressed their claims again on the Government.   But
in Silesia special attention was paid to the sale of raw material.
Sellers both of flax and of yarn had to be officially licensed ; and
the jobbers, who collected yarn from the peasants, were obliged
to sell it exclusively in the town markets and to the large merchants who dealt there, i.e. they must not themselves supply
yarn to weavers.   Moreover, there was a clause, of a kind familiar
in all the earlier struggles between merchants and craftsmen,
that no weavers must compete with the trading class by selling
yarn on their own account.   Obviously these clauses were drawn
up in the interests of wholesale dealers in yarn.

When the law began to take effect there were frequent complaints, and inspectors were sometimes driven out of the markets
by angry weavers.[2]   In 1793, five years after the issue of the
edict, more serious trouble occurred.   A dispute between
merchants and weavers in the market at Landeshut developed
into a riot : the market itself was wrecked, merchants were
attacked in their houses, the police fled, and a small force of
soldiers was driven off by the mob.   During the next four days
there were similar risings in other towns, such as Schmiedeberg
and Breslau, directed mainly against the yarn merchants, who
were compelled to make promises that they would supply the
weavers as cheaply as possible.   This outburst was partly
political, for the weavers gave cheers for the French people, and
used the catchwords of the Revolution.   The mixture of political
fervour with economic unrest is apt to be highly explosive, and
in this case it certainly added to the violence of the attack.

---

[1] Zimmermann, op. cit., pp. 176–82.
[2] For details of these troubles see Zimmermann, pp. 188–98 ; Horner,
pp. 410–15.

But the Silesian rising also resembled strongly the outburst in Lisburn in 1762. Weavers were again opposed to the merchant class ; there is at least a suspicion that the Silesian merchants were becoming industrial employers ; and in both countries one source of trouble was the supply of raw material. The Irish weavers complained that their masters had undue influence in the yarn markets and secured their own agents as inspectors, and they hinted that drapers were concerned in the import of flax seed.[1] The Belfast drapers themselves said that yarn was being sold by merchants at their shops.[2]

Whatever the relationship between merchants and weavers may have been in Silesia, it is clear that a change unfavourable to the weavers had taken place because of the import of yarn. A smaller proportion of yarn (perhaps absolutely a smaller amount) was produced at home, and weavers had to depend on the merchants for their supply of raw material.

When we return to this subject and trace the developments in Ireland after 1800 we shall find the custom of employment for wages still extending, so far as to cause a movement of population towards the chief centres of employment, the decline of open markets and of the old classes of drapers and independent weavers, and an important change in the methods of trade.

The Weaving Proletariat. In view of the growth of a weaving proletariat, and of the fact that the linen trade depended to such a large extent on cheap labour, it is natural to ask at what standard of comfort the weavers actually lived. As regards the hired labourers, their conditions must fairly completely have borne out the ' iron law ' of wages. A man whose wage was a shilling a day could afford, in face of the high prices of a hundred and twenty years ago, little more than the goods absolutely necessary for subsistence, even when his wife's earnings as a spinner added fourpence or sixpence a day to the household budget. He would generally have a small patch of land—no more than a few ' lazy-beds ' for potatoes, and grazing for a cow or one or two goats, perhaps by the roadside. His land and cottage might be held by ' dry-cot ', as a payment of part of his wages ; if not, about two shillings a week of his income would have to be deducted for rent. The goods which he bought at

---

[1] *Observations upon Materials,* pp. 8, 13.   [2] *Observations by Drapers,* p. 13.

fairs, such as household utensils and woollen cloth from Donegal or Connaught, would be cheaply made, but on the other hand Irish money had not quite the same value as English—the English shilling was exchanged for thirteen pence in Ireland.

Contemporary writers were divided in opinion as to whether weavers or agricultural labourers fared the better. Some agricultural labourers seem to have lived at a rather higher standard, because they had more perquisites. Those who held, with Sir Charles Coote, that weavers could earn more than twice as much as farm hands,[1] must have had in their minds either independent weavers or journeymen who made fine linens. It will be shown later that the wages paid for damask and the best plain linen compared favourably even with those of muslin weavers. The weaver of coarse or medium cloth had more of a struggle for existence, but even he was in a happier position than the peasantry in other districts, and it was only the best-paid farm labourers in Ulster whose condition could compare favourably with his. County Armagh included a large number of weavers working with coarse webs, yet it was of this county that Sir Charles Coote wrote : ' The miserable hovel of the lowest class, which so often wounds our feelings in other parts of Ireland, is scarcely to be seen here, nor does that squalid poverty or filth disgust the traveller, which more southern provinces too often display, and which is perhaps less to be found in Armagh than in any other county in Ulster.' [2]

Coote added that more flesh meat was consumed in this district than anywhere else in Ireland,[3] and that the cottages of ' wealthy weavers ' were very clean and comfortable.

One widespread peculiarity of the weavers, above all in Armagh and Monaghan, was their addiction to hunting hares on foot. Wakefield was told that when a meet was arranged every loom was deserted, and in Ulster, instead of ' running like a hare ', the phrase ' running like a weaver ' was in common use.[4]

The ' wealthy weavers ' to whom Coote referred would be journeymen working in higher branches of manufacture, and the more fortunate independent craftsmen. They would always have the possibility before them of acquiring more land and more

---

[1] Coote, *Armagh*, p. 214. [2] ibid., p. 134.
[3] ibid., p. 251. [4] *Account of Ireland*, ii. 732 ; cf. Young, p. 111.

looms and becoming small manufacturers. The independent
worker who used his own flax might make an additional profit
of two or three shillings a week ; and unlike the wage-earners, he
would benefit directly by any quickening demand, although
there would be a corresponding risk of loss when markets were
slack.[1] Further, these comparatively well-to-do workers would
not as a rule be tenants-at-will of a manufacturer : they would
have secure holdings and the other benefits of tenant right. In
the great slump of 1773, when hundreds of weavers emigrated
to America, many of them sold their tenant right for £30 or £40
and took the cash with them. Some, by selling cattle, horses,
and implements were able to take two or three hundred pounds.[2]
It appears that horse-dealing was a common trade among the
more prosperous weavers—chiefly, one would expect, among
manufacturers. They were both clever in their treatment of
horses—' as skilled as Spitalfields weavers in training pigeons and
singing birds ' [3]—and very dishonest in their methods of sale.[4]
But in spite of their guile they were able to maintain an active
trade in horses, especially with buyers in Scotland.

These small capitalists, however, were an aristocracy among
the weavers, and their way of life was not typical of the whole
countryside. Young indeed, writing in 1776, gave this favourable report on the general conditions in the north of Antrim,
where there were few manufacturers and not much of the finest
weaving, but many independent craftsmen : ' The food of the
poor people is potatoes, oatmeal and milk. They generally keep
cows : some of them will have a quarter of a side of beef in
winter, but not all. Upon the whole they are in general much
better off than they were a quarter of a century ago, and dress
remarkably well. The manufacture is at present very flourishing.' [5] Even this account suggests a rather low dietary, and all
the evidence goes to show that the benefits of an increase of trade

[1] In spite of Young's criticism it was well worth while for them to higgle
about ' one halfpenny or a penny a yard more or less '.
[2] Young, pp. 108, 125 ; pt. ii, p. 31. Cf. Wakefield, ii. 177.
[3] Wakefield, ii. 732.
[4] Coote, *Armagh*, p. 139. He suggests that as the linen laws prevented
frauds in weaving, the desire for dishonest practices found an outlet in ' jockey-
ing ' with horses. This is sound psychology, but in actual fact the impulse
to defraud seems sometimes to have found scope in both directions.
[5] *Tour*, p. 139.

were not at all evenly distributed over the population. Just as
the spread of factory production in England and Scotland led to
the growth of a huge mass of workers living at a very low standard,
so the increase of manufacture in Ulster implied for the majority
of weavers employment at a meagre wage ; but in their case
a rough subsistence farming both helped out their living and
kept down the level of wages. Wakefield, an equally ' wise and
honest traveller', was undoubtedly right in concluding that it
was the middle class, of bleachers, drapers, manufacturers, and
weavers of the finest linens—those who were ' engaged either in
the finer parts of the business or in finishing the prepared article
for market '—who really gained by the expansion of industry.[1]

NOTE TO CHAPTER VIII

Sales in Markets and by Private Contract

The following estimates, although they are partly based on
inexact information, may help to convey a general idea of the
scope of manufacture in Ulster, the importance of open markets
and independent weavers, and the gradual advance of capitalism
fifty or sixty years before the introduction of steam power.

Estimates of Trade in 1770

The one certain fact is that the exports for this year (or rather
for the year ending 25 March 1771) amounted to about 25,400,000
yards, valued at £1,691,800. In order to find the total output
in Ireland we need to know the home consumption as well.
Stephenson's estimate of home consumption was £833,333, or
12,500,000 yards, calculated on a basis of 6s. 8d. a head for a
population of 2,500,000. But the population at that time must
have been rather more than 3,000,000. Moreover, an estimate
for 1802 represented the home consumption to be about six yards
a head instead of the five yards allowed by Stephenson. We may
balance these two estimates, and give the amount for 1770 as
17,000,000. The total output would then be 42,400,000 yards.

Next, we have to find the total production of the southern
provinces. Stephenson said that the sales in southern markets
amounted to £502,000, but his figure was certainly too high.

[1] *Account of Ireland*, i. 699.

If we take the more reliable figures for 1816 and 1821 and make allowance for the difference of population and foreign trade in 1770, it appears that Stephenson's figure would represent more than the total southern output, market sales and private sales together. The actual total was probably about 8,000,000 yards. There would then remain 34,400,000 yards as the output of Ulster. This amount has to be divided between the markets and private sales. Stephenson again is misleading here. There was a rather larger export trade in 1784 than in 1770, and certainly a larger home trade ; yet Stephenson's estimate of market sales for 1770 is greater by £430,000 than Greer's figure for 1784. As the sales in Greer's table amounted to about 29,000,000 yards, it would be enough to give 27,000,000 yards as the quantity sold in 1770. There would then be left 7,400,000 yards as the amount of private sales, i. e. slightly more than a fifth of the total output in Ulster.

Estimate of Trade in 1784

Exports in this year were 26,700,000 yards. They had fallen off seriously during the American War, and were only beginning to recover at this time. Home consumption, on the basis that we took before, would be about 22,000,000 yards, and the total output for Ireland, 48,700,000. As for the trade of the southern provinces, it would be not much larger than in 1770, for production in the south had lost ground seriously after 1771, and we can hardly put it at a higher figure than 9,000,000 yards. Thus 39,700,000 yards remain to be divided between markets and private sales in Ulster. Greer gave the value of market sales as £1,214,560. At an average price of 10d. a yard, which is probably near the mark, this sum would be equivalent to 29,000,000 yards. The private sales in Ulster would then be roughly 10,000,000 yards, or about a quarter of the total output.

The estimates are given below in the form of a table :

	1770 yds.	1784 yds.
Exports	25,400,000	26,700,000
Home consumption .	17,000,000	22,000,000
Total output . . .	42,400,000	48,700,000
Total production in South .	8,000,000	9,000,000
Total production in Ulster .	34,400,000	39,700,000
Market sales in Ulster . .	27,000,000	29,000,000
Private sales in Ulster . .	7,400,000	10,000,000

Number of Weavers

The number of weavers in Ulster in this period can be roughly estimated by allowing for each weaver an average output of 20 yards a week, or 1,000 yards in a year. A good weaver, especially if he was making fairly coarse cloth, could produce at least twice this amount when he gave his whole time to the work. McCall gives some examples of individual output about the year 1800. He states that a weaver of fine cambric (17^{oo} cloth, $1\frac{1}{2}$ yards wide) worked for 8 weeks at a rate of nearly 23 yards a week; another made 27 yards a week for ten weeks, working with slightly coarser yarn (16^{oo} cloth, $1\frac{1}{2}$ yards wide); and it was not uncommon for weavers of yard-wide 10^{oo} handkerchief cloth to produce rather more than 40 yards a week. On the other hand, few weavers were able to give their whole time to manufacture. Even the regular employees generally did some work on the land. Independent craftsmen and small manufacturers would spend much time in attending markets and collecting yarn. Moreover, many of them were quite as much farmers as weavers. In the seasons of haymaking and harvest very little weaving would be done. Therefore an average output of 20 yards a week throughout the year seems a reasonable allowance, and it agrees with the statistics of the sale of webs and attendance of weavers in 1816.

The number of weavers in Ulster appears, then, to have been about 35,000 in 1770 and 40,000 in 1784. Their division into independent craftsmen and wage-earners can only be roughly guessed, because, in the first place, there is no indication of the number of weavers working for small employers; and secondly, the independent worker, being as a rule less of a specialist, would produce rather less than the average amount of cloth. In 1816 the number of employees working for small manufacturers was apparently about two-sevenths of the whole number of weavers. In the earlier years it might be a fifth or a sixth. Allowing for these factors, we may conclude that in 1770 about 35 per cent. of the weavers were employed by large or small manufacturers, and in 1784, rather more than 40 per cent.

IX

COMMERCIAL DEVELOPMENTS, 1760–1800

Hindrances to Trade. Although the linen trade in Ireland more than trebled in volume between 1760 and 1820, its progress was made in the face of constant difficulties. It is true that manufacture in Ireland was favoured by a mild and moist climate, a good supply of water, abundant raw material, and cheap but efficient production. There was further a strong demand for Irish linen in other countries. The hindrance lay in the machinery of trade, in the means of bringing manufactured goods from the scattered farmsteads in Ulster to the distant consumers ; and the main source of trouble was a lack of capital and credit.

In order to understand the causes of this great weakness we need to glance at the earlier economic conditions of Ireland. To examine the causes at all fully we should have to make a very long digression, but it is possible to state the chief points in a few sentences.

In the dark ages Ireland had benefited by her remote position. She avoided most of the troubles that beset southern and western Europe, and even the Northmen were only able to settle in a narrow fringe round the sea-coast. Therefore the Church in Ireland was left comparatively at peace ; and the clergy, carrying on Roman and Byzantine traditions, mingled with the best elements in Celtic culture, were able to maintain art and learning at a high level. In the Middle Ages, however, the isolation of Ireland began to tell against her. The sea no longer guarded her from invasion, but it cut her off to a large extent from the civilization and trade of southern Europe. The lack of inland transport was an equal barrier. There were no Roman roads, but only rough tracks cleared through forests or passing over mountains and moorlands. Only the sea-ports and the chief monasteries near the coast could keep at all closely in touch with European affairs. The export trade was in raw

materials. Merchants, such as the Staplers, collected wool and
leather all over the country, and sold them to traders from the
great manufacturing districts of the Netherlands, the Rhinelands,
and Italy. With the development of ocean routes the centre
of trading activity came nearer to Ireland, but she could not
take advantage of her position. The mass of the people were
quite ignorant of the world outside their own neighbourhood,
and their handicrafts, such as the weaving of bandle linen, were
designed to meet their own immediate needs. They had no
knowledge of the economic demands of other countries, or of
the methods of trade and industry which would serve to meet
those demands. Town life was little developed. About a dozen
towns, most of them very small, had some share in overseas
trade. But they always remained in outlook, interests, and race,
rather an exotic element in Irish life.

Communications were still so bad in the sixteenth century
that the Tudor Governments were driven to rule by means of
scattered garrisons, which often had to live by plundering the
natives, because they were completely cut off from sources
of supply. In the seventeenth century there came a great change.
Administration was vastly improved ; regular assizes were
established ; local government was organized through the agency
of grand juries, who were charged in particular with the business
of road-making. This branch of their work was by no means
perfectly done, but inadequate as it was, it made an immense
difference to the state of the country. Road-making was as
important to Ireland as it had been to the ancient Roman
Empire. It made possible the change from tribal rule, or inter-
tribal anarchy, to a comparatively efficient, centralized government. Moreover, the new roads served to open up the whole
country to trade to an extent that had never before been
approached. Progress was delayed, indeed, by the civil wars
and rebellions of the Stuart period, but with more settled conditions there came an increase of trade ; and at length, about
the beginning of the eighteenth century, a substantial growth of
Irish industries seemed possible.

Lack of Capital. Still, as regards the accumulation of capital,
Ireland in 1700 stood very nearly where the more advanced
countries of Europe had stood early in the Middle Ages. The

stock of capital had to be developed from a very small nucleus, and its investment had to be organized almost from the beginning. Under happier conditions there might have been great progress during the eighteenth century. Trading capital, acquired by traffic in raw material, would have found a natural outlet in working up this material, as it had done in many other countries, and as it actually did in the Irish linen industry. With success in manufacture, wealth would have increased rapidly, for the growing profits both of trade and of industry would have been used as capital to promote fresh enterprise. But, notwithstanding better communications and a quieter political state, the handicaps were still too heavy.

Their nature is more obvious to-day than it was in the eighteenth century. Contemporary writers believed the great obstacles to Irish trade to be the restrictive policy of England, and the constant draining away of wealth in payments to absentee landlords. Undoubtedly both absenteeism and the 'commercial restraints' were great evils; but, although their political effects were disastrous, there is reason to think them less important economically than they appeared to be at the time.[1]

Three other difficulties passed almost unheeded in the eighteenth century, but their consequences were serious and far-reaching. They were the agrarian system, the comparative dearth of towns, and the almost complete lack of banks.

Enough has been said already of the system of land tenure. We need only recall two points in this connexion : firstly, that rack rents and insecurity of tenure made any satisfactory growth of rural industry impossible ; and secondly, that the whole tendency of the time was for industry to spread over the countryside. It follows that this handicap alone was sufficient to keep the country poor.

Dearth of Towns. To understand the difficulty in regard to towns, we have to remember how trade had developed in other lands. The growth of rural manufacture, to which allusion has just been made, was in a sense a product of the capital and enterprise of townsmen. The village craftsman depended on manufacturers or factors in provincial towns, who sometimes

---

[1] See the note on absenteeism at the end of this chapter. The question of English policy, in so far as it affected the linen trade, is discussed in Chapter X.

paid wages and sometimes advanced capital in the form of raw material and implements. The provincial trader himself received credit from factors and merchants in the larger towns, and often drew capital for long or short periods from country bankers, who depended in turn on the great metropolitan banks. The general principle was that of capital flowing out from the towns over wide districts, for the nourishment of industries.

But in Ireland the towns were few and poor. Even Scotland, which in 1700 was accounted a poor country, presented a strong contrast to Ireland in this respect. Scores of corporate towns, well organized, and bound together by the powerful Convention of Burghs, represented in the total sum a large body of commerce and industry, including Continental trade ; and they were able to furnish capital for an immense economic advance during the eighteenth century. The Irish towns, moreover, were hampered by the action of their gilds, which not only kept a monopoly of trade, but excluded Catholics altogether from their membership. The narrow policy of craft gilds and companies is, indeed, a familiar fact in the history of every land ; but its chief effect was normally to drive out manufacture from the towns to villages, and to transfer commerce to new centres of exchange. In Ireland the land system prevented any such growth. Thus trade in Ireland was doubly handicapped : it could neither grow freely in towns nor in the country.

The one great exception was in Ulster. There industry could penetrate the country parts, and new market towns could grow without hindrance. In this respect the rise of Lisburn, Lurgan, and Ballymena was parallel to that of Manchester, Liverpool, Birmingham, and Leeds.[1]

Thus in the middle of the eighteenth century Ireland was still a country in which—owing chiefly to defects in social custom and government—a large part of the natural resources remained undeveloped.

---

[1] Carrickfergus might also be compared to Norwich, Bruges, and Ghent. It was an old town, with several gilds, and the centre of overseas trade for a wide area. The linen industry markedly avoided Carrickfergus, while it developed in places where communications with Great Britain were far inferior. Moreover, just as in the sixteenth century the manufacture of ' new draperies ', carpets, lace, and linen arose in the old Flemish towns, so the new and unregulated cotton industry took root in Carrickfergus at the end of the eighteenth century.

Lack of Credit. The third difficulty was that even the small amount of capital available found comparatively little outlet, because it was almost entirely unorganized. In this case Ulster was affected quite as seriously as the other provinces. The only remedy was the provision of a money market and a good banking system ; but this remedy was applied very late and after many unsuccessful attempts.

To realize what the lack of organized credit meant to Ireland, we have only to glance at contemporary affairs in Great Britain, where the need was already reasonably well supplied. It would be hard to over-estimate the importance of banking in the period of the Industrial Revolution. The great changes of that time—the perfecting of the steam engine and textile machinery, the development of mining, the metal trades and pottery, the building of canals, the improvement of agriculture—all were made possible by means of bank credits. For the foundation or growth of industries, and for the expansion of trade, an abundant supply of credit for long or short periods was one of the first necessities. It was through the London and country banks that this provision was made, out of money which, apart from them, would have been used haphazard, or hoarded and left unused. An excellent system of joint-stock banks virtually founded the fortunes of Scotland in the eighteenth century. The banks of Holland not only did immense service to their own country, but helped to restore the industries of the Austrian Netherlands,[1] and were of no little importance to the English and other Continental peoples as well.

By contrast with these ready springs of wealth and enterprise, the meagreness of Irish credit is all the more striking. Before the foundation of the Bank of Ireland in 1783 there were only two concerns in Dublin comparable to the great banks of London, and in the rest of the country no really reliable and permanent bank was to be found.

Evidence was given in 1804, before a Committee of the House of Commons, that there was only one private bank in the North of Ireland, and that was in Derry, far from the main centres of industry.[2] We may doubt the accuracy of this statement,

---

[1] Cf. Lewinski, *L'Évolution industrielle de la Belgique*, pp. 117, 118.
[2] Wakefield, vol. ii, p. 179. Apparently there was none at that time in Belfast. One bank, founded about 1752, closed in 1757 ; then there was a gap

but without question there was no approach to an organized money market in the northern counties, nor was there any agency for collecting and distributing capital. Bills were discounted, indeed : without discounting, overseas trade, or any trade on a large scale, would have been impossible. But the work was done by ordinary merchants, not by bankers. For instance, London bills were discounted in 1786 at the rate of 7½ per cent., by James Hogg and Joseph Nicholson, for J. & J. Richardson, a rising firm of bleachers.[1] Some years later John Bell, a cotton merchant of Belfast, had a considerable discounting trade, and caused trouble with his customers by charging more than the statutory rate of 6 per cent.[2] A Discount Company was formed in Belfast in 1793, but the enterprise was soon abandoned because some of the members wished to set up a bank.[3] In view of the scarcity of London bills and the absence of a regular money market, we cannot wonder that the rate of discount should exceed the arbitrary limit set by Parliament. Because of the difficulty of buying bills, it was apparently a common custom with traders who made frequent purchases from English firms, to lay in a stock of London bills when they were comparatively cheap and to send them at once to England, establishing a credit in advance of their purchases.[4]

It seems extraordinary at a first glance that the Discount Company which has just been mentioned should dissolve itself in order to undertake the work of banking, of which discounting is an important branch. Why could not the Company add deposit and issue to its other functions ? The answer is to be found in a remarkable measure, passed in 1755, which in itself must have gone far to prevent any healthy growth of banks in Ireland.[5] Within the previous five years, six of the leading banks had failed owing to the mismanagement of their issue. The remainder were refusing discount, and were so much shaken

---

of thirty years. Another bank was started in 1787, but only lasted until 1790 ; and there was another long interval, until 1808, when the Belfast Bank, the first really satisfactory concern in the town, was established. J. Salmon, *Early Irish Bankers* (*New Ireland Review*, vol. xii, pp. 70–2).

[1] J. and J. R., Cash Book.

[2] I am indebted for this statement to Professor G. W. Daniels of Manchester.

[3] Wakefield, vol. ii, p. 179.

[4] Mr. Daniels tells me that this method was used by the Irish customers who bought cotton yarn from McConnel & Kennedy of Manchester.

[5] 29 Geo. II, c. 16.

that Parliament had to guarantee their solvency.[1] In order to improve the status of Irish banks, and to avoid the issue of notes by speculative traders, it was enacted that no one should engage in banking without a licence, and that no licence should be given to any man who was carrying on another branch of trade.[2]

This measure certainly did not prevent speculation, for no banks in the world were less reliable than the Irish. Inexperienced landlords and adventurous rent-agents could still become bankers, and tradesmen could issue notes in the form of tokens. Failures of banks were especially common during the next half-century, and the usual cause of failure was speculative issue of notes, which were forced into circulation by means of bribes.[3] While incompetent or unprincipled men were not debarred from setting up banks, responsible tradesmen were prohibited. Now it was men of this type—the Barclays, Lloyds, Dales, Smiths, and Barings—who were the pioneers of banking in Scotland and England. They were traders or manufacturers, who adopted banking in the first instance as a secondary branch of their business. By their services to their own country we can judge the disservice to Ireland of this restrictive act. Moreover, joint-stock banking was prevented after 1783 by the monopoly of the Bank of Ireland. The rapid growth of joint-stock concerns after 1824, when the monopoly was reduced, suggests that they would have appeared earlier, to the immense advantage of Irish trade, if the law had not hindered them.

Reactions on Irish Trade. If credit had been available in Ireland as it was in England, the organization of the textile trades in this period would have been similar in both countries. In the cotton industry, manufacturers had long been in the habit of selling their goods by private contract to wholesale merchants, who distributed them over England and carried them abroad. The larger cotton manufacturers already had warehouses in London and branches or agencies in foreign towns, even as far distant as South America.[4] In the woollen trade,

---

[1] Wakefield, vol. ii, pp. 8, 162.
[2] ibid., p. 166 ; Salmon, op. cit., p. 69 ; Dillon, *History and Development of Banking in Ireland*, pp. 22-4.   [3] Wakefield, u.s.
[4] G. W. Daniels, *Early English Cotton Industry*, pp. 58-60.

even in Yorkshire, where production on a small scale was still common, many manufacturers were selling goods on their own account in London or abroad, or were dealing through factors who lived in the centre of the industrial district. Although open markets were still largely used, a considerable proportion of the goods must have been passing, long before 1800, direct from the manufacturers to wholesale merchants.[1]

By analogy we should expect to find the new class of linen manufacturers in Ireland turning to export trade, with the help of factors, who would be settled in Ulster, and would have connexions with London, Lancashire, Bristol, the Continental towns, the West Indies, and the mainland of America. But development on these lines was very slow. The want of credit reacted on the whole trade from top to bottom. It limited the sale of brown linen, and even a good deal of bleached linen as well, to cash dealings ; it hampered the work of drapers and bleachers ; it kept the manufacturing districts for a long time dependent on the Dublin market, and the whole export trade from Ireland dependent on factors and merchants in London.

These effects can be clearly seen if we follow the processes of sale, from the first disposal of brown linen in local markets to the export of finished cloth.

Processes of Sale: Jobbing. We will begin with the collection of cloth from the more distant markets. This work was in the hands of jobbers, whose function was to buy webs in outlying districts and dispose of them in the chief centres of trade. Any account of the sale of linen goods in this period must include a description of the jobbers, for they were the sole organizers of trade over a large area.

Their business was illegal : jobbing in general was condemned, for instance, in the act of 1764.[2] Jobbers were migratory and irregular in their habits, and therefore difficult to control. Greer, the Inspector, said of the markets of co. Donegal in 1784 : ' A great misfortune attending these two (the only linen) markets in the county is that they are chiefly occupied by jobbers, who buy up the linens for Londonderry market, and it is extremely difficult to enforce the laws.'[3] Moreover, the

---

[1] Heaton, *Yorkshire Woollen and Worsted Industries*, pp. 386-90.
[2] 3 Geo. III, c. 35, cl. III.　　　　　[3] *Report*, p. 10.

jobbers were sometimes guilty of the transgressions of fore-stalling (known in Ireland as ' morning jobbing ')[1] and regrating. But they were not suppressed, partly because there was no efficient means of carrying out the law, partly because their custom was necessary for the very existence of some of the smaller markets, and also because their cloths were a useful source of supply for drapers and bleachers—the only persons who would be likely to put the law in motion against them.

Therefore they continued in spite of the law ; and more than thirty years after Greer's visit, Corry, the Secretary to the Linen Board, found jobbers still pursuing the same methods.[2] According to his account they generally bought to sell again in another place, or in the same market at a later date, and no one raised any complaint against these practices. The only serious offence was that of forestalling the market and selling again in the same place on the same day. The weavers, no doubt, found it worth while to take a rather smaller price than the normal for the sake of a quick sale.[3]

In the market at Ballybay, co. Monaghan, Corry had a discussion with certain jobbers, who asked for the repeal of the law prohibiting their trade. ' They said they were a descrip-tion of traders, who, though neither countenanced by the law nor favoured by the regular buyers, were a very useful body to the poor weavers, who would often, but for them, be in need of a purchaser for their webs. They said that jobbers of their class, who never bought or sold in the morning,[4] but confined their traffic to the limits they described, were a useful class of under-agents, forming a low but necessary link in the chain of linen-traders, and were therefore entitled rather to the pro-tection than the punishment of the law.'[5] To this reasonable

---

[1] *Report*, p. 28.   [2] Corry's *Report*, pp. 10, 61, 62, 66, 72, 74, 75.
[3] But sometimes the jobber bought later and at a higher price. This curious instance is given by Corry (p. 84) : The Earl of Inniskillen proposed to move the market in his town from a narrow part of the street where the traffic was much congested to a wider place one hundred and fifty yards away. The drapers strongly objected. They explained that weavers, after agreeing to a price with regular buyers, would rub out the figures which were chalked on the roll and would often sell the roll at a higher price to a jobber. Although the market was quite close to the inns where payment was made, weavers were often intercepted by jobbers between the selling-place and the pay-tables. If the market were further from the inns there would be still more scope for this custom of ' selling a second time '.
[4] i. e. they did not practise forestalling.   [5] *Report*, p. 74.

statement Corry gave the unsatisfactory answer that the law against jobbing had been in existence for more than half a century, and seeing that the trade had made phenomenal progress during this period there could not be anything seriously amiss with the law.

The clause forbidding jobbing was not repealed, but neither was it enforced : therefore the jobbers were *de facto* free to continue their business as long as the brown-linen markets remained. Their work is an instance of the small scale of dealings and the absence of credit in the sale of brown linen, for they both bought and sold for ready money and only dealt in small amounts of cloth.

Markets for Brown Linen. The methods of trade were no more advanced in the larger markets, where drapers or bleachers bought cloth from weavers and small manufacturers. Arthur Young spoke of the weavers as ' always receiving money on the spot, as there is no credit '.[1] In an account of the markets in 1801, Sir Charles Coote, a member of the Linen Board, wrote : ' The trade depends on specie alone.' [2] He described how gold, received by the manufacturers and weavers, was paid to rent-agents, and handed on by them to drapers, in exchange for notes, at a premium of two to four per cent., ' the entire of the linen trade being carried on by specie only.' He added that ' at fairs or markets the purchasers must pay in specie or allow the discount, except there is a previous agreement that bank-notes will be taken '.[3]

We can easily understand why the working weaver had to sell his webs for cash. The small manufacturer was in a similar position. He had to pay wages and to buy yarn with ready money, and the slenderness of his resources compelled him to demand payment on the spot for his sales. If there had been country banks of the English type in Ulster,[4] the small manufacturer could have increased the scale of his business, and eventually he could have dealt directly with Dublin, England, and foreign countries, giving credit on his own account. But since manufacturers had to rely for capital on their own

---

[1] *Tour,* p. 107.   [2] *Survey of Monaghan,* p. 212.
[3] *Survey of Armagh,* p. 141.
[4] Or cash credits, according to the Scottish custom.

savings, their businesses grew slowly and never grew far. As no seller in the brown-linen markets could afford to wait for payment, the drapers had to take with them large supplies of ready money. Each of them would normally spend, towards the end of the eighteenth century, forty or fifty pounds a week.[1] For safety they commonly travelled in convoys from market to market.

Currency. It is not surprising that the drapers had to deal in coin rather than bank-notes, which would, of course, have been more convenient to them. At this time, when there was so little banking in Ulster, farmers were no doubt suspicious of paper money; and their mistrust was not unwarranted. Although some paper was quite sound—although, for example, receipts for guineas issued by the Bank of Ireland circulated at a premium, like the notes of the Bank of Amsterdam—a great amount of Irish paper money was of very doubtful quality. Besides the forced issues of many private bankers, forged notes were circulated ' to an extent ', as Wakefield said, ' of which no person in England can form an adequate idea '.[2]

On the other hand, if unsound paper was abundant in Ireland, metal currency was very scarce. The bad condition of Irish coinage in the eighteenth century is a familiar fact, of which no detailed evidence need be given here. The best gold was the Portuguese moidore : guineas were nearly all light and much worn. The shortage of silver was such that Spanish dollars, stamped with an artificial value, were used by the Bank of Ireland.[3] In most parts of the country tradesmen's tokens, each worth a few pence, were the regular medium for small payments. They were usually printed on paper, and in general resembled the little notes for half a franc or a lira, which are too familiar in Continental countries to-day. In 1795 when the Manchester firm, McConnel & Kennedy, asked one of their Belfast agents to send them a supply of silver, the answer was

---

[1] McCall, p. 55, gives approximate figures of the total sales and the number of drapers in attendance in the markets of 6 Ulster counties for the year 1800. The numbers vary from 50 drapers and an annual turnover of £100,000 in co. Monaghan, to 200 drapers and a turnover of £450,000 in co. Armagh. The average weekly purchases by each draper were : Armagh, £43 ; Antrim, £48 ; Down, £45 ; Derry, £42 10s. ; Tyrone, £44 ; Monaghan, £38 10s.

[2] Wakefield, vol. ii, p. 167. [3] ibid., p. 165.

that scarcely a sixpenny piece was to be found in the whole town.[1] This shortage of coins must have added greatly to the difficulty of the drapers' trade. It would certainly have the effect of favouring the large bleachers, who were more and more entering into competition with ordinary drapers in the open markets. Because of their large dealings with bankers in Dublin, and later with those in Ulster, they could more easily command a supply of coin ; and if they used paper money instead, their reputation would allow the weaver to take notes more readily from them than from a small draper.

The drapers, who were seldom wealthy men, had to make heavy payments in cash, both for their purchases of cloth and for their journeys to the markets or to Dublin. They had, moreover, to stand the cost of bleaching. Thus it is clear that they could not easily give credit to their customers. On the other hand, their customers often wanted credit.

Factors. The difficulty was met by the Dublin factors. It was a common custom among the factors to advance to the drapers who dealt with them either the whole or part of the value of the cloth, charging a discount for the loan, and a fee for storage.[2] This practice was greatly resented by the drapers, although some such help was essential to their trade. They argued, not very soundly, that the factor's capital was derived from them, so that he was growing rich at their expense and with their money. Nevill, the draper who made this accusation, added in an interesting note that many factors had acquired fortunes in a short time by means of their discounting business. ' Most of them ', he said, ' were known a few years ago to be as poor and needy as their neighbours.' [3]

Without doubt the factors grew rich, not only by acting as bankers for their principals, but by means of trading ventures of their own. The general distinction between a merchant and a factor is that the one buys and sells on his own account, whereas the other sells or buys on account of some one else, charging a commission on his dealings. But in many trades the two classes have often been more or less fused together.[4] A merchant

---

[1] G. W. Daniels, *Econ. Journal*, vol. xxv, p. 188 (June, 1915).
[2] Young, *Tour*, p. 107.   [3] *Seasonable Remarks*, p. 71.
[4] Several instances taken from the seventeenth and eighteenth centuries are given in Westerfield's *Middlemen in English Business*. Professor Daniels

may at times undertake sales or purchases for a principal. A factor, who must have an intimate knowledge of the state of markets, may seize a favourable opportunity to buy goods outright and sell them for himself. He may use his profits to expand this side of his business, and if it is successful it will soon be his chief concern and his largest source of income. There was certainly a give-and-take of this kind between merchants and factors in Dublin. In the early nineteenth century the term ' Linen Hall factor ' was used indiscriminately for all large dealers in linen, even for northern bleachers who had offices in Dublin.[1]

The factors' trade illustrates the value of banking in this period. They were able to make advances of cash because they had credit with the Dublin banks, whereas the drapers had not sufficient standing in Dublin to secure large credits.[2] For the same reason it was still necessary for a considerable part of the trade from Ulster to England to pass through Dublin : the fact that credit could be given there more readily than in Ulster served constantly to draw trade to the Linen Hall.

A provision of banks in Ulster would have been a great advantage. It would have enabled many drapers to become exporting merchants themselves. Or, when they dealt through the Dublin market, they would have had no need to ask the factors for ready money. The factors, in turn, could have offered more generous terms to their customers, and the volume of trade would have been greatly increased. In practice, the resources of the factors must often have been strained. Credit was demanded of them by buyers and sellers alike. There were only two or three trustworthy banks in Dublin from which they could draw their supplies ; and the Bank of Ireland was prevented from doing a large discounting business by a regulation limiting its rate to 5 per cent.

The buyers in Dublin were partly Irish retailers and partly English merchants or factors. About a third or a half of the cloth passing through the Linen Hall was sold for consumption

has found a similar gradation from pure factor to merchant in the cotton yarn trade in Belfast about the year 1800.

[1] There was a separate heading for Linen Hall factors in the Dublin Directories. The lists included Dublin merchants and northern bleachers.

[2] *Seasonable Remarks*, u.s.

in Ireland. There is hardly any information about the domestic trade, but it is probable that retailers, following the general custom of the time, would pay the factor as a rule in thirty-one day bills, drawn on Dublin.

Export. The export trade to England was managed on several different lines. English merchants still visited Dublin in considerable numbers at the times of the three chief markets, in February, June, and October. In June, when cargoes were being collected for foreign trade, most of the purchases were of goods stored in Dublin ; and this was the largest market of the year. In the other two markets, dealings were chiefly in the form of orders in advance.[1] The commonest form of payment was probably a short-dated bill drawn on London ; but cash was also used, at times when the cloth could be examined in the Linen Hall or in a private warehouse, and bought on the spot.[2]

English traders sometimes went beyond Dublin, and penetrated to the provincial markets. Besnard, in 1817, referred to this as an obsolete custom,[3] but in the previous year Corry had found a London factor in the market for brown linen at Cootehill, co. Monaghan, and did not mention the circumstance as anything unusual.[4] The business that would take such men to the local markets would be chiefly the purchase of brown webs for English bleachers.[5] Possibly English agents visited the bleach-works in Ulster to buy white linens. I have found no mention of such a practice ; but as bleachers, about the year 1780, were selling direct to customers in London, the supposition is not unlikely.[6]

On the other hand Irish traders, including bleachers, went

---

[1] Besnard, *Report*, p. 26.

[2] Young, *Tour,* p. 107. English traders similarly paid cash for their purchases in Silesia (Horner, p. 408).

[3] *Report*, u.s.   [4] Corry, *Report*, p. 63.

[5] Wakefield, vol. i, pp. 292–3. Wakefield said that English dealers were doubtful of the quality of Irish bleaching. He referred to ' an immense bleachgreen ' at Carshalton, ' where as much business is done as at any five in Ireland ', and to ' one equally large in the neighbourhood of Manchester '. As some of the finest bleaching in the world was done in Ireland at that time (1812), the first statement is at least open to doubt. The second statement is absurdly wrong : it shows that he had no idea of the output of the large bleachworks in Ulster.   [6] Young, u.s.

with selections of cloth to England, especially to Chester.[1] At each of the fairs, in July and October, about a million yards of Irish cloth were sold, and it was found worth while to build a linen hall in Chester to accommodate this trade.[2]

Foreign and Colonial Trade. The most striking point in regard to the export trade in Irish linen is its domination by English merchants. Not only were English people themselves by far the largest consumers, but even the cloth that was sent abroad went for the most part by way of London, Liverpool, or Bristol. Parliament and the Irish merchants alike were anxious to develop a direct export from Ireland to the Colonies and foreign countries. From 1780 onwards, for half a century, bounties were given for the export of linen to places outside the British Isles.[3] But the result was disappointing. In 1783 when trade with America and the West Indies began to revive, the exports to the rest of the world were about $5\frac{1}{2}$ per cent. of those to Great Britain.[4] During the first quarter of the nineteenth century the proportion varied from 4 to 14 per cent., with a distinct downward tendency towards the end.[5]

There were two main obstacles to direct export from Ireland. One, as we should expect, was the want of credit. Whereas merchants in Dublin, even as late as 1812, could only offer two months' credit to foreign buyers, London exporters were allowing credit for eight months.[6] The buyers would naturally wish to take advantage of the better terms offered in London. Although direct export would save the cost of carriage to England, the inconveniences must have outweighed this gain. It is interesting to notice that the export of linen goods from Silesia to Spain and America was controlled by London middlemen for precisely the same reason. The foreign merchants

[1] ibid., ' Some go over to Chester fair themselves.'
[2] Macpherson, *Annals*, vol. iv, appendix, s.v. ' Chester '.
[3] 19 & 20 Geo. III, c. 33.
[4] McCall, p. 68.
[5] See table given by Horner, p. 77. The amount was actually less in 1825 than in 1802. In 1802 it was 2,976,000 yards ($7\frac{1}{2}$ per cent.), in 1825 only 2,386,000 (4 per cent.). In the year ended 5 January, 1825, the amount of Irish linen sent abroad from Great Britain was 15,174,392 yards (*Account of Linen Cloth Imported into Great Britain*, 1825).
[6] Wakefield, vol. i, p. 692.

asked for six or eight months' credit, and the resources of Silesia were not equal to this demand.[1]

The second great hindrance to the Irish export trade was the lack of other goods which could contribute to mixed cargoes. Whole cargoes of linen would be difficult and expensive to provide, and still more troublesome to sell. English shippers could easily make up mixed cargoes of manufactures;[2] but in Ireland, apart from linen, there were scarcely any manufactured goods for export. The only other goods sent out of Ireland in any considerable quantities were meat, butter, and corn:[3] consequently a cargo containing linen cloth would have to be completed with these foodstuffs. But they were sent almost entirely to England. There was, indeed, some demand for butter and salted meat in France and the West Indies.[4] Trade with France, however, was impeded by tariffs and still more by war; and the cattle produce going to the West Indies was probably little more than ballast for cargoes of linen.

Similar difficulties hindered a direct export to Spain. In the latter part of the eighteenth century great efforts were made in Ireland to develop a Spanish market for linen.[5] But Irish

---

[1] Horner, p. 408.

[2] One reason for the great importance of Hamburg as an entrepot for the German linen trade was the ease with which cargoes could be made up there.

[3] Linen was always the most valuable export, as we may judge from the following table. The figures are taken from Wakefield, vol. ii, pp. 46–53. See also diagram II given below in Appendix II.

Value of Exports from Ireland.

	Linen and yarn.	Cattle, meat and dairy produce.	Corn.
1780	£1,500,000	£1,100,000	£100,000
1790	£2,700,000	£1,300,000	£600,000
1800	£2,500,000	£1,300,000	£100,000
1810	£2,600,000	£1,800,000	£700,000

Linen was also ' the greatest article ' of export from Belfast in 1774 (Young, p. 124). In 1810 linen was still far ahead of other commodities. The value of the cloth exported from Belfast in that year was approximately £1,100,000 (i.e. 15,150,000 yards at an average price of 1s. 6d. a yard). The corresponding values of other goods were : cotton, £250,000 ; butter, £210,000 ; bacon, £206,000. See Dubourdieu, *Antrim*, ii. 519. Dubourdieu estimated the value of the linen at twice the above figure, and his prices for the other commodities are probably too high as well. In that case the predominance of linen would be still more marked.

[4] Young, *Tour*, p. 124 ; Wakefield, vol. ii, p. 31.

[5] An early instance of an attempt on Spanish trade is mentioned in the Linen Board's *Proceedings* for 1763 (p. 104). The large firm of W. & J. Ogle, of Drogheda, received a grant of £66 for a calender, to enable them to prepare

trade had to struggle against the competition of goods from France, Germany, and the Netherlands, which paid smaller .duties.[1] Moreover, seeing that much of the Silesian cloth was carried to Spain by English merchants, Dublin and London were actually in competition in this market. Thus a Dublin exporter would generally find his cloth selling better in Spain if it went by way of London. A further handicap against Ireland was the difficulty of making up return cargoes. The Spanish had little that was of use to Ireland, except wine and barilla ashes, which were used in bleaching, whereas in England there was a strong demand for Spanish iron ore and wool.

The transatlantic trade of Ireland in this period was larger than the continental. The West Indies were commercially the most important of British colonies in the eighteenth century, and their sugar was by far the most valuable of colonial imports. Ireland was able to share in this trade to some extent, for there was a small demand, both in the West Indies and in the mainland of North America, for Irish butter and salted meat, as well as linen cloth. The return cargoes included sugar, rum, flaxseed, and in the last few years of the century, an increasing supply of raw cotton. In years of exceptionally good trade two or three million yards of linen might be sent direct from Ireland to America : normally the amount was from one to two million yards.

However, the course of transatlantic trade was very chequered —for several years it was seriously deranged by the War of Independence. The following figures show both the effects

cloth for the Spanish market. The amount of trade was very small in 1770. Stephenson, in an analysis of exports during that year, stated that less than 50,000 yards of linen had gone direct to Spain (*Observations*, 1784, p. 87). Young, in 1776, mentioned this trade as a new institution (*Tour*, p. 114). Its increase was urged seven years later by Nevill in his *Seasonable Remarks* (p. 19) ; and in a pamphlet published in 1790 particulars were given, by an Irish trader who had lived in Spain, of the kinds and make-up of cloth most in demand in the Spanish markets (*Informations to the People of Ireland*, by C. S. Merchant). The pamphlet is summarized in Horner's *Linen Trade of Europe* (pp. 557–60). The trade still continued in the early nineteenth century (see e. g. Wakefield, vol. ii, p. 18), but evidently on a very small scale. The Napoleonic War must have stopped it altogether for a time ; and the total export from Ireland after the war was so small that when allowance is made for American and West Indian trade, there is very little left for Europe as a whole.

[1] Horner, p. 78 ; Nevill, *Seasonable Remarks*, u.s. Nevill said that even trade from London was greatly hampered by discriminating customs duties.

of the war and the remarkable recovery after the Peace of Versailles.[1]

Export of Linen from Ireland to the West Indies and America :

	Yds.			Yds.
1780	. . 234,600	1783	. .	632,100
1781	. . 347,700	1784	. .	3,540,700
1782	. . 225,200			

Imports into Ireland from America :

				Tobacco. Lb.	Flaxseed. Hhds.
1780	.	.	.	—	1,775
1781	.	.	.	326,000	927
1782	.	.	.	296,000	868
1783	.	.	.	789,000	169
1784	.	.	.	3,077,000	21,184

This war, while it lasted, was a factor of great importance in Irish trade. It cut off a large market for linen and one of the chief sources of raw material. It was mainly responsible for a great slump in the linen trade in 1780, when the total exports were less than they had been in any year since 1764. The lucrative traffic in smuggled woollen goods was entirely stopped. Moreover, the ordinary trade to England was made very hazardous by the activity of privateers. The enterprise of American privateers during this war is notorious. They caused great loss to Irish shipping, not only by actual captures, but also by the delay due to travelling in convoys. The privateers which cruised near Ireland were the more efficient because they were manned largely by the Irish seamen who had formerly been smugglers. These men knew the coast thoroughly, and knew, too, how to prey with success on legitimate trade. In August, 1781, they actually blockaded Waterford Harbour.[2]

In view of all these dangers and difficulties it is easy to understand both the depression about 1780 and the great outburst of transatlantic trade in 1784. But the standard of this year was not maintained. The handicaps which affected all the

---

[1] Macpherson, *Annals*, vol. iv, p. 60. There had been direct trade with the West Indies and the mainland of North America for a considerable time before the war—as we may judge from the particulars of trade from Belfast given below. In 1779 Ireland was freed from most of the restrictions of the Navigation Acts, but this reform would not make much difference to export across the Atlantic, as linen, dairy produce, and salted meat were already exempted from the ban.

[2] For details of piracy in this period, see *31st Report of the Deputy of Public Records in Ireland*, pp. 92, 93 ; and Froude, *English in Ireland*, vol. ii, pp. 236, 237.

overseas trade of Ireland were enough to prevent any great development, and this particular branch was more difficult to maintain than any other. At the best of times it was highly speculative, and it involved many months, or even years, of waiting before there was any return for the original outlay. Hence, until the second quarter of the nineteenth century there was no general increase in the volume of exports across the Atlantic. The trade was injured by the Napoleonic War, and once more cut off almost entirely by the War of 1812–14. Even after the return of peace, the result of export to America was apt to be disappointing.

But, in spite of all the difficulties and hindrances, there was real progress during this period. In the first place, the volume of trade increased substantially. Although it is impossible to judge with any approach to accuracy the amount consumed in Ireland, we may be certain that it grew considerably between 1760 and 1800 ; and the export trade to England grew remarkably. The official figures show a gradual and rather unsteady advance from 1760 to 1780, then, after the end of the American War, an extraordinary increase, which continued until 1795. In that year the quantity of linen exported was more than three times as great as the export in 1780.[1]

Growth of Export from Ulster. This increase of output brought with it, in commerce as in manufacture, a development of methods and organization. Growing trade meant accumulating wealth ; greater wealth afforded stronger credit ; and the new credit was used to improve the system of trade. In a later chapter [2] we shall examine in some detail the methods in use early in the nineteenth century. For the present it is enough to notice the most striking change—a growth of direct trade with England and other countries from the northern ports, especially from Belfast. In the survey that we have made of the organization of trade in Ireland, Dublin has been treated as the chief market for export—and so it remained until about 1800. But all the time the position of Dublin was being assailed, and at the beginning of the nineteenth century its hegemony was transferred to Belfast.

In this period Belfast by no means dominated the economic life of Ulster as it did in the nineteenth century. Although

---

[1] See Table of Exports given in Appendix II.   [2] Chapter XIII.

there was a good deal of linen manufacture in and around the town and a flourishing brown linen market, for which a hall had been built in 1754,[1] several other markets had more trade.[2] Belfast had not yet gained a conspicuous lead in population,[3] and in 1762 the chief port for transatlantic trade was not Belfast but Londonderry. The growth of overseas traffic from Belfast was delayed by the shallowness of the harbour. At low tide there were only two or three feet of water at the quays. Even at high tide vessels of 200 tons had to unload half their cargo before they could come into the harbour : larger ships lay two and a half miles farther down the Lough.[4] Nevertheless Belfast was marked out by nature as the chief centre of export trade from the north of Ireland. The town had grown up at the point where river-borne traffic and sea-going traffic met. There was abundant manufacture in the immediate neighbourhood. Easy communications up the Lagan valley led into the heart of a great manufacturing district, and a few miles of road connected the Lagan valley with another area of weaving and bleaching, by the River Bann. Main roads from the north and west converged on Belfast, and a large traffic in both fine and coarse cloths, from North Antrim and the whole district around Lough Neagh, passed along them. From the sheltered waters of Belfast Lough the passage by sea, either to the north of England or the south of Scotland, was quite short. Thus communications both by land and by sea favoured the growth of a trade in linen from Belfast to Great Britain. Although a large and increasing proportion of the trade passed by this route, two other ports, Londonderry and Newry, had a considerable share. Newry was a convenient outlet for the manufactures of Armagh and South Down. Londonderry was the collecting point for yarn from Donegal ; it was centrally placed for a large area of weaving ; and the bleach-greens of Limavady and Coleraine were only a few miles away. The nearness of

---

[1] Owen, *History of Belfast*, p. 143.

[2] e. g. in 1784 sales in the Belfast market were equalled or surpassed by those in Lisburn, Ballymena, Lurgan, Armagh, Cootehill, Newry, Derry, and Dungannon (see Greer's Report, quoted below, Appendix I).

[3] In 1757 the population was estimated at 8,500 (Dubourdieu, *Antrim*, ii. 505). Several other towns must have had about a third of this population ; but by 1821 the census return for Belfast was 37,277, whereas no other town in Antrim, Down, or Armagh had more than about 8,000 inhabitants. Carrickfergus had 8,023 ; Newry, 7,470 ; Lisburn only 4,660.

[4] Young, *Tour*, p. 124.

bleach-greens was a great asset to these three ports, for it meant that they could easily develop an export trade in finished cloth. Moreover, bleachers were themselves the chief exporters.

This direct trade from the north of Ireland had apparently begun before the middle of the eighteenth century. In 1744 linen was being sent from Drogheda to Liverpool and Whitehaven for shipment to the Colonies,[1] and there would probably be a similar traffic from ports in Ulster, in addition to the export of yarn from Londonderry to Lancashire.

There is definite, though very incomplete, evidence of the growth of overseas trade from Belfast after 1760. The facts can best be arranged in the form of tables. The first table shows the number of trading vessels sailing regularly from Belfast in certain years. It enables us to judge not only the general course of trade from Belfast, but also the growth of the linen trade ; for, as Arthur Young observed, shipping and the linen trade varied exactly together.

Growth of Shipping from Belfast.

	Number of vessels.	Destination.	Tonnage.
1762 [2]	2	Liverpool	
	2	North America	250–300
1773 [3]	(Total) 50		20–300
1785 [4]	8	England	
	8	Europe	
	12	West Indies	
	15	North America	
	12	Coastwise	
	(Total) 55		(Total) 10,040
1791 [5]	4 (brigs)	London	(Av.) 160
	4 (sloops)	Liverpool	80
	(No particulars of transatlantic trade.)		
1811 [6]	8 (brigs)	London	270
	8 (sloops)	Liverpool	160
	2 (sloops)	Bristol	150
	12 (ships and brigs)	West Indies	350

[1] *H. of C. Reports*, vol. ii, p. 68.
[2] These sailings were advertised in the *News Letter*. In this summer eleven ships went from various ports in Ulster to America ; five sailed from Londonderry, two from Belfast, and one each from Newry, Larne, Portrush and Coleraine. The two vessels trading with Liverpool apparently crossed every month.   [3] Young, *Tour*, p. 124.
[4] Owen, *History of Belfast*, p. 164 ; Dubourdieu, *Antrim*, ii. 520.
[5] Owen (op. cit., p. 223), quoting William Ritchie, the pioneer of shipbuilding in Belfast.   [6] ibid.

We need not pay more attention to the transatlantic shipping beyond noticing that the large number of vessels in 1785 reflects the boom in trade after the war ; and that in 1811 traffic with the mainland of North America was stopped by the unfortunate dispute which led to the outbreak of war in the following year.

The export to England was more important. It was much greater in volume and had far more effect on the course and organization of trade. The most interesting point in the table is its indication that in traffic with English ports Belfast and Dublin were nearly equal in 1811. The total number of vessels crossing to England from Belfast in that year was 18. Three years earlier the corresponding figures for Dublin were as follows : [1]

Vessels sailing to London	. . . . . .	7
„ „ Liverpool	. . . . .	8
„ „ Bristol	. . . . .	4
	Total	19

The number would be about the same in 1811, consequently the cross-channel shipping from the two ports must have been almost equal at that time.

The next table shows the actual export of linen in certain years from Belfast and the three other main centres of overseas trade :

	Quantity (in yds.) of linen exported from :				Total from Ireland.	Percentage from Belfast.
	Belfast.	London-derry.	Newry.	Dublin.		
1773 [2]	3,713,822	—	—	—	16,916,674	22
1782 [3]	5,000,000 (about)	—	—	—	16,039,705	30 (about)
1792 [4]	—	1,153,000	—	—	43,312,057	—
1801 [5]	—	3,332,145	—	—	37,767,077	—
1807 [6]	16,735,582	3,000,000	3,000,000	12,923,678	40,901,442	40
1810 [7]	15,152,821	—	—	—	36,846,971	41

[1] *Dublin Directory*, 1808. One of the London brigs sailing from Dublin was significantly called the *Linen Hall*.

[2] Young, *Tour*, u.s. The exports from Belfast were two-thirds of the total from ports in Ulster. 'A little ' went from Londonderry, ' the balance ' from Newry.

[3] *Newry Magazine*, 1815, p. 316.

[4] Sampson, *Survey of Londonderry*, p. 382.   [5] ibid., p. 396.

[6] Newenham, *View of the . . . Circumstances of Ireland*, app., p. 11.

[7] Dubourdieu, *Antrim*, ii. 519.

These figures do not give by any means a consecutive view of trade, and it is unfortunate that nearly all the years mentioned here were years of depression. But the table suggests a steady growth in the volume of trade, both actual and relative, from northern ports. It also confirms the statement that, although there was a moderate export by way of Londonderry and Newry, a large proportion of the goods passed through Belfast. Further, it appears that about the beginning of the nineteenth century Belfast became the chief focus, not only in Ulster but in the whole of Ireland, for the overseas trade in linen. Dublin remained, of course, the great distributing centre for domestic trade in the southern provinces ; but in course of time the Linen Hall was altogether deserted.

How are these developments to be explained ? Seeing that Dublin had always been, before 1800, the chief emporium for domestic and foreign trade alike, there must have been some important changes towards the end of the eighteenth century which gave a preference to the ports of Ulster. These changes are to be found partly in England and partly in Ireland.

Trade with Liverpool. The chief new factor in England was the rapid growth of Liverpool. The fortunes of Liverpool were founded on trade to Africa and across the Atlantic, and we have already seen that Irish linen, bought by Liverpool merchants, contributed to this trade. In addition, the raw material of the great cotton manufacture, and the yarn or finished cloth for export, passed mainly through Liverpool. A large traffic in all manner of goods to and from the inland parts of Lancashire and the north of England as a whole had naturally grown up together with the staple trade. Thus Liverpool became a distributing centre for yarn and linen cloth from Ireland, taking over a large part of the connexion that had once been a monopoly of Chester.

Importation by way of Liverpool was made vastly cheaper and easier by the development of English canals. Evidence was given in 1751 that the cost of carriage from Liverpool to Manchester was almost prohibitive, and for this reason trade was driven round from the north of Ireland to Dublin and London.[1] Even the goods going to South Lancashire could be

[1] *H. of C. Reports*, vol. ii, p. 291.

sent at that time more cheaply and conveniently through Chester. This fact was a further reason for the concentration of trade in Dublin ; for the merchants of Chester had an ancient connexion with Dublin, and, as we have seen, were in the habit of travelling there twice a year to buy linen.

But with the opening of the Bridgewater, Grand Trunk, and Leeds and Liverpool Canals, the monopoly of the Mersey Navigation was broken. Easy ways were available from Liverpool to the manufacturing districts of Lancashire, Yorkshire, Cheshire, and the Midlands. This circumstance must have given a great stimulus to export from the northern Irish towns. Their trading relations with Lancashire were becoming very close in the last twenty years of the eighteenth century, because of the rise of a cotton manufacture in Ulster. Further, the Liverpool merchants, who were used to highly organized markets, would not be content to follow the old, clumsy system of trade through the Dublin Linen Hall if some more direct and efficient method were possible. The old system involved the cost of carriage by road to Dublin ; porterage of half-a-crown a pack at the Linen Hall ; the factor's commission, and his charge for warehousing ; more payments to porters and carters in Dublin when the goods were finally removed down the quays and placed in vessels bound for the English ports. These charges would be almost entirely avoided if the cloth could be ordered direct from the bleach-green, and carried only a few miles to a northern port.

But this more satisfactory method could only take full effect on two conditions. In the first place, there must be good communications and proper harbour accommodation in Ulster ; and secondly, there must be merchants in the north capable of carrying on overseas trade, and of allowing a credit at least equal to that given by the Dublin factors. It happened that both these conditions were fulfilled.

Communications in Ulster. In the matter of communications, both by road and by canal, Ireland was distinctly ahead of England. The Newry Canal, leading from Carlingford Lough up to Portadown, had been begun as early as 1730.[1] The Lagan

---

[1] Sanctioned by 3 Geo. II, c. 8 ; cf. Harris, *Co. Down*, p. 112.

Navigation, which connected Belfast with the manufacturing districts of South Antrim, Down, and Armagh, was begun in 1762. And a third, the Ulster Canal, from Caledon to Lough Neagh, was opened about twenty years later.[1] These water-ways provided a cheap means of bringing yarn to Ulster from the western counties, and of taking cloth down to the seaports.

Further, the harbour of Belfast was substantially improved before the end of the eighteenth century. In 1769 the Chichester Quay had been built to supplement the three or four small quays already in use.[2] The great defect of shallow water still remained ; but this fault was remedied to a large extent after 1785. In that year a Harbour Corporation, or Ballast Board, was given statutory powers to deepen the harbour and channel, excavate docks, build wharves, regulate the shipping, supply pilots, and in general undertake the work of a harbour board.[3] Within a few years the Board had built several new wharves and increased the depth of the channel by one-half. The harbour was not yet really satisfactory, for the channel was still winding. The two cuts which provided a straight and deep channel out to sea were not finished until almost the middle of the nineteenth century.[4] But in 1800 the harbour was at any rate available for ocean-going and cross-channel shipping.

Moreover, the Irish roads, although they could not compare in smoothness or durability with the ' county roads ' of the present day, were remarkably good according to the standard of that time. In many parts of the country, including the industrial districts of Ulster, the roads were very numerous, and there was a growing provision of stage and mail coaches, in addition to the service of carriers' carts.[5] Thus by 1800

---

[1] Owen, *History of Belfast*, p. 378. The canals were certainly of some value to the linen trade (e. g. Coote, *Survey of Armagh*, p. 369, mentioned the usefulness of the Ulster Canal to manufacturers) ; but they were by no means so important as those in the industrial districts of England, and they were not kept in good condition. Wakefield said that in 1809 the Newry and Ulster Canals were little used and were choked with weeds. The Lagan Canal was still unfinished, and its construction had come to a standstill. In 1827 complaints were made to the Treasury of the ' neglected state of the Newry Navigation ' (P.R.O. London, Treasury Letters, T. 14, 24, p. 215).

[2] Owen, op. cit., p. 163.

[3] 25 Geo. III, c. 64.

[4] ibid., p. 217 ; *Port of Belfast*, p. 15 ; *Belfast Directory*, 1819 ; Dubourdieu, *Antrim*, vol. ii, p. 526.

[5] See note II at the end of this chapter, and the map given in the Appendix.

Belfast was on the whole well supplied with means of communication.

Export by Bleachers. All these improvements, however, would have been of little use apart from the second condition that has been mentioned—the presence in Ulster of merchants capable of carrying on an export trade without the help of Dublin factors. It was no easy matter to undertake this trade. Because of the lack of banks in Ulster, the exporting merchant had to supply large consignments of cloth on long credit, relying almost exclusively on his own capital. The only persons in a position to undertake this task were a few of the more successful bleachers. In the Dublin linen market there were many pure traders who had no part in manufacture,[1] but if there were any at all in the north of Ireland their number must have been very small.

Thus bleachers were not only the largest manufacturers in Ulster, but they had become, before 1800, the chief linen merchants as well.

We have seen already that they were in the habit of supplying themselves with brown webs, bleaching on their own account, and selling the finished cloth. Originally the white linen was sent as a rule to Dublin. The bleachers themselves would travel up to Dublin, and would meet the English buyers, or their agents, in the Linen Hall. It has been mentioned that the buyers did not always purchase goods on the spot, but often gave orders in advance. When bleachers took to selling large quantities of their own cloth, and the buyers found themselves dealing directly with manufacturers, it would probably strike both parties as wasteful for them to travel to Dublin for the purpose of giving an order which could equally well be sent by post to the bleachworks in Ulster. In fact it was much better to avoid the Dublin market and to secure the economies of direct trade from the northern ports.

It was probably by some such process as this that the bleachers were first brought into touch with their customers in Great

---

[1] Forty-six dealers in the Linen Hall are mentioned in the Dublin Directory for 1808. A few were bleachers, but most were probably pure traders, although many of them no doubt dealt in other goods besides linen.

Britain. The methods of their trade will be described in a later chapter, dealing with the first quarter of the nineteenth century. It happens that there is a good deal of information on the methods in use in that period, but almost none relating to trade before 1800. We need only notice here that direct export by bleachers was already established in 1776, for Young stated that they regularly allowed seven months' credit for cloth sent to London.[1]

By 1783 export trade had developed so far in Belfast that it was felt to be worth while to build a special hall as a market for white linen. A sum of £10,000 was raised by public sub-scription; a hall was built (on the site of the present City Hall), and was opened with much ceremony in 1785.[2] The new enter-prise was strongly supported by the class of drapers. Their chief interest was to set themselves free from the Dublin factors, and from the necessity of travelling to Dublin with their goods.[3] They hoped, no doubt, to be able to sell their cloth for cash without the charge for interest which was demanded by traders in Dublin; and some of them may have expected to develop an export trade on their own account, dealing directly with buyers from England, and so avoiding the use of factors.

Their hatred of the factors was voiced by Nevill, who had evidently read some of the clothiers' pamphlets, reprinted in Smith's *Memoirs of Wool*; for he compared, with quotations, the drapers' escape from the Dublin factors with that of the woollen clothiers from ' those more than Egyptian taskmasters, the factors of Blackwell Hall '. In both cases one of the main grievances was the practice of advancing ready money at interest. He ended his invective by saying : ' I hope yet to live to see

---

[1] *Tour*, p. 107. Seven months' credit on the part of an Irish trader must have been quite exceptional at this time. Young was writing of the Armagh district, and he probably had in mind a few leading bleachers who had greens by the Bann, and were among the wealthiest men in the linen trade. In evidence given before the House of Commons Committee in 1773 it was mentioned that linens had recently been consigned to a London merchant from Lurgan via Belfast. They were carried from Belfast to London by sea. (*H. of C. Reports*, vol. iii, p. 118.) A large part of the 3,000,000 yards of linen exported from Belfast in that year was probably sold by bleachers.

[2] Horner, p. 74 ; *Select Papers*, p. 30 ; Charley, p. 6 ; Dubourdieu, *Antrim*, ii. 528.

[3] Also, as Nevill pointed out, from deterioration of goods on the journey to Dublin (*Seasonable Remarks*, p. 68).

the name of a linen factor sunk into that of factotum.'[1] The class of factors certainly survived his lifetime, but their trade in Dublin gradually declined, partly through the use of the Belfast Linen Hall and partly because of the growth of export in fulfilment of private contracts without recourse to any open market. Although much linen was still sent to Dublin, even from distant parts of Ulster,[2] either for sale in the southern provinces or for transmission to London, there is no doubt that trade was increasingly diverted to Belfast. It is significant that the amount of linen sent from co. Armagh to Dublin fell rapidly towards the end of the eighteenth century, notwithstanding that Armagh was on the southern edge of the linen-producing district, and had easy access to Dublin. In 1792 the value of linens going from Armagh to the Dublin Linen Hall was nearly £310,000. By 1800 it had sunk to £202,200, and by 1802 to £152,600, less than half the value sold ten years before.[3]

The Hall in Belfast continued in active use for many years, although it came more and more to consist of private warehouses and offices rather than a centre of exchange. Its chief function was always the collection and sorting of packs for transatlantic cargoes.[4] These cargoes were made up in Ireland as ventures ; they were not arranged to the order of customers in America. Therefore a merchant who wished to select a consignment would find it convenient to have before him in one place a large assortment of goods brought by many different bleachers and drapers.

For the English trade, however, more advanced methods soon came into use owing to the rise of bleachers as exporting merchants. The new methods did not involve dealings with the drapers, and in consequence the drapers must have been sorely disappointed with the result of their efforts to found a market for themselves in the north.

The fact that the Hall was largely used for colonial trade helps to explain the slump that occurred in its output in 1816, after a rush of business following the peace with America in

---

[1] *Seasonable Remarks*, pp. 67, 73.
[2] Cf. Corry's *Report* (1816). e. g. seven-eights webs from Omagh, co. Tyrone, and even a large quantity of yard-wides from Belfast, were sent to England via Dublin.   [3] Horner, p. 136.   [4] Charley, p. 6.

THE LINEN HALL, DUBLIN, 1783

THE WHITE LINEN HALL, BELFAST

1814.[1] It also goes far to account for the failure of the Linen Hall in Newry, which was built about the same time as the hall in Belfast ; for although Newry had a fair amount of direct trade with England it would have very little with the United States or the West Indies.[2]

NOTES TO CHAPTER IX

I. *Absentee Landowners*

The effects of absenteeism were more complicated than writers of the eighteenth century believed them to be. Irish economists such as Dobbs,[3] Prior,[4] and Newenham [5] were very much absorbed in studying the balance of trade. It appeared to them that the amount—over half a million pounds a year—paid to landlords living out of Ireland implied a dead loss of capital. Thus Prior in 1729 wrote in the strain of English pamphleteers of the seventeenth century : ' How we have been able hitherto to support all this I leave others to account for . . . it is impossible for us to subsist much longer under such a wasteful drain.' [6] A little later he stated that the export of coin ' must reduce our capital stock to nothing in a little time '.[7]

In actual fact the flow of coin would, of course, be regulated by the state of international trade. Any serious drain would tend to lower prices in Ireland and so to encourage exports, in return for which a stream of coinage would pass back into Ireland. A great part of the rents, however, were paid in kind. The rent agents would no doubt sell the goods to merchants and remit bills to the landlords. The merchants would send

---

[1] See figures given by Charley (u.s.) and in Bradshaw's *Belfast Directory* for 1819.

In 1815 the output was	636 packs		
,, 1816	,,	,,	374 ,,
,, 1817	,,	,,	626 ,,
,, 1818	,,	,,	1,241 ,,

[2] The Newry Hall was soon bought by the Government (as was the Dublin Hall nearly a century later) for use as barracks. Coote, *Survey of Armagh*, p. 342.

[3] *Essay upon the Trade and Improvement of Ireland.*

[4] *Observations on the Trade of Ireland*, and *List of Absentees of Ireland.*

[5] *View of the Natural, Political and Commercial Circumstances of Ireland.*

[6] Prior, *Observations*, p. 291 (in Thom's *Tracts and Treatises*, vol. ii).

[7] ibid., p. 294.

goods to England, so that in the long run the bills would be met by the export of agricultural produce. Therefore to a great extent produce instead of coin would leave the country, and in effect the payment to absentees would be an export of goods without any corresponding import. If the landowners had all lived at home, and invested their rents in local industries, there would have been a great addition to capital in Ireland, and absenteeism would have implied a corresponding loss. But actually a large part of the rents would have been spent in buying commodities from England and abroad. Thus in such cases the main effect of absenteeism would be that the landlord would consume English or foreign goods on the spot instead of having them conveyed to Ireland.[1]

Some writers have held that the chief evil of the absentee system was the indifference of landlords towards their tenants —an interest in the estate and its occupants merely as a source of rents. But in practice many absentee landowners treated their tenants well, gave long leases, and were zealous for improvements,[2] whilst many residents ground the faces of the tenantry and mismanaged their estates. The great evil was the system of tenure, which left the peasants entirely dependent on the will of individual landowners and agents.

II. *Communications by Road*

Since the time of Charles II, at least, road-making had been pursued as a matter of policy : good roads were a help towards efficient administration. The work was done by contract. It was supervised by the grand jurors in each county, who met for administrative purposes after assizes, just as county magistrates in England met after quarter sessions. As contracts were entered in the presentments of grand juries, road-making under this system was known as ' presentment work '. Payment was made from the local rates, or ' county cess', but each barony had to raise enough to pay for its own roads. Seeing that there

---

[1] There might be some further reactions ; for on the one hand the goods coming from England or abroad might have been met by increased exports from Ireland ; or if payment were made in coin there would be a fall in prices and a stimulus to export. But these effects would be complicated by such factors as restrictive policy, and the small range of exportable commodities in Ireland.

[2] Some outstanding examples are given by Young, *Tour*, part II, p. 59.

was no compulsory system of public aid in Ireland, the upkeep of highways was the chief business of grand juries, although they had many minor duties. Some parts of the main roads were taken over by turnpike trusts, and according to Arthur Young were generally neglected.[1] But he held that on the whole Irish highways were much better kept than English; and as he was a connoisseur of roads and had travelled widely in Ireland, we can accept the statement as true. His evidence is borne out by other writers. Wakefield, for example, said that many roads in Ireland were ' as smooth as gravel walks', and well supplied with sign-posts. On some of the main roads a traveller could go ' many miles without experiencing the inconvenience of a rut '. He commended the absence of trees and high hedges by the roadside, ' which in warm countries are considered as an agreeable shelter, but which here would prevent the wind and sun from drying them '.[2] Sampson, in the *Survey of County Londonderry* (pp. 320–3), mentioned the good quality of the roads, and the improvements that were being made at that time· He wrote of the neighbourhood of Kilrea and Magherafelt: ' I have seen no country more intersected with good roads.' One reason for the superiority of Irish roads was the absence of heavy wagons : carts drawn by more than one horse were rare. Carriers going with linen, corn, and dairy produce from small market towns to Dublin, Belfast, or Derry apparently used light vehicles, not the huge wagons drawn by half a dozen horses which were common in England (cf. Young, *Tour*, ii. 39 sqq.).

There was, of course, a considerable waste of money on ' road-jobbing '—more perhaps in the nineteenth century than the eighteenth ; but on the whole the ' presentments ' for road-making seem to have been spent to good purpose.

Services of stage and mail coaches were being organized about the end of the eighteenth century, but coaches were very rare in comparison with those in England, and there were hardly

---

[1] The enclosure of roads by turnpike trusts was resisted in Ireland as it was in Great Britain. There are many references in the *Belfast News Letter* to the work of Levellers in Ulster between 1760 and 1770. But Wakefield said that turnpikes were by no means common in Ireland. Payments of cess for road-making and regulations for the maintenance of roads (e. g. the prohibition of narrow-wheeled carts) were also strongly resented. They were among the grievances of the Hearts of Steel in Ulster.

[2] *Account of Ireland*, vol. ii, pp. 658, 659.

any cross-country services from one provincial town to another. Even from Dublin there were in 1811 only about 20 coaches daily, whereas Brighton at the same time had 29, and London had 1,400.[1] The following lines of coaches were serving Belfast in 1812 :

> To Dublin, one coach daily at 10 a.m., another thrice weekly.
> To Lurgan and Armagh, five times a week.
> To Donaghadee, every evening, with the English and Scottish mails.
> To Londonderry, every afternoon at 4.0 (arriving at 10 a.m.).
> To Coleraine, three mornings a week at 8.0 (arriving in the evening).
> To Larne, thrice weekly at 4 p.m. (arriving at 9 p.m.).
> To Downpatrick, a coach going and returning daily.
> To Lisburn, a coach going and returning daily.
> (Dubourdieu, *Antrim*, ii. 328.)

These coaches may have been of considerable use to drapers and linen merchants. But some, having dispatched their cloth by carrier's cart, preferred to ride on horseback, even for long distances. For instance, William Coulson, the damask manufacturer, added to his fame when he was an old man by riding from Lisburn to Dublin in a single day.

---

[1] *Account of Ireland*, vol. i, p. 669.

X

POLICY OF PARLIAMENT AND THE LINEN BOARD, 1765–1800

Political Changes. The last thirty-six years of the eighteenth century were a period of great importance in Irish political and social history, a period of emancipation and of active legislation. Most of the penal laws were repealed. In particular, long leases of land were allowed to Catholics ; and as these leases, from 1793 onwards, carried with them a parliamentary franchise, the power of granting them was used to a considerable extent by landowners. In 1782 the Irish Parliament itself was set free from the veto of English ministries, which had been in force since 1719. Before this political restraint was removed, a series of economic measures had done away with nearly all the undue restrictions on Irish trade. Already in 1759 the Cattle Acts had been repealed. During the next ten years free export of beef, butter, and bacon was allowed.[1] In 1779 and 1780 freedom was extended to the export of several manufactures, notably woollen goods, as the result of an agitation led in England by Rockingham, and in Ireland by several prominent statesmen and officials.[2] Politicians and traders alike made active use of their freedom. Bounties and grants were offered by the Irish Parliament for the encouragement of many industries and of overseas trade. By Foster's Corn Law of 1784[3] similar bounties were given for the export of agricultural produce in times of good harvest. The grant, made in 1795, of £96,000 for the promotion of textile and metal manufactures,[4] and the present of

---

[1] These two measures had the curious result of stirring up jealousy between dealers in meat and dealers in cattle. Drovers who were taking cattle to the coast towns for export were attacked by mobs, led presumably by butchers. Consequently the cattle had to be taken to northern ports, where the main interest was not in meat or dairy produce, but in linen (Stephenson, *Letter to Trustees*, 1789, p. 19).

[2] These reforms were effected by the statutes 20 Geo. III, cc. 10 and 18 (Brit.).

[3] 23 & 24 Geo. III, c. 19.

[4] 25 Geo. III, c. 48.

£25,000 to a single firm of cotton spinners,[1] are typical of the new spirit in Irish politics.   Other signs of the same impulse were the foundation of the Bank of Ireland in 1783,[2] the formation of a separate Post Office in the following year,[3] and the improvement of harbours, which brought so much benefit to trade in Ulster.[4]

Increased Prosperity.   Moreover, this activity on the part of the Government was matched by an actual increase of industry. There was, as we have seen, a great rise in the export of linens between 1780 and 1795.   Woollen exports, or more accurately, those recognized by the law, grew from something quite insignificant in 1779 to 800,000 yards in 1784.[5]   Cotton manufacture was springing up rapidly in several parts of Ireland. Trade in agricultural produce was also making good progress.

Economic advance in Ireland was for a time so striking that certain commercial groups in England took alarm.   The Chamber of Manufactures, which included some of the leading figures in British industry, made loud and ungenerous protests against the freedom of the Irish government.   It was feared that Irish industry, with the help of cheap labour, substantial bounties and protective duties, would soon advance so far as to do serious damage to trade in Great Britain, and would draw capital and enterprise away from the mother country.   There seemed at the time to be some reason for these fears.   Irish trade was progressing ;   protective duties were being levied ;   bounties were being paid ;   labour was distinctly cheaper in Ireland ;   and some capital had actually migrated.   Several important firms in the linen trade, such as those of Sidebotham, Coulson, Richardson, Barbour, and Cruikshank, were founded with money brought from Great Britain.   Some cotton manufacturers had followed suit, and English capital had been invested in Irish banking and Irish land.   Policy before 1779 had unduly favoured British producers, as against the Irish.   Now it seemed likely that the position would be reversed.   Pitt's attempt, in the

---

[1] 23 & 24 Geo. III, c. 12.   The grant was made for Brooke's undertaking at Prosperous, which is described below, Chap. XII, p. 230.
[2] The original Bank Act was 21 & 22 Geo. III, c. 16.
[3] 23 & 24 Geo. III, c. 17.
[4] 25 Geo. III, c. 11.   An Act for cleansing the Ports, Harbours, and Rivers, &c.   [5] Murray, op. cit., p. 269.

Commercial Propositions of 1785, to frame a compromise between the interests of the two countries, had failed. Therefore the Irish government was left with the power of shaping its own economic policy, and the desire of the Chamber of Manufactures for equal commercial laws throughout the British Isles became a strong force in favour of a parliamentary union.

Before long—even before the Union—there were signs that Irish competition would not be formidable. England had a very long lead in respect of capital, credit, and commercial organization, and the introduction of steam power gave her a still greater advantage. The metal, glass, and pottery trades in Ireland never had more than a trifling development. The woollen manufacture very soon shrank in face of the competition of English and Scottish mills.[1] The cotton manufacture gave greater promise, but it never made any approach to rivalry with the industrial centres of Lancashire and Lanark. The silk industry was always a small affair, confined to the neighbourhood of Dublin.

These limitations, however, were not so clear before 1800 as they are to-day. At that time it seemed quite possible that Ireland might become a great manufacturing country, and there could be no question that the Government was working towards this end. ' Parliamentary Colbertism ' had become as strong a force in Ireland as in any country of Europe.

If we were dealing with the general economic history of Ireland in this period, it would be necessary to follow in detail the movements which have been outlined here.[2] But these changes in domestic policy and international relations probably affected the linen trade less than any other. The removal of commercial restraints could have little direct influence, for the import of Irish linens into Great Britain had been free, with slight exceptions, since 1696. Nor was encouragement by means of protective duties, grants, and premiums a new thing : it had been in progress throughout the eighteenth century. Therefore it is enough for our purpose merely to understand

---

[1] From 1785 to 1791 the export was fairly stable, nearly always between 300,000 and 400,000 yards in a year. Then there was a rapid fall, and by 1799 the export was only 35,000 yards.

[2] Some further discussion of the ' commercial restraints ' is given in the note at the end of this chapter.

the outlook and aims of the Irish government, and to see how their treatment of the linen industry was connected with their general policy. Perhaps the shortest and clearest statement of this relationship would be that from 1779 onwards the governments of Great Britain extended to Irish trade as a whole the policy which had long been applied to the linen trade. The widening of governmental interest in economic affairs by no means caused Parliament to neglect the leading manufacture, for more than twenty statutes relating to the linen industry were passed between 1780 and 1800. But in order to gain a proper view of these measures we must return to the point at which our survey of policy was broken off.

Slackness of Trustees. After their great effort in passing the regulating act of 1764, both Parliament and the Trustees rested for a time from their labours. During the next sixteen years only three minor acts were passed, dealing with matters of detail, such as the easier transference of land which was to be used for manufacture or bleaching. The Trustees, having set up the new system of inspection in brown linen markets, appointed a large number of sealmasters, and sanctioned Stephenson's schemes for 'premium markets' and the saving of flaxseed at home, began to lose interest in their duties. They relapsed into many of the bad habits for which they had been severely criticized a few years earlier. Their attendance became very irregular; their finances fell into confusion; lavish grants were made without due inquiry; large sums were entrusted to officials, who were seldom called upon to account for them. Even the crisis of 1773 made little impression on them. They made no move until a group of merchants in London asked them to send witnesses to appear before the parliamentary committee of inquiry. At first the Trustees nominated two Dublin merchants, Stephenson and Carleton, as their representatives. But after a few days, at the request of the northern drapers, Carleton was replaced by Henry Betty, of Lisburn, who had had a large share in drafting the Act of 1764. The Board provided them with a few historical documents, some rather shallow arguments, and £100 each for their journey.[1]

[1] *Proceedings*, 1773, pp. 1-3, 10-11, 21, 27-30, 38-9. In this year the Board held few meetings and did very little business.

But apart from this deputation no attempt was made to understand or relieve the depression in trade.

The slackness of the Trustees at this time must have led to a great waste of their funds, but perhaps its worst result was the effect on their officials. The cost of the Linen Office,[1] the Linen Hall, and the head-quarters staff was always a heavy drain on the Board's revenue. For instance, in the year ending 25 March, 1786, the expense of central administration was approximately as follows : [2]

	£
Paid to Architect (fees, and contracts for alterations and repairs)	5,000
Legal expenses (prosecutions, law officer's fees, &c.)	3,000
Head-quarters Staff and London Agent . .	1,400
Stationery	600
Rent and taxes	300

Three years earlier there had been a stringent reduction of costs ; therefore it is highly probable that the corresponding expenditure between 1764 and 1782 was even greater. These were largely ' overhead ' charges, which did not directly benefit the trade. Moreover, the drapers and factors who used the Linen Hall paid no fees, so that the cost of upkeep was a dead-weight on the funds of the Board. Thus there was every reason for economy in administration, but before 1782 there was hardly any attempt at economy. The architect's accounts were accepted year by year without comment. Large perquisites were allowed to the chief officials. Three or four of them had free houses and coals. When utensils were distributed, they received a generous grant : the Secretary's share was worth £50 or £60 a year. The Chamberlain had both a house rent-free and an allowance of £40 for rent.[3] The Secretary received an annual bonus which more than doubled his salary.[4] There were other additions in the form of travelling expenses and extra payment for special work. But, above all, the disbursement of over £20,000 a year was left to

[1] i. e. the Secretary's department. The market and warehouse accommodation was in charge of the Chamberlain.

[2] Stephenson, *Letter to the Trustees*, 1789, p. 6. These expenses would amount to nearly half the Board's revenue for the year.

[3] *Proceedings*, 1782, p. 184.

[4] His salary was £200 a year, his gratuity was generally between £225 and £250.

the Secretary and Chief Inspector. Like Paymasters-General in England, they controlled large sums which they were not obliged to spend at once. They knew that if the money were spent according to the Board's directions much of it would be wasted. They knew also that the Board was very unlikely to ask whether its orders had been fulfilled or not. There was every inducement to slackness, and an easy opening for dishonesty.

In 1773, after an interval of nearly twenty years, a committee was appointed to examine into the accounts.[1] The reason of this appointment may have been that Stephenson, in preparing his evidence for the inquiry in London, had found a recurrence of the faults which he had laid bare in his report of 1755.[2] The committee certainly discovered that all the Board's affairs were once more in the utmost confusion. There was no annual balancing of accounts. The payment of grants and premiums was constantly in arrears, and when payment was made no receipts were kept. The Secretary had incurred a debt to the Board of over £2,600. He was not yet accused of dishonesty, and the Trustees contented themselves with a resolution that no money should be voted for grants in any session until the last year's grants had been fully paid.

Eight years later there was a fresh inquiry into the state of the linen trade by a committee of the Irish House of Commons. Evidence given before the committee showed that both the late Secretary, Broghill Newburgh, and his successor, Henry Archdall, had misappropriated large sums. Archdall, who had been responsible for the cutting and distribution of brown and white seals, had added substantially to his income by charging much more than the statutory price.[3] This fact throws light on the remarkably free issue of seals after 1764. It was to the

---

[1] *Proceedings*, 1773, pp. 15–19. Stephenson said that a committee was appointed in 1771 to inquire into the Board's expenditure (*Observations*, 1784, p. vii). But as I have found no other mention of a committee in this year, and as Stephenson did not allude to the committee of 1773, he apparently made a mistake in the date.

[2] Stephenson was appointed early in April, but he did not go to London until November. The Committee also brought in their report in November, so that there was ample time for both Stephenson and the committee to examine the Board's accounts. The Chairman of the Committee was David Latouche, the banker, who became Treasurer to the Trustees.

[3] *Commons Journals*, 1779–82, pp. 320–1, and Appendix, p. ccccxix.

interest of every weaver to have a brown seal, and of every small draper to have a white seal, and they were prepared to pay something extra for the privilege. Archdall traded on their willingness to pay, and reduced the system of inspection to an absurdity for the benefit of his own pocket. Both officials were prosecuted : both went bankrupt, and litigation about their debts continued for more than a quarter of a century.[1] A good deal of the blame for this calamity must rest with the Trustees, whose carelessness exposed their servants to a very strong temptation.

Change of Policy. The period of slackness came to an end about the year 1779. At that time the interest of many Trustees, and other members of Parliament, in Irish trade was quickened by the negotiations for increased freedom of trade with England. Another source of energy was the addition to the Board of a man of strong and active public spirit, John Foster, son of the former legal adviser to the Trustees.[2] As the ground landlord of an important manufacturing centre, Collon, co. Louth, he had a personal interest in the linen trade. He was also, like his father, a keen agriculturist ; indeed, he is chiefly remembered as the author of the important Corn Law of 1784. He had a seat in the House of Commons, and became one of the most prominent figures in Grattan's Parliament. His presence among the Trustees undoubtedly gave a new vigour to their policy.

It has been mentioned that the reforms of 1779 affected the linen and hempen industries less than many others. But there were two reforms which directly concerned the Linen Board and roused it to fresh activity. In the first place, the prohibitive duties levied in Great Britain on coloured, striped, checked, and

---

[1] *Proceedings*, 1808, pp. 49–51. James Corry (father of the Secretary to the Linen Board) was one of the assignees for Newburgh's property (*Proc.*, 1782, p. 232), and his death seems to have caused fresh legal complications.
[2] Corry, *Report*, 1822, p. 12. He was thirty-nine years of age at this time, and he had been in Parliament for ten years. In 1784 he became Chancellor of the Exchequer, and in 1785 was elected Speaker, in succession to Pery. He was a strong ministerialist, and resisted the measures for relief of Catholics in 1793 ; but he was also an opponent of the legislative union. Nevertheless he consented to sit in the British Parliament, and was made Chancellor of the Exchequer for Ireland in 1804. In 1821 he was raised to a peerage of the United Kingdom, and took the title of Lord Oriel. In his old age he still kept up a connexion with the Linen Board by means of correspondence. He died in 1828, the year of the Board's dissolution. (See *Dict. of Nat. Biogr.*)

printed linens from Ireland, were removed.[1] Secondly, Irish shippers were admitted on more generous terms to foreign and colonial trade. The Navigation Acts had already been modified to some extent, and their force had been largely defeated by smuggling ; but it was a great advantage, on moral, political and fiscal grounds, that the traffic which had been contraband should be made legitimate.

Printed Linens. In regard to printed and dyed linens, their free export had been urged by the Trustees as early as 1719,[2] and the demand was pressed sixty years later by the Irish Lord Chancellor and others.[3] When freedom of export was allowed, the Trustees gave their support to the manufacturers by means of special grants, and premiums for the production of dyestuffs.[4] The result was rather disappointing, but hardly surprising. Although linen printing was an established industry in Ireland, coloured cloths found only a very small market overseas. The reason was, no doubt, that in Great Britain machine printing, with cylinders, had come into common use, whereas the work was still done in Ireland on a small scale, by hand. It was not until printing and dyeing were taken up by bleachers and large manufacturers, towards the middle of the nineteenth century, that the export trade in coloured linen made any substantial progress.

Bounties for export of Linen and Sail Cloth. The second political change of this period, the freedom of foreign and colonial trade, led to a fresh scheme of bounties for linen goods. Linen was the chief article of export from Ireland, both to Great Britain and to other countries. Therefore if a large foreign trade from Ireland were to be developed the linen merchants

---

[1] The duties had been imposed in 1711 (10 Anne, c. 19, Brit.).

[2] A copy of the petition of 1719 was supplied to Stephenson and Betty to support their evidence (*Proceedings*, 1773, pp. 38, 39).

[3] Official Papers, 1760–89, 236/2, summary by Lord Chancellor Lifford.

[4] e. g. the bounty paid for export of coloured linens was only £33 in 1780-1, and £8 in 1783–4. In the years 1801–3, when the average export from Ireland of plain linens was nearly 36,000,000 yards, the amounts of coloured and printed cloth exported were :

1801	.	.	.	142,853
1802	.	.	.	128,879
1803	.	.	.	137,489

Account of Irish Linen Exported, Parliamentary Papers, 1803-4, no. 186.)

must be chiefly responsible for its success. For their encouragement bounties were offered, varying from ½d. to 1½d. a yard,
for exported linens, up to the value of 1s. 6d. a yard.[1] These
bounties were payable only for the coarser kinds of cloth, partly
because the scheme in Great Britain was limited in the same
way, and partly because coarse linen was likely to be in greatest
demand. In normal times a considerable amount of fine linen
was sent to North America, usually by way of Liverpool. But
Spain and Portugal seemed to offer a more hopeful field for direct
export than the distant and uncertain markets across the
Atlantic. The exploitation of Spanish trade was being actively
discussed about the year 1780, and it was well known that coarse
cloths, similar to the 'Germany narrows', would have the
largest sales in Spain.

At the same time a bounty was offered for the export of sail
cloth. An attempt made in 1745 to give bounties for Irish
sail cloth had come to grief. The British Parliament played a
counter-stroke in 1750 by levying import duties equal to the
bounties paid in Ireland.[2] Seeing that nearly all the sail cloth
sent out of Ireland would have to go to Great Britain, the
bounties were dropped, and the import duties were withdrawn
as well.[3] But the position in 1780 was different. The bounty,
of about 1d. a yard, was confined to sail cloth exported to places
outside the British Isles, and as this measure did not invite any
serious rivalry with British manufacture it was not opposed
in England.

An attempt was also made to promote the supply of raw
material by giving premiums for the cultivation of hemp, and
for the export of hemp to Great Britain. These offers, however,
met with very little response.[4]

---

[1] 19 & 20 Geo. III, c. 33.

[2] The principle involved was no doubt that in time of war Great Britain
should be as nearly self-supporting as possible in the matter of naval stores.
Reliance on Ireland was not to be encouraged because a naval war would
always disorganize the cross-channel traffic. There would also be an outcry
from British manufacturers against a bounty-fed rival.

[3] The bounties were offered under 19 Geo. II, c. 6 (Irish) : the duties were
imposed under 23 Geo. II, c. 33 (Brit.).

[4] Stephenson pointed out (*Letter to Trustees*, 1789, p. 10) that even with the
help of the premiums hemp growing in Ireland would not pay, except now and
then on rough ground as a preparation for superior crops. Hemp was used for
this purpose in England. Stephenson's statement is borne out by the fact
that in 1808, when there was a shortage of foreign hemp, only 525 (statute)

Effect of Bounties. The bounties for linen and sail cloth were renewed from time to time. They continued through the remainder of the eighteenth century and the first quarter of the nineteenth. But it cannot be said that they had any satisfactory result. We have seen already that neither the Spanish nor the transatlantic trade flourished during the period of the bounties, and we have noticed some of the difficulties which prevented the growth of direct export. An actual instance of transatlantic trade, taken from the nineteenth century, will throw further light on these difficulties.

The firm of J. & J. Richardson, whose business is described in Chapter XIII, made an effort, after the end of the American and French wars, to restore their trade with the United States and the West Indies. For several years they sent cargoes of linen to Jamaica and to various ports on the mainland, and they received the premium due for each consignment. It is interesting to see how the system of bounties affected their enterprise. In 1819, when they consigned £545 worth of goods to Jamaica, bounty was paid on £300 worth. Its amount was £8 9s. 5d., about 1·5 per cent. of the total outlay, and little more than half the cost of insurance. Their bounties for American trade were even smaller. The following figures are taken from three successive 'American Consignment' accounts. They show the extent of the bounty, and the net loss on each venture, when the bounties have been added to other receipts :

Loss.			Bounty.		
£	s.	d.	£	s.	d.
275	2	8	7	6	1
191	3	7	3	2	2
107	8	0		Nil.	

A gain of £10 8s. 3d. is to be set against a loss of nearly £600. Although the firm would be glad enough to reduce their losses by £10 at the public expense, we cannot imagine that this payment would have the effect, desired by the Government, of stimulating them to send larger amounts of linen to America. The Richardsons seem to have fared exceptionally badly because they dealt largely in fine qualities of linen, whereas the bounties

acres were sown with hempseed in Ireland (*Proceedings,* 1808, App. III). Notwithstanding their small effect, bounties of various kinds for hemp cultivation were continued for more than forty years.

were paid for coarser qualities of cloth. Statistics for the whole of Ireland during the first quarter of the nineteenth century show that the bounties were on an average from three to five per cent. of the total value of the exports.[1] But these subsidies were no guarantee against loss ; and it is not surprising that Irish traders were unwilling to risk more than a small part of their stock in the speculative undertakings for which bounties were paid. There was a much greater chance of profit in the regular lines of trade, through London, Bristol, and Liverpool.[2]

Saving of Flaxseed. Discussion of the bounty system has taken us beyond the chronological limit of this chapter, and we must return to the events of 1780. At that time the War of American Independence was seriously impeding both English and Irish trade. The linen trade was affected not only by the loss of an important market but also by a shortage of raw material, for in normal years a great part of the supply of flaxseed came from America. The amount of flax available in Ireland had probably fallen off during the war ; English and Scottish manufacturers were making large purchases of Irish yarn, no doubt at a very high price ; [3] and it will be remembered that the output of linen in Ireland was less in 1780 than it had been at any time in the previous fifteen years. The question of flax supply was considered in Parliament, and it was resolved to stimulate as far as possible the saving of seed and the growth of flax at home. By the statute of 1780, which established the bounties for direct export, two further grants were made to the Linen Board. The first grant, of £7,250, was to encourage the saving of seed ; the other, of £7,000, was to be spent in premiums for flax grown from Irish seed.

This was a reversal of policy. Stephenson's bounties for home-saved seed had been abandoned before 1773, and the earlier practice of paying premiums for imported seed was revived. Now there was yet another change, and bounties similar to Stephenson's were set in operation again. Some such

---

[1] See table given by Horner, op. cit., p. 77. The percentage varied from year to year according to the proportions of fine and coarse cloth exported.
[2] There was the further inducement that bounty could be claimed on cloth exported from England.
[3] The export of Irish yarn (largely to Great Britain) reached its maximum (42,370 cwts.) in 1779–80 ; and it was very high (37,202 cwts.) in 1780–1.

policy was necessary in war-time, when foreign supplies were cut off : it was adopted during the Napoleonic War, and once more during the recent war. But the statute of 1780 was not meant to be only an emergency measure, for the bounties were continued for several years after the return of peace.[1] They were abandoned, however, in 1791.[2] Apparently the Trustees had become convinced that it was useless to expect any great proportion of the flaxseed sown in Ireland to be produced at home. Stephenson himself, the author of this system of bounties, had turned against it. Experience had taught him that foreign seed was cheaper and more satisfactory than Irish, and he told the Trustees that their large expenditure on home-grown seed was a pure waste of money.[3] It was probably his advice that persuaded the Trustees to bring this costly experiment to an end.

Regulating Act of 1782. The bounties devised in 1780 had no appreciable effect. But the renewed interest in the linen trade had a more important outcome—a fresh regulating act, passed in 1782.[4] This measure was drafted by Foster : it was known among the Trustees as ' Mr. Foster's Act ', and it certainly owed a great deal to his enterprise and reforming spirit. Its character, however, was decided by a parliamentary committee, which issued a report early in the same year. There were several reasons for the appointment of this committee. It was felt to be appropriate, at the beginning of a new era of economic freedom, that the linen industry should be put under the best possible regulation. The cases of Newburgh and Archdall had recently shown how lightly the Trustees had been taking their responsibility. Inspection of linen, both brown and white, had become a formality. It served, not as a guarantee of quality and measurement, but merely as a source of revenue to Archdall and a swarm of sealmasters. The bleachers were urging, as they had done twenty years earlier, that the system of sealing should be made really effective. It is also highly probable that some of them were anxious to repeal the law against bleaching

[1] They were renewed for two years in 1781 and again in 1783, and afterwards for a year at a time.

[2] Or rather, the grant of £7,250 was absorbed in the general revenue of the Board.

[3] *Letter to the Trustees*, 1789, p. 8.   [4] 21 & 22 Geo. III, c. 35.

with lime. Their influence is shown in the fact that nearly all the witnesses summoned before the committee were bleachers, and in the substance of the statute, which in most respects was clearly designed for their benefit.[1]

Regulations for Lappers of White Linen. The statute, like that of 1764, was a long and comprehensive measure. Its most important clauses dealt with the inspection of linen. All seals, brown and white alike, were to be surrendered by 1 August, 1782.[2] New seals would then be issued on certain conditions, and the terms laid down for holders of white seals were very strict. Each applicant must offer security of £200 on his own account, and must name two other guarantors of the same amount. All bleachers were to be registered in a list kept in the Linen Office, and no cloth was to be sealed for any one except a registered bleacher.[3] Heavy fines were imposed for violations of the rules for sealing. Every lapper was to promise on oath that he would obey all the regulations and orders of the Trustees.

Inspection of Brown Linen Markets. Sealmasters of brown linen also came under a stricter regulation. Until this time, sealmasters had worked on their own responsibility. If they transgressed, by sealing webs of short measure or poor quality, it was left to private informers to secure their conviction and punishment. Now, in order to prevent ' frauds in the sale of brown linens, whereby bleachers and drapers are often imposed on ', inspectors were to be appointed to supervise the whole system of sealing. Each inspector had charge of the markets in a county, or a group of counties. The inspectors themselves were put under the control of two inspectors-general, one for Ulster and one for the other provinces.[4] The chief duty of

---

[1] The bill was presented on 8 March, and discussed simultaneously by Parliament and the Trustees. It followed very closely the committee's recommendations (*Proceedings*, 1782, pp. 36–8).

[2] An order to this effect was issued by the Board on 20 March (ibid., p. 42).

[3] The register was drawn up on 1 May, 1782 (ibid., p. 43).

[4] The law provided either for one Inspector-General for the whole country, or for one official for Ulster, and one for the other province. The Board adopted the second alternative. John Greer, of Lurgan, was the first Inspector-General for Ulster, John Arbuthnot the first for the rest of Ireland. Two additional officers were soon added, one for each section. By a statute of 1804 (44 Geo. III, c. 69) the Trustees were allowed to appoint a Chief Inspector for the whole country, and two Provincial Inspectors. Charles Duffin, who had served in the southern provinces, was promoted to this post, and he was

county inspectors was to visit the markets, intervene if disputes should arise, and report faults in sealing to a magistrate, who had power to decide the case summarily and inflict a fine. The Act did not prescribe any use for the fines, but in practice they went either to the inspectors, or to deputy-inspectors.[1] Other duties of the inspectors were to make monthly returns to the Linen Office of the volume of trade in their markets, and annual returns of the flax crops in their counties. The method of appointing inspectors was significant. They were nominated by the registered bleachers. In each county or district the bleachers chose three candidates, and the final selection was made by the Linen Board. The bleachers had always had a great interest in the system of sealing. But the Act of 1764 was not quite satisfactory to them. It left them responsible, when the cloth which they had bought proved to be defective, for finding out the offending sealmasters and reporting the case to a magistrate ; and the increasing number of sealmasters made the position still more difficult. Under the terms of the new statute, this work was to be done for them at the public expense. Thus the appointment of inspectors was distinctly to the advantage of the bleachers, and of drapers as well.

Bleaching with Lime. Another part of the Act was much less welcome to the bleachers. The first two clauses reasserted the old rules against bleaching with lime, and gave to inspectors and Trustees a right of entry into bleachworks, in order that they might search suspected premises for lime. In a later clause the Linen Board was authorized to spend £4,000 a year in premiums for the production of ashes. It was believed that an abundant supply of potash and other salts, obtained by kelp-burning, would take away the temptation to use the alternative reagent, lime.[2]

joined after a few years by his son. When Duffin resigned, in 1810, because he was found to have misappropriated the Board's funds, his post was abolished. From this time until 1828 there were two Inspector-Generals in the south and one in Ulster.

[1] As the county inspectors could not attend all the markets, they were allowed to appoint their own deputies.

[2] The full title of this statute was : ' An Act for Prohibiting the Use of Lime in Bleaching, regulating Sealmasters of Linens, encouraging the home Manufacture of Ashes for Bleachers' Use, enlarging and rendering more commodious the Linen Hall in the City of Dublin, and other Purposes therein mentioned.'

There lay behind these clauses a long history, of which only a slight indication need be given here, because most of the detail belongs to the technique of bleaching. It will be remembered that lime had been banned in the very first linen law of the eighteenth century, and the prohibition had been renewed several times. One of the renewals was in the Act of 1764. It happened that experiments in bleaching were being made at that time by Dr. Ferguson, in Belfast. He was impressed with the fact that certain compounds made from lime, when properly used, were safe, effective, and economical.[1] His discoveries were made known to bleachers in the district—among others to John Williamson of Lambeg, who had been mainly responsible for the new statute. According to this Act, lime might be used to a limited extent with the approval in each instance of five or more Trustees. Williamson applied to the Board for a licence, and was given leave to bleach 160 pieces with lime, on condition that he should report the result.[2] But soon demands for licences began to pour into the Linen Office, and the Board scented danger. A committee appointed to deal with the applications suggested that no firm should be allowed to bleach more than ten pieces with lime, and that every piece should be officially marked in advance. Accordingly, leave was given to nine firms, including Williamson's, to bleach not more than ten pieces each.[3] Williamson's earlier licence was superseded and he naturally protested against this violation of the Board's promise to him. In a short time his protests led to a personal quarrel. The Board resolved that as he had written an insolent letter to one of its members, his licence should be cancelled altogether until he had made submission.[4] But Williamson, as we have seen, preferred exile to surrender. He handed over his business to his sons, and went to live in London. This was not quite the end of his connexion with the linen laws. As late as 1779 he sent a petition, this time to Parliament, asking that the prohibition of lime in Ireland might be removed.[5] The question was discussed by the committee which prepared the Act of 1782.[6] Stephenson and others spoke in favour of lime-bleaching, and

---

[1] McCall, p. 23.   [2] *Proceedings*, 1764, p. 53.
[3] ibid., pp. 117, 161–3.   [4] ibid., p. 180, 8 March, 1765.
[5] *Commons Journals*, 1779–82, App., pp. ccccxxix-ccccxxx.   [6] ibid.

pointed out that it was regularly and freely practised in England and Scotland. On the other hand, much evidence was offered of damage to cloth, which was alleged to have been caused by lime. The committee were strongly impressed with this evidence, since it agreed with their own prejudices. They reported that although lime appeared to be of some use in bleaching, it had serious disadvantages. Therefore they recommended that the prohibition should remain, and Parliament acted on their advice.[1]

The bleachers were not able to repeal the law against the use of lime ; but fortunately they proved to have enough influence to prevent the law from being enforced.[2] If it had not been so, the bleaching industry in Ireland would soon have collapsed.

Regulations for Trustees. The other chief subject of legislation was the conduct of the Trustees. It was provided that they must meet regularly in future, on the first Tuesday in every month, and at certain other stated times. Money was only to be voted at monthly meetings, and at these meetings there had to be a quorum of twelve. Members of the Board who failed to attend any meetings for a year, and could offer no good excuse, were to be removed from office. To prevent a recurrence of the fraud and waste of earlier years an audit was prescribed, to take place every six months, and the Trustees were forbidden to spend more than £3,000 a year on looms, spinning-wheels, or other utensils.

These measures, and the public inquiry which preceded them, had an immediate, though not an enduring, effect on the Trustees. Their meetings became more frequent. Whereas in earlier years they had met very seldom between May and October, some attempt was made from this time to keep the Board in active being throughout the year.[3] Members who failed to attend were duly struck off the list : in some years more than twenty names were removed. But at this rate the Board would have shrunk before long to a small committee, and the rule

---

[1] *Commons Journals*, 1779-82, p. 320.

[2] e. g. thirteen years later the Inspector-General complained about lime bleaching in Cork (*Proceedings*, 1795, p. 119).

[3] The chief officials had sometimes had several months' leave of absence during the summer.

A BLEACH-GREEN IN COUNTY DOWN, 1783

was perforce relaxed. Minute books of the early nineteenth century show that almost any excuse was accepted. Apparently a Trustee was sure of his position so long as he took the trouble to send a letter of apology once a year.[1]

The Board's financial methods underwent a similar change. Accounts were duly audited, and in June 1782 the whole system of administration was reformed. The officials lost many of their needles perquisites, and the headquarters staff of twenty-four was reduced to fourteen.[2] The spirit of retrenchment, however, did not last long. Indeed, Parliament itself, while preaching economy in some directions, was urging expenditure in others, such as the inspection of markets, and the useless schemes of bounties for flax, hemp, and ashes. It is hardly surprising that the Trustees should follow suit. They soon began to vote more than the prescribed £3,000 for utensils, and they were induced to spend large sums, as they had often done before, on specious projects, which brought no return. For instance, in their zeal to prevent lime-bleaching by increasing the supply of ashes, they wasted much money in wild schemes for burning potato-stalks, hay, rape, and all manner of weeds. An adventurer named Clarke proposed to them a plan for mixing ashes and lime into a kind of mortar, which, as Stephenson said, might have made a good manure, but proved to be of no value for bleaching. The Board resolved in 1783 to spend a sum not exceeding £700 on his project; but by 1785 they had given him more than £5,000.[3] Parliament had not succeeded in bringing about any improvement in the methods of the Trustees. When we come to deal with their work in the nineteenth century we shall find that the same methods continued to the end.

Opposition of Drapers. In another respect the Act of 1782 failed to carry out the purpose of its authors. The new rules for lappers of white linen were strongly resented by the whole class of drapers. At the beginning of May, when the old seals

---

[1] The Act of Union made attendance more difficult : as long as there was a Parliament in Dublin the meetings of Trustees were most frequent, and there was the fullest attendance, while Parliament was in session.

[2] It was probably no more than a coincidence that these changes occurred at the same time as the 'economical reform' preached by Burke and undertaken by Rockingham.

[3] Stephenson, *Letter to the Trustees*, 1789, pp. 6, 11, 13.

were called in, it was announced that the revised regulations would be strictly enforced.[1] During the summer, meetings of drapers were held in various parts of Ulster, and several petitions against the regulations were sent to Parliament.[2] The answer was a fresh announcement by the Board, on 23 July, that the law must be observed.[3] This measure only urged the drapers to more decisive action. At a mass meeting, held in Armagh on 5 August, a declaration was drawn up stating that the signatories would buy no more brown linen until the new restrictions were repealed. The document was signed by 437 drapers —quite half the total number in Ulster—and there can be no doubt that the whole body of drapers were unanimous in their opposition.[4] The main stumbling-block was the oath to obey all the linen laws and all instructions of the Linen Board. It was pointed out that every draper taking such an oath would be guilty of perjury. Yarn was not reeled according to law ; cloth was not of statutory breadth ; bleachers had every intention of using lime ; and drapers could not undertake to seal always in their own premises.

The declaration was sent to the Linen Board, and with it went a letter from the Inspector-General for Ulster, pointing out the danger of the position.[5] At length the Board came to terms. The drapers had no need to resort to violence, as the weavers had done twenty years earlier : their threat to paralyse the whole trade was enough. The Trustees met in haste and sent an immediate answer.[6] They had found on investigation, they said, that an oath would not be necessary for the holders of white seals ! They promised further to do what they could to have the clauses relating to securities modified. In making this answer they were acting in flat contradiction to the law, and were assuming a power which had been denied even to the Crown since 1689. However, it was certain that if they did not put the law into force no one else would do so. Therefore

[1] *Proceedings*, 1782, pp. 104, 119.
[2] Four of these petitions are mentioned in the *Commons Journals*.
[3] *Proceedings*, 1782, pp. 214–18. The Trustees were acting on a resolution passed by the House of Commons on the previous day (*Commons Journals*, 1779–82, p. 320).
[4] ibid., p. 226 ; McCall, pp. 23, 24.   [5] *Proceedings*, u.s.
[6] The answer was dated 7 August, only two days after the meeting in Armagh.

the outcome of the drapers' resistance was that, as far as the sealing of white linen was concerned, the statute of 1782 became a dead letter.

Inspection Established. The new law failed to alter the habits of Trustees, bleachers or drapers. Its only important effect was to provide a staff of inspectors for brown linen markets. This change was permanent, for as long as the Board existed, that is until 1828, the inspectors continued in office. It seems rather strange at a first glance that their appointment should not be resisted by the weavers, or at least by those who were sealmasters. But in reality the system gave little cause for complaint to the manufacturing classes, and it probably made no difference to most of them. If they had woven or sealed defective cloth, and were fined for the offence, it would not matter to them whether the law was set in motion by an inspector, a bleacher, or a draper. The appointment of inspectors would slightly increase the likelihood of punishment for faults, but this was an improvement on which no protest could be based. The wage-earning weavers, who had had the strongest grievance in 1762, were not affected by the new system. They had no direct concern with sealing. Their main interest was in trade unionism, which was not touched by the statute of 1782. There may have been some alarm among sealmasters when their seals were called in, especially as the Act provided that new seals should only be given to those who were approved by ' the principal drapers and bleachers in their neighbourhood'. But anxiety on this point would soon be allayed, for in practice the seals were dealt out with considerable freedom.[1]

Settlement of Revenue. The statute of 1782 was the last important linen law of the eighteenth century, and it remained in force, or at any rate unrepealed, until 1825. The remaining acts dealt only with matters of detail. The number of inspectors

---

[1] Seals were allotted by a committee of drapers—most of them no doubt bleachers as well—who met once a week for the purpose and continued the work for several weeks. One or two sealmasters in each town agreed to be present at the markets to examine any cloths that had not been stamped. But ' private ' seals were given out so freely that most manufacturers and weavers were able either to stamp the cloth themselves or to have it stamped by a neighbour before it was taken to market. (See Corry, *Report*, 1822, p. 149, quoting a memorial from a meeting of merchants and manufacturers held in Belfast in July, 1821).

was slightly increased on three occasions,[1] and their duties were more strictly defined.[2] In 1784 a fresh set of rules for the reeling of yarn was issued, and the Trustees were ordered to spend £2,000 on the distribution of ' statutable ' reels—a con- fusing measure, and one not likely to give satisfaction, seeing that the custom of the trade had never agreed with legal require- ments.[3] In 1788 the revenue of the Linen Board was settled on what proved to be its final basis. From this time onwards it was a fixed sum of £21,600, recommended each year by the Lord Lieutenant in his speech from the throne, and duly voted by Parliament.[4]

The use of this revenue continued on traditional lines. Premiums were paid for seed and flax, grants were made to individual firms, and every year thousands of implements were distributed. In 1795, after voting £4,000 for wheels and reels and £1,260 for looms, the Trustees suddenly changed their minds. They drew up an elaborate scheme, including premiums

[1] In 1784, 1786, and 1787. The total number of inspectors in 1787 was twenty-eight.

[2] 34 Geo. III, c. 17, an Act for a more effectual redress in cases of fraudulent or damaged linens, and for enforcing County Inspectors to an effectual Execu- tion of their Duty.

[3] 23 & 24 Geo. III, c. 53.

[4] Since 1719 a substantial part of the Board's income had been derived from duties on tea, coffee, and cocoa. There was added in 1723 (10 Geo. I, c. 1) a grant of £2,000 to encourage cultivation of flax and hemp, and ten years later (7 Geo. II, c. 1) another £2,000 to be spent in the southern provinces. These two grants were renewed for short periods, and continued until 1807, when they were merged in the general grant. The revenue from tea grew steadily. In 1766 it reached £15,000 ; but this was more than enough for the Board, and the Government was in great need of money, for it had been unable to balance the budgets since 1759. Therefore the allowance from tea duties was limited to £10,000 (7 Geo. III, c. 2). By an Act of 1780 (19 & 20 Geo. III, c. 33) the sum of £7,250 was voted to encourage the use of home-saved seed. This grant also became part of the permanent revenue. Finally, in 1788 (28 Geo. III, c. 7) the Board's share of coffee duties was reduced to £350. Thus, the regular income was composed as follows :

	£
General grant . .	10,000 (after 1780 paid out of general funds instead of tea duty)
For flax and hemp .	2,000
For southern provinces	2,000
For saving seed . .	7,250
From coffee duty .	350
Total . . .	21,600

In practice the different sections of the revenue were not strictly appro- priated to the uses for which they had been voted.

for hemp, scutching of flax, fine spinning, production of ashes for bleaching, and the manufacture of candlewicks. The expenditure on looms was increased to £1,890—allowing fifteen looms to each Trustee ; and the grant for wheels and reels was reduced to £1,000.[1] The reason of this alteration was probably that there was already a fair amount of spinning in the southern provinces—more than enough to supply the decreasing export trade—and it was thought more important to encourage weaving and other enterprises than to add to the number of spinners. As a matter of fact the new scheme was not important, for the premiums had no appreciable result.[2]

Experiment in Sealing. The only other change of interest before 1800 was an attempt, in 1798, to improve the sealing system still further. Seeing that a large proportion of the brown seals were in the hands of manufacturers, who stamped their own cloth, the addition of a stamp to a web could hardly be said to carry any public guarantee of its quality or dimensions. In order to increase the usefulness of sealing, the Trustees, advised by John Greer, the Inspector-General for Ulster, called in the existing seals, and announced that in future sealing would only be allowed in market towns : no manufacturer might stamp cloth on his own account.[3] At the same time the issue of new seals was begun. Immediately there was a great outcry. Experience had abundantly proved a generation earlier that sealing in market towns alone was not practicable. Weavers could not spare the time for special journeys to the sealmaster's house ; or if the inspection were made on the market day it would be so hurried as to lose all its value. A large proportion of the cloth would probably be sold and taken away unsealed. Moreover, the manufacturers—many of them quite large employers —resented the idea that they could not be trusted to examine and guarantee their own cloth.

Once more the Board gave way. In 1799 the regulations of the previous year were cancelled, and yet another issue of seals of a new pattern was ordered. Old seals, however, came

---

[1] *Proceedings*, 1795, pp. 56, 57, 69–72.
[2] But there was some sense in increasing the number of looms, for the export trade in linen cloth was exceptionally large at this time.
[3] Corry, *Report*, 1822, pp. 16–18.

in slowly, the distribution of new seals was still more gradual, and it was badly organized.[1] Consequently the system of inspecting brown linen was in a state of confusion at the end of the eighteenth century.

NOTE TO CHAPTER X

It is beside the purpose of this chapter to discuss in detail the effect of the restrictions on Irish trade or the circumstances of their repeal, although some of the events, such as the famous parade of Volunteers before the statue of King William, the impassioned debates in the Irish Parliament, and the refusal, or partial refusal, of supplies, are of great interest. But it may not be inappropriate to mention a few facts which illustrate the economic state of Ireland about the year 1780.

The most instructive documents connected with the movement for freedom of trade are the eleven letters written in 1779 to Buckingham, the Lord Lieutenant, by various prominent Irishmen.[2] Rockingham, in the English House of Lords, had

---

[1] Corry, *Report*, 1822, p. 149.

[2] The writers were : Sir Lucius O'Brien, an active member of the Linen Board ; the Lord Chancellor ; Pery, Speaker of the House ; the Archbishop of Armagh, who professed ignorance of economic affairs ; W. Hussey Burgh, the Prime Serjeant, whose speeches in the House of Commons aroused great enthusiasm ; Patterson, the Lord Chief Justice, who would not give a definite opinion ; Lord Annaly ; the Rt. Hon. John Foster ; J. Hely Hutchinson, Provost of Trinity ; and the Commissioners of Revenue (Lord Naas, Lord Clifden, Sir Hercules Langrishe, Monck Mason, and Robert Waller). Hely Hutchinson's letter was the ablest and most interesting. It was an elaborate survey, historical and economic, including the most important features of his book on *Commercial Restraints*, published in the same year.

The original letters, written in May and June, were kept by Buckingham, and preserved among the *Official Papers* in the Dublin Record Office (Series of 1760-89, 236/2). The copy, in the Public Record Office, London, was used by Froude (*English in Ireland*, vol. ii, pp. 241-9). See also Murray, op. cit., pp. 208-10. The copy sent to London was by no means complete. Although it contained a letter from Hood, which was not kept in Dublin, it left out the opinions of the Archbishop of Armagh, the Lord Chief Justice, Foster, and the Commissioners of Revenue. A more important omission was that of the Lord Chancellor's list of recommendations, which is summarized below. His earlier private letter, quoted by Froude, was too vague and cautious to be of any value. Lecky evidently saw the collection in Dublin, for he mentioned Foster's letter, which was not sent to London. He was greatly impressed with the ability of several of the writers, and said quite truly that the letters were ' well worthy of publication ' (*History of Ireland*, ed. of 1892, vol. ii, p. 173).

At the time when this note was written I supposed that Lecky's suggestion could never be carried out, for the original letters were destroyed very soon

secured the promise of an inquiry into the condition of Ireland. The Lord Lieutenant was asked to collect information for the purpose of this inquiry, and these letters were written at his request. A copy of some of them was sent to Weymouth. A few months later, a useful series of recommendations was drawn up by Lifford, the Irish Lord Chancellor. His proposals were apparently the basis of the reforms carried out between December 1779 and March 1780.

The writers agreed in saying that the political troubles in Ireland had a basis in economic distress. Both the Government and the nation as a whole were in difficulties. Some part of the distress was due to the American War, but it was felt that there must be some deeper and more permanent cause. The drain of payments to absentee landlords, and of pensions to residents in England were mentioned, together with a more important trouble, the lack of capital in Ireland. Both low rents and high rents were also blamed, and two writers thought it worth while to point to ' the licentiousness of the common people, which has increased extremely within the ten years last past '. Lord Annaly urged that the frequency of parliamentary elections helped to corrupt and intoxicate the people. But the majority held that commercial restraints were the most serious evil, and that their removal would be the only radical cure. The partial relaxation of 1778 had been of no value—' not one shilling of benefit '. There was an immediate need either of complete freedom, which was most to be desired, or of very wide concessions. As Hussey Burgh said, ' It is now come to this : England must either support this kingdom, or allow her the means of supporting herself.' [1]

The necessary concessions were laid down in the Lord Chancellor's summary.[2] They were briefly :

(i.) Free export of coarse woollen goods. It was well known

after I had read them. But by good fortune transcripts of several of them had already been made by Dr. G. O'Brien, and these have recently been published in the *English Historical Review*, vols. xxxvii and xxxviii (Oct. 1923 and Jan. 1924).

[1] Cf. Foster's statement : ' I am clear in opinion that a total repeal of all the restrictions on our trade will be beneficial to Britain : certainly it will be so to us, and must conduce to the common strength and wealth of both kingdoms.'

[2] This summary was dated 17 September. The other letters were written in May and June.

that the Woollen Acts of 1699 and 1700 had led to a migration of Irish manufacturers and traders to France, Germany and Spain, who ' by their correspondence (had) laid the foundation for the running of wool thither, both from England and Ireland, highly to the prejudice of Britain '. Dobbs, whose words are quoted here, had pointed out these facts as early as 1729. The illicit trade had increased ; wool was smuggled not only to Great Britain and the Continent, but also across the Atlantic. The writers now put forward the demand, to quote Sir Lucius O'Brien's letter : ' That we might be indulged in such low Branches of the woollen Manufacture, and to such Markets, as we have all along enjoy'd permissively and by connivance, tho' against the Letter of the British Law, and which England seems to have lost entirely.'

(ii.) Free export of printed and coloured linens.

(iii.) A preference for Irish corn in Great Britain—e. g. an earlier opening of ports to Irish than to Continental corn— in order that Ireland might become ' one of the granaries of Europe '.

(iv.) An open trade with the colonies and foreign countries, especially Spain, Portugal and the West Indies, and freedom for the import of such goods ' as may give it a back carriage '. There had actually been a large smuggling trade, in other com-modities as well as wool. It was larger, perhaps, in imagination than in fact. But Hely Hutchinson said : ' It appears probable that the existence of Ireland has depended upon an illicit commerce ' ; and the Lord Chancellor mentioned the stoppage of smuggling to America as an important cause of distress.

(v.) The encouragement of brewing by cheaper import of hops. There was certainly some ground for holding that whisky —' that cursed liquor ', as Lord Lifford called it—had become a serious social evil, and, in Ireland as in England, the brewing of better and cheaper beer was regarded as a measure of temper-ance, because it would reduce the consumption of spirits.

Other proposals were a tax on the rents of absentees, which was not likely to be imposed, as it had been rejected by Parlia-ment ;[1] and the formation of a national bank, to help the

---

[1] A tax on absentees was discussed in the Irish House of Commons in 1773, but it was rejected as the result of several discreditable manœuvres (Froude,

LINEN EMBROIDERY IN THE ARDS DISTRICT

A MODERN BLEACH-GREEN

Government with its finances, and the private trader with the provision of capital. This was, I believe, the first official suggestion of a Bank of Ireland.

These recommendations were largely carried out. Freedom of export was allowed for woollen goods in general, for glass, and for printed linens. Colonial and foreign markets, including those in the Mediterranean lands, were thrown open to Irish trade. The prohibition of export of gold and silver from Great Britain to Ireland was removed. Import of foreign hops into Ireland was allowed. The Irish Government was further left free to levy protective duties and to offer premiums for the encouragement of particular industries.

The economic results of these measures, as we have already seen, were not very striking. Agricultural exports increased, chiefly because of the great demand in England. Brewing also grew to such an extent that high duties on hops were continued under the terms of the Act of Union ; but it is not certain whether the greater consumption of beer was a substitute for, or an addition to, the use of whisky. The Bank of Ireland was founded within four years from the date of Lifford's proposal. Foreign and colonial trade, however, did not develop far, neither did the sale of glass, nor the export of printed linens. The woollen manufacture was soon depressed by competition from England, especially as the coarse trade, in which Irish makers were chiefly interested, was the first to be affected by factory production.

Several of the Lord Lieutenant's advisers had prophesied that British trade would not be injured by Irish freedom. Hely Hutchinson argued with much force that woollen manufacturers in Scotland, after seventy years of free trade, had only gained a small share in the industry, and that no greater result could be expected in Ireland.[1] He also argued, quoting Adam Smith,

op. cit., vol. ii, pp. 163–71). The main reason for the defeat of this proposal is significant : a rumour was spread that the tax would be followed by a general tax on Irish land, and the threat was enough to drive many members into opposition.

[1] Cf. Wealth of Nations (Cannan's edn.), vol. i, p. 345. This comparison suggests that if the Irish woollen trade had been throughout the eighteenth century as free as the Scottish, it would still have been limited by the same conditions. In all probability the volume of exports would not have been very much greater than the actual volume of clandestine trade.

that there was no need to fear permanent competition from cheap labour in Ireland, because an increase of prosperity would soon lead to higher wages : in a country the resources of which were being newly exploited, wages would be exceptionally high. Other writers said that English traders ought, in their own interests, to welcome any growth of prosperity in Ireland. ' It cannot injure the community', wrote Foster, ' that Ireland should undersell Lancashire, more than that Lancashire should undersell Norwich. Were this kingdom not separated by sea, no man could doubt a restriction on her wealth to be a restriction on the wealth of the Empire, equally with any on Lancashire or Norwich.'

These arguments, although they may have influenced the English government, could not alter the prejudices of British merchants. But their truth was shown by experience. The industries newly emancipated made comparatively little progress : those which advanced most rapidly after 1780—agriculture and the linen and cotton trades—had hardly any direct connexion with the measures of reform. The conclusion is that those measures had not for the time being any great economic im-portance. Their immediate effect was mainly political : together with the freedom of legislation granted in 1782, they helped to allay discontent, to consolidate national feeling, and to break down the old idea that Ireland was a colony, to be subjected in all matters to English interests. Ultimately, of course, it was of great importance that the overseas trade of Ireland should be unimpeded, and that the old colonial system should be jettisoned. It was in helping to establish these new traditions that the changes of 1779–80 were of real value.

One of the most striking features of the discussions in 1779 and 1785 is that agrarian reform, the measure needed above all others for the welfare of Ireland, was never mentioned.

XI

THE FRENCH AND AMERICAN WARS

Effects in Great Britain. In the last quarter of the eighteenth century the chief industries of Great Britain made remarkable progress. A glance at statistics, such as those of overseas trade, the import of raw cotton, or the output of coal and iron, is enough to show what a ferment of industrial activity had spread through the country. It was not only that there was a great advance in the efficiency of the extractive and manufacturing industries. The development of national and international markets, the accumulation of capital, and the services of metropolitan and country bankers, were helping both to augment the supply of goods and to facilitate their sale. Peace with the United States and Pitt's commercial treaty with France brought a great immediate gain, and showed what vast benefit might result from a period of unimpeded trade.

But progress was suddenly stopped by the Revolutionary War. Overseas trade ceased to grow and soon fell away. Shortage of supplies, high prices, and difficulty of marketing caused great dislocation, and conditions became worse as the war proceeded. A great part of the social distress of this time has been attributed to the industrial revolution, but in all probability most of it was due to the war. If the country had been at peace between 1800 and 1815, the gains of the industrial revolution would have been more conspicuous than its ill effects. In the actual course of events the depression was so deep, and recovery was so slow, that the early promise of the great inventions was not realized until the middle of the nineteenth century.

Difficulties in Ireland. The Irish linen industry, which depended so largely on the demand of English merchants, could not escape the widespread difficulties of this time. Its development, in fact, closely followed the general trend of trade in Great Britain. After a gradual increase during four-fifths of the eighteenth century, there was a short period of rapid progress between 1783 and 1795. Then came a sudden check, and there was no further expansion for more than twenty years.

The following table shows clearly how the growth of trade was arrested until after 1815 :

Average Annual Export of Linen from Ireland.

					yds.
1791–5	.	.	.	.	44,300,000
1796–1800	.	.	.	.	35,515,000
1801–5	.	.	.	.	39,443,000
1806–10	.	.	.	.	39,553,000
1811–15	.	.	.	.	38,500,000
1816–20	.	.	.	.	46,600,000

Other causes helped to increase the depression. The political upheaval of 1798, in which many of the northern Presbyterians were involved, must have injured the linen trade. In the two following years a general failure of harvests spread famine over the whole country. The farming population in Ulster suffered severely. There are no figures to show whether flax crops were as bad as the corn crops, but in any case the weavers at such a time could hardly keep up a full production of cloth. These troubles, however, soon passed. The competition of cotton, which will be discussed later, was a more permanent factor ; but the steady recovery of trade after 1815, in spite of the rapid growth of cotton manufacture, shows that this competition was not the main obstacle to progress.

The war did not lead to any actual breakdown. Even in 1811, the year of the worst depression, exports of linen were more than two-thirds of those in 1795, the best year of the eighteenth century. Certain reactions in this war, as in the Seven Years' War, helped to maintain the volume of trade. The restriction, or complete stoppage, of imports from France, the Netherlands and Germany, would cut off a large part of the normal competition. The classes of landowners, government contractors, and others, who had profited from rising prices, could well afford the luxuries of fine linen, cambric, and damask. Moreover, the great demand for Irish agricultural produce, although much of the gain was absorbed in rent, must to some extent have encouraged the domestic trade in linen.[1]

Price of Raw Material. At the same time, the war raised great

---

[1] Table II, in Appendix II, shows how agricultural exports, including cattle and dairy produce, increased after 1801.

difficulties for the producers of flax and linen. The special difficulties were the high cost of raw material, and the necessity for keeping the price of finished cloth as low as possible. In view of the growing competition of cotton, the demand for several kinds of linen was bound to be elastic. There were no important Government contracts, apart from those for sail-cloth, to maintain the strength of demand. Thus there was a great need for economy in production.

The difficulty in regard to raw material can best be understood by means of a diagram, showing the course of prices of Russian

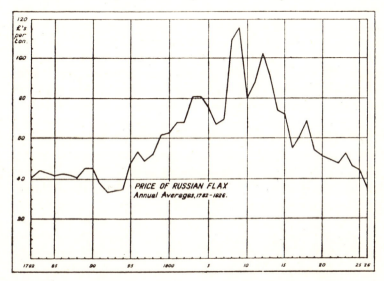

PRICE OF RUSSIAN FLAX
Annual Averages,1782-1826.

flax between 1782 and 1825.[1] The price rose from about £34 a ton in 1792 to £63 in 1802, and again to £115 in 1809. After the Peace of Tilsit in 1807, there was obviously a great scarcity of Russian flax, until the reaction in Russia against Napoleon's Continental System led to a furtive renewal of trade with England in 1810; and the export had scarcely been established again when it was stopped once more by Napoleon's Moscow campaign. It was not until the last year of the war that the Russian trade

[1] The materials for this diagram are taken from Tooke's *History of Prices*, vol. ii, p. 403. They are all for the same quality of rough flax (St. Petersburg 12 hd.). Tooke gave the prices, so far as they were available, in January, March, July, and November of each year. I have taken an average of these prices, to represent a general level for the year. Later prices for various qualities are given by Tooke, vol. iii, pp. 296–7, and vol. iv, p. 428.

returned to anything like a normal state. The effect of this shortage was more serious, it is true, in Scotland than in Ireland. The Scottish manufacture, which was mainly of coarse linen, depended to a great extent on supplies of Russian flax. According to William Marshall, an inspector to the Linen Board, the price of Russian flax in Scotland rose at one time to £150 a ton, and three-quarters of the millowners went bankrupt.[1]

But in Ireland the reactions were serious enough. There was, of course, a large supply of home-grown flax, which could be, and was, increased by more abundant sowing—as it was in the recent war, when the trade in flax from Belgium and Russia was cut off. The area under flax varied considerably, but in several years it was more than 100,000 acres.[2] It was not, however, always a simple matter to grow a large amount of flax in Ireland. Most of the seed came in normal times from the United States. But the dispute in regard to the search of neutral vessels led in 1809 to an embargo on exports from the United States to the British Isles, and three years later to war. The importance of American seed to Ireland is shown by the fact that it was used again as soon as possible after 1814. Of about 46,000 hogsheads of flax-seed sown in Ulster in 1816, nearly 39,000 hhds. came from America.[3] Thus the stoppage of American supplies had very serious results in Ireland. Even the alternatives of Dutch and Riga seed were cut off by Napoleon's Continental System,[4] and although the Berlin Decrees were already losing their force when the American War began, the years from 1809 to 1814 were an exceptionally difficult time for produce in Ulster. They were driven to rely, first on old stocks of flax and seed, and afterwards very largely on home-grown flax and home-saved seed.[5] The position was made even worse for manufacturers, though not for the growers,

---

[1] *Report on a Tour in Yorkshire and Scotland*, 1817, p. 22. Marshall was at this time the port inspector of Londonderry, but shortly afterwards he became Inspector-General for Ulster. A copy of *Precedents and Abstracts*, now in the Linen Hall Library, Belfast, used to belong to him, and has many notes and additions in his handwriting.

[2] e. g. in 1810 (Wakefield, p. 683), and in 1815 and 1816 (*Account of Flax Seed Imported and Sown*, 1824, and Horner, p. 172) : probably also in some other years.   [3] Horner, pp. 171, 172.

[4] The price of Dutch seed, which was six or seven guineas a hogshead in 1805, had risen by 1809 to thirty guineas (McCall, p. 101).

[5] Further details of this crisis, and of the measures of relief adopted by the Linen Board, are given in Chapter XV.

by the fact that English and Scottish spinners were buying large amounts of Irish flax at a time of great stress, in 1812 and 1813.[1] The table of exports of Irish linen shows that the five years, 1809 to 1813, were a period of bad trade ; but before the end of 1813 conditions had begun to improve, and from that time there was a steady advance, with only one short set-back, caused by speculative trading.

Thus the difficulties were met, on the whole, with fair success. The main reason for this success was, apparently, that in spite of the high cost of flax and seed, the price of finished cloth did not rise by any means in proportion. There are no published figures which gave any clear indication of the course of prices, but the general impression conveyed by many casual references is that the price of linen did not increase during the war by more than fifty per cent.[2]

Methods of Economy. The continuance of low prices is to be explained largely by the cheapness of labour. It will be shown later that the wages paid for plain weaving seem scarcely to have risen at all. The low earnings of labour—whether that of inde-

[1] See table of exports of flax given below, p. 259, and Appendix II. The prices of Irish and Russian flax seem to have moved closely together. e. g., in 1810 the average price of Irish flax was given as 10s. 6d. per stone of 16 lb. (See Wakefield, u.s.) This is equivalent to £73 10s. a ton. The cost of Russian flax fell in this year from £100 to £68, the average being £79 16s. In 1816 the price of flax in Ulster varied from 5s. to 12s. a stone, for different qualities. The average was apparently about 8s. a stone, or £56 a ton (McCall, p. 105). The average price of Russian flax in that year was £54 12s. Thus growers in Ireland might profit considerably by the shortage of foreign flax.

[2] In the *Newry Magazine,* 1815 (p. 316), it was stated that a cloth which in 1794 (just before the rise in prices) had cost from 1s. 7d. to 1s. 9d. in Armagh market, would be sold for 2s. 2d. or 2s. 3d. in 1814 ; and again, that webs bleached near Belfast in 1782 were worth on an average £2 10s. each, but in 1814 the average value was £3 6s. 8d. In each case the reference is to bleached cloth, and in each the increase in price is only 33 per cent. Prices would be rather higher between 1809 and 1812, when both flax and cotton were very scarce. Young, in 1776, gave the price of 12°°s in co. Down as 26s. a piece, or about 1s. a yard. The prices shown in Corry's *Reports* for 1816 and 1820 are 1s. 4d. and 1s. 5d. But all the official statements of market prices are given so vaguely as to make comparison very difficult, and the prices fixed by the customs authorities are even less of a guide. The price generally taken for exports of finished cloth in this period was 1s. 4d. a yard. Wakefield (vol. i, p. 695) said that it ought to be at least 1s. 6d. This estimate was possibly too low as well ; but it is clear that the authorities in Dublin were not conscious of any great rise in prices, for the official value half a century earlier had also been 1s. 4d. According to Dubourdieu (vol. ii, p. 387), the official value was kept at 1s. 4d. from 1781 to 1795, but after that time an attempt was made—not very successfully—to give the real values.

pendent workers or of employees—can be accounted for, in turn, by local supplies of foodstuffs and of flax. In the Napoleonic War, as in the recent European war, the pinch of high prices was not felt to such an extent in Ireland as it was in England, or rather in the English towns, because the bulk of the population could supply themselves, apart from a failure of crops, with at least a bare subsistence by their own direct labour on the land. In the case of a northern weaver, if he could grow enough potatoes and oats to supply the staple food of his household, and could graze a cow, or one or two goats, he would be comparatively little affected by the level of food prices. If, in addition, he was able to raise a small crop of flax, particularly from home-saved seed, his position would be still stronger.

However, even the small farmers, who could cultivate flax and foodstuffs, would not maintain their normal standard of life, and the workers who depended largely on money wages must have suffered severely. They did not, like the textile operatives in England and Scotland, resort to strikes, riots, and machine breaking, and their hardships may have been less than those of the linen workers in Silesia; but the stress of war-time conditions must have told heavily upon them.[1]

Low prices were the result not only of cheap labour, but also, to some extent, of greater efficiency. The improvement of communications by land and water, increased use of machinery, better methods of buying in brown linen markets and of selling for export, all implied economy and helped to keep down the cost of production. But low wages were probably the chief cause, and we should take account of this fact in estimating the state of trade during the war.

[1] There was more trouble in the cotton industry directly after the war. The industry was concentrated in a small area, and most of the weavers worked for large employers. In the linen trade, on the other hand, only a minority were employed by large firms, and these weavers were comparatively well paid. Those who worked for small manufacturers were so widely scattered that they would find it difficult to combine. It will be shown later that quite a third of the linen weavers were still working on their own account.
In 1815 there was serious trouble among cotton operatives in Belfast and Lisburn. Certain employers were boycotted. The house of one of them was twice attacked. Two ringleaders were executed; and great indignation was aroused by the murder of Gordon Maxwell, a trade union official and a man of high character. Three years later there was a strike in the cotton trade which lasted several weeks. (McCall, pp. 165, 168.)

XII

THE COTTON INDUSTRY IN IRELAND

In the half-century from 1770 to 1820 the most striking feature of Irish industry was the rise of a great cotton manufacture, centred in Belfast. It is difficult to realize this fact to-day. The reputation of Belfast depends on the linen manufacture, shipbuilding, and three or four other flourishing industries ; but from the time of the cotton famine until 1914 scarcely any pure cotton goods were made in Belfast, or anywhere else in Ireland.[1] Nevertheless, from about 1790 to 1860 cotton was regarded as one of the staple manufactures of Ulster ; a century ago it was the most valuable product of Belfast ; and it is no exaggeration to say that the fortune of the city was largely founded on the cotton trade.[2]

The growth of a second textile manufacture in the heart of the linen-producing district was bound to react seriously on the linen industry. The two trades were to some extent rivals. They competed for the supply of capital, management, and labour ; and, in a time of rising prices, cotton served as a cheap substitute for several kinds of linen goods. Our chief concern here is with this competition, and a full account of the Irish cotton trade would be beyond the range of our subject. But in order to understand the effects on the linen industry we must at least have a general idea of the progress of the cotton manufacture in Ireland.

Rise in the South. The manufacture seems to have begun about the year 1750, as a part of the economic revival in the southern provinces.[3] As it first appeared in Leinster and Munster,

---

[1] Much cotton is used in Ulster in the manufacture of unions; and during the last few years linen manufacturers have been driven by the shortage of flax to make pure cotton goods. But this is an exceptional state of affairs.

[2] Cf. Wakefield (vol. ii, p. 701), who said that the prosperity of Belfast and the neighbourhood was due, not to linen, but to ' commerce and cotton '. McCall (*Staple Manufactures*, p. 156) wrote : ' Belfast owes more of its local greatness, and more of its commercial glory, to the working of the cotton manufacture, than its leading men have yet had the gratitude to acknowledge.'

[3] At this time, and for the next thirty or forty years, nearly all the so-called cotton cloth was really a mixture of linen warp and cotton weft.

we will deal with its development there, and afterwards we will follow its later and more rapid growth in the north-eastern counties. Stephenson, on his first tour of inspection, in 1755, found that cotton yarn was used in weaving by Curry and by Newson & Co., in Cork.[1] In Drogheda and Dublin, William Bryan & Co., a large firm of bleachers and manufacturers, made plain linen, damask, kenting, fustian, and cotton. Their chief trade was in cotton goods, of which Stephenson wrote : ' As those manufactures are in great measure new to this kingdom, from the improvement and extent of them they are justly deserving of public notice.'[2] A few years later the manufacture had spread farther inland. It was carried on, together with a trade in coarse linens, near Clara, King's County, and at Hackettstown, co. Carlow.[3] Further, James Sidebotham, the bleacher from Manchester, was finishing large amounts of cotton goods for Dublin manufacturers.[4] After his tour in 1760 Stephenson said in regard to cotton : ' This article is becoming of great consequence to the kingdom.' The village of Balbriggan, on the coast between Dublin and Drogheda, was already a centre of linen weaving and bleaching. In 1770 the manufacture of calico and stockings was started there, and it met with considerable success.[5] At the present day a kind of knitted fabric, named after this village, is in common use.

After 1780, when trade in Lancashire was advancing at a prodigious rate, there was also much activity in Ireland. The Linen Board and the House of Commons were besieged with petitions for help with the making of mixed fabrics.[6] At first the Trustees were inclined to take the cotton industry in general under their protection ; but by the Act of 1782 their grants were restricted to cloth of which at least two-thirds was composed of linen or hempen yarn.[7] This limitation, however, had no great effect : it apparently left the Trustees free to give grants for cloth made of linen warp and cotton weft. Only a few weeks after the passing of the Act they announced that they

---

[1] *Journal*, p. 182.   [2] ibid., p. 168.   [3] *Report*, 1760, pp. 74, 76.
[4] ibid., p. 84.   [5] McCall, p. 150.
[6] e. g. large sheaves of petitions considered by the Trustees in May 1782 and March 1784 (*Proceedings*, 1782, pp. 133, 146 ; 1784, pp. 45 sqq.) ; twenty petitions to Parliament in 1784 (*Commons Journals*, 1783-5, pp. 243-6).   [7] 21 & 22 Geo. III, c. 35, cl. 37.

would pay three-quarters of the cost of machines for making mixed fabrics, and they immediately made payments to eighteen firms.[1] Seeing that nearly all the applicants wished to buy jennies and carding machines, these grants meant in practice the direct endowment of cotton spinning.[2] The weaving of pure cottons was beyond the reach of the Board's generosity, but Parliament itself supplied the funds. In 1785 a sum of £96,000 was voted to support the manufacture of wool, cotton, thread, cambric, iron, copper, and silk,[3] in addition to bounties of 5 per cent., for the production of mixed linen and cotton goods.[4] These efforts to promote home industries were, of course, in part a result of the legislative freedom of 1782, and the debates on Pitt's propositions in 1785. As far as the metal trades were concerned, they only expressed a pious hope.[5] But the growth of a cotton trade was an established fact, and there was no lack of claimants for the bounties.[6]

In regard to the southern provinces, all the existing evidence goes to show that its development was similar to that of the linen industry : many enterprises were started by large employers and ran for a few years, but the manufacture never gained a firm hold. Among those who received grants from the Linen Board in 1782 were manufacturers in Meath, Kildare, Waterford, and Cork. Nearly twenty years later, Wakefield visited cotton mills at Mountmellick, Queen's County, at Bandon, co. Cork, at Collon, co. Louth, and at Stratford, co. Wicklow. The workers at Stratford were a colony of Scotsmen from Paisley, and Ulstermen from Hillsborough. The mill had been set up there because of the supply of water power, and a lease of the land in perpetuity. The workers, who were five hundred in number, were attracted by high wages and good conditions

---

[1] *Proceedings*, 1782, p. 146.

[2] The first roller-spinning machine in Ireland was set up in 1784. There is no evidence to show whether the carding machinery was made according to Arkwright's design (of 1775), or was of the earlier and less efficient type, which had been used in Lancashire since 1760 (Daniels, pp. 78, 81).

[3] 25 Geo. III, c. 48.

[4] In the year ending 25 March 1786 these bounties amounted to £2,500.

[5] In the next year a special Act was passed, in vain, for the encouragement of copper mining (26 Geo. III, c. 36).

[6] The same was true, at the time, of the wool trade, which had a short period of prosperity before it was set back by the competition of steam power in England and Scotland ; of the silk trade, which flourished in Dublin ; and of the manufacture of thread and cambric.

of employment. The organization included a benefit society and a library.[1]

The most notable concern in the southern provinces was that of Robert Brooke, founded in 1782 at Prosperous, co. Kildare. Brooke evidently had high ambitions and influential friends. His works were of a type which was common in the south—a vertical combination, including all branches of the trade, from machine spinning to bleaching and printing. But he was by no means so generous in his wages as the firm at Stratford. His spinners received only 10s. a week, his weavers 7s.[2] Indeed he seems to have ground the faces of the poor as keenly as any of the millowners in Lancashire. Lord Sheffield, after visiting the works at Prosperous, and those at Balbriggan, wrote in 1785 : ' The pleasure of seeing children advantageously employed in these works, was greatly diminished by learning that part of them work all night, even so young as five or six years old, and the wages so low as sixpence per week, and from that price to thirteen pence per week in some places.'[3]

Nevertheless, the Government strongly supported Brooke's enterprise, perhaps as a means of employment for poor children from Dublin. He first applied, no doubt successfully, for a grant from the Linen Board.[4] In 1785 he was presented by Parliament with £25,000 towards his capital expenditure. And in the two following years two other Acts were passed for his benefit.[5] Moreover, he received more than a quarter of the total sum granted for bounties on mixed linen and cotton goods.[6] At the outset, as we should expect, his concern deserved its name—at any rate from the point of view of the owner, though scarcely from that of the workers : he had ' a pretty large factory, fully employed '.[7] But the success was not lasting. After eighteen years the firm collapsed, and the inhabitants of the village were in great distress.[8]

It is easy to understand both the early appearance and the small success of the southern cotton trade. Seeing that the

[1] *Account of Ireland*, vol. i, pp. 705–7. [2] McCall, p. 150.
[3] Lord Sheffield, *Manufactures of Ireland*, quoted by Horner (p. 54).
[4] 23 & 24 Geo. III, c. 12. [5] 25 Geo. III, c. 41 ; 26 Geo. III, c. 42.
[6] *Commons Journal*, xii. 102. [7] McCall, p. 150.
[8] *Official Papers*, 1790–1831 (P.R.O. Dublin), no. 637.

raw material had to be imported, manufacture could most easily be conducted on a large scale. In the middle of the eighteenth century large-scale production and employment for wages were far commoner in the southern provinces than in Ulster. Consequently there was more inducement for the pioneers of cotton manufacture to set up their works in the south. If a patron or projector were planning to start an industry near one of the chief ports, where supplies of cotton wool or yarn were available, he could as readily embark in the cotton trade as in the linen—in some ways more readily, for cotton is a more tractable material. But it proved easier to start enterprises than to continue them. The obstacles that hindered the linen trade were almost equally crippling to the cotton trade. In both there was the same periodical rise and fall of manufacturing concerns, the same long struggle, always renewed but never successful.

Cotton Manufacture in Ulster. In Ulster the trade began much later, but it rested on a firm foundation and grew rapidly. Its late appearance was probably due to the fact that all the spare capital and enterprise had been able to find safer employment in the growing linen industry. Contemporary writers were agreed that the actual beginning was made, in a rather curious manner, in 1777. Certainly Arthur Young, who visited Belfast in the previous year, and carefully examined its industries and overseas trade, made no mention of cotton as an article either of import or of manufacture.[1]

The foundation was an act of public service. Four or five years earlier the population of Ulster had been hard hit by the commercial crisis which has already been described. Trade had scarcely recovered when the American War brought fresh trouble by cutting off an important market and source of raw material, and by interfering with every branch of overseas trade. In England, distress due to the war led to the passing of Gilbert's Act in 1782 ; in Ulster it led to the foundation of the cotton industry as a means of relieving unemployment and preventing emigration. Soon after the outbreak of war, Robert

---

[1] On the other hand he wrote (*Tour*, p. 124) : ' It is curious to see . . . how the trade of this place had vibrated with the linen manufacture.' This statement is in striking contrast with Wakefield's remark quoted above, p. 227 *n.*

Joy,[1] a citizen of Belfast, was travelling in Scotland. He noticed that the Scots, with a small population, had flourishing manufactures of wool, cotton, and iron, as well as linen, whereas in Ireland a much larger population had scarcely any alternative but linen and farming. Thus he formed the opinion, strongly expressed two years later by Hely Hutchinson, that it is much better for a country to depend on several manufactures than on one. On his return he started a cotton manufacture in Belfast, with the help of two partners, McCabe and McCracken. The firm had workrooms in the Charitable Institution, and, after the English fashion, employed pauper children to serve under the minders.[2] Machinery for carding and spinning was supplied by Nicholas Grimshaw, an English calico printer, who had settled in Belfast as a printer of linens.[3] In 1784 Grimshaw himself, in partnership with Nathaniel Wilson, set up at White-house, between Belfast and Carrickfergus, the first twist-mill in Ulster driven by water power.[4]

The idea of a cotton manufacture in Ulster had already caught the public imagination. In 1782 grants for cotton-spinning machinery were made by the Linen Board to nearly a dozen firms besides that of Robert Joy.[5] Most of these firms

---

[1] The same Robert Joy, I believe, who was an official printer to the Linen Board.

[2] It is interesting to notice that one of the earliest spinning machines, made by Lewis Paul, was used in a workhouse. He also tried to introduce one into the Foundling Hospital in London (Daniels, op. cit., p. 77).

[3] For accounts of this undertaking see article in the *Belfast News Letter*, 1 May 1805, reprinted, with notes, in the *Belfast Magazine*, Nov. 1809, pp. 342–4. The former article was used by Dubourdieu (*Survey of Antrim*, vol. ii, pp. 400–11), McCall (*Staple Manufactures*, pp. 133–58), and Horner (*Linen Trade of Europe*, pp. 132–3) ; the latter by Wakefield (*Account of Ireland*, vol. i, pp. 703–8). The firm sent a skilled mechanic to Lancashire, and he came back with information about improvements in carding machinery, which they adopted. These may have been Arkwright's crank and comb device, and his method of feeding the machine. At any rate this statement suggests that the grants of 1782 had been made for the earlier type of machine.

[4] Lewis, *Top. Dict.*, vol. i, p. 35. In the evidence given against Arkwright in his third lawsuit (June 1785) it was said that spinning frames which infringed his patent were being worked without hindrance in Scotland and Ireland. The argument was advanced that unless there were a similar freedom in Lancashire, Scotland and Ireland would capture the industry (Daniels, p. 106). Grimshaw's mill (founded by a Lancastrian) was no doubt the basis of this argument, as far as Ireland was concerned. When the cotton manufacture developed in Ulster, Grimshaw added his old trade of calico printing to his other undertakings. Cf. McCall (p. 174) : ' In the trade of printing calicoes Messrs. Grimshaw took the lead, and were popularly distinguished for the style and execution of the goods brought out at their establishment.'   [5] *Proceedings*, 1782, p. 146.

were in co. Down; a few were in Armagh and Monaghan. In 1784 almost all of the numerous grants were made to manufacturers in the north.[1] Two years later direct import of cotton wool from America began, and from that time onwards the manufacture spread rapidly. It soon invaded the chief centre of the linen trade in Lisburn, where James Wallace, a Yorkshireman, set up a spinning mill in 1790. The site which he secured was not conveniently placed for water power. Therefore Wallace, who like Robert Joy had travelled in Scotland, and had seen steam engines at work in mills, bought a small Boulton & Watt engine, the first ever used in Irish industry, and worked it successfully with the help of two mechanics from Glasgow.[2] The introduction of steam power caused great excitement in the district, and crowds came to watch the engine at work.[3]

The extraordinarily quick growth of cotton manufacture in Ulster is shown by Grimshaw's estimate that in 1800 it was giving employment to 13,000 people, and indirect employment to another 14,000, within a radius of ten miles of Belfast.[4] By 1811 Belfast was importing nearly a quarter of a million pounds' worth of raw cotton, besides a great quantity of yarn brought from Lancashire or Scotland.[5] Within the same radius of ten miles there were fifteen mills driven by steam power, and eighteen worked by water, horse, or hand. These mills contained 150,000 spindles and gave direct employment to 22,000 persons. In a single mill there were 14,000 spindles [6]—more than twice the number of linen spindles driven by mechanical power in the whole of Ulster.

---

[1] ibid., 1784, p. 45.

[2] McCall, p. 152. Wallace showed great enterprise, for the steam engine had only been introduced into Lancashire in 1789.

[3] Cf. the custom of stopping stage coaches in Stockport (in 1791) so that the passengers might see the Boulton & Watt engine in Oldknow's mill (*E.H.R.*, vol. xxxvii, p. 391). In 1789 the use of steam power had been foreseen by the owners of the Drumglass Collieries, who petitioned that a road might be made from their pits to the Newry Canal. One ground of the petition was that the increase of manufacture might soon necessitate the use of steam power. In 1797 the Linen Board was given authority to make grants up to £350 to any firms setting up steam engines. Presumably these grants were to be applied to mills for cotton spinning.

[4] Dubourdieu, *Antrim*, vol. ii, p. 404.

[5] Lewis, *Top. Dict.*, u.s.

[6] Dubourdieu, op. cit., vol. ii, p. 405. This mill belonged to McCracken.

The following figures will help to show how rapidly the cotton manufacture grew in Ireland :

Cotton Wool and Yarn Imported into Ireland.[1]

			Wool. cwt.	Yarn. lb.
1772	.	. .	1,717	6,045
1783	.	. .	4,550	6,316
1790	.	. .	11,911	77,687
1800	.	. .	14,853	976,466
1805	.	. .	18,183	1,149,004
1810	.	. .	49,786	1,114,879

Two facts, in addition to the growth of manufacture, are indicated by this table. In the first place, it shows that the use of imported yarn increased much faster than the spinning of raw cotton ; in other words, that weaving developed more rapidly than spinning,[2]—no doubt on account of the more efficient spinning machinery and cheap coal in Lancashire on the one hand, and on the other the abundant supply of skilled weavers in Ulster. Secondly, it is clear that most of the manufacture was carried on in Ulster, in all probability more than three-quarters of the total manufacture of Ireland.[3] Thus the linen and cotton industries were localized in the same district, and it must next be shown what were the reactions of one industry on the other.

Effects on the Linen Trade. One obvious effect was that the cotton manufacture set an example of advanced methods, such as mechanical spinning, the use of steam power, and probably the use of the flying shuttle. It is true that the flying shuttle was first applied in Ireland to the linen manufacture. It was introduced in 1776 by McMullan, a teacher in the Moravian settlement at Grace Hill, near Ballymena.[4] But linen weavers

[1] Wakefield, vol. ii, p. 45.

[2] But the cotton spun at home was still much greater in volume than the imported yarn. According to Dubourdieu, the proportion about the year 1810 was 2 : 1.

[3] In 1811 the total import of cotton wool into Ireland was 53,133 cwt. Some of this cotton would be re-exported. In Belfast the proportion of re-exports was 21 per cent. If we allow the same proportion for the whole country, the amount remaining is about 42,000 cwt. The value of this amount would probably be rather less than £300,000. But in this year the raw cotton imported into Belfast, and retained for manufacture in Ireland, was valued at £226,000. Thus it appears that more than three-quarters of the raw cotton came to Belfast, and nearly all would be used in the neighbourhood.

[4] Stephenson, *Select Papers*, p. 26. McCall (p. 33) gave the date as 1778,

were slow to adopt the device : between 1807 and 1809 the Trustees were trying to encourage its use by means of premiums.[1] On the other hand, the flying shuttle was very soon employed for cotton weaving by Joy, McCabe and McCracken. Moreover, cotton manufacturers were anxious to try new methods. They kept a close watch on the cotton industry in England, where the flying shuttle had already been common for many years. Therefore they would be disposed to bring it as quickly as possible into general use.

In regard to spinning machinery, although it was applied very late to the production of linen yarn in Ireland—about a quarter of a century after the foundation of Joy's cotton firm in Belfast, and ten or twelve years after the first use of steam power for flax spinning in England—yet, without doubt, the presence of cotton mills in Ulster must have encouraged the early experiments in flax spinning. It is significant that the pioneer of steam spinning in the Irish linen trade had himself been a cotton spinner.

The advanced methods were not only a matter of technical processes ; they included the organization of trade as well. It is true that the system in Ireland was far less elaborate than that of Lancashire, where even the pedlars had large credit dealings,[2] and the profits of manufacture furnished the wealth of Arkwrights, Peels, and Rothschilds. Whereas many manufacturers in Lancashire not only exported goods, but had their own agencies abroad, nearly all production in Ireland was for the home markets : goods were either supplied locally to the retailer, or were sent to Dublin and sold by factors. Instead of the import of raw cotton by Liverpool brokers or great merchants in Manchester, who had credits in America, the cotton

but as Stephenson wrote nearly fifty years earlier, and would himself remember the circumstances, his date is more likely to be right.

The flying shuttle, although it was so slow in reaching Ireland, caused great excitement when it arrived. ' Crowds came to witness the new process of weaving ' ; and an old countrywoman, when she first saw the invention in use, exclaimed : ' Well, well, the works of God's wonderful, but the contrivance of man beats Him at last.' (Hume, *Spinning and Weaving*, p. 4).

[1] One reason for this delay was that, apart from damask and sheetings, most of the Irish linens were narrow enough to be woven by one man on looms of the old type. Nevertheless the flying shuttle would have made the work much lighter. It was on account of the comparative lightness of the work that the Linen Board wished to persuade women to weave with flying shuttles.

[2] Daniels, op, cit., p. 65.

was often brought to Belfast as a venture by shippers, who sold it on the wharf as best they could.[1]

However, in one or two respects the Irish cotton trade as a whole was from the beginning distinctly more advanced in organization than the linen trade. The raw material was all imported in bulk. Raw cotton was bought by the owners of spinning mills. The imported yarn was either bought straight from the spinners in Lancashire or Scotland, by manufacturers who had credit with them, or was sold by the spinners, through commission agents, chiefly in Belfast, to the manufacturers.[2] These methods of sale implied that the weaver could not provide his own yarn, but must depend for his supply on some one with larger capital. In that case the weaver would almost necessarily work for a wage, and in the Irish cotton trade employment for wages seems to have been practically universal.

This growth of capitalism in Ulster had different, in fact conflicting, influences on the linen trade. In the first place, there was a fresh, and very attractive, field for investment of capital. For a time a certain amount of capital which would otherwise have been applied to linen manufacture must have been drawn away to the rival industry. In this way the spread of capitalism in the linen trade would be delayed. But before long the handsome profits made by successful cotton manu-facturers would begin to provide a surplus which could find an outlet in other lines, and thus might actually benefit the linen producers. For instance, one of the great banks in Belfast was founded, I believe, with capital largely drawn from the profits of cotton spinning.

Wages in Linen and Cotton Industries. If there is some doubt about the effect of this competition on capital, there is none at all about its main effect on labour. It is a familiar fact that the finer branches of the cotton trade, in the early days of machine spinning, not only yielded large profits to millowners,

---

[1] There is evidence of this custom in advertisements in the Belfast news-papers, e. g. the *Commercial Chronicle*, from about 1800 to 1809.

[2] Both these methods were practised by McConnel and Kennedy, of Manchester, in their dealings with the north of Ireland.

but at the same time allowed a substantial income to weavers.[1] The statement is no less true of Ireland than of Lancashire, Cheshire, and the West of Scotland. Although there is not enough evidence to form an ordered account of the level or movement of wages in the two industries, the following particulars will at least serve to show that the weaving of cotton— especially muslin—offered a better livelihood than any but the highest grades of linen weaving.

At the time of Arthur Young's visit to Ulster the normal earnings of a weaver of plain linen were 6s. or 6s. 6d. a week.[2] In 1811, notwithstanding the rise in prices, they were little higher. Some weavers were even earning less than 6s.[3] An ordinary wage for coarse goods seems to have been from 6s. to 7s. 6d., and for fine goods from 8s. to 9s., or rather more. Wakefield was told, in answer to a questionnaire, that weavers of such fine cloths as 16°°s, in Antrim and Armagh, would receive only 6s. 4d. or 6s. 8d. a week, and that ' weavers who could do this were called good and industrious workmen '.[4] But as these particulars were given during a long spell of bad trade, the earnings must have been exceptionally low. It was stated by Sir C. Coote that a weaver of the best linen goods could earn even more than a cotton weaver ;[5] and Coulsons, of Lisburn, were paying some of their employees as much as 30s. a week.[6] Such wages, however, were earned only by a very few of the most highly skilled makers of damask and fine diapers.

Between 1800 and 1811 weavers of fustian and corduroy were earning from 9s. to 15s., and calico weavers from 12s. to 15s. a week.[7] Muslin weavers received from 18s. to 21s., with an addition for winding the yarn.

The contrast in wages for spinning was quite as striking. Linen spinners in Young's time had about 1s. 6d. a week.[8]

[1] Radcliffe's well-known account, written in 1822, of the prosperity of cotton weavers at the time when he was a young man, is discredited by the evidence published by Professor Unwin in the *E. H. R.*, vol. xxxvii (1922), pp. 216–18 ; but this evidence confirms the view that, in general, cotton weaving was a better-paid occupation than linen weaving.
[2] *Tour*, pp. 116–25.
[3] Dubourdieu, *Antrim*, ii. 394.
[4] Wakefield, i. 685.
[5] *Armagh*, p. 267.
[6] McCall, p. 47 ; Dubourdieu, *Antrim*, ii. 394.
[7] Dubourdieu, *Antrim*, p. 411.
[8] *Tour*, i. 125.

Between 1800 and 1811 their normal earnings appear to have been from 1s. 6d. to 3s.; [1] and, according to McCall, a very good spinner of fine yarns might make 6s. [2]

In the cotton mill at Randalstown (in 1811) women were earning from 5s. to 16s.; [3] and minders in general were paid a net wage of about 30s. [4]

The natural result of these differences of income was that men and women alike turned to the manufacture of cotton in the places where raw cotton or yarn was available.

The response to the new opportunities was well described by Dubourdieu, in his *Survey of co. Down* :

' Muslin weaving', he wrote, ' very soon on its appearance detached a number of workmen from the linen trade ; and a great many others, who would have applied to the latter, finding it much more easy to acquire a knowledge of weaving muslins, and better wages, gave themselves up entirely to that trade. . . . It must be allowed that the introduction of a muslin loom into a family must be an object of considerable importance : indeed the change of dress and deportment in this class of persons was very obvious to everyone, and a smart young cotton weaver became no slight attraction in the eyes of a country belle.' [5]

Linen displaced by Cotton. This passage, however, does not show by any means the whole effect. Cotton had virtually driven the linen manufacture out of Lancashire and some parts of the west of Scotland. In a single parish of Glasgow, for example, ' nearly 3,000 looms were in 1780 employed in linen fabrics. . . . Ten years later, however, cotton had almost entirely superseded flax, and the weavers were mostly occupied in making muslins.' [6]

A similar change soon took place in the north of Ireland. Successive inquiries, made in Belfast by private investigators before the first official census, showed the following as the number

[1] Wakefield, i. 684, 685.   [2] McCall, p. 108.

[3] Wakefield, i. 705 n.   It is interesting to notice that wages were higher in the coarse branches of the linen and hempen trade in which large scale production had begun.   The *average* wage of women spinners in linen mills was said to be 4s. (Wakefield, i. 684) ; and weavers of canvas, made from machine-spun yarns, earned from 7s. to 21s. (Dubourdieu, *Antrim*, ii. 411).

[4] *Antrim*, ii. 406.

[5] Op. cit., pp. 236–7.

[6] Bremner, *Industries of Scotland*, p. 230.

of looms, and in two cases the number of jennies, at work in
the town :

	LINEN. Looms.	COTTON. Looms.	Jennies.
1760 [1]	400	—	—
1776 [2]	500	—	—
1782 [3]	388	not stated	25
1790 [4]	130	500	—
1791 [3]	129	522	229
1798 [1]	10	not stated	—
1807 [3]	4	629	—
1810 [2]	6	860	—

This eviction of linen by cotton was particularly marked in
Belfast, but the movement was widespread, and it is worth
while to notice which districts were most affected. Briefly
they were the parts of the north-eastern counties lying near
the coast ; that is, the parts which could readily be supplied
with raw material. Bangor, the small port and seaside resort
on the south side of Belfast Lough, was filled with cotton manufacture.[5] The Hannay family, who were customers of McConnel
and Kennedy, of Manchester, had two spinning mills there, and
employed several score of weavers in the town.[6] In Larne, the
chief port between Belfast Lough and Fair Head, the main
occupation was cotton weaving ; [7] and at Carrickfergus, which
had failed to draw more than a very small share of the linen
trade, there were 127 cotton weavers in 1812.[8] The rapid growth
of population in Carrickfergus, from about 3,400 in 1812 to
8,023 in 1821, must have been largely due to the new manufacture.[9]

The census returns of 1821 show that the industry reached
some distance inland where there were easy communications
with the ports, but was less in evidence as the distance from

[1] McCall, p. 32. [2] ibid., 39.
[3] Dubourdieu, *Antrim*, vol. ii, p. 505. The returns for 1782 and 1791 were
made by Hyndman, the Chief Constable, those for 1807 by A. Thomson.
[4] McCall, p. 152.
[5] In 1821 there were 283 weavers of muslin, 77 weavers of linen.
[6] Professor Daniels has found among the papers of McConnel and Kennedy
much interesting correspondence with the Hannays, showing the rapidly
increasing volume of their trade and strengthening of their credit. The
census returns suggest vividly the extent to which their works dominated
the industrial life of Bangor.
[7] Dubourdieu, *Antrim*, vol. ii, p. 483.
[8] ibid., p. 485. In the same year there were only 24 linen weavers.
[9] Of 3,724 persons who were employed, 2,020 were engaged in manufacture.

the coast increased.[1] In the parish of Annahilt [2] in the middle of co. Down, out of a total of 319 weavers, 108 were entered as working with linen, 51 as working with cotton, and 160 were simply called weavers. If these undifferentiated weavers were employed in about the same proportion as the others, we could assume that there were two weavers of linen to one of cotton. In Tullylish, a parish in the north-west of co. Down, including some of the bleachgreens on the Bann a few miles from Lurgan, there were many weavers of linen and none of cotton. Thus the districts in which the linen and cotton industries came into competition seem to have been the eastern half of co. Down and co. Armagh, and the coast of co. Antrim. The difficult hill country of co. Antrim prevented the cotton industry from reaching inland, except in the neighbourhood of Belfast.

Although cotton weaving was spread to some extent over the countryside, the large number of weavers in Belfast, Bangor, Carrickfergus, and Larne shows that it was more of an urban industry than linen weaving. One reason was that the yarn, whether imported or locally spun, was supplied in comparatively few centres. But further, the weaving was organized on a large scale by manufacturers, who found it most convenient to live in towns, and the workers would naturally live in the neighbourhood of their employers' warehouses. In Belfast in 1819 there were fifty-five cotton manufacturers ; in Lisburn there were eleven, who must have employed nearly all the 142 weavers in the town, and probably many more who lived near at hand.[3] Several of the spinners, following a practice which was common in Lancashire, employed weavers to work up their yarns. Eight of the manufacturers in Belfast were spinners as well. John Bell, who has been mentioned already as a discounter of bills,

---

[1] Wakefield mentions a flourishing cotton industry in Randalstown, at the north-east corner of Lough Neagh (vol. i, p. 705 *n*.) ; but Randalstown had an easy connexion by road with Belfast. There was also some cotton weaving in the interior of county Armagh (Coote, *Armagh*, p. 267). In this case the yarn would be imported through Newry, and brought inland by road or canal.

[2] Dubourdieu, who wrote the *Surveys of Antrim and Down*, was the rector of this parish. He had an ancestral connexion with the linen trade, for his grandfather was the first minister to the Huguenot colony in Lisburn.

[3] Bradshaw, *Belfast Directory*, 1819.

combined the trades of yarn merchant, spinner and manufacturer.[1]

Reactions on Wages. It was only in certain places,
especially in towns, that linen was really ousted by cotton.
Elsewhere, while the cotton trade was growing, the linen trade
still held its position, and the fact that two textile industries
were thus intermixed had rather complicated effects on wages
and employment.

In the first place, weavers of coarse linen commonly learnt
to weave cotton as well, turning from one line to the other
according to the state of markets. Many weavers of fine linen
also found it worth while to learn muslin weaving. Hence there
was great mobility of labour between the two trades.[2]

The new demand for labour in the cotton industry would
naturally tend to give a scarcity value to linen weaving, and
so to increase the weavers' wages. Dubourdieu said that wages
in the linen trade did actually rise because of the competition
of cotton in the labour market; and that after a time, when
much labour had been transferred, there was some readjustment,
and a slight fall in the wages for cotton weaving. No figures
are available to show the extent of the changes; but, for the
following reasons, they must have been considerable. It
happened that the chief districts of cotton manufacture—south
Antrim, north and east Down, and Armagh—were also those
in which the fine and coarse branches of the linen trade were
carried on. Seeing that neither coarse canvas nor the finest
linens, diapers, and damasks could be replaced by cotton goods,
there would still be a firm demand for labour in these branches.
Wages therefore could be raised with comparative ease, and
they would have to increase because there was an alternative,
and well-paid, occupation.[3]

Moreover, the weavers in these districts had been used to
employment for wages, and for at least half a century they
had had some form of trade union. They were evidently
pressing their claims by means of collective bargaining, in spite
of the Combination Acts. This fact is proved by Sir C. Coote's

---

[1] ibid.
[2] Coote, *Armagh*, pp. 267, 341 ; Dubourdieu, *Down*, pp. 235–37.
[3] The contrary effect of the subsequent fall of wages in the cotton industry
is discussed below, Chap. XVI.

invective against the weavers of county Armagh : ' Tradesmen should be prohibited to form themselves into societies. It is well known they subscribe weekly sums, under the pretence of supporting their families in sickness, or procuring for them decent funerals, at the joint expense of the body or trade to which they belong ; although their real design is to consult how they can best pillage the public by combination for encrease of wages ; which when they have determined on, they resist work until their unlawful demands are complied with.' [1]

On the other hand, cotton would compete seriously with the lighter linens of medium quality. Therefore there would be a downward pressure on wages, or prices in the open markets, in these lines, while wages in the coarse and fine ends of the trade remained comparatively high. As far as possible, labour would forsake the less promising branches for better-paid work, whether in linen or cotton manufacture,[2] and there might be some actual movement of population.

Pressure of Competition. If cotton and linen were rival claimants for the factors of production, they competed still more strongly as goods for consumption. Certain properties of linen, such as the beauty of its finish, its strength, durability, and power of absorption, have always given it a secure place among textile fabrics ; and it has just been mentioned that there was a comparatively clear field for the sale of some of the finest and coarsest kinds of linen. Nevertheless cotton must have been a serious competitor for such uses as wearing apparel, sheetings, linings, upholstery, and many others. It is impossible to judge the strength of its influence on the demand for linen. But seeing that the price of cotton goods was actually falling between 1790 and 1815, when most prices were rising substantially, cotton would very often be preferred, even for purposes for which linen was intrinsically better suited.

In the last chapter it was pointed out that the difficulties of a time of war raised a very urgent problem of economy in

---

[1] *Survey of Armagh*, p. 262. Nothing more is heard of this union. If it continued through the first half of the nineteenth century it would gradually lose its membership as power looms, managed by women, came into use.

[2] Or perhaps for farming. Agricultural prices were high, and the real wages of farm labourers at that time were quite equal to those of many linen weavers.

the making of linen. The most obvious means of economy was the payment of the lowest possible wages ; but seeing that the level of wages was being driven up by the growing demand for labour in cotton manufacture, the leaders of the linen industry were forced to pay more and more attention to efficient, rather than merely cheap, production. Thus the cotton trade did the great service to its rival of compelling reforms, particularly the improvement of organization and the use of machinery. These reforms, which brought about the change to the factory system and modern methods of trade, will be the subject of the remaining chapters.

The cotton industry continued to flourish and expand in Ireland until about 1830. In 1823 the duty of 20 per cent. *ad valorem* on imported cotton goods was removed, but this change did not check the growth. According to McCall,[1] the exports of muslin from Ireland to Great Britain were as follows :

1823	.	.	560,000 yards
1824	.	.	3,840,000 ,,
1825	.	.	6,500,000 ,,
1830	.	.	8,000,000 ,,

But the manufacture of coarse cotton goods must already have been affected by the competition of power looms in Great Britain ; and after 1830 the muslin manufacture gradually declined for the same reason.[2] Seeing that the linen industry was advancing rapidly at the same time, it was left without any serious competitor in Ireland.

NOTE TO CHAPTER XII

Manufacture of Unions. One result of the growing supply of machine-made cotton twist in Ireland was the use of cotton as warp for mixed fabrics. During a great part of the eighteenth century the so-called cotton goods made in the British Isles were really composed of linen warp and cotton weft. The mixed linen and cotton cloth, sold in a special department of the Dublin Linen Hall, was of this kind. But the fabrics which

---

[1] *Staple Manufactures*, p. 176.
[2] Cf. Pim, *Condition and Prospects of Ireland* (1848), p. 151 : ' Perhaps the main cause of the decay of both the woollen and cotton manufactures in Ireland, has been the growth of the factory system.'

came to be known as ' unions ' had a cotton warp and a linen weft. It is not known when the manufacture of unions began : their invention was not publicly announced because they were originally sold by unscrupulous dealers as pure linens. Seeing that the first complaints against the sale of unions reached the Linen Board in 1823, the practice must have been fairly new at that time.[1] On the other hand, the Board was told by two prominent bleachers that the manufacture of unions ' was carried on to a very great extent in some of the northern counties.[2] Unions may first have become common during the slump of 1819–20. At that time cotton twist was once more cheap and abundant. The demand for linen of good quality was very small ; and it may well have occurred to some manufacturers that there would be a readier sale for a mixed fabric which looked like linen but cost considerably less.

There was nothing inherently wrong with the manufacture. The only grievance was that unions were sold at first as pure linens. They soon became a recognized class of textiles, and an important adjunct to the linen industry.

[1] *Proceedings*, 1823, pp. 102, 211, 228. Complaints came from leading merchants and manufacturers in Belfast, Ballymena, and counties Down, Monaghan, and Armagh. Other complaints reached the Board from Great Britain and America.

[2] ibid., p. 232.

XIII

THE TRADE OF BLEACHERS

Progress of Bleaching. Seeing that, through all history, increase of trade has been the main underlying cause of progress in economic organization, we ought not to expect any great development in the methods of making or marketing linen during the early years of the nineteenth century. As a matter of fact several of the chief features of the old system continued with very little change down to 1820. A large proportion of the spinning was still done by hand ; weaving remained a domestic industry, spread over the whole countryside ; brown linen markets not only flourished, but actually increased in scope ; purchases of brown linen were still made with ready money ; much of the exported cloth passed through the Dublin market, and the Linen Hall was in regular use.

Nevertheless, while the general appearance of the industry was little altered, certain improvements were quietly taking place, not in order to cope with increasing trade, but to save the industry from being overborne by hostile forces. The measure of their success is the comparatively small reduction in sales during the Napoleonic War, and the great expansion of trade when once the worst effects of the war had passed.

The chief responsibility for measures of improvement fell on the bleachers, who had already been for half a century the dominant class of manufacturers. In their case there was a special need for economy, because the cost of bleaching had apparently risen more in proportion than that of weaving, spinning or flax preparation.[1] There were also special opportunities for progress. As the result of much experiment in several countries, notably in France, a great advance had been made in the chemistry of bleaching. Above all, a means had been devised, between 1785 and 1799, of using chlorine com-

---

[1] Sampson, *Survey of Londonderry*, said that a piece which in 1784 would have cost 3s. 9½d. to bleach, would cost 6s. 6d. in 1802 : a rise of more than 70 per cent. If the piece in question were a seven-eights web, about 25 yards

mercially in the form of chloride of lime.[1] The most efficient chemicals were expensive ; but those who could afford to buy them could save an immense amount of time—and economy of time was one of the main problems of bleaching. Further, machinery had been devised to replace the old methods of washing by hand and trampling with the feet. Other machines were used for rubbing, calendering, and beetling. These machines again were expensive. We have noticed already that for a well-equipped bleach-yard, about the year 1800, they would cost £3,000.

During the last few years of the eighteenth century some of the more enterprising firms discovered that the new methods would enable them to break through an ancient custom of the trade, and bleach throughout the winter months.[2] This was another great economy. Together with the improvements already mentioned, it had the effect of preventing any appreciable rise in the cost of bleaching after 1800.[3]

Increasing Scale. But there was an additional effect which to many people was less welcome. Since the new methods involved both capital and enterprise, trade was bound to be engrossed by the larger and more progressive firms at the expense of the smaller and more backward. If trade had been expanding the change might have been gradual. But as the demand for linen was not increasing, the existing trade fell rapidly into the hands of a few large firms. This movement is reflected in the diminishing number of bleach-greens, and the growing individual output. In 1782 there were 39 bleach-greens within eight miles

in length, the expense of bleaching in 1802 would thus be about 3*d.* a yard. Warden (p. 410) said that this was the price early in the nineteenth century, but he did not mention a date. According to Wakefield (vol. i, p. 693), the cost of bleaching and finishing was 4*d.* a yard. In recent years it has been 2*d.* or less (Horner, p. 170).

[1] There is a considerable literature on this subject. All the standard writers (e. g. McCall, Charley, and Horner) devote a good deal of attention to methods of bleaching. For methods in use at the beginning, middle, and end of the eighteenth century, see respectively Crommelin's *Essay* (1705), Stephenson's *Journal* (1755), and *The Theory and Practice of Bleaching* (1799), by William Higgins, Professor of Chemistry to the Royal Dublin Society. It is interesting to notice that James Watt was responsible for introducing the use of chlorine for bleaching into Scotland (Horner, p. 68).　　[2] McCall, pp. 23, 55.

[3] And of reducing the cost after 1815, when materials would be cheaper. According to Warden (p. 410), the cost fell in a few years from 3*d.* to 1¼*d.* a yard.

of Belfast, with an average annual output of 4,400 pieces. By 1814 the number had fallen to 17, but their average production for several years had been 11,400 pieces.[1]

It was said in the last chapter that the economies of this period were not only in processes of manufacture, but also in methods of trade. We have seen, further, that bleachers had had a large share in the direct export trade from the north of Ireland. The fact is that the commercial enterprise of the great bleaching firms was as important as the industrial side of their work, and helped quite as much in their rise to power.

Records of a Firm of Bleachers. Their position and influence in this period could hardly be understood if it were not for the fortunate chance which has preserved the ledgers, for the years 1815 to 1822, of a large firm of bleachers and merchants, J. & J. Richardson—a firm which is still (under the title of Messrs. Richardson, Sons & Owden, Ltd.) one of the leading concerns in the Ulster linen trade.

Their works were set up about the middle of the eighteenth century. They secured from the Marquis of Hertford a lease of land near Lisburn, by the River Lagan, close to the site which Crommelin had chosen for his bleach-yard. Near at hand was the thread-mill of John Barbour, and before long there was added the mill of William Barbour, which stood on the ground formerly used as a bleach-green by Crommelin's brother-in-law, Nicholas Delacherois. Other neighbours were the Williamsons of Lambeg, sons of the bleacher who had played a leading part in the dispute of 1762 ; James Hogg of Lisburn, a prominent bleacher ; and William Coulson, the famous damask manufacturer. The works were in an excellent position, near one of the chief markets for brown linen ; they had easy communications by road and canal with the industrial districts of county Down and county Armagh, and still better communications with Belfast, which could be used for the purpose of direct export. Moreover, the head of the firm, Jonathan Richardson, was a man of enterprise and ability, a pioneer in the new methods

---

[1] *Newry Magazine*, 1815, p. 316. The same movement continued later. In 1832 the eleven bleach-greens in the parish of Belfast had an average output of 23,600 pieces (Marmion, *Maritime Ports*, p. 358) ; and whereas in 1790 there had been about 80 greens in county Antrim, in 1850 there were only 20.

of production. He and his friend John Hancock were the two
first bleachers to keep their greens employed in the winter.
Moreover, he was evidently active in working up a trading
connexion. His efforts were certainly successful. In the years
1785–87 the turnover was £16,000, £20,000 and £43,788.[1] By
1819 the turnover on trading concerns alone, apart from bleaching,
was nearly £40,000 ; and in 1820, by no means a good year
for the trade in general, it had grown to more than £48,000.[2]
At that time the bleach-works and the commercial branch were
almost equally important : sometimes one and sometimes
the other proved at the end of a year to have been the more
profitable.[3] The bleach-green must have had an output of
about 20,000 pieces in a normal year—a curious contrast to
the ' vast quantity ' of 3,000 pieces produced by the ' very
extensive bleacher ', Barclay of Lambeg, half a century earlier.[4]

In every branch of the firm's undertakings there are signs
of enterprise and experiment. A few years after the period
of the ledgers the linen industry entered an era of profound
and rapid change, beginning with the introduction of steam
power. But the change was only possible as a result of many
years of gradual development. The Richardsons' methods of
trade throw considerable light on this process of preparation.

Linen Buyers. In the first place, their means of securing
unbleached cloth was different from any that we have yet
noticed. It was a common practice among bleachers to supply
themselves with part of their brown linen by direct employment
of weavers, but there is no sign that the Richardsons manu-

---

[1] Cash book of J. & J. Richardson, 1785–87.
[2] Ledgers of J. & J. Richardson, 1815–22. All the account of this firm
given in the remainder of the chapter is drawn either from the cash book or
from the ledgers.
[3] In 1817, a year of very active trade, when there was a great demand for
bleached goods for foreign cargoes, the profits were :

Bleach-yard.	. £4,242 18s. 7½d.
Trading .	. £3,945 18s. 6½d.

In 1818, when the slump had begun, the figures were :

Bleach-yard.	. £1,780 10s. 0½d.
Trading .	. £2,342 11s. 0d.

and in 1820 :

Bleach-yard.	. £1,694 8s. 8d.
Trading . ·	. £2,847 19s. 11½d.

[4] McCall, p. 22.

factured on their own account. The whole of their stock seems to have been bought, and Corry mentioned them as buyers in all the chief linen markets of Ulster. The ledgers show that their purchases were made in the following way.

Nearly all the brown linen was supplied by eight men. Five of them seem to have bought goods on commission : the other three, who did the greater part of the buying, were not given a commission, but received a regular salary.[1] These eight men represent two divisions of a class which had recently become very prominent in the linen markets of Ulster. The five in the former group were independent traders, but they did not, like the drapers, undertake buying and selling on their own account : they were factors for the large bleachers and merchants. The other group were members or employees of the bleaching firms. Wakefield wrote in his account of the linen trade, as it was organized in 1811 : ' Among the Presbyterians of the north there is a description of men called linen buyers, who in rank are considered to be one step below merchants.' [2] There can be little doubt that the Richardsons' agents all belonged to this class.

Decline of Drapers. In buying through their own agents the firm were helping in a movement which changed the whole commercial organization of Ulster ; for the linen buyers were doing work which had once belonged to drapers. During the first quarter of the nineteenth century, the scope for the drapers' trade was fast diminishing, and their numbers were shrinking in proportion. There were still, about the year 1800, a large number of drapers in Ulster—perhaps four hundred in the whole province—who did no bleaching, but lived solely by their trade as middlemen.[3] Their chief function was to serve as a link

---

[1] One certainly received a salary. The others received periodical payments of round sums, which were probably in part instalments of salary, though they were not specified as such in the ledgers.

[2] *Account of Ireland*, vol. ii, p. 723.

[3] According to McCall (p. 55), there were 156 drapers in county Antrim in 1800. At that time there would be fewer than 80 bleachers. Thus there must have been about 80 drapers who were not bleachers. Similarly in county Derry there were 130 drapers and less than 60 bleachers. In six counties (Antrim, Armagh, Down, Londonderry, Monaghan, and Tyrone) the total number of drapers was given as 766 ; and as, in all probability, a slight majority were pure traders, we can assume their number in the whole of Ulster to have been at least 400.

between the linen-producing districts and Dublin. But when bleachers or their agents were buying brown linen for their own works and for direct export they had no need of the draper. Even if they wished to deal through the Dublin Linen Hall they could send goods on their own account, as the Richardsons did ; or they might, like the Coulsons, of Lisburn, and Edward Clibborn, of Banbridge, set up offices in Dublin, and become ' Linen Hall factors ' themselves.[1]

If it had been possible, the drapers could best have defended their position by returning the attack and combining their trade with bleaching. But not many could succeed in such a venture. Few had enough capital. The volume of trade could not be increased to support new undertakings. Moreover, those drapers who already owned small bleach-greens were being crushed out by the competition of the large firms.

The whole of this movement—the accumulation of capital, the rise of bleachers, and the decline of drapers—is reflected in an enthusiastic account of the draper's trade written in 1815, the year of the Richardsons' first ledger :

' When we rise on the scale to the linen-draper, what occupation can be conceived more enviable ? Of all ranks in the community he may perhaps be the most independent. He need be under little obligation to anyone. His purchases are made without favour or affection, from the multitude of weavers in the open market ; his goods are again offered to sale in their finished state in whatever great mart best answers him ;[2] their intrinsic merit is supposed to sell them, nor is the seller under obligation to him who purchases to the amount of thousands.[3] All is a pleasing reciprocity of interest, from one end of the manufacture to the other ; and before luxury overspread the land, the draper, by attending markets himself, promoted his health by the same activity that laid the foundation of his fortune.'

The drapers are treated thus far as an important and apparently flourishing class. But in a later passage the writer

---

[1] See *Dublin Directory*, 1819.

[2] As Dublin and Belfast were the only ' great marts ' for white linen in Ireland, this statement suggests that there was still some custom for drapers in the White Linen Hall in Belfast.

[3] This rather dark saying must imply, I think, a contrast between the independent draper and the linen buyer, who acted under orders from his principals.

shows how their position was being weakened, and confesses himself a *laudator temporis acti* :

' (The trade) was formerly in the hands of a much greater number of drapers, which may in some part be thus accounted for. Forty years ago they consisted of a body of active working men, who attended markets themselves, and superintended the manufacture in all its parts. The result is what might naturally have been expected. They became wealthy, and respectable at home and abroad. The consequence, however, of their increase of substance, was luxury and ease in the succeeding generation.[1] The purchase of cloth from the weaver devolved on hired buyers, enhancing the cost to the consumer—at least not improving the selection,[2]—while too much was entrusted to the management of others, and too much relaxation indulged (in) by the master . . . At length it has in a considerable degree been given up to the most perseveringly industrious ; a small number comparatively with their precursors, but doing individually much more business, and deriving emoluments greatly exceeding what at former periods had been experienced by others.' [3]

The days of the small dealer were nearly at an end. As the independent weaver was gradually giving place to the manu-facturer, so in every branch of their work the ordinary drapers were more rapidly yielding up their trade to the great firms. Those who were beaten in the struggle would have to abandon the linen trade, or become agents for their successful rivals, and the young men of their class would be trained, not as drapers, but as linen buyers.

There yet remained, it is true, some scope for the drapers' services. A certain amount of trade of the old type still passed through the Linen Halls of Dublin and Belfast, especially for distribution to retail shops in Ireland. In some districts of Ulster, such as north Antrim and Tyrone the organization of industry was very stable. The markets were supplied largely by independent weavers, and there was work for the drapers in connecting these outlying markets with Dublin and Belfast. A note in Richardsons' cash book, dated 1817, mentions the

---

[1] This sentence explains the previous allusion to the spread of luxury.

[2] The writer seems to have been conscious that there might be a flaw in his economic theory.

[3] *Newry Magazine*, 1815, pp. 317-18. These passages occur in a general description of the linen trade. But apart from an account of the rising in 1762, the article contains little else that is new : it is nearly all based on Dubourdieu's *Surveys of Antrim and Down*.

bleaching of 9,736 pieces for eight firms. Some of these firms may have been bleachers, sending goods for a particular type of finish in which Richardsons had specialized; but more probably they were drapers, following the century-old methods of trade.

Nevertheless, the class of drapers was declining fast during the early years of the nineteenth century. Instead of one or two hundred drapers who were to be found in each county in 1800, Corry's report of 1816 shows only a few dozen buyers, even in the chief markets for brown linen ; and the same names —often of large bleaching firms—recur in one market after another. Moreover, the census returns of 1821 mention a large number of linen buyers, but very few drapers. If John Nevill, the pamphleteer of 1783, had been able to look ahead to a distance of twenty years, he would have felt less enthusiasm for the new Linen Hall in Belfast, less fear of the Dublin factors, and more concern on account of the growing power of the northern bleachers.[1]

Trade with England. We have seen something of the new methods of trade, both in the purchase of brown linens and in the process of bleaching. We must turn next to the sale of finished cloth. On this point the Richardsons' accounts give very full and useful information : apart from them, indeed, it would be impossible to offer more than a few allusions to the subject.

Bleachers have already been described as pioneers of direct export from Ulster, and it has been shown that in the period covered by the ledgers, the exports of linen from Belfast were greater than those of Dublin. Even so, it is rather surprising to find the extent of the trade carried on by this firm with buyers in England. It is clear that the great majority of the pieces sold by them were not only sent to England, but were sent straight to the customers, without the intervention of a factor. Although at various times they had dealings with four factors in Dublin and three in London, these dealings, even in the aggregate, were not very large. An important part of their trade was with two English customers : the great firm of Marshall, Hives & Co., of Leeds, the largest linen dealers in

[1] Evidence of the decline of the drapers' trade in Dublin is given below, p. 298.

England during the first half of the nineteenth century ; and Parsons, Hurles & Co., of Bristol, who were probably West India merchants. The former bought from Richardsons £11,000 worth of linen and flax in a year ; the latter bought £8,000 worth of bleached and brown linen. Besides these two valuable customers there were several who bought to the extent of £1,000 or more in a year, and many occasional purchasers in England of £50 or £100 worth of assorted goods—a number of them evidently shopkeepers in provincial towns—who found it economical to deal directly with the bleachers.

Several features of overseas trade from Belfast are illustrated by a list of thirty customers, which was written in the Richardsons' cash book.[1] The list is entitled : ' Names and abodes of Persons we send Linens to, and manner of dealing with them.' It is far from exhaustive,[2] but it is representative enough to show the wide extent of their trade, the method of conveying goods, and the system of payment. Twenty-eight of the customers lived in England : eight in the north-eastern counties, seven in the north-western, seven in London, five in Bristol, and one in the Midlands.

In regard to the means of transport, the most striking fact is that in quite half the cases goods were consigned by way of Liverpool, which was a general focus for trade, not only to Lancashire and Yorkshire, but also to a place as far north as Kendal,[3] to Cheshire and the Midlands, and often to London. From time to time a consignment was sent round by sea from Belfast to London ; but as a rule goods for London would go by sea to Liverpool, and then across country by canal. We can see the use of the Bridgewater and Grand Trunk canals in the case of the brown linens sent to Nantwich. This example also suggests that sales in the Chester Linen Hall were being replaced by orders for whole packs, to be sent through Liverpool.

The importers in Bristol, such as Parsons, Hurles & Co., had probably been in the habit of buying linen in Dublin, for export

---

[1] The cash book was laid aside for twenty-five years, and then, from 1812 onwards, was used for miscellaneous notes. This list seems to have been written in 1813. The full list is given in a note at the end of this chapter.

[2] e. g. no mention is made of Marshall, Hives & Co., or of Moore, Stanger & Co., who bought goods to the value of £2,000 to £5,000 a year.

[3] In this case the customer seems to have had a family connexion with Benson, the shipping agent.

or for sale at the Bristol Fair, but had found it worth while to dispense with the Dublin factor when bleachers were able to sell on equally good terms.

Maryport was evidently the chief centre for distribution over the four northern counties. Goods would no doubt be taken from Maryport to Carlisle, and thence by one of the two main roads to Newcastle.[1]

For the success of this direct trade with England two by no means easy conditions were essential. In the first place, the cloth had to be properly standardized and of good quality. Detailed entries in the ledgers show that the webs were always accurately described ; and, although there is no definite evidence on this point, there can be no doubt that the firm had its own lappers, of the modern type, who examined all the cloth before it left the warehouse. Their work would be better done than that of the sealmasters of brown linen, because they had a direct inducement to do it efficiently. Thus the purchasers had a reasonable expectation of getting precisely the goods which they desired.

System of Credit. The second condition was credit, and in this matter the list is more informing. It shows that credit was given for periods varying from three weeks to nine months. It is interesting to find that the usual method was that of the ' two and two months '—two months' credit, followed by a draft for 61 days—which was also the commonest form of payment in the cotton trade at that time.

In view of all that has been said about the difficulty of credit in Ulster, it is natural to ask how this firm was in a position to give credit regularly for several months for nearly all its seals. The question is vital, since without this fund of credit the direct export to England, which comprised a great part of the Richardsons' trade, would have been impossible.

The answer is given in their account with the firm of Henry Montgomery & Co. In the second ledger the name of the firm changes to Orr, Sloan & Co., as the result of an amalgamation. This name continues through the third ledger, and if the next,

---

[1] An entry in one of the ledgers also shows direct traffic with Stranraer, probably from Donaghadee. There were several customers in Scotland who do not appear in this list.

covering the years 1824 and 1825, were still extant, we should find a new amalgamation and a fresh title, the Northern Banking Company. The Northern Bank was one of three private banks founded in Belfast early in the nineteenth century.[1] In the year 1824, three years after the Bank of Ireland's monopoly had been limited to a radius of fifty miles round Dublin, the Northern Bank became the first provincial joint-stock bank in the country.[2] At the time of which we are writing the Northern Bank was still a private concern, but it was none the less of the greatest importance to the Richardsons in every branch of their business. Their own large payments were regularly made by drafts on the bank, and the bills received from their customers were presented to it for discount. From its own resources the firm could have given a certain amount of credit, but the management of bills and the supply of ready money would have been a continual difficulty. The added resources of the bank were an immense advantage ; indeed it is to the growth of sound banking and an organized money market that we must look for the main underlying cause of the increased export from Belfast.

Most of the Richardsons' payments were made in Ireland, so that it was possible to use drafts on the bank, which were simply cheques under another name. But as there was no clearing house in England that included the Irish banks, their customers had to pay in bills of exchange. The common practice, as we should expect, was for Richardsons to send drafts at the end of the period of credit, either on a London accepting house, or on the firm of purchasers, but payable in London. Three accepting houses are mentioned in the list, but another which is not mentioned—Smith, King & Smith—did the greater part of this business, and often arranged the insurance of the goods. Nearly all the bills used in Ireland for overseas trade seem to have been drawn on London,[3] a fact which further emphasizes the dependence of the Irish markets on London credit.

[1] The other two banks existing in 1812 were the Belfast and the Commercial (Dubourdieu, *Antrim*, vol. ii, p. 528).

[2] According to the Act of 1821 all shareholders in Irish joint-stock banks had to be resident in Ireland. This senseless restriction was removed in 1825, and a great increase of joint-stock banking followed.

[3] Thirty-one days' bills on Dublin were a common form of currency for internal trade.

Sale of Brown Linen. A curious feature of the Richardsons'
trade with England, which may or may not have been common
to other exporters, was the difference between their dealings
in brown and in white linen. All the white cloth sold by them
was their own property, whereas the brown linens were bought
on account of English firms, in return for a commission of
2½ per cent. In other words, the Richardsons were merchants
of white linen and factors of brown. This distinction probably
arose in the following way. The firm at first had no interest in
brown linen except as material to be bleached. Their trade
was in white cloth. But as certain of their customers found it
convenient to order bleached and unbleached cloth from the
same firm, and to have them consigned together, the agency
for brown linen was undertaken, perhaps at the customers'
request, as a subsidiary line of trade.[1]

Transatlantic Trade. A considerable amount of the cloth
sent to Liverpool and Bristol was re-exported to the United
States, the West Indies and Africa. Light, but comparatively
coarse, cloths from many districts in Ulster were used in tropical
and sub-tropical lands, no doubt to a large extent by negroes ;
but there was a good demand in America for the fine seven-
eighths webs of north Antrim and Londonderry, and the fine
yard-wides of Lisburn and Belfast, ' for the wear of the better
sort of people '.[2] We have noticed the attempts made, with
no great success, by Irish exporters to secure a share in transatlantic trade. After the peace of 1814 there was a special
effort to recapture the American market, and this effort was
partly responsible for overtrading during the next few years,
and for the slump which followed.

The Richardsons' accounts give us some insight into the
methods and difficulties of this enterprise. The firm apparently
took no direct part in the speculative trade immediately after
the war : if they had done so they would have lost heavily.[3]

---

[1] It was never as important as the trade in bleached linen. e. g. the dealings
with Parsons, Hurles & Co. (the largest buyers of brown linen) would yield
on an average a profit of about £300 on the sales of white cloth, and a commission of only £75 for the purchase of brown. A large part of the brown
linen seems to have been dyed in England, and used for shirtings and linings.

[2] Corry, Report for 1816.

[3] Their caution is illustrated by the remark which James Richardson—a
senior partner at this time—made to his son : ' There never was a big war

But from 1819 to 1823 (the end of the period covered by the ledgers) they were sending assorted goods both to New York and to the West Indies. During these years separate accounts were kept, with the headings 'American Consignment' and 'Jamaica Adventure'.

In both cases the linens were sold on commission by agents, of whom some at any rate had family connexions with the Irish linen industry. The agents in America were Paxton & Gregg, Abraham Bell of New York, and Magwood & Patterson, of Charlestown. Eleven cargoes were sent to Jamaica in four years, and eight to the United States. They were insured by John Pim & Sons, of Dublin, but the ships belonged to Belfast. Most of the consignments to Jamaica went in the *Marathon*, owned by Thomas Bell, which made three voyages in a year. The charge for freight was quite reasonable; for instance, the cost of carriage to Jamaica of cloth worth £545 12s. 6d. was £2 16s. 6d. Insurance, which came to £14 3s. 5d. for the same goods, was a more serious expense.

The cloth could only be sold very gradually: its dispatch was a poor speculation; there was no established market; and the agents had to find custom as best they could. In America sales were particularly poor, and a large prat of the goods had to be dumped at less than the cost price. Hence there were heavy losses on the American Consignment, as the following table shows:

1819	Loss	£86 2s. 1d.
1820	,,	£275 3s. 8d.
1821	,,	£191 3s. 7d.
1822–3	,,	£107 8s. 0d.[1]

The Jamaica Adventure was more prosperous, and showed a gradually increasing gain:

1819	Profit	£6 8s. 1d.
1820	,,	£16 14s. 1d.
1821–3	,,	£135 5s. 9d.

Thus the net loss on five years' transatlantic trade was on the average slightly over £100 a year. Ten years later, when steam

in modern times which was not followed by a commercial panic . . . not necessarily commencing in either of the two nations engaged, but it spreads' (J. N. Richardson, *Reminiscences of Friends in Ulster*, pp. 69–70).

[1] Accounts for America were made up in this case at the end of two years, and for Jamaica at the end of three years, to allow time for sales.

spinning began to lower the price of cloths, the scope for sales in the West Indies and America would no doubt increase : still more after the middle of the century, when the power loom was beginning to take effect, and steam transport was reducing both the cost of carriage and the period of waiting.[1] But in these early days any Irish linen merchant who tried to build up a distant market for his goods was bound not only to wait for many months, or even years, for his return, but to be prepared in the long run for a loss on his outlay.

Export of Flax. In addition to their trade in bleached and brown linens, the Richardsons were engaged in several smaller undertakings. The chief of these was their export of flax to England. They supplied, on commission, over £5,000 worth of raw flax in a year to Marshall, of Leeds. The flax was collected by their linen buyer, Samuel Quin, probably from the flax markets, which were often held in conjunction with the markets for brown linen. Marshall's purpose in importing flax was to provide raw material for his spinning mill. He had already been spinning by machinery for nearly thirty years, and had a very large output. The rise of his firm, and of machine spinning in general, must be described later. But it is worth while to notice here the reaction of this new development on the production of flax and yarn in Ireland.

Throughout the eighteenth century English and Scottish manufacturers of linen, or mixed linen and cotton goods, had maintained a steady—though never a very large—demand for Irish yarn. From the last few years of the century, however, they were able to provide themselves very cheaply with coarse machine-made yarns spun in Great Britain. Therefore they bought only the finer counts from Ireland, and Irish exports of yarn fell correspondingly. After 1790 they never exceeded 30,000 cwt. ; the demand became very irregular—varying

---

[1] But as late as 1850 the direct export abroad seems to have been trifling in comparison with the trade of England. The estimate of £50,000, given in the *Dublin Directory* for 1851 (p. 237), may have been too low, yet the fact that such an estimate was possible shows that the actual export—from Dublin at any rate—must have been small. At the price of 10*d.* a yard, assumed for exports in that year, the amount would be 1,200,000 yards. If these figures are anywhere near the truth, they can only be explained on the assumption that there was still a great advantage in sending goods abroad by way of England.

during the war inversely as the continental trade in raw material ;
and at length in 1820, when import from the Continent was
re-established, the amount fell to 5,553 cwt.

English and Scottish spinners used chiefly flax from the
Baltic States, which was cheap and well suited for coarse yarns.
Between 1790 and 1800, when the normal import of flax into
Great Britain from St. Petersburg alone amounted to 5,000 tons
a year, the average import from Ireland was only 4 tons. But
there followed the Armed Neutrality, the Berlin Decrees, the
entente between Alexander I and Napoleon culminating in
the Treaty of Tilsit, the renewed hostility between France and
Russia, and Napoleon's Moscow Campaign. Thus trade with
Russia became precarious, and British spinners were driven to
make more use of Irish flax, which was in general finer than
the Russian.

The effect of the Moscow Campaign is clearly shown in the
following statistics of rough flax exported from Ireland : [1]

1810	.	.	1,073	cwt.
1811	.	.	14,334	,,
1812	.	.	65,651	,,
1813	.	.	69,191	,,
1814	.	.	24,363	,,

It happened that between 1810 and 1820 the gradual introduction of gills, or combing frames for drawing out and spreading
the stricks of hackled flax, enabled machine spinners to deal
with finer qualities and to produce higher counts of yarn.[2]
Therefore their demand for Irish flax increased, and it was
maintained after the Napoleonic War. In 1820, for example,
the export from Ireland was well over 3,000 tons.[3] Corry, writing
in 1817, lamented the fact that the export of flax was ' unregulated '. As an official of the Linen Board he naturally wished
to see a system of inspection and sealing applied to the flax
markets, although the expert buyers were quite competent to
see to the quality and make-up of the goods. The interesting
point, however, is not the absence of inspectors, but Corry's
explanation—that the trade was ' of modern date ', and therefore
had not come within the cognizance of the Board.[4] It was this
trade which had attracted the enterprise of the Ulster bleachers,

[1] Horner, p. 206. The total output of rough flax in Ireland in 1812 and
1813 was about 20,000 tons.   [2] Horner, pp. 259, 260.
[3] ibid., p. 206.   [4] Report, pp. 44, 94.

and Richardsons appear to have had no small share in the export ; for, at the rate of 8s. a stone of 16 lb., their purchases for Marshall, Hives & Co. would amount to about 90 tons a year.[1]

Bleaching and Farming. We have still to notice three or four minor undertakings of the Richardsons' firm. They had a corn mill by the Lagan which yielded a profit of more than £300 ; they had a boat, apparently a barge on the Lagan, for carrying their cloth to Belfast ;[2] and they grazed sheep on the land that was not in use for bleaching. Many, perhaps all, of the bleachers carried on farming as well ; and conversely, in certain districts by the Rivers Lagan and Bann, nearly all the farmers were bleachers. This point may be illustrated from the census returns of 1821 for the parish of Seapatrick, co. Down, which included most of the town of Banbridge and a stretch of five miles of the River Bann, bordered with a succession of bleach-greens. The following list shows the chief farmers in this parish, with the area of their land and the description of their work given in the returns :

Francis Mulligan.	.	22¾ a.	Linen merchant and farmer (bleacher).[3]
John Mulligan	.	28½ a.	Farmer and cloth merchant, bleach mills.
Abraham Russell	.	17 a.	Farmer, linen merchant, has corn and scutching mills.
James Charles Mulligan		19¾ a.	Farmer and linen merchant (bleacher).
Hans McMurdy .	.	39½ a.	Farmer, bleach mills.
Walter Crawford.	.	112 a.	(Farmer and bleacher).
George Crawford.	.	68½ a.	Farmer and linen draper.
Thomas Crawford	.	—	Linen buyer.
Wm. Hudson	.	61 a.	Linen merchant, and has bleach mills.
Gilbert Mulligan .	.	67½ a.	Linen merchant and farmer, and has bleach mills.
Henry Stirling	.	14 a.	Farmer and cloth merchant (bleacher).
Samuel Law	.	22½ a.	Farmer, has bleach mills.
William Hayes .	.	93 a.	Linen merchant and farmer, has bleach and corn mills.
Edward Clibborn	.	21 a.	Farmer, has flour mills and bleach mills.

(Walter Crawford, George Crawford, Thomas Crawford are marked as *Brothers*.)

The only other holders of 10 acres or more are one who is described as a shopkeeper, another who was a tobacconist and

---

[1] This is about the average of a list of prices in Ulster, in 1816, quoted by McCall, p. 108. The average export from Ireland from 1811 to 1820 was 2,000 tons.

[2] Or rather, they seem to have had a monopoly of a particular boat, and to have worked by contract with the owner.

[3] The words in brackets are based on evidence in other parts of the census ; e. g. Henry Stirling is not called a bleacher, but other men are described as bleachyard workers employed by him.

chandler, the postmaster of Banbridge, and a farmer of 10 acres, whose son was a linen buyer.

In the year 1817 the Richardsons, as a branch of their American speculation, tried the experiment of importing tobacco and flax-seed, to the value of £356, in part payment for their linen. But they lost slightly on this experiment, and did not repeat it. Some other merchants, however, seem to have had better fortune, for Corry observed in 1817 that it was not uncommon for exporters of linen to import flax-seed.[1]

This survey has shown something of the widespread activity of the great bleachers early in the nineteenth century, and of the growth of capital and credit in Irish trade. In the next chapter we shall trace the extension of more advanced methods through the linen trade as a whole, before the era of steam power and factory production.

NOTES TO CHAPTER XIII

(i.) The following is the list of customers, written in J. & J. Richardson's cash-book :

The names and abodes of Persons we send Linens to, and manner of dealing with them :—

Richard Arrowsmith, Preston, Lancs. 4 mos. credit. Generally after 2 mos. draw 61 days' bill on London. Shipped Belfast— Liverpool, c/o Richard Roskill.

Hadwin Bragg, Newcastle-upon-Tyne. 21 days' bill on shipping. Draw on Nicholson, Haydon & Co., London. Goods via Maryport, c/o Wilkinson Ostle. Commn. 2½ p. c.

Edward Bellis, Nantwich, Cheshire. 21 days' bill on shipping on Lilwall and Moline, London. Commn. 2½ p. c. Via Liverpool, c/o B. Greenwood, thence by canal, via Chester.

James Burn & Co., London. Credit 4 mos. After 2 mos., 2 mos. bill. Or (to Portugal) 21 days' on shipping. Commn. 2½ p. c. Ship at Belfast for José Bento de Arajno, merchant.

Robert Benson & Co., Kendal. C/o Hodgson & Benson, Liverpool.

Bates & Winkes, Nottingham. 4 mos., 2 mos. and 61 days, payable in London. Belfast to Liverpool, c/o Sugden & Pearson.

Cater Marshall (Cater & Humphries, London). 6 mos., 4 mos. and 61 days, on London. Ex. 8¼. Via Liverpool, B. Greenwood.

John Coleby, London. 9 mos., 7 mos. and 61 days, on London. Via Liverpool, c/o Benjamin Greenwood.

[1] *Report*, p. 36.

Cleugh, Teale & Groves, London. 4 mos., 2 mos. and 61 days, or 3 mos. and 21 days, on London. Via Liverpool, c/o B. Greenwood.

Dickson & Watson, Stockton-on-Tees. 4 mos., 2 mos. and 61 days, on Nicholson Haydon & Co., London. Via Maryport, c/o John Gillespie.

Dunn & Dixon, Durham. 4 mos., 2 mos. and 61 days, on London. Via Maryport, c/o Wilkinson Ostle, and to Newcastle, c/o Nichol & Ludlow.

George Binns & Co., Sunderland. 4 mos. They remit us. Via Maryport, c/o Wilkinson Ostle.

Foster, Fisher & Co., Bristol. 4 mos., 2 mos. and 61 days. Ship Belfast to Bristol.

Fenton, Sadler & Sadler,[1] Leeds. 4 mos., at end of which draw at 21 days on Sir Richard Carr Glynn & Co., London. Shipped at Belfast by Robert Delap, for Liverpool.

William Green, Bristol. Credit 6 mos., 4 mos. and 61 days. Ship Belfast to Bristol.

Benjamin Greenwood,[2] Liverpool, 6 mos., 4 mos. and 61 days. Ship to Liverpool.

Jno. & Geo. Gradwell, Preston, Lancs. On shipping @ 21 days. Commn. 2½ p. c. Draw on Jos. Dennison & Co., London. Ship to Liverpool, c/o Anthony Swainson.

E. & A. Jacob & Co., Waterford, 4 mos. from receipt of goods. They remit. Forwarded c. p. Dublin.

Jenkins & Walduck, Bristol.

James Jackson, Lancaster. Credit 4 mos.

John Janson & Co., London. 21 days on shipping. On London. Via Liverpool c/o B. Greenwood.

Wilson, Johnston & Co., Dublin. 4 mos., 2 mos. and 61 days.

Lucas & Procter, London. 2 mos. and 61 days. Via Liverpool, c/o B. Greenwood.

Metford & Lansdown, Bristol. Buy brown goods for them on commn. 2½ p. c. 21 days on Bristol, payable in London. Ship to Bristol.

Martindale & Bragg, Manchester. 4 mos., 2 mos. and 61 days, on Manchester, payable in London. Via Liverpool.

Richard Markham, Sunderland. 4 mos., 2 mos. and 61 days, on Sunderland, payable in London. Via Maryport, c/o Wilkinson Ostle.

Oldham & Ravenhill, London. Buy Hillsboroughs [3] on

---

[1] A branch of the Sadler family was afterwards engaged in the linen trade in Belfast.

[2] He was the shipping agent for a large part of Richardsons' goods, and bought linen himself to the value of about £2,000 a year. He may have acted as a buyer for Liverpool merchants who were engaged in American and colonial trade.

[3] These were the coarse cloths known as Hillsborough haggs, or huggs.

commn. 2½ p. c. 21 days on London for these. White goods, 2 mos. and 61 days. Send by Wm. Phelps from Belfast.

Orton & Beckwith, Sunderland. 4 mos., 2 mos. and 61 days on Sunderland, payable in London. Via Maryport, c/o Wilkinson Ostle.

Parsons, Hurles & Co., Bristol. Browns on commn., 21 days on Bristol, payable in London. Whites, 4 mos., 2 mos. and 61 days. Ship to Bristol.

Procter & Spence, North Shields. 4 mos., 2 mos., and 61 days.[1]

(ii.) *Export of Yarn from Silesia.* In connexion with the decline in the export of yarn from Ireland, it is interesting to notice that there was a similar, and apparently a much greater, fall in the production of yarn in Silesia. The effects there were more serious for three reasons. In the first place, export of flax was forbidden, so that the farmer had not even the consolation of selling raw material in place of partly manufactured goods. Secondly, during the period of war it was difficult to find a market for linen cloth, and there was a general decline in the whole industry, involving a smaller demand for flax. Thirdly, in spite of constant efforts on the part of their rulers, the peasantry clung persistently to the old method of spinning with distaff and spindle, refusing even to use the wheel. Their yarn was very soft and easily bleached, but the coarser counts could not possibly find a sale in western markets in competition with machine-made yarn. In 1797 the minister, Hagen, who knew something of the development of steam-power in England and Scotland, told the Silesian Chamber that the days of hand-spinning were numbered; but his proposal to set up publicly owned mills was strongly resisted by the merchants and bleachers. His agitation led to nothing more than a revival of spinning schools, and the spindle and distaff remained in general use (Zimmermann, op. cit., p. 214). The Silesian farmer-weavers, deprived within a few years of a great part of the demand for raw flax, yarn and cloth, must have suffered terribly during the war.

---

[1] In a later list there is a repetition of the six months' credit to B. Greenwood of Liverpool and Wm. Green of Bristol. Similar credit (four months and a 61 days' draft) is given to Broadhurst, Morris & Co. (Lancashire ?), Stockdale & White (Yorkshire ?), and John Wilson, a large customer in London. Cadbury & James receive five months' credit (four months and a 31 days' draft). The senior partner in this firm was probably Benjamin Cadbury, who at that time had a linen-draper's shop in Bull Street, Birmingham.

XIV

GROWTH OF CAPITALISM, 1800–25

DURING the first quarter of the nineteenth century bleachers were the dominant figures in the Irish linen industry. Bleaching and finishing were the only processes of manufacture controlled entirely by large employers. But already there were signs of change. Between 1800 and 1820 capitalism, in the sense of factory production, appeared in all the remaining branches of manufacture—flax preparation, spinning, and weaving.

Scutching by Water Power. The idea of machines for flax preparation was by no means new. Even before 1740 there were some scutching mills in Ireland, but apparently little machinery was used at that time.[1] In 1760 Stephenson remarked on a mill in co. Mayo, ' on the old horizontal model,'[2] and in the following year he mentioned a great number of mills in Donegal and Londonderry.[3] But the eighteenth-century mills did such poor work that, according to Young, it was found actually more economical to scutch by hand.[4] It seems to have been the great need of flax in Scotland that led to the invention of more efficient machinery early in the nineteenth century. Marshall, the inspector to the Linen Board, in his report of a tour in Scotland, printed in 1817, said that there were more than four hundred scutching mills in the country, with from four to nine workers in each. Most of them were of a type with vertical shafts, which was evidently new in Stephenson's time, and had been in fashion ever since. But improved machines—fitted, like those first designed, and like the machines in use to-day, with horizontal shafts—had recently been set up in some Scottish mills, and at the time when Marshall wrote, four had been ordered for use in Ireland. The practice of scutching by water-power spread rapidly during the next few years,[5] and it would undoubtedly help to bring down the price of home-grown flax.

---

[1] *Thoughts on the Importance of the Linen Manufacture* (1739), p. 13.
[2] *Report*, 1760–1, p. 63.   [3] ibid., p. 89.   [4] *Tour*, p. 110.
[5] e. g. some of the Livery Companies of London encouraged the use of scutching mills among their tenants in co. Derry (Charley, p. 25). For the action of the Linen Board in regard to scutching machinery see below, chap. xv.

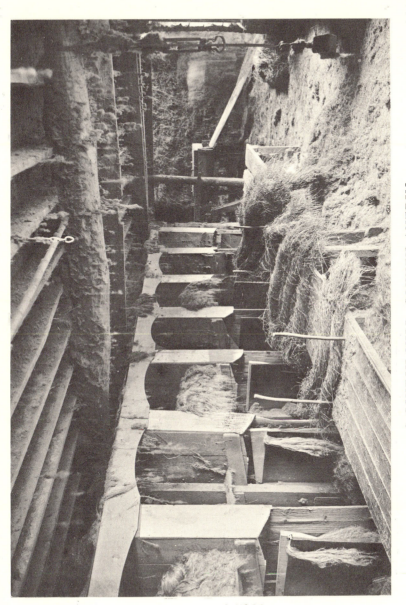

A SCUTCH MILL, COUNTY ANTRIM

Machine Spinning: its origin. The use of scutching mills was
encouraged by the strong demand for flax in Great Britain. This
demand, in turn, was due to the practice of machine spinning.
There was also, in 1817, a certain amount of machine spinning in
Ireland ; but in this matter Ireland was far behind Great Britain.
There was a strong contrast, too, between the backwardness
of flax spinning and the rapid advance of cotton spinning in
Ulster. In order to appreciate these differences we must first
trace the origin of machine spinning in England and Scotland.

The competition of cotton goods with linen, intensified by the
use of water-frames and mules for cotton spinning, led after
1780 to attempts on the part of English linen dealers to produce
linen yarn by machinery. In 1787 a practicable method was
patented by Kendrew, an optician, and Porthouse, a cloth
manufacturer, both of Darlington. The general principle of
their invention was the same as that of the modern spinning
machinery : the hackled flax was drawn into a sliver by successive rollers, and twisted on spindles. Their patent was worked
in the following year by John Marshall, in a small mill near Leeds.
In 1791 he set up larger works at Holbeck, driven at first by a
Savary steam-engine, helped out by water-power ; but in 1792
he introduced improved machinery, with 900 spindles, worked
by a Boulton & Watt engine. During the next thirty years
other firms in Leeds started spinning by machinery, although
Marshalls continued to make about a third of the yarn produced
in the town. Their yarn was supplied chiefly to manufacturers
of coarse linen goods in Barnsley. Gradually machine spinning
spread to other parts of the country, especially to Lancashire,
where linen mills were worked beside the cotton mills of Bolton,
Manchester, and Preston.[1] At the same time spinning machinery
was spreading in Scotland. The first mill, worked by Sim and
Thom of Kincardine, under Kendrew and Porthouse's patent,
was actually set up a few months before Marshall's.[2] Three
years later Ivory & Co. of Brigton, Forfarshire, followed suit,
and in 1792 they installed a steam-engine.[3] The spinning
industry developed chiefly in the eastern counties, because linen

---

[1] For a detailed account of the machinery, and a description of Marshall's
work, see Horner, chap. xxix.
[2] Bremner, p. 228.   [3] ibid., p. 219.

manufacture in general, which had previously flourished in Renfrew, Lanark, and Ayr, was being driven from the western counties by the more remunerative trade in cotton.[1]

Spinning Mills in Ireland. Thus, before the end of the eighteenth century machine spinning and steam-power had already made a considerable impression on the linen trade in England and Scotland. In Ireland there was probably no mechanical spinning at all at that time. As for steam-power, although it was in use for cotton spinning in Lisburn as early as 1790, it was not introduced into the Irish linen industry until almost forty years later. There is reason to believe that spinning mills, driven by water-power, were first used in Ireland shortly after 1800. Dr. Stephenson, writing in 1808, said that there were already some ' very extensive mills ' in Antrim, Armagh, and Tyrone ; [2] but they must have been quite new, for it was stated by a competent witness, in 1811, that there was no machine spinning of flax in Ireland ' till within these few years '.[3]

By 1803 the Linen Board had become interested in the subject, and just as it had given grants in earlier times for the building of bleach works, so now it offered bounties for linen mills, usually of 30s. for each spindle. The general bounties continued from 1803 to 1811, and afterwards special grants were made to individual firms. Some firms received substantial help. Crookshank, Kennedy & Co., of Buncrana, co. Donegal, were given £2,600 ; two others, Ferguson of Belfast and the Nicholsons of Bessbrook, received over £1,000 each ; and in three cases the Board supplied half the entire capital.[4]

An account of these grants, presented to the Board in 1811, shows that only twelve firms, working on an average 530 spindles each, existed in the whole of Ulster.[5] Six years later Corry mentioned three other spinners, who were still working on a comparatively small scale. All the mills at that time, and for another twelve years, were driven by water-power, and produced only the lowest counts of yarn for sail-cloth and coarse canvas.[6]

---

[1] As raw cotton and yarn were chiefly imported into Glasgow, the cotton trade naturally grew up in the west ; and the import of Russian flax similarly drew the linen manufacture to the East.

[2] *Select Papers*, p. 23.   [3] Wakefield, vol. i, p. 684.

[4] A further description of these bounties is given in chap. xv.

[5] Horner, p. 186.   [6] Corry, *Report*, pp. 6, 7, 28–30.

The reason why machine spinning made such slow progress was well stated by one of the largest spinners, Joseph Nicholson of Bessbrook, who wrote in 1811 :

' The leading cause against the extension of machinery is the low price of labour ; yarn spun by women is sold here much cheaper than the same article manufactured by machinery in England. ... To one unacquainted with Ireland the small earnings of the poorer females—frequently not more than two pence per day working diligently from morning to night, for months together—must appear very extraordinary ; and under such circumstances, it is unlikely that this trade should increase so much as it might, though spurred on in the beginning by offers of large premiums from the Linen Board.'

Nicholson added that although one person working with a machine could produce ten times as much as a hand-spinner, he would estimate the economy of machine production over hand-labour as no more than a halfpenny per hank (i. e. $8\frac{1}{2}$ per cent.), in the case of 12 lea yarn. Wages and overhead expenses were much higher in the mill, and the handworker, from any given quality of raw material, could produce a yarn perhaps four or six times as fine as the machine-made goods. The saving in England would, of course, be larger, because of the higher wages for hand-labour.

There was something to be said on the other side. The machine spinner had greater facilities for buying flax, and his goods were generally of sounder quality than those made by hand. Consequently there was a strong demand for them for use as warp. Further, the large dealer could find a readier market, by trading over a wider area and giving credit—and, the writer might have added, he could draw a fresh profit by employing weavers to work up his yarns. Therefore Nicholson concluded, rightly, that the advantage on the whole lay with machine spinning, and that ' this improvement would, one time or other, become a source of prosperity to the country '.[1] But that time was not to come until the invention of wet-spinning had enabled machines to produce finer yarn, and until their productive power had been

---

[1] Nicholson's observations are quoted by Horner, pp. 251-2. Wakefield, who knew Nicholson personally, and described him as ' a very intelligent manufacturer ', drew similar evidence from him (*Account of Ireland*, vol. i, p. 684).

increased by the use of steam-engines, supported by a cheap and abundant supply of coal.

Weaving Factories. In the weaving of coarse cloth, production on a large scale had made some progress in Ireland, but less, as we should expect, than in Great Britain. A Scottish spinner, Wilson of Brechin, actually used power-looms with success, from 1810 onwards, although they were hardly known in Ireland before 1850. Wilson gave as the reason of his experiment that the labour of hand-loom weavers was scarce and expensive.[1] This seems at a first glance a surprising statement, seeing that employment in the linen trade was reduced by the war. But the fact is that Scottish manufacturers, who specialized in coarse cloths, would be kept busy, as were the makers of sail-cloth in Cork, by Government contracts. This fact also explains the statement that the general use of power-looms had been prevented by a fall in the wages of hand-loom weaving ; for after the war, when orders from the Government ceased, employment would be reduced, and wages would fall in consequence.

By 1817, when the account of this enterprise was written, small weaving factories, furnished with hand-looms, had appeared in Ulster. They were the result, not so much of war-time conditions, as of machine spinning. The owners of spinning mills in Ulster, like the great cotton spinners in Lancashire, soon found it ' more profitable to work up the yarn into saleable cloth, than to dispose of it to the small hand-loom manufacturers through the country '.[2] Some of them, such as the Nicholsons of Bessbrook, co. Armagh, employed only spinners in their mill, but gave out yarn to domestic weavers, who worked for wages. Others had looms on their own premises. Samuel Smith, of Ballymoney, for example, had both a mill with three hundred spindles, and a weaving shed with thirteen looms.

Some other firms did no spinning, but employed weavers in their own factories, buying all their yarn from the spinning mills. Francis McCracken and Thomas Ekenhead, of Belfast, carried on this kind of business. McCracken bought his raw material from

---

[1] Marshall, *Report of Tour*, 1817, p. 25. Wilson used the labour of boys and girls, with one supervisor to twelve of them, and he found the quality of the cloth quite satisfactory. One horse-power was enough to work six looms.   [2] Charley, op. cit., p. 89.

Samuel Smith and from two other spinners, one in Ballymena and the other in co. Armagh.[1] These factories were clearly the outcome of machine spinning. The supply of yarn in bulk, for them as for the ' factory masters ' of co. Louth, was an economy which enabled them to pay sufficient wages and still to have a profit from the use of hand-looms.[2] On the other hand, it was a great convenience to the spinners to dispose of their yarn in large amounts.

Capital in Fine Manufacture. (i.) *Damask.* These new concerns all dealt with low counts of yarn, and hteir significance may be summed up by saying that capitalism had appeared in the manufacture of coarse linen. In some other branches of the industry production on a large scale was old-established : in some it was beginning at this same time. Damask weaving, for instance, was a slow and expensive process, and we have seen that the weavers were very early employed for wages. By 1820 Coulson's business in Lisburn had been in existence for more than half a century. Although the elaborate Jacquard looms seem not to have been used in Ireland before 1823, the old-fashioned damask loom, worked with the help of draw-boys, was none the less beyond the resources of the ordinary weaver.[3]

(ii.) *Thread.* Thread-making, again, had been attempted on a large scale since about 1750. It seems to have been a favourite undertaking of ladies, because it was a means of giving employment to poor women. We have noticed the striking enterprise of Sarah Smith & Co., in Waterford. In 1760 Stephenson mentioned a mill in co. Longford, owned by Mrs. Bond, and two years later a small concern managed by the Misses Harris in Queen's County.[4] The fashion soon spread to Ulster. In 1763 and 1764 considerable grants were made by the Linen Board to Elizabeth Hare, of Moira, and Esther Cherry, of Acton, co.

---

[1] Corry, *Report*, 1817, pp. 28–30.

[2] It will be remembered that they paid higher wages than those of domestic workers.

[3] Michael Andrews, of Ardoyne, who had set up a damask factory in Belfast in 1810, introduced two Jacquard looms in 1823 (Horner, p. 135). In 1827 the Linen Board paid £37 to Richard Robinson for setting up a damask loom in the Dublin Linen Hall, and in the same year they gave £140 to private manufacturers to help in the purchase of new damask looms. These looms were probably all of the Jacquard type. In several other instances the Trustees exhibited specimens of new kinds of machinery in the Linen Hall.

[4] *Reports*, 1760–1, pp. 80, 81 ; 1762, p. 2.

Armagh, for the equipment of thread-mills.[1] Nearly twenty years later there was a fresh outburst of enterprise, probably as a result of the introduction of cotton spinning machinery. Ten applications for the endowment of thread-mills were received in 1782 by the Linen Board. One firm at least proposed to use water-power.[2] But apparently these attempts had no great importance. Most of the thread used in Ireland was still imported from the neighbourhood of Aberdeen,[3] and a large amount was sold in Ireland by Marshall, of Leeds.[4]

The first permanently successful thread-mill in Ulster was founded in 1784 by a Scotsman, John Barbour. His works were at Plantation, near Lisburn ; they were moved in 1831 to Hilden, and they have remained on the same site to the present day.[5] Early in the nineteenth century another thread-mill, which is also still working on a large scale, was started in Lisburn by Robert Stewart ; and by that time a great number of women, perhaps 2,000, were employed either in spinning yarn for these mills or in the actual making of thread.[6] The industry lent itself to factory production because the thread was not only spun, but also bleached or dyed and finished, on the premises, so that a thread-mill implied bleachworks and expensive machinery.

(iii.) *Cambric.* The production of cambric, which had previously been in the hands of small manufacturers, was first undertaken on a large scale by T. McMurray, of Dromore, co. Down, whose business was founded in 1803. Soon after 1820 two other cambric concerns were started, one of them owned by a branch of the Richardson family.[7]

(iv.) *Diaper.* The making of fine diapers, which involved the use of expensive looms, was also undertaken by large employers, in the north of co. Armagh. Sir Charles Coote wrote in regard to

---

[1] *Proceedings*, 1763, pp. 47, 195 ; 1764, pp. 120, 129, 181.
[2] ibid., 1782, pp. 76, 146 sqq.
[3] Bremner, op. cit., p. 228 ; Horner, p. 305.
[4] McCall, p. 109 ; Warden, p. 384.
[5] Owen, *History of Belfast*, p. 376. The Hilden works were established by John Barbour's son William. Another son, John, kept the original mill at Plantation until his death in 1831. Then the whole plant was brought to Hilden, and the two firms were combined as Wm. Barbour & Sons.
[6] McCall, u.s.
[7] ibid., p. 79. McMurray's firm became McMurray & Henning, and it has been continued by Messrs. Henning & Co. to the present day.

this manufacture : ' The yarn is always the property of the merchant, who gives it out to the weavers on task work.' [1]

These particulars show that employment for wages had become common in both the coarse and the fine branches of manufacture ; and although plain linens were probably made to a great extent by independent craftsmen, we should remember that many bleachers were supplying themselves with cloth of this kind by the direct employment of weavers. In addition, the bleachers had under their control large staffs of bleachyard workers, clerks, warehousemen, and linen buyers. Thus it is clear that in the linen trade as a whole, and in almost every section of it, there was already, before 1820, a strong movement in the direction of modern capitalism.

Employment for Wages. The proof is not only in the presence of large bleachgreens and mills, but also in the various reports on brown linen markets, which, like Greer's report of 1784, afford a rough indication of the amount of employment for wages. Their evidence points to the following conclusions, which may be stated in the form of a table, showing approximate averages for the period 1816–21 : [2]

	yds.
Linen exported	46,200,000
Home consumption . . .	38,600,000
Total output	84,800,000
Manufactured in South . . .	14,300,000
Manufactured in Ulster . . .	70,500,000
Sold in markets in Ulster . .	44,100,000
Sold out of markets in Ulster. .	26,400,000

The sale of cloth outside the markets, that is, by private contract, meant practically the sale of cloth manufactured on a large scale ; for weavers would very seldom dispose of their linen privately to a dealer unless they were employed by him for wages. Hence it appears that rather more than a third of the linen produced in Ulster about the year 1820 was made by large manufacturers who dealt outside the markets.

Employment by Small Manufacturers. But there is another important point to be considered. We have thus far made a

[1] Coote, *Survey of Armagh*, p. 340.
[2] The method of arriving at these figures (which represent only a rough approach to the facts) is given in a note at the end of the chapter.

broad distinction between the craftsman working for the open market and a journeyman working for his employer. A closer examination of Corry's report for 1816 proves, however, that the markets were by no means entirely served by independent weavers. Corry mentions the average attendance of sellers and the average number of webs sold in each market. In many cases a seller disposed of two or three webs together, and in Armagh the proportion was nine webs to each seller. Now it would normally take a weaver two or three weeks to finish a piece. A weaver, helped by one or two members of his family, might send on an average one piece to market each week ; but when two or more webs were sent the seller was obviously a small employer— in Armagh some of the dealers must have employed from a dozen to twenty men. According to Corry's statements, half the sales in Ulster were made in markets in which two or more pieces were sold by each man. It does not follow, of course, that every dealer was a small capitalist, but neither does it follow that in the other markets every seller was a working weaver. We may balance the exceptions one against the other, and conclude that about half the sales were made by 'manufacturers', and therefore represented goods made by journeymen.

The statistics thus suggest that the linen produced in Ulster about the year 1820 could be classified into three nearly equal groups, the first consisting of cloth made by small craftsmen and sold in the market, the second of cloth made for small manufacturers and sold by them in the market, the third made for larger employers and sold privately, or made for the bleachers by direct employment.

The classification is clearer since each of these methods of production was typical of particular parts of Ulster ; and in order to gain a more exact idea of the growth of capitalism we need to distinguish between the areas of rapid change, in which production on a large scale was common, and the conservative districts, where capitalism had made little headway.[1]

---

[1] The whole study of economic history is complicated by the irregularity of changes. In the later Middle Ages, for instance, while the smaller towns of Europe maintained a simple system of local trade the great towns, such as Florence, Venice, Augsburg, Cologne, Bruges and Ghent, had developed overseas markets, bills of exchange, joint-stock companies, and funded debts. Serfdom disappeared from Flanders about five centuries before its abolition

Local Differences. (i.) *Districts of Bleaching.* In the first place, the bleachgreens all lay along the lines of rivers : on the lower course of the Lagan, especially between Lisburn and Belfast ; on the upper Bann, in the neighbourhood of Banbridge, Moyallon, and Lurgan ; on the lower Bann, about Coleraine ; and on the River Roe at Limavady. In these districts employment on a large scale was the most abundant, and changes, both industrial and commercial, were the most rapid. It happened that the southern bleaching districts were also centres of the more advanced kinds of manufacture—damask and fine linens near Lisburn, cambric, lawns, and diapers near Lurgan—which involved either expen-sive machinery or the use of imported flax, and therefore lent themselves to organization on a large scale.

Thus we may mark out the east of Londonderry, the south of Antrim, the centre and west of Down, and the north of Armagh, as districts in which capitalism was the most fully developed.

The fact that so many of the employers were bleachers had an interesting effect on the grouping of population. In earlier times, when practically the whole demand for brown linen came through the open market, weavers would naturally wish to live near to a town, for convenience in selling their cloth and buying flax or yarn. But with a steadily increasing demand on the part of bleachers for the direct supply of cloth by means of hired labour, weavers gradually settled in larger and larger numbers in the neighbourhood of bleachgreens. The census returns show time after time a bleachyard, the owner's house, and a little community of bleachyard workers and weavers settled round them.[1] McCall, in describing the organization of the linen trade about 1800, mentioned the migration of weavers from towns to the country. Their destination is shown by his statement that ' wheresoever an enterprising merchant was found at work, drapers were certain to congregate, and weavers as rapidly

in France and Prussia. In England, during the fifteenth century, the growth of trade on a national scale, with central markets in London, had most involved and varied effects in different parts of the country. There was a fresh set of complications when the centres of industry began to move from the south and east of England to the north and the midlands. Thus the local differences in Ulster illustrate on a small scale one of the chief characteristics of economic development.

[1] To give one example out of many, close to the bleachgreen of William Hudson, near Banbridge, nineteen households of his employees—bleachyard hands and weavers—were settled.

increased '.[1] Towards 1820, the persons congregating in new centres of trade would be linen buyers rather than drapers. The 'enterprising merchant' in almost every case would be a bleacher, and the migration of weavers meant a concentration round the bleachgreens.

There were, it is true, comparatively large manufacturers who had offices and warehouses in the towns to which weavers would bring their cloth, taking away with them fresh supplies of yarn.[2] Such concerns, although they would tend to destroy the open markets, would not draw weavers away from the towns ; but direct employment by bleachers was apparently large enough to cause a considerable movement of population.

(ii.) *Districts of Independent Weavers.* There was a sharp contrast to all this change and activity in the simple and stable organization of some other areas, notably north Antrim, Tyrone, parts of Londonderry, and the outlying districts in general. In these places trade was still in the hands of independent weavers, drapers, and jobbers.

This local distinction had already appeared in 1762, for it will be remembered that in the north of Antrim at that time the regulations for sealing were neglected, and there was no sign of disturbance or agitation.[3] The trouble was all in the more advanced districts, where weavers were falling into subjection to employers. But in north Antrim the old system of trade was so firmly fixed that, nearly a century later, when brown linen markets had nearly disappeared elsewhere, the market in Bally-mena was still flourishing. The fact was that the wide plain lands served by the markets of Ballymena, Ballymoney, and Ahoghill were distant from the centres of bleaching ; cut off by mountains from the coast, and therefore free from invasion by the cotton trade ; so far also from the centres of direct export that there was still scope for drapers to connect the weaver and the merchant—the more scope since many of the cloths from north Antrim were exported unbleached.[4] The same conditions

---

[1] op. cit., pp. 32, 53.

[2] cf. McCall (p. 71) : ' Some of the more extensive class of manufacturers had warerooms in certain towns, where on market days they sold their goods to regular customers.' [3] *A Brief State of the Debate*, p. 9.

[4] See Corry's list of local manufactures in his *Report* for 1816.

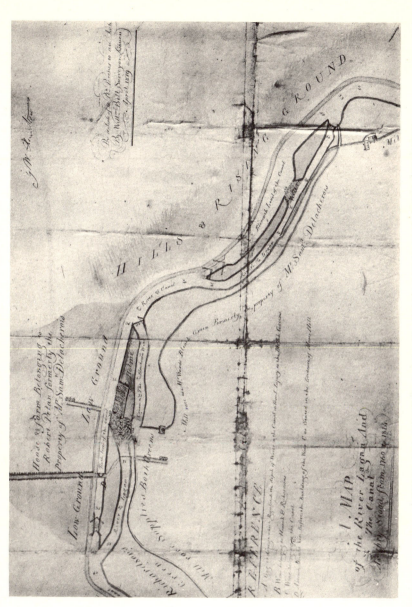

MAP OF RIVER LAGAN, SHOWING BLEACH-GREENS

held, *mutatis mutandis*, in the other districts lying outside the bleachers' sphere of influence.

(iii.) *District of Small Employers.* Near the southern boundary of Ulster, in south Armagh and north Monaghan, there was a peculiar system, not found elsewhere to anything like the same extent. Arthur Young had noted the abundance of ' manufacturers ' in co. Armagh ; [1] a quarter of a century later Sir Charles Coote had remarked on the same point ; [2] and the statistics of sales in the great market at Armagh—as we noticed earlier in this chapter—prove the presence of many small employers.

Nearly all the coarse linens produced in this district were made in the south of Armagh and the north of Monaghan, and a great proportion of the coarse cloth was sold in the market at Armagh.[3] A working weaver could not easily travel so far to market, and in all probability a good deal of flax from the southern provinces or from the Baltic States was used. On both these grounds there was an economic gain in marketing by small manufacturers ; but the manufacturer had not yet such facilities for credit and accumulation of capital that he could develop trade on a large scale, and deal directly with exporters, or export on his own account. Therefore his sales were still made for cash to drapers or linen buyers in the open market ; and as the market of Armagh was one of the largest in Ulster, there must have been a numerous body of manufacturers dealing there.[4]

Decline of Open Markets. It is worth while to notice one other movement, which in this period was confined to co. Down. In the east and centre of the county the cotton trade was competing with the manufacture of linen, and machine spinning had begun to affect domestic production. The west and north were areas of bleaching and of the finest branches of the industry.

[1] *Tour*, pp. 103 sqq.   [2] *Survey of Armagh*, pp. 138–41.

[3] Coote, *Survey of Armagh*, p. 267. Most of the trade in this market was in coarse cloth. The estimate of webs sealed in a year was 260,000 at a price below the average (10·83*d.*), and 52,000 at higher prices. Nothing worth more than 1*s.* 4*d.* a yard was sold in Armagh, whereas the finer linens in Lurgan, Lisburn, and Belfast cost from 1*s.* 6*d.* to 2*s.* a yard.

[4] Corry's Report for 1816 shows that there were settlements of manufacturers in co. Down, especially near Banbridge, Kircubbin, and Newry. In the neighbourhood of Belfast and Lisburn there were ' richer manufacturers ', who took to market packs containing from ten to forty pieces. But these large dealers must have been few in number ; for in Belfast and Lisburn the pieces offered by each seller averaged only 2½ and 4 respectively.

Consequently the system of trade was changing more rapidly there than in most districts of Ulster. In particular the brown linen markets were falling into disuse. The only markets of any importance remaining in 1820 were held in the towns of Banbridge and Newry.[1] They were maintained because there was a certain demand for brown linen for export from Newry, and because bleachers found it worth while to make some purchases in the markets through their linen buyers. But the old methods of trade were clearly passing out of fashion. Of the eight other markets which had once existed in the county, three had disappeared by 1820, and two were near to dissolution.[2] Whereas the sales in the markets of Ulster as a whole increased in value between 1784 and 1816 by 89 per cent., the increase in co. Down was only 15 per cent.

The movement which had already taken effect in co. Down gained in force and extent during the next thirty years. It led to a general disappearance of open markets and independent weavers, to the establishment of factory production, and the growth of a modern organization of trade.

NOTES TO CHAPTER XIV

I. *Statistics of Employment*

The basis of calculation is contained in three reports by James Corry, Secretary to the Linen Board, on the brown linen markets in Ulster during the years 1816, 1820, and 1821, and the reports of Besnard and Corry on the southern provinces in 1816 and 1821. The reports give estimates of the value of weekly or yearly sales in all the markets of Ireland. The reports of 1820 and 1821 for Ulster are very detailed : they state the value of all the different kinds of cloth sold in each market, and the normal price per yard of each kind. By dividing the total value of any quality by the price per yard, we can find the estimated amount of that quality sold annually in any given market ; and then, by adding together

---

[1] In 1784 these two markets had rather more than half, in 1820 about five-eighths of the total trade of the county.

[2] Seeing that the markets remaining in 1820 were all within the area of cotton manufacture, the change could not be wholly due to the competition of cotton : it must have been quite as much the result of capitalism in the linen trade.

the amounts of all qualities in all the markets we may estimate
the total sales in open markets in the whole of Ulster.[1] This
calculation yields the result that in 1820 about 41,000,000 yards
were sold for £1,850,000, an average price of 10·83 pence per yard;
and in 1821, about 45,000,000 yards were sold for £2,073,000, an
average price of 10·97 pence per yard.

The average price in 1816 would be rather higher. In 1820
there was a slump in fine linens,[2] so that an abnormally large
proportion of the cloth sold in that year would be coarse, and
therefore cheap. We should not be far wrong in assuming a price
of slightly over 1s. a yard in 1816. At these prices the quantities
sold in the Ulster linen markets would be as follows :

	Value. £	Yds.
1816 . .	2,324,000	46,000,000
1820 . .	1,850,000	41,000,000
1821 . .	2,073,000	45,400,000
		(Average, 44,100,000)

In order to find approximately the total output of Ulster we
need to estimate the output of the whole country and that of the
other three provinces. As we noticed in Chapter VIII, the total
production for Ireland in 1802 was estimated at 70,000,000 yards.
In that year the exports were 37,800,000 yards, so that 32,200,000
yards would remain for home consumption. The population of
Ireland increased between 1802 and 1821 from slightly over
5,000,000 to 6,800,000. Therefore we should expect a considerable growth in the domestic demand. But the growth would not
be proportionate to that of the population—partly because of
the increasing use of cotton goods, and partly because a great
part of the expansion of population would be among the poorest
of the peasantry. Allowing for these factors, we may make the
following estimates :

	Export. yds.	Home consumption. yds.	Total output. yds.
1816 . . .	45,600,000	36,400,000	82,000,000
1820 . . .	43,500,000	39,500,000	83,000,000
1821 . . .	49,500,000	40,000,000	89,500,000

[1] The table for 1821 gives as well the number of webs of each quality sold
in the different markets, and the average length of each kind of web ; so that
in this case the number of yards sold can be found either by multiplication
or by division.

[2] See below, note ii.

As for the output from the other three provinces, these estimates were given by Besnard and Corry :

	In open markets.	Outside markets.	Total.	Yds. at 10·83d. a yd.
	£	£	£	
1816 (Besnard)	456,080	195,600	651,680	14,300,000
1821 (Corry)	471,000	(202,000)	(673,000)	(14,500,000)

Corry does not give an estimate of sales outside the markets, but I have supplied a figure proportionate to that of 1816. The sales in 1820 would be smaller than those of 1821 ; and we may assume without much error that the total output in 1820 was about 14,000,000 yards.

The output from Ulster would then be :

				yds.
1816	.	.	.	67,700,000
1820	.	.	.	69,000,000
1821	.	.	.	75,000,000
			(Average,	70,500,000)

A small amount of the exports for each year would be manufactured in the previous year, and as the markets were glutted in 1820 the proportion carried over to 1821 would be rather larger than the normal. But it is hardly worth while to allow for this difference, seeing that the adjustment would not affect the average figures. Therefore we may accept the figures as they stand, and conclude that the amounts of cloth sold privately in Ulster (the differences between the total output and the market sales) were as follows :

				yds.
1816	.	.	.	21,700,000
1820	.	.	.	28,000,000
1821	.	.	.	29,600,000
			(Average,	26,400,000)

Thus it appears that about 36 per cent. of the cloth produced in Ulster was sold privately, outside the open markets.

The conclusions drawn from these accounts are confirmed by Corry's statement of the webs sold weekly in the various markets of Ulster in 1816 and 1821. According to his information, the total weekly sales amounted in 1816 to 24,150 webs, and in 1821 to 22,765 webs. As it took normally about a fortnight to weave a piece, these webs would represent the weekly work respectively of 48,300 and 45,530 men. If the weavers serving open markets were two-thirds of the total number, the total would be from 68,000 to 72,000. There are several indications that the average output of a weaver was approximately 1,000 yards a year. Hence the output of all the weavers in Ulster would be, on an average of the two years, about 70,000,000 yards—a result which corresponds closely with that of the other calculation.

It seems probable, then, that there were about 70,000 weavers in Ulster at that time, and that rather more than a third of their output was produced on a large scale. The number of weavers of the three different classes (independent craftsmen, employees of small manufacturers, and employees of large firms) would not be exactly proportioned to their output ; for the wage-earners would give most of their time to weaving, whereas the independent craftsman would have to devote some time both to farm work and to attending markets. Therefore a third of the weavers, and perhaps rather more, may still have been independent.

II. *The Trading Depression of 1820*

It has been mentioned that the export markets were overstocked in 1820, and that the trouble seems to have affected chiefly the finer branches of the industry.[1] The following figures illustrate these two points:

Estimated Trade in Brown Linen Markets

	1816	1820	Increase or decrease
	£	£	per cent.
Co. Down	174,252	216,260 [2]	+ 24
„ Armagh	353,600	554,180	+ 57
„ Antrim	697,600	273,460	− 61
„ Tyrone	559,260	363,560	− 36
„ Londonderry	176,160	192,030	+ 9

Of the counties which showed an increase, Armagh was very largely supplied with coarse cloths from the southern districts and from Monaghan ; Londonderry and Down produced both fine and coarse cloths. In Down, as in north Armagh, there was

[1] Mr. Horner (op. cit., p. 198) suggested that the decline was due to a rapid increase of weaving for large manufacturers ; but this idea is disproved by the recovery of the markets in 1821, when the quantity of cloth sold in them was almost equal to the quantity sold in 1816.

[2] In this estimate I have corrected the mistake in Corry's return for Downpatrick (see table in Appendix I). But it is shown in the notes on the table that the returns for the whole of the markets in south Down were probably exaggerated in this year.

a fine manufacture; but to an increasing extent it was in the hands of large employers, who did not sell in the markets. There were also in co. Down small manufacturers of fine linen, but they supplied chiefly the markets of Belfast and Lisburn, which were in co. Antrim. In these two markets, which depended chiefly on fine linens, there was an extraordinary falling off. In Lisburn the figures for 1820 were less than a third of those for 1816 (£83,000 instead of £260,000) ; in Belfast the proportion was a little less than two-fifths. Dungannon, co. Tyrone, was another important centre of fine manufacture. The turnover there in 1816 was the same as that of the Belfast market, £4,000 a week. It is significant that the decline of trade in Dungannon was also almost the same as that of Belfast : the turnover in 1820 was £1,583 a week in Belfast, £1,560 in Dungannon. A great slump in fine linens and a good demand for coarse would explain the above figures, and would help to account for the fact that exports in 1820 were not much smaller in volume than in 1816.

XV

THE LAST YEARS OF THE LINEN BOARD (1800–28)

The Act of Union. From 1801 onwards, control of the Linen Board, and of the linen industry as a whole, passed to the British Parliament. The Act of Union, however, made no appreciable difference to the industry. The fuller freedom of trade between Great Britain and Ireland might have been expected to increase the export of goods in general, linen goods among the rest ; but any such tendency was defeated by the difficulty of overseas trade in time of war. The administrative system was hardly changed at all before 1823. The Linen Board remained in office and received annually its fixed grant of £21,600.[1] The regulating Act of 1782 was still in force—or as much in force as it ever had been. Inspectors and sealmasters continued their work. Bounties for export of sail cloth and coarse linen were still paid, and in 1805 they were renewed for an indefinite period.[2]

The only changes in the system were made in the first four years. In 1802 the Trustees were allowed to appoint inspectors in the chief seaports to examine imported seed, flax, hemp, and yarn.[3] By an Act of 1804 they were given leave to raise one of their provincial inspectors to the position of Inspector-General for the whole of Ireland.[4] In the same Act it was provided that if a buyer of Irish linen in England complained of any piece of cloth, the London agent of the Linen Board should summon a few experts—from three to five merchants, drapers or bleachers—to examine the cloth and report their verdict to him. The Trustees, acting on the report of this jury, would award any damages that might be due. The Act also gave formal recognition to the use of hydrochloric acid in bleaching, but ordered that on every piece of cloth treated with this acid the word 'muriatic' should be stamped under the bleacher's name. The use of lime was not yet admitted.

---

[1] The grant was £19,938 in English money, the equivalent of £21,600 Irish.
[2] 45 Geo. III, c. 18.
[3] 42 Geo. III, c. 75. Arrangements for import were further defined in 1804 (44 Geo. III, c. 42).   [4] 44 Geo. III, c. 69.

During the next twenty years only one other statute was passed dealing with the Irish linen trade—an emergency measure of 1809 making a special grant of £20,000 to encourage the saving of flaxseed at home.[1]

As Parliament was content to make its annual grants without passing any regulations, the policy of this period is simply that of the Board of Trustees ; and the Trustees themselves only undertook two new functions of any importance—the encourage-ment of machine spinning and the endowment of mills for scutching—both of which were mentioned in the last chapter. But it is worth while to examine the main features of their policy, old and new, in order to see how far they were able to influence the course of trade, and why their organization was dissolved.

Inspection of Brown Linen. Ever since 1762 one of the Board's most important duties had been the regulation of brown linen markets. The system of sealing had been strengthened in 1782 by the appointment of county and provincial inspectors ; but we have seen that it was in an unsatisfactory state at the end of the eighteenth century. Further changes were made in the next twenty-five years. It will be remembered that new seals had been issued in 1798 and again in 1799. There was a fresh distribution in 1802, for the Board had decided that a distribution every three years would enable them to keep a tighter hand over the sealmasters. However, this plan was abandoned at the earnest request of the bleachers, who pointed out that the old seals were not in fact returned, so that they themselves were at a loss to know which webs were legally stamped and which were not.[2] There was no general re-issue of seals after this time, and for fifteen years the business of sealing continued quietly and without any change of system.

But in 1816 the Board showed a sudden revival of activity, owing probably to the increase of export trade and to a desire to reorganize the industry after the war. The Secretary, Corry, was sent on a tour of inspection throughout the industrial districts of Ulster ; a few months later Marshall, the Port Inspector of Londonderry, was sent to Scotland and Yorkshire ; and Besnard, one of the inspectors-general, made a similar tour

---

[1] 49 Geo. III, c. 29. The use made of this grant will be described later.
[2] Corry, *Report*, 1822, pp. 19–20.

through the southern provinces. The special mission of Corry and Besnard was to find whether the system of open markets could be improved. Markets in the south were few in number, and most of them were small. But in the larger markets of Ulster there was without doubt much irregularity in the way of ' morning jobbing ', sale of unsealed cloth, and sealing of defective webs. Since 1802 more than 1,600 brown seals had been issued.[1] Although the fines levied in Ulster for selling or stamping unstatutable cloth amounted to £700 or £800 a year, the inspectors were not able to supervise at all closely the large number of sealmasters, and not all of them tried to do their full share of the work. In order to meet the complaints of buyers, and to limit more strictly the granting of seals, a regulation was made in 1817 that every application for a brown seal must be signed by five registered bleachers.[2]

Sole Sealmasters. But this was only a partial measure. A more drastic reform had already been tried at the instance of Pollock, the Inspector-General for Ulster. The new method was to appoint a single person as sealmaster for a market or a group of markets. The ' sole sealmaster ' could employ assistants, but he would be personally responsible for their work. The Trustees may well have been encouraged to try this method by the example set in Scotland. The whole work of sealing was done there by about eighty ' stampmasters ', and the yarn was examined by twenty inspectors ; whereas the Irish Linen Board had in its service perhaps 1,200 sealmasters and a staff of sixty inspectors.[3] The idea of adopting a method similar to the Scottish soon found favour among the bleachers and drapers in Ulster. The experiment was made in co. Cavan in 1816.[4] During the next two or three years many petitions were sent to the Board asking that the sealing in particular markets should be entrusted to a single official. These petitions were naturally approved by the Trustees. In one district after another ' sole

[1] id., *Report*, 1816, p. 114.   [2] id., *Report*, 1822, p. 21.
[3] *Proceedings*, 1820, App., pp. 60–2.
[4] ibid., p. 29. A sole sealmaster had been appointed in Drogheda as early as 1778 (ibid., p. 11). In 1808 the sealing in Newtown Stewart, co. Donegal, was handed over to two men, W. and R. Chambers (*Proc.*, 1808, p. 32). This was done at the request of the buyers, probably to avoid ' morning jobbing '. But the serious trouble which followed seems to have given a check to the system, for there were very few appointments of sole sealmasters before 1818.

sealmasters' were appointed, and seals of the old type were cancelled.[1]

The new system was unpopular. Hundreds of former seal-masters lost the privilege of stamping their own cloth, and lost the income that they had made by stamping cloth for others. Moreover, the new officials were given a monopoly, which soon became a means of extortion. Although the statutory fee for sealing was either 1*d*. or 2*d*. for each web, charges of 3*d*. or more were not uncommon : some sealmasters even demanded 4½*d*. The victims, who were men of little substance—independent weavers and small manufacturers—found redress very difficult.[2] They had no organization, and hardly any influence with the Linen Board. The authority of bleachers and permanent officials was all on the side of the sealmasters. In co. Monaghan, where there were many dispossessed sealmasters, a violent attack was made on the monopolist at Ballybay ; but this show of ill-feeling only hardened the opposition.[3] By the beginning of 1821 sole sealmasters had been set in charge of forty out of the fifty-two linen markets in Ulster,[4] and several other appointments were made during the year.

There was one quarter, however, in which the new regulations were resisted more strongly, and with success. The large manu-facturers of Armagh and Down, who still dealt to some extent in the open markets, naturally protested against the appointment of sole sealmasters in their districts. It would be a great indig-nity to them to have their cloths inspected by men whose standing in the trade was inferior to their own. After a long controversy the Trustees came to a compromise. They kept to their determination to put nearly all the markets under sole sealmasters, but they allowed manufacturers who owned or employed forty looms to have 'private' seals, and to stamp cloth on their own premises.[5]

---

[1] This was the chief topic discussed in the Board's meetings from 1818 to 1820, and the main reason for Corry's visits to Ulster in 1820 and 1821.

[2] e. g. in the case of W. and R. Chambers at Newtown Stewart, it was only after a long delay that the Trustees were persuaded to appoint another seal-master, and even so, the Chambers brothers apparently kept their seal (*Proceedings*, 1809, part i, p. 182).

[3] *Proceedings*, 1821, p. 58.   [4] Corry, *Report*, 1822, p. 118.

[5] *Proceedings*, 1821, pp. 216-51. The final decision is not clear. Corry reported in 1822 (op. cit., pp. 191-3) that all the seals in Belfast, Lisburn,

There was great competition for the new posts, as might be
expected, seeing that the sealmaster in a market of average
importance would have three or four times the income of a
county inspector.[1] Many of the candidates were linen buyers,
and it is significant that every one canvassed the support of as
many bleachers as possible. Daniel McClure, the linen buyer for
J. & J. Richardson, was nominated by his employers and by
more than fifty other registered bleachers, for the appointment
in Tanderagee.[2]

The only other change in the sealing system before 1828 was a
change of title. The Board adopted a proposal, made by Corry,
to substitute the word ' public ' for ' sole '. ' Public sealmaster '
was felt to be a pleasanter expression because it carried no
suggestion of monopoly.[3] But it did not alter the fact.

Value of Sealing and Inspection. We have already examined
the value of sealing as it was practised before 1782. The system
was designed as a means of enforcing regulations. At the outset
the Trustees had given orders that the inspection should take

and cos. Armagh and Down were in the hands of manufacturers. But
the Board had already appointed several ' public sealmasters ' for markets
in Armagh and Down ; and in the following year a committee of manufacturers
and merchants complained of the tyranny of the sole sealmasters in Belfast
(*Proceedings*, 1823, p. 311).

[1] The average of weekly sales in 1816 was 530 webs in a market. At the
rate of 2d. for a web the annual income from fees would amount to £230.
The sealmaster might have to pay two or three assistants, but even so he
would probably have a net income of about £150. The salary of county
inspectors was £40, but they also had a share of the fines. An inspector for
co. Down told Corry in 1816 (*Report*, p. 18) that his share was about
£15 a year. There were also travelling expenses, amounting on an average
to about £20 a year, and another £9 or £10 for branding utensils distributed
by the Board (Treasury Accounts A.O. 17, 428). Some inspectors had the
good fortune to become sole sealmasters themselves—the work of their
inspectorships must have left them a good deal of time to spare. Corry
(*Report*, 1822, p. 79) gives particulars of the income of the sole sealmaster
for north Londonderry :

	£	s.	d.
Salary of inspectorship	40	0	0
Travelling expenses	27	6	0
Revenue from fines	55	8	9
Net fees for sealing (after paying salaries to assistants)	224	16	4

Some minor sources of revenue brought up his whole income to over £353.

[2] *Proceedings*, 1821, p. 237. McClure was not elected, although on paper
his qualifications seem to have been stronger than those of his successful
rival. His colleague, Samuel Quin, signed one of the petitions against the
appointment of sole sealmasters (ibid., p. 245).

[3] Corry, *Report*, 1822, p. 118.

place between market days, so that there should be time for a thorough examination, and that seals should be held by a comparatively small number of reliable men. But very soon the Board had to allow sealing on market days ; and as it was impossible for a few men to do all the work that was needed in the rush of an open market, seals were distributed in large numbers. Although the multitude of sealmasters were almost as difficult to control as the whole body of weavers, the institution of sealing had one advantage : it gave to the buyer a definite legal guarantee, so that if his cloth were unsatisfactory he could recover damages by a simple process.

The staff of inspectors established in 1782 was intended to make the control of sealmasters more effective, and it certainly would have this result to some extent. It is doubtful indeed whether they were ever responsible for checking the measurement or testing the quality of cloth stamped by sealmasters. According to the Inspector-General for Ulster, the usual procedure was for the buyer to examine his purchases at home, and to report any faults in sealing to the inspector.[1] It was the inspector's duty to lodge a complaint before a magistrate, and presumably to collect the fine. Thus the chief work of the county inspectors seems to have been to act as legal agents for the bleachers and drapers. They were present in the markets not so much to detect faults in cloth as to settle disputes between buyers and sellers, or between weavers and sealmasters, and to see that the law against forestalling and regrating was observed.

When sole sealmasters were appointed the position was changed. The sealmaster was a public official, and he was personally responsible for the quality and measure of all the cloth sold in his market, except the goods stamped privately by manufacturers. The new system left very little scope for an inspectorate. It was hardly necessary to keep a staff of eleven inspectors in Ulster, whose main duty was to receive complaints against a few among the seventy sealmasters.[2] In several counties

---

[1] Letter from James Greer (son and successor of John Greer) to the Linen Board (*Proceedings*, 1810, p. 133). As Greer was writing to support a petition of his staff for higher salaries, he would not understate the amount or value of their work.

[2] Corry's *Report* of 1822 shows that at that time there were 70 sole sealmasters and 266 assistants.

of the middle and south of Ireland the inspectors had even less responsibility : once a month they entered ' Nil ' in their books as their report on markets to the Linen Office. If they had not had a strong vested interest, and some casual duties in connexion with the payment of premiums and grants, they would probably have lost their positions after the parliamentary inquiry of 1825.[1] Their actual dismissal came three years later, when the Board itself was dissolved.

It is difficult to judge how far the sealing system as a whole served to raise or maintain the quality of Irish linen, for no one can say what the standard would have been apart from sealing. The quality was certainly well maintained. Stephenson, who could speak with authority, said that there was less trouble with defective cloth in Ireland than in any other country.[2] The question remains whether this satisfactory state of affairs was due to regulation and inspection or to other causes. Much of the credit ought to be given, I think, to the weavers themselves. Although some of them used nefarious means of doctoring their cloth—especially by filling out the material with paste—the great majority must have kept up a very good tradition of crafts-manship : it was only a minority who needed compulsion.

There was clearly vigilance, too, in dealing with this minority ; but it is doubtful whether the sealmasters did very much to prevent the sale of defective cloth. Their work was necessarily done in haste, and we have seen that they generally relied on the weavers' statements.[3] The inspectors formed the next line of defence, and they regarded themselves as the chief guarantors of sound manufacture. They wrote, for instance, in their petition for an increase of salaries : ' Through the humble but useful

---

[1] They did not escape criticism at this time. e. g. Trant said in the House of Commons that ' he had himself conversed with some of what were called inspectors, who knew nothing of linen ' (*Parl. Debates*, 1st Series, xii, 1079).

[2] Stephenson, *Observations*, 1784, p. 10.

[3] On the other hand, sealing may have given some protection to manu-facturers and drapers against their agents in Dublin.   In 1809 thirty-three cotton manufacturers of Belfast petitioned that the system of sealing might be extended to the cotton trade. The only reason for their demand was that factors in Dublin counted one yard less than the true measurement of each piece, and kept the price of this yard as part of their commission.

The cotton factors had rooms in the Linen Hall : there are many allusions to the cotton department in the *Proceedings* for this period.   It was presumably the ' Linen and Cotton Mixed Hall ' mentioned in the *Proceedings* for 1809 (Appendix XXI).

exertions of these Inspectors, instructed and aided, by their superior officers, a more general conformity to all the wise and wholesome regulations of the Law has been everywhere enforced.'[1] But the statement of the Inspector-General, that a quarter of the pieces sold in the markets of Ulster were not sealed at all,[2] does not suggest any great enterprise on the part of county inspectors ; and if, as seems to have been the case, they only exerted themselves at the instance of bleachers or drapers, the real safeguard was a thorough examination in the warehouses and bleachworks.[3] The work of sealmasters and inspectors was scarcely more than a means of helping buyers of brown linen to recover damages.

The records of the Linen Board confirm Stephenson's statement that there was remarkably little trouble with defective cloth in Ireland. The amount of the fines levied in Ulster implies that about one piece in two thousand five hundred sold in the markets was condemned—by no means a large proportion considering all the chances of error in weaving and sealing.[4] Hardly any bad material was allowed to pass the private examination in the exporters' warehouses, for there were never more than two or three complaints in a year from the juries of merchants in London.

Public officials, however, contributed little to this success. We can hardly agree with Stephenson's assertion that county inspectors were first appointed to cover the ignorance of the Inspector-General.[5] But their dismissal in 1828 made no

---

[1] *Proceedings*, 1810, p. 117. The meeting at which this petition was presented was attended by only one Trustee, Lord Northland ; therefore no action could be taken at the time. However, the inspectors were allowed some additions to their salaries, which drew an annual complaint from the Commissioners of Public Accounts. In 1813 the Board tried in vain to have the limit of £40 removed by statute : the change was made ten years later by the Act 4 Geo. IV, c. 90.

[2] Corry, *Report*, 1822, p. 21.

[3] Cf. the evidence given to Corry (op. cit., p. 78) by drapers in Ballymena : ' A buyer seldom discovers a deficiency till he has got his cloth to the green.'

[4] The fines for false sealing were from 10s. to £5. If we take £2 as being roughly an average fine, the total amount of £770 implies rather less than 400 convictions in a year, and about a million webs would be sold in a year at the time (1808-9) for which statistics of fines are available.

[5] *Observations*, 1784, p. ix. John Arbuthnot, the Inspector-General for Leinster, Munster, and Connaught, was Stephenson's greatest enemy at this time. He had been a linen printer at Carshalton ; but he had failed in business and lived for some time on the Continent. He secured the favour of Lord

appreciable difference to the trade, and they might equally well
have been dismissed at any earlier time.

Regulation of Yarn. Besides its constant concern with the
inspection and sealing of cloth, the Board was still responsible,
as it had been from the beginning, for the regulation of yarn ;
and in this period it undertook fresh duties in connexion with
flax and seed. Since 1784, when the law relating to the reeling
of yarn was revised, the Trustees had not been greatly exercised
with the old problem of suppressing unstatutable yarn. There
were no special inspectors of yarn markets, and the county
inspectors had been appointed primarily to deal with brown
linen. As they had no information about the sale of yarn the
Trustees were content to let the matter rest. But the revival of
interest after the Napoleonic War, which led to the new system
of sealing brown linen, had also a sensational effect on the yarn
trade.

The Board may have been impressed with the fact, which they
probably learnt from Marshall, that there were twenty inspectors
of yarn in Scotland. The chief impulse, however, came from
Besnard's report of 1817. In his tour through the southern
provinces Besnard had noticed several times that, though it was
often of good quality, the yarn was not made up in the manner
prescribed by the Act of 1784, and when he visited the Yarn Hall
in Dublin he was distressed to find how greatly the export trade
had fallen away. The decrease, as we have seen, was caused by
the growth of machine spinning in Great Britain, but Besnard
told the Board that it was entirely due to the bad making up of
Irish yarn.[1]

Although the Trustees made no move for some months, their
action when they did move was drastic. In March, 1818,
members of the head-quarters staff raided the Yarn Hall and
seized £7,000 worth of goods. If the yarn had been confiscated
outright the owners, or some of them at least, would have been
ruined ; therefore the yarn was restored on condition that it

---

Loughborough, was brought by him to Ireland, and through Loughborough's
influence was appointed to this lucrative post (ibid., pp. 10–11). According
to Stephenson, he knew nothing about the linen trade apart from printing ;
but his chief fault seems to have been his disagreement with Stephenson's
schemes for the southern provinces.

[1] *Report*, 1817, pp. 26, sqq.

should be reeled again in a statutable manner ; but the factors who had had it in their possession were fined nearly £300.[1] This show of violence was grossly unfair, although it may have been legal. The Act of 1784 had laid down regulations which were not desired by spinners, manufacturers in Ireland, or importers in England. It was a long time since the Board had tried to enforce the regulations, and every one regarded them as a dead letter.

It is not clear to what extent the law was enforced after 1818. But seven years later a committee of the House of Commons reported that the regulations were unsuitable and ought to be amended.[2] They were altered accordingly in the statute of 1825.[3]

Regulation of Flax and Flaxseed. The sale of flax was on a different footing. From time to time the Trustees had shown an interest in teaching farmers how to prepare flax for spinning, but they had never prescribed rules for the handling of flax before it had been made into yarn. Even in the case of yarn, their atten-tion was almost confined to the export trade ; and flax preparation was unregulated because there was only a trifling export of flax before 1811.[4] It will be remembered that Corry, after his visit to Ulster in 1816, urged the regulation of this trade. The Trustees, however, had not the power of making by-laws without the sanction of Parliament, and the question was in abeyance for some years. There was evidently a fresh move in 1823, although the only record of it is a protest by growers in Londonderry and Donegal against the proposed regulations.[5] The parliamentary committee of 1825 found evidence that Irish flax was often carelessly cleaned ; but it was not until 1828 that any definite law was passed to safeguard the quality of flax. A clause in the statute of that year provided that all flax sold in the open market should be evenly cleaned, but the enforcement of this rule was left to private informers.[6] Thus the regulation of the flax trade had a very short and slender history.

The Trustees were more interested in the examination of imported yarn, flax, and seed. We have seen that they were

---

[1] *Proceedings*, 1818, pp. 50, 192-215, App., p. 1.
[2] ibid., 1825, App., p. 52.   [3] 6 Geo. IV, c. 122, sec. 15.
[4] See table given below, App. ii.   [5] *Proceedings*, 1823, p. 68.
[6] 9 Geo. IV, c. 62, secs. 3 and 4.

allowed by Parliament to appoint ' port inspectors ' for this purpose in 1802. The work was not apparently of any great importance, and some of it at any rate was not effective. In 1809, for instance, six merchants of Dublin informed the Trustees that a large amount of seed passed by the inspectors, and branded by them as sound, had proved to be worthless.[1] The parliamentary committee of 1825 decided that this inspection of imported flaxseed was not needed, and it was abandoned in the following year.[2] Port inspectors were retained in Belfast, Londonderry, and Newry, probably to examine Irish and foreign yarn or flax ; but the nature of their duties is not clearly stated.[3]

Lime bleaching. In 1815 the Trustees had a last encounter with their old enemy, lime. A bleacher in co. Armagh had been privately accused of using lime, and the magistrate before whom the charge was made sought advice from the Linen Office. A conviction, he said, would mean the loss of a hundred pieces of cloth and a fine of £1,000, but according to the statute of 1782 he ought to convict. Evidence was given that the charge had been brought maliciously, to pay off a personal grudge. Eleven bleachers of co. Armagh stated that lime bleaching was the safest and best method ; that it had been in common use for many years ; and that it had done more than anything else to keep down the cost of white linen.[4] The bleacher was not fined, and although the law of 1782 remained on the statute book for ten more years, no further attempt was made to enforce it. The r egulating Act of 1825 repealed all earlier statutes, and did not renew the prohibition of lime bleaching. So the long controversy came to an end.

---

[1] *Proceedings,* 1809, p. 166.
[2] ibid., 1825, p. 48. The Act of 1825 (sec. 42) directed that there should be no more inspection after 1 July 1826.
[3] The Board showed great consideration for the officials who were dismissed. In April, 1826, while they were still at work, the Treasury was asked to compensate them for the loss of fees. The Treasury ' saw no reason for compensating flaxseed inspectors ' (P.R.O. Lond., Treasury Letters T 14, 24, pp. 96–7). But the Linen Board persisted in its claim, and a year later the Treasury agreed to consider the question. In May, 1827, it was agreed that the Board should make payments to the inspectors from its annual grant (ibid., pp. 201, 208). The amount given in 1827 was £793 19s. 2d., divided among rather more than a dozen men, in proportion to their previous income from fees (Treas. Accts., A.O. 17, 428, Account Roll for 1827).
[4] *Proceedings,* 1815, pp. 131–5.

Supply of Raw Material. We will turn from the work of regulating to that of promoting various branches of the industry. It was mentioned in an earlier chapter that the supply of raw material caused great difficulty during the latter years of the Napoleonic War. The crisis gave the Trustees an opportunity of useful service, and for a time they were very active in helping to relieve the shortage. In the summer of 1808 they learnt that there was only half the normal supply of home-grown flax in the country.[1] The outlook for the next season was not at all promising, for the stock of imported seed was low—35,000 hogsheads instead of the usual supply of over 40,000.[2] In 1809 the position was much worse, for the embargo on exports from the United States had cut off the main source of flaxseed.[3] A report reached the Trustees that 10,000 or more hogsheads were available in England, and although the price was extravagant they determined to secure the seed. Three inspectors were sent across. They travelled over a large part of England examining and buying seed—not without great expense, for their journey alone cost over £600.[4] In the course of a hundred days they were able to provide a useful amount of seed for distribution in Ireland.[5]

There was still a great shortage, and if an absolute famine of raw material was to be avoided in 1810 it was imperative to save a large stock of seed at home. The Board was fortunate enough to secure from Parliament, probably with the help of Foster, a special grant of £20,000 for this purpose.[6] The money was used to pay premiums of 35s. a hogshead for all seed saved from the crop of 1809, whether it was rippled or stacked with the flax.[7] The high cost of bought seed, and the great profit to be made by selling flax were still stronger inducements.

Figures are not available to show exactly what followed. It appears that 10,000 hogsheads, or perhaps rather more, were saved ; but as this was less than a quarter of the usual supply,

---

[1] *Proceedings*, 1808, p. 42.

[2] ibid., App. iv. Between 5 July 1808 and 18 March 1809 only 2,406 hhds. were imported (*Proc.*, 1809, ii, App. xxiii).

[3] ibid., 1809, p. 44.   [4] ibid., pp. 15–16, 43, 115–16, 132–4,140.

[5] Some of the seed would not grow and its failure caused the complaint mentioned above. But the Inspector-General reported that the crops of 1809 had been good on the whole (*Proc.*, 1810, p. 11).

[6] Foster, who was Chancellor of the Irish Exchequer at this time, had helped the inspectors during their tour in England.

[7] ibid., 1810, pp. 8, 40.

some seed, perhaps from the Baltic States, must have been secured by the regular importers.[1] Although the seed grew well there was evidently a serious lack of raw material in the next winter. Hardly any flax and yarn were exported, but still the output of linen was lower in 1811 than it had been for almost a quarter of a century. Conditions improved, however, in the next two years : the Inspector-General had foretold that more seed would be saved, and he appears to have been right. When trade with America was re-opened in 1814 the supply of seed and flax quickly became normal.[2]

In this instance the Trustees did a real service in helping the country over a serious crisis.[3] Apart from the crisis they did little to encourage the production of raw material. The premiums for imported or home-saved seed, and the prizes for flax culti-vation, which had been given for long periods in the eighteenth century, were no longer offered in the nineteenth. The only efforts in this direction were made in the last five years of the Board's existence. In order to improve the cultivation of flax the Trustees decided in 1823 to spread a knowledge of Dutch methods. Almost exactly a century before, their predecessors had sent Richard Hall to Holland, but this time three farmers were brought from Holland. The Board's agent in London sent an interpreter with them, but as it was found that the ' Dutch Boers ' could make themselves well understood without help, the interpreter was sent home. They went on tour through Ulster, accompanied by Besnard, and they seem to have given great satisfaction.[4] Besnard himself naturally gained a thorough grasp of their system, and he wrote a book to perpetuate the know-ledge.[5] This was a sound method of helping the industry, but as

[1] Out of the grant of £20,000, the Board paid £1,659 12s. 8d. in special salaries to officials. When the premiums had been paid, there remained a balance of £3,059. Therefore the amount spent in premiums was £15,281. At the rate of 35s. a hhd., this amount would imply that 8,732 hhds. were saved—a quantity sufficient to sow about 17,500 acres. But the Inspector-General reported that farmers had saved a good deal of seed without claiming any premium.

[2] From July 1814 to July 1815 more than 49,000 hhds. were imported : 28,500 hhds. came from America, and 11,400 from Holland (*Proceedings*, 1815, App., p. 29 ; Corry's *Account of Flaxseed Imported*, 1824).

[3] Seeing that they had a balance in hand they could hardly be blamed for spending a sixth of the money in giving a bonus to their ill-paid inspectors.

[4] *Proceedings*, 1823, passim.

[5] *Report . . . on the Treatment of Flax as practised in the Netherlands*, 1823.

the results were intangible it is impossible to say how much permanent improvement followed the Dutch farmers' visit.

Two years later the parliamentary committee recommended the extension of linen manufacture in the south and west of Ireland, as though it were a new thing. Although the Board had worked vainly at this problem for a century, it was felt that something should be done to carry out the wishes of the committee.[1] Seeing that the statute of 1823 had put an end to bounties for weaving, there was little scope except in encouraging the supply of raw material. Therefore in 1826 premiums of £1 an, acre, payable only in the southern provinces, were offered for flax cultivation.[2] After two years they were cut short by the reduction of the Linen Board's grant. In any case they could have little importance, because they were only awarded for a minimum of three acres of flax on each farm, whereas the average area of flax on farms in the southern provinces was only half an acre.[3]

Scutching Mills. More was done in this period for flax preparation than for flax growing. The Trustees learnt in 1817 that ' the scutch mills of Scotland were very superior in their construction and efficacy ' to any scutching machinery known in Ireland.[4] Therefore Marshall, one of the three inspectors who had been commissioned to buy seed in 1809, was sent across to Scotland to examine the new methods. His report was very favourable, and he brought back five machines, which were first exhibited in the Linen Hall, then granted to private persons for erection in each of the provinces.[5] There were twelve applicants for the five sets of machinery. One of the earliest to apply was Samuel Smith, of Ballymoney, who has already been mentioned as a linen manufacturer and a pioneer of flax spinning by water-power.

The mills did excellent work and were soon in great demand.

[1] In 1823 there were 81,000 acres in Ulster under flax, and only 41,500 acres in the rest of Ireland (*Proc.* 1823, App., pp. 62–7). It was no doubt for this reason that the Dutch farmers confined their attention to Ulster ; but the fact that Ulster had received special help would make it seem all the more important to encourage flax-growing elsewhere.

[2] ibid., 1825, App., p. 78.

[3] ibid., 1810, App. i and xx. The amount actually paid in 1826 was less than £300, and a considerable part of it went to large landowners.

[4] ibid., 1818, App., pp. 63 sqq.

[5] ibid. There were already in 1817 over 400 scutching mills of the improved type in Scotland (Marshall's *Report*, p. 14).

One of them had been granted to John Foster, and set up near his home at Collon. This mill was so much approved by local farmers that they brought more than enough flax to keep it fully employed, whereas a neighbouring mill of the old type was standing idle.[1] After 1818 the Board distributed no more scutching machines, but gave grants, nearly all of £100, for the erection of mills. By 1823 they had endowed in this way 109 mills at a total cost of £11,266.[2] Five officials were constantly employed in touring round the country to explain and super-intend the use of the machines.[3]

If the Board had done nothing to help in this matter, the new methods of scutching would doubtless have come into use in Ireland before long. But the ready advance of capital, and the expert advice on fixing and working the machines, must have given strength to the movement. The new mills, in turn, benefited farmers by scutching their flax more thoroughly and so raising its market value. They were probably an important factor in the striking increase of flax production between 1800 and 1825.[4]

Machine Spinning and Coarse Weaving. Some years before this change in flax preparation was brought about, manufacture on a large scale had begun, as we have seen, in the coarse branches of both spinning and weaving. The Trustees were interested in these developments as well. Their bounties of 30s. for each spindle driven by water power have been mentioned already. The bounties were first offered in 1803, and continued until 1811. During the first six years, five-sixths of the spindles were set up in the southern provinces, especially for the sail-cloth manu-facture in Cork ; but after 1808 the fashion spread to Ulster, and there was a rapid growth of machine spinning in the north. Grants were made altogether to twelve firms in Ulster, five in Cork, and two in Leinster.

They were closely connected with another set of bounties,

---

[1] ibid., 1821, p. 25.   [2] ibid., 1823, App., p. 93.

[3] ibid., p. 19. The Commissioners of Public Accounts protested against the continuance of their salaries, because their temporary posts showed signs of becoming permanent.

[4] There was an increase of about 50 per cent. The area under flax varied a good deal from year to year ; but 80,000 acres were a normal amount at the beginning of the century, and 120,000 acres, or more, were common after 1820.

offered for the manufacture of canvas, sail-cloth, and duck.[1] Bounties for spinning and for weaving were established in the same year, and they were both meant to strengthen the policy of helping the coarse branches of manufacture. Moreover, the recipients in both cases were practically the same persons, for nearly all the spinners had weaving factories, or at least employed domestic weavers. The grants for spinning were probably dropped in 1811 because it was felt that there was enough yarn to supply the weavers, and because the grants for cloth were indirectly an endowment of spinning as well. The payment of bounties for cloth continued until 1823, and the Trustees would evidently have liked to carry them on indefinitely, for the usual bounties figured in the scheme of payments for 1824. But parliamentary opinion by that time had turned against them, and they were forbidden by statute.

In any case these grants had little permanent effect. So long as a squadron of the Channel Fleet was stationed off the south coast of Ireland, there was a steady, though limited, demand for naval stores. But we have seen that the coarse manufacture declined after the return of peace. In normal times it was difficult to maintain more than a very small trade for the supply of the home market. The Irish manufacturers had no established connexion with dealers in sail-cloth or other coarse goods in Great Britain. They had to compete with manufacturers in England and Scotland who had larger capital, readier credit, and easier access to supplies of raw material from the Baltic ports. After 1818 the annual output of cloth eligible for premiums was less than 700,000 yards.[2] Even this small amount was artificially maintained, and when the premiums were withdrawn the coarse manufacture shrank to an insignificant scope.

Ever since the middle of the eighteenth century it had been a settled feature of the Board's policy that the only hope of spreading the linen and hempen industries all over Ireland lay in the promotion of coarse manufacture. The attempt to carry out

---

[1] At first the bounty was at the rate of 2d. a yard. But in 1818 it was 1½d. for sail-cloth, and 1d. for duck and canvas; in 1821, only 1d. for coarse cloth of every kind.

[2] The premiums paid, at the rate of 1½d. or 1d. per yard, were between £2,000 and £3,000, implying, probably, an output of 500,000 to 700,000 yards a year.

this policy had been one of the most constant activities of the Trustees, and during the last twenty years it had been their main preoccupation. But the effort was made in vain; indeed, its failure, and the waste of public money which the failure implied, must have done great damage to the Board's reputation.[1]

Other Premiums. We have noticed the most important branches of policy, but a few other interests of the Trustees should be mentioned. The distribution of wheels, reels, looms, and hackles went on, though rather irregularly. In some years only a few hundred pounds were spent in this way, in other years many thousands.[2] Premiums were given for various offshoots of the linen industry, such as the making of bobbin lace, candle-wicks, and carpets of flax or hemp. For a few years, women who wove two hundred yards of cloth with a flying shuttle were rewarded with the gift of looms or other implements. There was still some endowment of the teaching of spinning in schools. Prizes were occasionally offered for fine spinning.[3] In 1818 an experiment was made in the use of wheels for two-handed spinning, which had been brought from Scotland, and were strongly recommended by Marshall.[4]

The Linen Hall. One of the largest and most expensive of the Board's undertakings in this period was the upkeep of the Linen Hall in Dublin. The Hall was so much used in the latter part of the eighteenth century that it was enlarged several times. In its final form the building, together with its courtyards, covered four

---

[1] Cf. Charley's statement (op. cit., p. 10): 'It is a singular fact that perhaps the most backward part of the Irish manufacture now is the very one that received most money for encouragement during the ten years previous to 1828—namely, sail-cloth and canvas.'

[2] e. g. in 1808 only £320, in 1823 over £7,000.

[3] e. g. in 1815, when there were 17 claims, all from co. Down. (*Proc.,* 1815, App., p. 12.) The finest work was done by Rosanna McKenny, who made yarn of 272 leas to the pound. The third in order of merit was Ann McQuillan, a member of a famous family of spinners, living in Comber. The count of her yarn was 144, but she contrived later to spin 768 leas to the pound, by splitting the yarn with a needle. (McCall, p. 101.) This, I believe, was the finest yarn ever spun in Ireland; although the sample of 760 lea yarn shown at the 1851 Exhibition was more wonderful, because it was made by a woman of 84 (Charley, p. 99).

[4] See his *Report,* p. 21. A hundred of these wheels were tried in Ireland (*Proc.,* 1818, App., pp. 60 sqq.). For many years before machine spinning became general the value of double spinning by hand was under discussion. Most people held that it was not economical, because the yarn was nearly always uneven.

acres.[1] It was three stories high, and contained 550 rooms. The main courtyard of the linen market was surrounded by an arcade, and above the arcade, on the two upper floors, there were open galleries. The chief building, known as the Old Hall, was used for linen ; halls for yarn and mixed goods of linen and cotton were built round the smaller courts ; and in addition to offices and warehouses there was a board room, a coffee room, and houses for six members of the staff.[2]

Such a large building could not be kept in repair without considerable expense, and the cost to the Trustees was very heavy. During the last ten years of the Board's existence the annual expenditure on the Linen Hall seems to have been about £3,500, practically one-sixth of the Board's revenue. A few years before it had been much greater. From 1806 to 1808, for example, the actual cost was £24,000 ; an account for £2,000 was outstanding, and the architect had submitted a fresh estimate of over £8,000.[3] Expenditure on this scale might be justified if the Hall were overcrowded with business, and additional rooms were needed ; but from the beginning of the century trade in the Hall was steadily declining, so that there was a constantly growing element of waste in the cost of upkeep.

The reason of this decline has been shown already. The Hall was originally used for the trade of northern drapers and Dublin factors. But since bleachers had taken to exporting on their own account, there was no longer so much scope for the work of drapers.[4] Corry wrote in 1825 : ‘ The country drapers who now attend are so few in number, and so limited in their dealings in this market, that the whole body of them taken together . . . are

[1] i. e. 2½ Irish acres.

[2] *Proceedings*, 1809, App. xxi ; 1825, App., p. 14 ; Cromwell, *Excursions through Ireland*, vol. i, pp. 147-8.   The officials who had houses in or near the Hall were the Secretary, Inspector-General, Chamberlains of the Linen and Yarn Halls, the Port Inspector, and the Coffee-Room Keeper.

[3] ibid., 1808, pp. 23, 69, App. i, v ; 1909, App. xviii.

[4] Cf. the evidence of Thomas Oldham before the Linen Board's committee (*Proceedings*, 1825, App., p. 25) : ‘ Thirty years ago the principal part of the linen-business of Ireland was done there (in the Linen Hall), and it was there that all the orders from America were executed. . . . The manufacturers, that is, the bleachers, have become great exporters themselves on their own account, and send the goods direct from the nearest port, say Belfast or some other port, or send them to Liverpool, and from thence to America.’ Oldham was a linen factor of London. His warehouse was in Bucklersbury. He was described by a contemporary writer as ‘ a great wholesale dealer in Irish linen ’ (Memorandum by W. Salisbury, P.R.O. London, H.O. 37, 100, 216).

not supposed to occupy more than 20 to 25 rooms.'[1] A generation earlier they had needed 131 rooms for their accommodation.
The Hall was still used by factors as a store for the domestic
trade; and owing to the variety of cloths stocked by various
dealers, it was patronized, like the White Linen Hall in Belfast,
by merchants who wished to make up assortments for export.[2]
The factors were evidently securing most of their goods straight
from the bleachworks, without the intervention of drapers.

But the factors themselves were losing custom. In 1808,
although Dublin had ceased to be the chief centre for export
trade, forty-six factors were still dealing in the Linen Hall.[3]
By 1825 their number was reduced to thirty, and of 447 rooms
available for trade, 177 were empty.[4] Thus the maintenance of
the Hall simply meant that the Board was providing a small
group of privileged traders with free warehouse accommodation
—much more than they needed—and a staff of porters.[5] The
parliamentary committee of 1825 made the reasonable suggestion
that a small rent should be paid by the factors. The Trustees,
advised by the factors themselves, objected to this change, on the
ground that it would injure the trade by raising the price of linen.[6]
They might not be expected to understand why such a result was
impossible; but they knew that in Belfast, where a rent of £2 a
year was paid for each room in the Linen Hall, prices had not
been affected, and the commission charged by factors was the
same as the commission in Dublin.[7] Their resistance was in vain.
By the Act of 1825 they were compelled to charge rents for the
use of the Hall—in practice the same as the rent paid in Belfast—
and to offer the vacant rooms on seven years' leases for any
suitable purpose.[8]

---

[1] ibid., App., p. 9.   [2] Thomas Oldham's evidence, u.s.

[3] *Dublin Directory*, 1808.

[4] As early as 1789 Stephenson said that the Yarn Hall was unnecessary
(*Letters to Trustees*, p. 28). In 1811 Wakefield expressed the same view of
the Linen Hall as a whole : ' However unpopular the measure, the Linen
Hall might be sold, and all the officers attached to that establishment might
be dismissed, without the least injury to the trade, or to the interests of the
country ' (vol. i, p. 697).   [5] *Proceedings*, 1825, App., p. 63.

[6] They appointed a committee of their own, which recommended that no
charge should be made for rooms in the Hall.

[7] Evidence given before the Board's committee, *Proceedings*, 1825, App.,
p. 19.

[8] The rents received in 1826 amounted to £774 11s. 6d., and in 1827 to
£1,165 2s. 11d. (P.R.O. London, Treas. Accts., A.O. 17, 428).

Negligence of the Board. By this time the Board itself had nearly run its course. The main reason for its dissolution was the doctrine of *laissez faire* ; but the Board invited opposition, and hastened the end, by its constant waste of funds. It is true that ever since 1711 waste had proceeded steadily, with no worse result than an occasional outburst by critics, such as Stephenson, and some minatory clauses in statutes which were not strictly enforced. But opinion in the eighteenth century had been kind to the Trustees : although they might be extravagant, most people believed that they were doing a great amount of good. Nineteenth-century opinion, however, held that they were extravagant and did no good.

Some evidence of their wastefulness has been shown in this chapter. The work of their inspectors was of doubtful value. Many of the implements distributed year by year must have gone to people who made no good use of them ; and there was no rational ground for making these presents, unless the Government was prepared to do the same for every trade—to give sheep and cows to farmers, nets to fishermen, saws and planes to carpenters. The large sums paid for coarse manufacture were spent to no purpose. There was a great amount of needless expense, and in all probability some jobbery, in connexion with the Linen Hall. The cost of printing and stationery was no less remarkable.[1]

Not all of these defects were the fault of the Trustees, but there certainly was great negligence among them—more, perhaps, than in any previous period. In the volumes of minutes it is no uncommon thing to find a list of agenda followed by the entry ' No business ', because there was not a single member present. In other cases there are minutes of a meeting and a list of those present, although no meeting was held. The minutes were drafted by the Secretary and signed at odd times by two or three members.[2] Quite important work was done in this way, notwithstanding the rule that five members should be a quorum for ordinary business, and twelve for financial business.

---

[1] One of the many attacks by the Commissioners of Accounts was directed against the cost of stationery (*Proceedings*, 1818, App., pp. 20–9). The expenditure under this heading in 1816 was over £1,400. It is significant that the architect's bills were much reduced after the Commissioners had called attention to their extravagant size.

[2] This custom is mentioned by W. Williams (*Correspondence with the Rt. Hon. Robert Peel*, p. 9).

Every year the books of the Linen Office were examined by the Commissioners of Public Accounts, and the audit resulted in an annual censure. The Commissioners' criticisms were almost exactly the same as those which Stephenson had made half a century earlier. For example, they wrote in 1810: ' The Trustees are too numerous, too fluctuating, have too great a variety of opinions, and frequently counteract each other. They seldom attend in proper numbers ; they frequently, in our opinion, act in direct opposition to law.' [1] As a result of this slackness nearly all the responsibility was left, as it had often been before, to paid officials. Fortunately for the Trustees their Secretary, James Corry, was an able and honourable man, or the consequences would have been much worse than they actually were. Even the Commissioners of Accounts more than once spoke highly of Corry's character and ability.

It was otherwise with the Inspector-General, Charles Duffin, who had much more authority than Corry. His position had been very comfortable. He had a salary of over £1,000 a year, and a house rent free.[2] His duties were not onerous, and he shared them with his son. But like Newburgh and Archdall, he was tempted to abuse his trust. The Commissioners found that he had been taking receipts in duplicate and telling the Board that each receipt represented a separate payment. At first he was only accused of carelessness, but he soon showed himself to be thoroughly dishonest. He was probably in league with a firm in Cork which had made doubtful claims for bounties ; he certainly gave lame excuses and tried to make light of the affair.[3] When two men came to Dublin to give evidence in regard to their receipts, Duffin tried to keep them from meeting Corry, and urged them to make false statements to a committee of the Linen Board. He was not brought to law, but he was compelled to resign ; and the post of Inspector-General was abolished.[4]

As the funds were so loosely administered, many rascals besides Duffin must have succeeded in gaining a share of them. Two important cases became public. The firm of E. & H. Shanahan, of Cork, which had been suspected of fraud in 1810,

---

[1] *Proceedings*, 1810, App. xix.   [2] ibid., ii, p. 95.
[3] ibid., 1810, pp. 166–7.   [4] ibid., App. xix, part ii, pp. 6, 93–5.

was openly accused five years later. Their partner, Williams, had grown suspicious and left them. In 1815 he found that they had obtained £7,000 by means of false claims for bounties, and gave information to the Board ; but the Shanahans disappeared with their booty.[1] In the same year another firm which had secured £1,030 in bounties admitted that they were only entitled to £204.[2]

In past times the Trustees had often adventured large sums in projects which proved useless, although they were not fraudulent, and similar mistakes were made in this period. The most striking instance was the purchase, in 1815, of machinery for flax preparation invented by James Lee, of Merton, Surrey.[3] This machinery was recommended, after a cursory examination, by R. Williamson, a member of the bleaching firm of Lambeg. Lee claimed that his device made the flax remarkably clean, and much easier to manipulate at all stages of manufacture, including bleaching.[4] The Board eagerly took up the invention, and spent more than £5,000 in erecting and working the machines. But, as the Commissioners of Accounts reported, the machines ' completely failed in effecting the purpose for which they were purchased '.[5] The capital for the experiments had been advanced by a merchant in Dublin named Joseph Williams, who acted as Lee's agent. He was the chief sufferer by this failure, for the Trustees did not repay him fully until 1827.[6]

The Trustees treated their misfortunes lightly, and were in no

---

[1] W. Williams, op. cit., pp. 9, 32–46 ; *Proceedings*, 1815, pp. 20, 286 ; ibid., 1818, App., p. 10. The Board held a committee of inquiry, and Corry visited Cork three times to collect information. Williams sent word to Dublin Castle, and a grand jury in Cork indicted the Shanahans. But they had taken alarm and fled. A reward of £300 for their apprehension had no result.

[2] Williams, op. cit., p. 40.

[3] It is interesting to notice that at this time linen manufacture, particularly finishing and printing, was carried on to a considerable extent in Mid-Surrey. We may recall Wakefield's allusion to a large bleachgreen at Carshalton, and the fact that Arbuthnot, an inspector-general to the Trustees, had been a linen printer in the same place.

[4] *Proceedings*, 1815, p. 169, App., p. 28.   [5] ibid., 1823, App., p. 18.

[6] ibid., 1818, p. 377. Williams wrote a pathetic letter, saying that as he had no mechanical knowledge he ' could not have formed an idea of the failure of the system introduced by Mr. Lee '. He stated that only half his loan to the Board had been repaid, and he urgently needed the remainder. But the Trustees, although they had a large sum in hand, gave no answer. In 1821, when Lee himself was dead, Williams applied again for the money. He seems to have recovered most of it at that time, for there is a mention, in the statement of accounts for 1821, of £2,171 10s. 10d. for Lee's machinery (ibid., 1823, App., pp. 16–17). It is difficult to understand why he should not

way ashamed of their slackness. Indeed, they demanded in 1813
that they should be allowed to meet at longer intervals and with
a smaller quorum, and that the statutory restrictions on their
expenditure should be removed.[1] Every year the Commissioners
of Accounts disallowed some part of the expenditure, and
criticized the Board's policy. The reports were printed in the
Board's proceedings, but with few exceptions they left the
Trustees entirely unmoved. In their report for 1823 the Commissioners wrote : ' We find that none of our disallowances are
refunded by the parties, that they all remain unnoticed by the
Trustees, and have no influence on their past or present ex-
penditures.' [2]

Opposition in Parliament. Although these repeated attacks
made no impression on the Trustees themselves, they were
observed in other quarters. Both the ministry and the opposition
in Parliament had learnt in some degree the principle of *laissez
faire.* Moreover, in face of a vast national debt, they were
anxious to stop all needless outlay of public funds. Neither the
granting of premiums nor the regulation of manufacture was in
accordance with the trend of public opinion, and the Linen
Board made itself doubly obnoxious by carrying on these works
without any attempt at economy.

The first signs of opposition appeared in 1822, when a Bill was
passed directing that the bounties for export of linens from
Great Britain should continue only so long as the Irish bounties
remained.[3] In the same year a committee was appointed to deal
with certain questions relating to the linen trade. Its chief
findings were embodied in a statute of the following session.[4] In
some ways the statute was generous to the Trustees. It cancelled
many of the surcharges made by the Commissioners of Accounts ;
it allowed the payment of higher salaries to officials, and removed

have received the whole sum of £2,500 which was due to him. Five years
later it was pointed out by the Commissioners of Accounts that the balance
was still unpaid (A.O. 17, 428). In August, 1827, the Board made a final
payment of £2,000 for Lee's machinery (ibid.). As the amount due to Williams
was only £328 9s. 2d., the Trustees had apparently incurred a considerable
debt in some other quarter.

[1] ibid., 1813, App., p. 62. Heads of a Bill for relieving the Trustees, &c.
This bill does not seem to have been presented to Parliament, but some of the
proposals were included in the Act of 1823.

[2] ibid., App., p. 19.   [3] 3 Geo. IV, c. 28.   [4] 4 Geo. IV, c. 90.

the limit of £3,000 for the expenditure on utensils. But in one important matter their power was very much reduced : they were no longer free to give premiums for the manufacture of any goods for which bounties were paid on export. Thus their long struggle to promote coarse manufacture was brought to an end.

In the same year, 1823, the regulations for the linen manufacture in Scotland were repealed, and the compulsory stamping of cloth was abolished.[1] The Irish Linen Board was left in an anomalous position. Its work of regulation had now no parallel in the textile trades of Great Britain ; premiums of the type which it was still allowed to grant for certain purposes were falling into disuse there ; and it must have occurred to many of the Board's critics as strange, that the Irish industry which least needed artificial support should be the one most freely subsidized with public money. The Board was left at peace for another year ; but during that year the reaction against bounties came to a head. It was decided that from 5 January 1825 there should be an annual reduction of one-tenth in the bounties on exported linens.[2] The process of attrition went on until 1830, when payments were abandoned.

This measure did not directly affect the Trustees ; but in March, 1825, a frontal attack was made in the House of Commons by members of the opposition. When the usual grant of £19,938 was proposed in committee of supply, Hume moved a reduction of the grant by £10,000.[3] He was supported by Lord Althorp and several other Whigs, who ' denounced the Linen Board as utterly incompetent to the task which it had undertaken '. The Government, while refusing to sacrifice the Linen Board, made two significant statements, showing their general agreement with Hume's point of view. Robinson, the Chancellor of the Exchequer, claimed that ministers had ' not been asleep on their posts ', and alluded to the limits already set to the system of bounties. Peel, who had a first-hand knowledge of the Board's methods, said still more plainly that he ' hoped that this short

---

[1] 4 Geo. IV, c. 40 ; Bremner, op. cit., p. 220.

[2] 5 Geo. IV, c. 43. In accordance with the statute of 1822, the decision applied equally to Great Britain and to Ireland. If the bounties had been withdrawn at once the Trustees would have been free to renew their grants for coarse manufacture ; but before the bounties ceased the Board itself was dissolved.   [3] *Parl. Debates*, 1st Series, xii, 1078-81.

discussion would be taken as a notice in Ireland that Parliament had turned its attention to the subject '.

Report and Statute of 1825. Only a month later, the House of Commons appointed a committee to inquire into the state of the Irish linen trade.[1] The committee's findings fell into three groups, dealing respectively with the linen laws, the Trustees, and the whole organization of the industry.[2]

In the first place they recommended that the import duties still levied on raw material should be reduced ; that the inspection of yarn, flax, and seed at the ports should be abolished; and that substantial changes should be made in the regulation of manufacture. They regarded the sealing of white linen as a needless formality. Modified rules for the making of yarn and brown linen might be retained as long as domestic production on a small scale was common, but the penalties should be light, and the rules should apply only to goods sold in the open markets.

The committee was not specially charged to consider the work of the Trustees, but the members gave it as their opinion that the annual grant should be continued, and that a Board would be needed to administer the grant, supervise officials, and hear claims. The Trustees were urged, as we have seen, to encourage manufacture in the southern provinces, but they were warned against persistence in their old custom of giving away utensils. Finally, certain changes already described were recommended in the use of the Linen Hall.

In regard to the organization of industry the committee were struck with the large proportion of hand-spinning and of domestic weaving on a small scale in Ireland. They were anxious to see the old system replaced by factory production, although they admitted that such a change could not be brought about by Parliament. They stressed, quite rightly, the improvements made in machine-spinning during the last twenty years, and mentioned the likelihood of further great advances.[3] A similar

[1] ibid., 1340 (14 April).
[2] The report was sent to the Trustees, and printed in the *Proceedings* for 1825, App., pp. 47–53.
[3] They had probably heard of the invention of wet-spinning which was patented in this year. However, they evidently thought that fine yarns would always be made by hand, for they said that the increase of mills ' would

change in the system of weaving seemed desirable. The committee noted with satisfaction that such a movement was actually taking place. ' There are extensive manufacturers ', they wrote, ' who buy and give out the yarn to weavers to be woven into cloth, and have become a numerous class of persons in the north ; and the more they increase the more it will be for the benefit of Ireland.' They were impressed with the evidence of a Scottish witness, who said to them : ' The best sheeting that I have ever seen made in Ireland is made by a manufacturer who employs a number of weavers, and which cloth never came to the brown markets, but was sold directly to the bleachers.'

No time was lost in carrying out the Committee's proposals : they were included in a regulating Act passed on 1 July 1825.[1] This statute left the Trustees and their staff in office, and laid down new rules for the sale of yarn and brown linen in the open markets. But the use of white seals and the inspection of raw material were abolished, and the trade of manufacturers outside the markets was freed from regulation or inspection.[2]

The Linen Board had received a new lease of life ; it is doubtful, however, whether the committee expected the lease to run for long. They had stated as a guiding principle that a government ' never should concern itself, except when it was absolutely necessary, with the internal management of any manufacture '. They might, and apparently did, think that regulation was necessary as long as cloth was made by small craftsmen ; and the weak organization of Irish industry might justify grants from the public funds. But if, as the committee hoped, Irish industry were soon put on a firmer foundation, the need for state intervention would cease. Peel probably had the same thoughts in his mind when he said in Parliament that ' it was necessary to have a Board to protect the interests of the small manufacturers '.[3]

not interfere with the interests of the spinner of hand-spun yarn '. Three years before, Radcliffe had written in the same way of the relations between power looms and hand looms.

[1] 6 Geo. IV, c. 122.

[2] Like most of the earlier laws this measure was discussed in advance by the Trustees and drafted by their legal adviser.

[2] *Parl. Debates*, 1st Series, xii. 1081. Parliament had recently set members of trade unions free to defend their own interests, and it was about to legislate for the protection of children in factories. Peel may well have thought that the system of sealing was in keeping with this policy ; that the public guarantee of cloth was a safeguard to the weaver.

As a matter of fact the Board's régime ended sooner than either Peel or the committee had anticipated. Perhaps it had been found that the small manufacturers themselves had no wish for the Board's protection. They could no longer ask for implements from the Trustees. They had lost the right to seal cloth on their own account. The Board could only be connected in their minds with regulations and fines.

But the ministry would hardly be likely to consult the lower industrial ranks. They were probably content to follow the custom of the Trustees themselves by merely sounding the opinion of bleachers and large manufacturers.[1] They did make such an inquiry, and they found that although the sealing of brown linen was still considered a safeguard, no importance was attached to the premiums and grants.

There was certainly no strong feeling in the industrial districts of Ireland in favour of continuing the Linen Board or the system of state control. Moreover, many of the Trustees had come to the conclusion that their services were not needed, and Corry, to his credit, agreed with their view.[2] A few months before the Board's dissolution he wrote : ' That the prosperity of the linen manufacture of Ireland has been greatly advanced by the wisdom of the laws which have governed it, cannot be denied ; but there is a popular opinion now abroad in which I feel that I participate, that, after a certain point of prosperity has been attained, the less any manufacture is encumbered with legislative regulations the better.' [3]

Dissolution of the Linen Board, 1828. The Government decided on a change early in 1827. In the estimates for that year the grant to the Trustees was reduced to £10,000, and even this partial grant was not meant to be permanent : it was only given to keep the Trustees in funds while their affairs were being wound up. Robinson said, in his speech proposing the vote : ' As to the

[1] They took the opinions of sixty-eight bleachers or manufacturers, of whom about two-thirds lived in Ulster (Horner, pp. 211–13). We have seen that parliamentary committees on the linen trade regularly chose men of this type as their witnesses. There is abundant proof in the *Proceedings* that the Trustees gained information in the same way. e. g. Corry in his *Report* of 1822 often referred to the views of bleachers as ' the opinion of the trade ', and said that it was always worth while for the Board to weigh carefully advice coming from such a respectable quarter.

[2] Horner, p. 208.   [3] Quoted by A. S. Moore, *Linen*, p. 43.

Linen Board, he could assure the House that it was the last time of its appearing on that stage. The abolition of that establishment was resolved on.'[1]

Accordingly, no grant was proposed in 1828. Instead, it was enacted ' that the powers . . . executed by or under the authority of the Trustees for encouraging the said manufactures should cease and determine ', and that the Trustees and their staff should go out of office on 5th September.[2]

It was thought desirable, however, that the work of small craftsmen should be kept under public control. In all probability many members of the Government would have been glad to abolish the whole system of state intervention. But the Board had been asked for advice, and the Board wished that some form of public control should be retained.[3] To follow this advice could do little harm, and it would conciliate those supporters of the Government who disliked the growing spirit of *laissez faire*. Therefore the regulations of 1825 for flax, yarn, and cloth sold in the markets were continued, and sealmasters of brown linen remained at work. As there were no inspectors the law was to be enforced by means of complaints made directly to a magistrate ; and magistrates were given the power to order an examination of the flax or cloth in dispute by three experts.[4] Sealmasters were to be appointed and controlled by a committee in each county, nominated by the Lord Lieutenant.

These regulations for local markets were all that remained of the Board's former work of stimulus and control. They were renewed for terms of three years in 1831, and 1834, and for five years in 1837.[5] But at the end of this fourth term they were allowed to lapse. The linen markets, for reasons which will be shown in the next chapter, were steadily passing out of use, and the legal restrictions had no longer any importance.

Experience soon proved that the Act of 1828 had done no injury to the linen trade. At the very time when the Act was

---

[1] *Parl. Debates*, 1st Series, xvii. 245.   [2] 9 Geo. IV, c. 62.

[3] A year earlier the Board had recommended that the regulations of 1825 should continue in force, and that a staff of twenty-two inspectors and two inspectors-general should remain in office. The first recommendation was adopted, but the second was not (Horner, pp. 209–10).

[4] This regulation was based on the custom of appointing panels of experts to examine linen in London.

[5] 2 & 3 William IV, c. 77 ; 5 & 6 William IV, c. 27 ; 1 & 2 Vict., c. 52.

passed wet-spinning was being introduced into Ireland without any public subsidy. Steam power was first used in an Irish linen mill in the next year, and the expansion of trade which followed was greater than any that had been known while the Trustees held office.

Influence of the Linen Board. Opinions of their work varied greatly at that time. When Sir George Hill maintained in Parliament that ' the Linen Board had already produced the greatest advantages by augmenting the trade from a few hundred thousand pounds to five millions annually ', Hume retorted that the volume of trade would have been six million pounds instead of five if the Board had never existed.[1] The truth lay between these two statements. Hume was not justified in thinking that the regulation of brown linen markets had seriously reduced the output or sale of cloth. It was even of some benefit to drapers and bleachers, and the cost of sealing was so small that it could not affect the price of linen. On the other hand, the Board's influence was not the great constructive force imagined by Hill and by all the supporters of the old system. Encouragement had been given in three ways—by the award of prizes; by instruction, especially in methods of growing and preparing flax ; and by the provision of capital, in the form of money, flaxseed, utensils, or machinery for mills. The educational work had been spasmodic, and as far as it is possible to judge, not very effective. Prizes were no more than an embellishment. Capital was sometimes applied to good purpose—for instance, to the erection of bleach-works and scutching mills. But grants were given with so little discrimination that they were to a considerable extent wasted.

Whatever moderate degree of success the Board might have had in earlier times, it was certainly no longer needed in the second quarter of the nineteenth century. The trade was able to flourish without bounties. In the matter of capital and credit, the joint-stock banks did a greater service than any that the Linen Board could have done. Good technical education would have been valuable, but it was not forthcoming at that time, and the Board was not the authority best fitted to supply it. The work of regulation, as we have seen, was rapidly losing all importance. Trade was deserting the open markets ; and a manufacturer who

[1] *Parl. Debates,* 1st Series, xii. 1081.

had a reputation to maintain stood in no need of supervision by inspectors or sealmasters. In a few years' time industrial regulation turned to the more useful line of factory inspection.

One monument of the Board's work long survived as a forlorn relic. The Linen Hall was transferred in 1828 to the keeping of the Lord Lieutenant.[1] It was still used as a warehouse for factors, but it had ceased to be a market. With the steady development of direct export from bleachgreens, factories, and warehouses in Ulster, the number of vacant rooms in the Linen Hall grew from year to year. Thackeray, who visited the Hall in 1842, described it as ' that huge, useless, lonely, decayed place, in the vast solitude of which stands the simpering statue of George IV, pointing to some bales of shirting, over which he is supposed to extend his august protection '.[2]

In 1852 only ten factors stored their cloth there, in 1858 only seven. By 1870 the linen factors in Dublin were reduced to six, three of them with rooms in the Hall.[3] Four years later no one remained there, and the empty Hall was transformed into barracks.[4]

NOTE TO CHAPTER XV

EXPENDITURE OF THE BOARD, 1826 AND 1827

The two following tables may help to give a clear view of the Linen Board's policy in the latter years of its existence. The first table shows the premiums proposed for 1826, the amount estimated under each heading, and the amount actually paid either in this year or the year following. The second table gives a summary of the Board's income and expenditure for 1827, the last full year of its work. The plan and estimates of premiums are taken from *Proceedings*, 1825, Appendix, pp. 78–84 ; the sums actually paid are from the detailed account rolls (P.R.O.

---

[1] He appointed a committee to take charge of the Hall. The committee's accounts down to 1832, which are filed with the later account rolls of the Linen Board (A.O. 17, 428), show that the cost of up-keep was slightly larger than the income from rents.

[2] *Irish Sketch Book*, 1843, vol. ii, p. 324. In 1825 Corry mentioned that officials at the Hall were ' clearing a space for the King's statue '. (*Proceedings*, 1825, App., p. 7).

[3] *Dublin Directories.*   [4] O'Reilly, *The Dublin Linen Hall*, p. 36.

London, A.O. 17, 428), which are also the source of the second table.

I. PREMIUMS FOR 1826

	Estimated expenditure. £	Actual expenditure. £
1. Sowing flaxseed, £1 per acre for a minimum of 3 acres (in Leinster, Munster, and Connaught) . . .	1,000	295 19 3
2. Extensions of scutching mills	400	102 6 0
3. New scutching mills . .	3,000	688 8 11
4. Cleaning flax [1] . . . { 600 at ports / 1,000 in inland markets }		219 10 8
5. Mill-spinning of fine yarns [2].	3,000	492 6 0 in 1827
6. Bleaching of yarn . .	1,000	400 0 0
7. Utensils [3]	2,000	{ 1,841 in 1826 / 4,251 in 1827
8. Improved looms, for damask, &c.[4]	1,000	177 in 1827

The most striking feature of this table is the very small amount actually paid in premiums. It is clear that although the Board's payments at this time benefited a few individuals they could have no appreciable effect on the general course of trade.

The second table is mainly of interest as showing the staff employed by the Trustees. Apart from salaries and allowances the Board's chief expenditure, in this year as in many others, was on utensils.[5] Grants for utensils could easily be administered by the permanent officials, without any discussion of policy, and they continued as a matter of routine from year to year. Of the premiums given in 1827 a large part (87 per cent.) consisted of grants to large manufacturers. The rest had probably been earned before 1827, but had remained unpaid.

For at least thirty years the Trustees had had a substantial balance in hand. It had been reduced early in the century by

[1] The parliamentary committee of 1825 had complained that Irish flax was badly cleaned.

[2] The committee had suggested that machines were capable of spinning yarns up to 50 leas. They were probably alluding to Kay's process, and the grants made in 1827 were given to spinners who used this invention.

[3] It was resolved that utensils should only be given to public bodies or charitable associations ; but this regulation was very loosely interpreted, e. g. nearly £2,000 worth went to individual trustees.

[4] Probably Jacquard looms.

[5] As the inspectors received a branding fee for each utensil they would be inclined to encourage expenditure in this line.

extravagant charges for building ; but the economies urged by the Commissioners of Public Accounts led to a fresh increase. Although the parliamentary grant for 1827 was only £10,000 instead of £19,938, the Trustees, by drawing on their balance, were able to spend nearly as much as in a normal year. Their expenditure had been for many years between £18,000 and £23,000 (English).

II. Accounts for 1827

REVENUE :		£	s.	d.
Balance from 1826		19,924	5	3
Parliamentary grant		10,000	0	0
Rents for use of Linen Hall		1,165	2	11
Total		31,089	8	2

EXPENDITURE.

Premiums and Grants :	£	s.	d.	£	s.	d.
Flax-growing	234	4	6			
Cleaning flax	2	10	0			
Saving seed	5	7	0			
Hackles for flax growers . . .	7	10	9			
New scutching mills	1,222	3	9			
Extension of scutching mills. . .	306	10	7			
Temples for weaving [1]	78	2	4			
Fine spinning by machinery :						
Wm. Hudson	250	0	0			
Crosthwaites	142	6	0			
Jos. Nicholson.	100	0	0			
Damask looms	140	0	0			
Do. in Linen Hall	37	0	0			
Total of Premiums and Grants				2,525	14	11
Utensils :						
General	2,255	17	8			
To Trustees	1,970	5	8			
Total of Utensils . . .				4,226	3	4
Establishment :						
Linen Office :						
Salary of Secretary (James Corry) .	553	16	11			
First Clerk	184	12	3			
Second Clerk . . .	156	18	5			
Third Clerk . . .	156	18	5			
Messenger	55	7	0			
Office Keeper . . .	14	15	4			
Linen Hall :						
Chamberlain	276	18	4			
Gate Keeper	46	3	0			
First Watchman	46	3	0			
Second Watchman	46	3	0			
Sweeper of Courts	27	13	8			
Sweeper of Galleries	24	15	0			

[1] A device for stretching the web in a loom while the weft thread last inserted is being packed into position. Temples were invented by a mechanic of Dromore, co. Down, who was rewarded by the Linen Board with £100. They were soon applied to looms for all kinds of textiles.

Yarn Hall :	£	s.	d.	£	s.	d.
Chamberlain	136	12	0			
Gate Keeper	46	3	0			
First Watchman . . .	46	3	0			
Second Watchman	46	3	0			
Craner	9	4	4			
Three Inspectors-General . . .	692	6	0			
Pension	112	3	5			
County Inspectors (38) . . .	1,605	13	9			
Port Inspectors	235	8	9			
London Agent	75	0	0			
Revenue Accountant . . .	10	10	0			
Architect	46	3	0			
Engineer and six Firemen . . .	21	1	0			
Total of Establishment . .				4,572	15	7
Allowances :						
Travelling : Inspectors-General . .	957	12	0			
County Inspectors . .	723	17	10			
Fees for branding utensils [1] . .	361	2	10			
Clothing for Gate Keepers, &c. . .	79	7	6			
Repair of trucks and cranes . .	69	4	6			
Coffee-room Keeper	36	18	4			
Corry (for house and coals) [2] . .	249	4	6			
Hibernian Gas Light Co. [3] . . .	5	1	6			
Total of Allowances . .				2,482	9	0
Miscellaneous :						
Two scutchers from Scotland . .	130	15	8			
Dutch flax dressers and assistants [4] .	53	19	11			
Buildings	299	16	8			
Ground rent [5]	149	16	2			
Taxes	97	1	11			
Printing	499	4	9			
Stationery	125	18	5			
Bookbinding	56	1	7			
Postage	636	2	0			
Advertising	142	8	8			
Legal [6]	52	10	0			
Insurance	61	14	6			
Newspaper [7]	11	11	3			
Carriage of parcels	25	9	10			
Sundries	119	12	0			
Total of Miscellaneous Expenses				2,462	3	4
Total Expenditure [8] . .				16,369	6	2

[1] These fees were paid to the county inspectors.

[2] Including coals for the Office and Board Room.

[3] It is added in a note that the cost of gas for the whole year was £20 9s. 0d. The payment mentioned above was for four months.

[4] Balance owing since 1823.

[5] For extensions to the Linen Hall.

[6] Chiefly payment to Gervase Bushe, the Board's Counsel, for drafting the Act of 1825.

[7] *Freeman's Journal*, probably supplied in the Coffee Room.

[8] The total given in the original roll is £16,368 13s. 9d. The difference was probably due to some small adjustments made by the Commissioners.

A separate roll continued the accounts to 5 September 1828, the day on which the Board was dissolved. The expenditure during the last eight months was £7,346. Some premiums were still paid, and a few utensils were distributed, but the greater part was spent on salaries, allowances, and upkeep of buildings. The Board left a credit balance of £4,217.

There is no record to show what happened to the sixty or more officials whose appointments came to an end in 1828. As they are not mentioned either in account rolls or in the Treasury correspondence, they evidently had no compensation in money, although other posts may have been found for some of them. Corry and his clerks remained at work for eight months at least after the Board's dissolution, and a small staff was retained at the Linen Hall. The Treasury gave £1,500 as a contribution towards their salaries and the upkeep of the Hall. In addition, the rent of rooms in the Hall and the balance left by the Trustees were available to meet these expenses. By 5 April 1829 the balance was reduced to £2,424, and it had been further reduced by 1832. As soon as it was exhausted the committee in charge of the Hall would have to bring down the cost of administration to the amount received in rent, for the grant from the Treasury was not repeated.

XVI

STEAM POWER AND ITS REACTIONS

Improvements after 1825. The special subject of this volume is the period of domestic production in the Irish linen trade ; and the domestic system, at any rate in its full form, did not survive long after 1825. But it will not be out of place to offer a short survey of events during the next thirty or forty years ; for to stop short at the point which we have reached would be to leave the story without its denouement.

We have seen many changes in the early years of the nineteenth century : the development of credit and private banking ; the rise of bleachers to power as the chief buyers of brown linen, as manufacturers and exporting merchants ; the accumulation of capital, shown in the case of bleachers, large manufacturers, and mill-spinners ; the growth of classes of employers and employees; and the influence of capitalism in the cotton industry. These movements were gradual ; they did not effect any sensational changes ; they left the markets still open, the linen halls in Dublin and Belfast still active, and multitudes of independent craftsmen still at work. But from our standpoint it is clear that they were preparing the way for more rapid changes in the succeeding decades.

Even before 1830 four great innovations were made : joint-stock banking ; a striking advance in mechanical spinning ; the use of steam power ; and the beginning of steam transport.

Joint-stock Banking. The establishment of joint-stock banks is put first because it was in a sense the foundation of all further progress. Just as private banks had made possible the growth of direct export from Ulster, and all the consequent changes in organization, so now the greater resources of joint-stock banking were the means of a fresh advance, which was invited by the gradual recovery of trade after the Napoleonic War. In 1821 the monoply of the Bank of Ireland, which had been similar to that of the Bank of England, was restricted to a radius of fifty miles round Dublin. Therefore bankers in Belfast were free to form joint-stock companies with limited liability. As long as the right was confined to companies with capital subscribed in Ireland, only one concern was founded, the Northern Bank, which was re-established on a joint-stock basis in 1824. But in the next year the restriction on shares was removed, and there followed a great outburst of activity in the founding of joint-stock banks, nearly all of which proved to be sound and successful undertakings, of incalculable benefit to the country. Two of the new concerns, the Belfast and Ulster Banks, had their head offices in Belfast, and others set up branches in the chief industrial towns in Ulster. Thus, by 1830, the linen trade had at its disposal far greater financial resources than had ever been available before. One result of this new acquisition of strength was a huge increase in direct export from Belfast. In 1810 the export of linen was a little more than 15,000,000 yards, a figure which was then considered very respectable.[1] By 1835 it had more than trebled in amount : the exact figure was 53,881,000 yards, a much larger quantity than the total for all Ireland in 1810, or for that matter in 1820.[2] But it was not merely a question of facilities for short credit, although they were essential for the purchase of raw material and the direct sale of cloth to customers overseas. When the full history of the rise of banking in Ireland is written, it will probably be found that the banks did an immense service in the advance of capital for long periods, for investment in buildings and machinery. At any rate, the credit given by joint-stock banks must be set down as one of the chief agents in the increased efficiency of production, and the great expansion of trade, which came about between 1825 and 1865.

Machine Spinning. Credit was needed above all for exploiting two improvements in spinning. The first was the invention of wet-spinning by James Kay, of Preston, in 1825. Flax fibres are difficult to spin because they contain a kind of gum. The original fibres are only an inch or two long, but the gum binds different fibres together so effectively that they can be drawn out into strands eighteen inches or more in length. In order

---

[1] Dubourdieu, *Antrim*, ii. 591.   [2] Warden, p. 403.

to form these strands into a continuous yarn they must be both twisted together, and made to slip past one another as the yarn is pulled out ; but as the strands are slightly viscous they stick together and resist the roving action. The hand-spinner could move them gently with her fingers ; but the action of machinery, in the early days, was rougher, and resulted, when any attempt was made to spin fine counts, in uneven yarns and much breakage. The gill frames, by presenting finer fibres for the silver, enabled the machine-spinner to make medium counts with some success, even before 1820. Fine yarns, however, were still spun entirely by hand. In 1825 Kay discovered that a thorough soaking in cold water, although it did not injure the yarn by dissolving out the gum, made the fibres more slippery, so that they could be drawn by machinery into a really fine yarn.[1] Owing to a flaw in his specification Kay was unable to take out a patent, and his invention—like Cort's invention of iron-puddling—was the more readily adopted by manufacturers, so that the public benefited at Kay's expense.

The invention of wet-spinning was no accident. Although the special difficulties caused by the war had passed, the com-petition of cotton goods remained and grew stronger. The demand for linen was gradually increasing, but the trade was by no means in a safe position. On the other hand there was a prospect of much larger sales if production could be made cheaper ; and the most obvious way of reducing the cost of production was the improvement of machine spinning.

The invention was soon adopted by Irish manufacturers. There were many large employers who could afford the capital needed for working the new process. Some were spinners already, such as Joseph Nicholson, of Bessbrook, and the Crosthwaites of Dublin. Others were bleachers, such as William Hudson, of Banbridge, who set up a branch concern for spinning in Bess-

---

[1] The development of spinning machinery is well described by Mr. Horner (chaps. xxix and xl). The first idea for mechanical spinning of flax had been to dissolve out the gum completely, leaving only the short ultimate fibres, which could then be treated as if they were cotton. But this process only resulted in turning ' good flax into bad cotton '. In the latter years of the Napoleonic War, Philippe de Girard, a prolific inventor, made a machine furnished with a wet roller. His machine lubricated the flax a little and enabled finer counts to be spun. Consequently he claimed that Kay had pirated his invention ; but it was rightly held that Kay's method of steeping the flax for six hours was a different and much more important discovery.

brook. They were helped, as we noticed in the last chapter, by grants from the Linen Board, given on the advice of the parliamentary committee of 1825.[1] In 1828, without any support from public funds, Murland set up in the beautiful little town of Castlewellan, co. Down, a mill which was at that time by far the largest in Ireland.[2] The economy of machine spinning reinforced by Kay's invention, had evidently caused a rapid growth of mills, and it led very quickly to the next great advance, the introduction of steam power.

Steam Spinning. In 1829 John Mulholland, who had been a cotton spinner and a user of steam power, set up a mill in York Street, Belfast.[3] His cotton mill had been burnt down, and he decided to turn to the linen trade and try the experiment of applying the new motive power to the new wet-spinning machinery : wisely, as the event showed, for as a cotton manufacturing concern his business could hardly have survived more than thirty years, whereas his linen mill became, and still remains, the greatest in the world.

The success of Mulholland's enterprise gave a still further impulse to the use of spinning machinery. Mills, independent of a head of water, could be set up on any convenient site, and their spindles could produce fine counts of yarn. Consequently the number of mills soon increased. There were forty in Ireland in 1838 ; by 1853 the number had grown to 80.[4]

Progress is shown, however, more clearly in the number of spindles than the number of mills. England and Scotland had

[1] Crosthwaites received a grant of £142 in 1827. In this year and the next Hudson and Nicholson had grants of which the totals were respectively £312 10s. 0d. and £600. In the case of Nicholson it was stated definitely that the money was given for spinning by Kay's process. Hudson's house and bleachyard, near Banbridge, were mentioned in Chapter XIII, as the centre of a small colony of artisan bleachers and weavers.

[2] McCall, p. 112 ; Charley, p. 36.

[3] McCall, p. 113 ; Charley, u.s. ; Owen, *History of Belfast*, p. 297.

[4] Warden, p. 403. The fact that there were only 40 spinning mills in Ireland, as compared with 169 in England and 183 in Scotland, misled Kane (*Industrial Resources*, pp. 320, 321) into the idea that the whole manufacture in Ireland was much smaller than that of either England or Scotland. He believed—though it is difficult to understand why—that the relative output of the three countries was ' exactly shown ' by statistics of horse-power and employment in the mills. Consequently he held that Ireland was ' almost as much behind in this as in every other branch of industry '. It is interesting to notice that the Irish mills were on an average considerably larger than those in Great Britain. Although only 10 per cent. of the mills in the British Isles were in Ireland, these mills had 18 per cent. of the horse-power, and 21 per cent. of the employees.

had a long start in steam spinning; but after 1830 Ireland steadily gained upon them, about 1850 actually passed them, and apparently captured trade from the spinners in Great Britain.

The relative positions may be judged from this table, which shows the number of spindles working at various dates : [1]

		England.	Scotland.	Ireland.
1844		—	—	155,000 (in Belfast)
1850		266,000	303,000	396,000
1853		—	—	581,000
1854		300,000	350,000	—
1857		442,000	—	—
1861		—	—	—
1862		344,000	312,000	593,000
1868		474,000	264,000	905,000

There was an actual decrease in Great Britain before 1862. During the boom between 1862 and 1865 there was some fresh expansion; [2] but by that time the output of yarn in Ireland must have been as great as that of England and Scotland together. A favourable climate, local supplies of flax, and production as efficient as that in Great Britain, and probably cheaper, had at length told decisively in favour of Ireland.

Export of yarn was also increasing, no doubt for use with power looms in England and Scotland—for Irish manufacturers were behindhand with power-loom weaving, as they had been at first with machine spinning. Exported yarns, which had scarcely exceeded 4,500,000 lb. in the days of hand spinning, amounted in 1857 to 9,000,000,[3] and, according to an estimate of 1865, they rose in that exceptional year to 28,000,000 lb.[4]

[1] The figure for 1844 from Kane's *Industrial Resources*, p. 320 ; those for 1850 from Riordan's *Modern Irish Trade and Industry*, p. 107 ; for 1853 from Owen's *History of Belfast*, p. 300 ; for 1854, from McCall, p. 114. Warden (pp. 387 and 439) gives the figures for England in 1857 and 1862, and for Scotland in 1861. The Irish output in 1862 and 1868 is given by Murphy, *Ireland, Industrial, Political and Social*, p. 42. It is interesting to note the production in France in the same period. Steam spinning was very little developed in 1840, but by 1849 there were about 250,000 spindles, and by 1866, 907,000. But after drawing level with the Irish output production in France fell away ; and in 1904 there were only 450,000 spindles (Clapham, *Econ. Development of France and Germany*, pp. 69, 255).
[2] Warden mentioned a rapid growth both in England and in Scotland in 1862 and 1863.   [3] McCall, p. 115.
[4] Owen, op. cit., p. 298. The export in 1912 was estimated by Mr. J. H. Stirling (*The Times*, 4 Nov. 1919) to be rather more than 23,000,000 yards. See also Chart, *Economic History of Ireland*, p. 127.

This was probably a maximum figure, because the decline of weaving in Great Britain, and its increase in Ireland, would tend to keep the yarn at home.

There was an advance in quality as well as amount. Whereas in the first quarter of the century spinners seldom tried to produce from machines anything finer than 36 lea yarn, by about 1850 the invention of wet-spinning and later improvements had enabled them to make yarn of 220 or more leas to the pound—a yarn which would be considered very fine if it were made by hand.[1]

Transport. The progress of spinning, and of trade in general in the neighbourhood of Belfast, was greatly helped by improvements in transport after 1820. At that time the passage from Liverpool to Belfast had very recently been made by a steamship, and in 1824 a regular service of cargo steamers between the two ports was organized.[2] A quick, cheap, and reliable system of conveyance to the English markets—improved in a few years' time by the opening of railway communication from Liverpool—must have been a boon to exporters in Belfast, and it was undoubtedly a main reason for the increase of direct trade which has just been noticed. Moreover, the use of steam power for cotton spinning had led already to the organization of a coal supply, especially from Whitehaven and the Ayrshire coast. After 1830 there was a rapidly growing import of coal as fuel for the linen mills.

In the same connexion we should note that great improvements in the harbour of Belfast were begun in 1839, an extension of docks and quays, and above all the cutting of a straight channel from the main quays out to the deep water of the Lough, so that large ships could be moored at any time within a few hundred yards of the centre of the town.[3]

---

[1] McCall, p. 114.

[2] Marmion, p. 358. The steamer which made the voyage to Liverpool was the *Waterloo* (200 tons), the largest steamship in the British Isles. A smaller steamer, the *Greenock*, had been plying betwen Belfast and Bangor since 1816. Two years later it was joined by the *Rob Roy*. In 1819 two other steamers began regular crossings to Glasgow (Owen, *Hist. of Belfast*, pp. 264–6). In 1826 a steam packet service was organized between Portpatrick and Donaghadee. Considerable sums were spent on the improvement of the harbours for this purpose. (See correspondence in Treasury Letters, T. 14, 24.)

[3] For a full account of the improvements see Mr. D. G. Owen's *History of Belfast*, pp. 226–32, and his *History of the Port of Belfast*, pp. 32–6. There had been much discussion, since about 1820, of proposals made by

Concentration in Towns. These improvements in transport, together with the growth of joint-stock banking, the spinning of fine yarns by machinery, and the use of steam power, gave an impetus to trade all over Ulster. But above all they were of benefit to Belfast. Before 1820 Belfast had been the centre of cotton manufacture, and little more than an emporium for linen. Now it became the chief seat of linen manufacture as well. About the middle of the century more than a third of the mills in Ireland were in or near Belfast, and as these mills included most of the large concerns, their output would probably be well over half the total output of the country.

This concentration of industry is readily understood. Linen spinning was becoming more and more dependent upon coal supply, and as coal could be had more cheaply at the quayside than further inland, spinning mills were naturally built near to the ports, especially Belfast. It followed that yarn was most easily available in the coast towns; therefore not only spinners but weavers as well flocked to the neighbourhood of those towns. As long as yarn was spun in cottages and was available at home or in local markets in every part of Ulster, the weaver or small manufacturer could remain on his farm, for he never needed to travel more than a few miles in search of raw material. Now that the supply of yarn was becoming more and more concentrated in large stocks at a few centres, weavers had to migrate to the sources of supply.[1]

A generation earlier there had been a movement of population towards the bleach-greens : now there was a return movement

the great engineers Rennie and Telford for floating docks, and a ship canal to the deep water at Garmoyle. But in 1831 the simpler project of Walker and Burgess, for a deepening of the channel, was sanctioned by a private Act. Negotiations for the work lasted for seven years, and involved the passing of a second Act. The enterprise was carried out in two main stages : the first cut was opened in 1841 ; and the second, the Victoria Channel, in 1849. The effect of these improvements, together with the growing industry of Belfast, may be judged from the following figures :

Tonnage cleared from Belfast Harbour.

1837	.	.	288,000
1847	.	.	538,500
1857	.	.	797,000
1867	.	.	1,372,000 (Owen, *Port of Belfast*, p. 48).

[1] The opening of a railway from Belfast to Lisburn in 1839, and its extension to Lurgan two years later, would facilitate the carriage of coal and raw material inland (see Owen, *History of Belfast*, pp. 248, 249). But this change did not prevent a great concentration of industry in Belfast.

to the towns. Linen manufacture was following the lead given by cotton ; only in the case of linen it was import of coal rather than import of yarn that was causing a concentration of industry near the coast.

The result is seen in a great increase of town populations, notably in Belfast. A rather generous estimate by Hyndman in 1791 gave the population as 18,320. Thirty years later the first census returns showed a population of 37,117. Between 1831 and 1841, when steam spinning was being introduced, the growth was extraordinarily quick—from 48,224 to 75,308 ; and by 1851 the number had just turned 100,000.[1]

Employment of Weavers. The example of the cotton trade was followed in another respect, and again it was the supply of raw material that caused the change in organization. We have noticed several times that the purchase of raw material in large quantities from a distance tends towards employment of workers for wages, and we have seen that capitalism soon appeared in cotton weaving for this reason. Even in the more conservative linen trade the use of yarn from foreign countries or from Connaught had tended towards a wage system. Now that linen spinning on a large scale was firmly established, weavers fell more and more into the position of wage-earners.

As early as 1811 machine spinners were branching out into manufacture of cloth. Between 1830 and 1850 they were doing so to a much greater extent, and were replacing bleachers as the chief employers in the weaving industry. In some cases, however, perhaps in many, bleachers themselves were undertaking the manufacture of yarn, thus forming vertical combinations, which included every process of manufacture as well as the marketing of finished goods.[2] There must have been a strong inducement to the owners of spinning mills to take up cloth manufacture. Spinners could hardly move to the neighbourhood of the mills unless the men of their households moved with them.

[1] The increase shown in 1851 is all the more striking since the potato famine and emigration had caused a great reduction in the population of Ireland as a whole.

[2] The growth of machine spinning in Banbridge, about 1850, was probably due to the enterprise of bleachers. Sometimes spinning mills were set up in villages, as at Bessbrook and Gilford, where coal could easily be supplied from Newry ; and these undertakings, again, seem to have been closely connected with bleachworks. (See McCall, p. 73 ; Charley, p. 79.)

Thus spinners would not be forthcoming unless employment were found for weavers as well.

These profound changes in methods and organization led to the disappearance of several old customs. In the first place, women all over Ulster, and in Connaught and some other parts of the southern provinces, lost the pittance of wages which they had made by hand-spinning. The loss in terms of money was small because wages were extremely low, but a shilling or two more or less made a great difference to the household budget of an Irish labourer. Two circumstances, however, helped to temper the blow. There was a growing demand for machine spinners, at higher wages, in the towns ; and those women who remained in the country found fresh scope in the embroidering or ' flowering ' of muslin or linen—still an important domestic industry at the present day.[1]

With the new movement of population, weaving became more and more an urban industry, and manufacture by peasant farmers declined. The Devon Commission, making their tour of inquiry shortly before 1845, found that in certain districts of Ulster manufacture had almost disappeared. In one part of south Down, for instance, although they were told that many farmers were still weavers, their informant added : ' A change has passed over the province of Ulster in the staple manufacture, and affected it very seriously.' [2] The change was clearly the urbanization of industry, as a result of spinning by steam power. In a neighbouring district a witness said, ' Manufactures are extinct, or at least there is very little employment in that way.' [3]

The forces which were gradually driving manufacture out of the country districts in Ulster had a still greater and more disastrous effect in the other provinces. The ' yarn counties ' had depended for their trade on the demand for hand-spun yarn in Ulster and Great Britain. As that demand was rapidly failing, spinners, ' grey merchants ', and exporters alike were losing their means of

[1] The census of 1821 shows that ' muslin flowerers ' were already almost as common as spinners in some districts.

[2] Report of Devon Commission, i. 403.

[3] ibid., i. 405. Ten years later the process had gone further. Tooke (op. cit., vol. vi, p. 530) said that the class of farmer-weavers was disappearing from Ulster as a whole. Many weavers had emigrated after the famine. A considerable number had transferred their labour to the woollen industry in Bradford (ibid., p. 533).

livelihood. Although a few large firms in the south, such as Crosthwaites of Dublin, had taken to machine spinning by water power,
most of the factory masters and all the small manufacturers
still drew their supplies from the old centres of hand-spinning.
Their trade kept a certain number of spinners at work ; but
they were finding it more and more difficult to compete with
the cheap goods produced by mill-owners. By 1826 unemployment among the southern weavers had become a serious problem.
There was acute distress not only in Dublin, Drogheda, and
Cork, but in all the rural districts of manufacture as well.[1]
Several public subscriptions were raised for the relief of manufacturers, and the Government was besieged with petitions from
the unemployed. The King himself gave a donation of £500,
but his ministers could do little to heal the injuries, or even to
palliate the suffering.[2] Nor were they in a mood for intervention.
It was in this same year that they decided to dissolve the Linen
Board ; and although various schemes were put forward by
private persons for the promotion of industry in southern Ireland,
not one of them was carried even to the stage of experiment.[3]

Part of the trouble may have been due to the financial crisis
of 1825-6, which had given a serious check to manufactures
in England, but the main causes were deeper and more permanent. Conditions in Ireland were as bad in 1830 as they
had been four years earlier.[4] In fact, there was no recovery
from the depression. The destitution of those who had once

---

[1] e. g. at Clonakilty, co. Cork, it was said that 500 looms were standing idle.

[2] In the Home Office correspondence (H.O. 100, 216) there is a bundle of
documents dealing with the distress of manufacturers in Ireland. The bundle
includes several petitions for relief, some of them addressed to Peel because he
was the only minister personally known to the writers.

[3] There was, of course, good reason for ignoring these proposals, for many
similar schemes had come to grief under more favourable conditions. Moreover,
the Government was preoccupied with the conduct of O'Connell and the
Catholic Association. Examples of the proposals made about this time are
A. M. Creevy's plan for encouraging linen manufacture in the west (Official
Papers, Dublin, 1790–1831, no. 475) ; a project of central woollen and cotton
markets in Dublin (ibid., no. 641) ; W. Salisbury's suggestions for flax and
hemp cultivation and several minor rural industries (memorandum in H.O.
100, 216).

[4] A short account of conditions in southern Ireland about 1830 is given
by Dr. G. O'Brien in his introduction to Mr. Riordan's *Modern Irish Trade
and Industry*. There is an excellent description of social conditions in the
rural districts of Ireland at this time in Dr. D. A. Chart's *Economic History
of Ireland*, pp. 92–8.

been spinners and weavers merely increased the mass of social misery, which reached its climax in the great famine.

Disappearance of Open Markets.   While southern enterprise was failing under the stress of these misfortunes, trade in Ulster was growing, but under constantly changing conditions.   We have seen how the use of steam power in spinning mills drew weavers as well as spinners to the towns, and caused weaving to be organized more and more by large employers.   Another outcome of the same movement was the decay of brown-linen markets.   There was no catastrophic fall.   In the bleaching districts open markets had begun to decline long before the introduction of steam power, and thirty years after the opening of Mulholland's mill a certain amount of cloth was still sold by the old methods.   But during these thirty years yarn markets were being steadily replaced by spinning mills, and the increasing production of cloth by large manufacturers was doing away with the need for open linen markets.

The change was irregular as well as gradual, for the old local distinctions remained.   In the less progressive districts—north Antrim, Tyrone, Londonderry, and south Armagh—where small manufacturers could still provide themselves with yarn, markets were more freely used.   About ten markets remained in these districts in 1855, and six or seven of them had some trade as late as 1862.[1]   But in co. Down there was apparently none at all.   In south Antrim the market of Lisburn, which had been the largest in Ireland fifty years earlier, had entirely disappeared, and the Belfast market was almost extinct.   The few buyers still dealing in this market were commission agents of the large exporting firms.[2]

Power Looms.   The last stage in the decline of open markets, and of the domestic system as a whole, set in about the middle of the century with the introduction of power looms.   In Scotland, as we have seen, the first experiments in steam power for weaving had been made during the Napoleonic War.   In England the use of power looms had been gradually spreading for about twenty years.   It was encouraged by the invention, soon after 1830, of a vibrating roller, which kept an even tension

---

[1] McCall, pp. 70, 71 ; Charley, pp. 8, 99.   See also Table of Markets given below in Appendix I.   [2] McCall, u.s.

on the warp, and so enabled the looms to weave comparatively fine linens with success.[1]

In Ireland power looms came into general use much later. They appeared, indeed, as early as 1826, when the firm of T. & A. Davison, of Laragh, co. Monaghan, set up ten looms for the manufacture of wide cloths, probably sheetings.[2] But this seems to have been an isolated enterprise ; for another twenty years practically all the linen made in Ireland, fine and coarse alike, was woven by hand.

The main cause of this delay was the low level of wages. Although the wages of weavers had risen to some extent during the Napoleonic War, the rise was only temporary. It would be natural to expect that machine spinning, by producing a great supply of cheap yarn, would cause a strong demand for weaving, and so would lead to a rise in the weavers' wages. That would have been a repetition of the course of events in the cotton manufacture.

But although there must have been a tendency of this kind, it was more than counteracted by other forces. The competition of cotton had grown keener because of the spread of power-loom weaving in Great Britain. The problem of cheap production, which had been acute through transitory causes during the war, became after 1820 a permanent difficulty. Steam spinning, machine scutching, and improved methods of bleaching offered a partial, but not a complete, solution. If the market for linen goods were to be preserved and enlarged, some economy in weaving was needed as well.[3] English and Scottish manu-

[1] Charley, p. 90.

[2] Linen Board's Account Roll for 1826, P.R.O. London, A.O. 17, 428. T. & A. Davison received a grant from the Board of £6 (Irish) for each loom. It was officially stated that there were 100 power looms in Ireland in 1835 (Prof. L. Knowles, *Ind. and Comm. Revolutions*, p. 55). But we may well doubt whether so many were actually in use before 1850.

[3] We may take an example from the cambric trade. A cut of cloth for handkerchiefs, which in 1833 cost 16s. 3d., brought only 6s. in 1853 ; and the corresponding prices of the finest cambric were 40s. and 22s. (McCall, p. 81). The reduction in one case is 63 per cent., in the other 45 per cent. In practically the same period the cost of yarn fell by about 50 per cent., as is shown by the following figures, which may be taken as fairly representative :

Price of a bundle (4 hanks) of 40 lea yarn.

1834	.	.	10s. 0d.	to 11s. 0d.
1840	.	.	7s. 0d.	,, 7s. 6d.
1847	.	.	4s. 9d.	,, 5s. 0d.
1854	.	.	4s. 10½d.	,, 5s. 3d.

facturers met the difficulty by introducing steam power into their own works.[1] In Ireland, however, the downward pressure on prices was allowed simply to reduce the level of wages. It is said that between 1828 and 1852 piece wages for cambric weaving fell by 69 per cent. for fine cloth, and by about 40 per cent. for coarser counts. These figures may be exceptional, for cambric was probably affected by the competition of cotton goods more than most kinds of linen ; and they may be exaggerated.[2] But it is certain that the wages of linen weavers in general remained very low until 1845, and were lower at that time than they had been twenty years earlier.

The reduction of wages, which at the outset were by no means high, was only possible because there were weavers in Ulster prepared to work for a mere pittance, and to eke out their living by subsistence farming, or by the still smaller earnings of the women and children of their households. Contemporary writers were agreed that the miserable wages paid in the second quarter of the century called forth an abundant supply of labour— according to some, a redundant supply ; so that, in spite of the increased production of yarn, the labour of weavers was far from acquiring a scarcity value. The copious supply of cheap labour was due, no doubt, to two factors. The first and more obvious was the rapid growth of population. The second was the use of power looms for cotton weaving in Great Britain, which steadily drove down the wages of handwork until they fell below the level of subsistence. . It is highly probable that many Irish weavers of muslin and calico, when their wages fell to a certain point, would turn to the linen manufacture,

This reduction could not account for the whole decrease in the cost of finished cloth : there must have been a reduction also in the cost of the later processes.

In the example given above, the slight increase shown in 1854 is not surprising. General prices had risen since 1850 because of the discoveries of gold.

[1] Their action would intensify the problem of keeping down prices in Ireland.

[2] McCall, p. 79. The reduction was from 60s. to 40s. for a piece of the finest cambric. For the coarser cambric wages rose from 17s. to 18s. for a piece, but in the meantime the length of the piece was increased from 58 yards to 104 yards. McCall does not say whether these measurements applied only to the coarser cloths ; it is highly probable that fine pieces were a good deal shorter. Therefore his statement in regard to wages for fine weaving is open to doubt.

and by their competition would still further reduce the wages of linen weavers.[1]

This wretched state of affairs continued until 1845. But in the next five years there was in Ulster, as in the rest of Ireland, a vast social upheaval—famine, followed by emigration on a huge scale. Thousands of weavers were among the emigrants. With their departure labour became scarce, and wages began to rise : they increased to the extent of twenty or thirty per cent. in five years.[2] The result was an increased cost of production. Moreover, the shortage of labour made it difficult to fulfil contracts. Therefore the manufacturers were driven to the adoption of steam power, to the economy of efficient machines instead of the economy of cheap labour. The change in circumstances is well described in the following account, written by one of the manufacturers of this period :

' So long as a man's labour could be had at the handloom in Ireland for a shilling a day, it was felt no power loom could work much, if at all cheaper ; but when wages, some few years back, began to advance, and the population to decrease, instead of increase, it was admitted that the power loom was at length required.' [3]

The use of steam power had been long delayed, but when the fashion had once been set it spread rapidly, because there was an urgent need of increased production. Eighty power looms were said to have been erected in 1847 by Giles Haworth, an engineer who was brought across from Blackburn for the purpose.[4] There was only a slight increase during the next three years, but in 1852 a firm of machine makers in Leeds found it worth while to set up a branch in Belfast.[5] In 1853 it was reported that power looms were ' now rapidly extending themselves in Ulster '. By 1860 several thousands had been set up, and in 1868 the number of power looms in Ireland was almost

---

[1] Cf. Riordan, op. cit., pp. 22, 24 (Historical Introduction by Dr. G. O'Brien): ' The cotton manufacture began to decline about 1830, and this decline caused many weavers to turn to the linen manufacture.'

[2] Tooke, op. cit., vol. vi, p. 530.

[3] Charley, p. 88.

[4] ibid., p. 90. According to Sir R. L. Patterson (*British Industries*, p. 141) the two pioneers in Belfast were Craig and Currell, who each set up forty looms.

[5] Tooke, vol. vi, p. 531, quoting the *Belfast Linen Trade Circular*, October 1852. The attraction seems to have been the supply of power looms, but there would, of course, be a good demand for spinning machinery as well.

equal to the number in Scotland, and far ahead of the figure for England.[1]

We have seen the extension of capital and machine production to all the chief branches of linen manufacture. Practically all the yarn was now produced in mills, a large proportion of the cloth in factories, and bleaching had long been the business of large employers. Even printing, which had always been undertaken by small craftsmen (apart from early and unsuccessful experiments in the south), began, about 1840, to be transferred to the bleachworks as a branch of the finishing trade.[2] Flax preparation, moreover, was partly taken out of the hands of the small farmers, for scutching mills had spread all over the flax-growing districts.[3] Although they were seldom large concerns, they represented none the less an increase of capital and machine power.

Flax Growing. The only section of the industry which remained to the farmers, and the only section in which there was no substantial growth, was the actual cultivation of flax. But this was a branch rather of agriculture than of manufacture. Supplies of cheap flax from abroad, especially from Russia, discouraged production at home. So also did the strong demand for corn and other agricultural produce in Great Britain, before the development of the great corn lands in America. The southern farmers almost completely abandoned flax growing :

[1] The following table shows the earlier development of power-loom weaving in Great Britain, and the rapid progress in Ireland, especially after 1860.

Number of Power Looms for Linen Manufacture.

	England.	Scotland.	Ireland.
1835 .	41	168	100 (?)
1850 .	1,131 (911 in Yorkshire)	2,529	88
1853 .	—	—	218
1856 .	—	—	1,871
1857 .	1,787	—	—
1859 .	—	—	3,633
1861 .	—	8,510	4,933
1862 .	2,160	—	6,000
1866 .	—	—	10,804
1868 .	5,086	12,985	12,969

These figures are taken from Warden, pp. 387, 421, 439 ; Charley, p. 89 ; Murphy, *Ireland Industrial, Political and Social*, p. 43 ; Owen, *History of Belfast*, p. 292 ; Ashley, *British Industries*, p. 141.

[2] Charley, p. 110.   [3] ibid., p. 35.

in 1870 less than 1 per cent. of the arable in the southern provinces was under flax.[1] Even the farmers in Ulster, who could more readily have their flax crops scutched and put on the market, were always more or less doubtful of the wisdom of sowing large quantities. It was commonly said about the middle of the century that the area under flax varied inversely as the price of corn. This lack of interest in a staple raw material was viewed with alarm by many leaders of opinion in Ireland. They made experiments and calculations to show the great profits which might result from flax farming.[2] In 1841 a Flax Improvement Society was founded in order to teach the best methods to farmers in all parts of the country. But the society did not justify the high hopes of its founders, and in 1859 it was dissolved.[3] Up to that time the area under flax had seldom exceeded 150,000 acres. During the cotton famine it suddenly increased twice that figure. But as soon as the emergency was over the area rapidly shrank, and in recent times—until the fresh emergency of the European war—the normal area of flax growing was only 50,000 acres.[4]

Recent Developments. We have traced the gradual development of modern methods of trade and credit, and following them, the introduction of steam power for spinning and weaving, the appearance of large factories, and the concentration of workers in industrial towns. By 1860 a great part of the industry had been transformed to an organization and methods similar to those of the present day.

---

[1] Murphy, op. cit., p. 39.

[2] e. g. Kane, *Industrial Resources*, pp. 308 sqq. Kane quotes an instance showing a certain yield of £25 and a probable yield of £30 an acre.

[3] Kane, u.s. ; Charley, p. 37 ; McCall, p. 92. McCall said of the Society, ' (It) has performed a greater amount of good in this country . . . than all the Linen Board was able to achieve during its entire existence.'

[4] Warden (p. 411) gives particulars of the area under flax, showing the following annual averages :

1817–23	.	131,000 acres
1847–53	.	102,000 ,,
1857–63	.	138,000 ,,

In 1864 the acreage increased to 301,700, but it had fallen to 206,400 in 1868 (Murphy, op. cit., p. 40) and to 34,500 in 1897 (*British Industries*, p. 131). A table given by Mr. Riordan (op. cit., p. 115) shows the average area under flax, from 1898 to 1914 (inclusive), to have been almost exactly 50,000 acres. In 1918 the area had grown to 143,000 acres, but in the first year of peace it fell to 95,600.

During the next few years the cotton famine gave a great
impulse to linen manufacture. But the prosperity was short-
lived and by no means healthy. The inevitable reaction caused
serious distress and dislocation of trade. ' No fewer than thirty-
six spinning mills were brought to insolvency, or at least to
such financial difficulty that eighteen of them, with 200,000
spindles, ceased to exist. . . . One of the largest mills lived through
a long-protracted crisis in so crippled a condition that it was
unable to pay any dividend to the shareholders during twenty
consecutive years.' [1]

In the last three decades of the nineteenth century there was
not only a recovery of the cotton trade after the famine, but
also a great advance in the technique of manufacture, which
made cotton a more formidable rival than ever to linen. If there
had been no corresponding reforms in the linen manufacture,
it would have lost ground seriously. But fortunately there has
been considerable enterprise and progress during the last sixty
years. Methods of sale have been improved, especially in regard
to facilities for credit, and agencies in other lands. Joint-stock
companies have become common, and many individual concerns
have gained great distinction, both for the volume of their trade
and the quality of their work.[2] The concentration of bleach-
greens has continued : there are now about the same number
of greens in the whole of Ulster as there were seventy years
ago in co. Antrim alone. The business of printing and dyeing
has substantially increased, and it has given rise to the important

[1] A. S. Moore, *Linen, from the Raw Material to the Finished Product*, p. 62.
Cf. Sir R. L. Patterson (*British Industries*, pp. 127, 134), who said that since
the cotton famine he could remember the closing of forty spinning mills in
Ireland, more than twenty in Scotland, and more than a dozen in Yorkshire.
There was a great fall in the price of yarn, and only those firms of spinners
survived which could produce yarn very cheaply. e. g. the price of a bundle
of 80's line yarn fell from 6s. 7½d. in 1864 to 2s. 10½d. in 1897 (ibid., p. 140).
  The number of spindles working in Ireland in 1868 was 905,000. By 1871
it had fallen to 866,500. After some fluctuations it gradually fell to 841,600
in 1902. Then there was a recovery, and between 1912 and 1918 the number
was rather more than 950,000. This figure is only 5 per cent. higher than
the figure for 1868 ; but the actual output of yarn increased in a greater
proportion, because the modern spindles are more efficient than those in
use half a century ago. (See Chart, *Economic History*, u.s. ; Riordan, op. cit.,
p. 111.)
[2] One of the first joint-stock concerns to be set up in the linen trade, after
the passing of the Companies Consolidation Act, was the York Street Flax
Spinning Company, formed to carry on the work of Mulholland's firm.

trades of shirt and blouse making. There have been many improvements in methods of manufacture, some of them—such as the machinery for hackling and the wonderful devices for embroidery—involving processes of great beauty and delicacy.

Perhaps the most remarkable change of the last sixty years has been the steady growth of power-loom weaving, a growth which is the more striking because it continued after the American Civil War, when there was a long depression in the spinning industry.

Its persistence may be judged from the following figures :

				Power looms in Ireland.[1]
1868	.	.	.	12,969
1871	.	.	.	14,834
1881	.	.	.	21,779
1890	.	.	.	26,592
1899	.	.	.	32,245

From 1911 to 1918 the number was about 37,000.[2] Thus in the half-century following the year 1868, while the spindles in Ireland only increased in number by 5 per cent., power looms increased by 185 per cent. This advance was accompanied by the gradual decline of hand-loom weaving in Ireland and of the linen manufacture as a whole in England, France, and Germany. The linen trade of Yorkshire, which was still considerable in 1860, gave way before the growing strength, improved technique, and greater attractiveness of the woollen, worsted, and wholesale clothing industries. In France and Germany the linen manufacture was very conservative. Power looms—and in Germany even spinning machinery—came in remarkably slowly. Moreover, in both countries other industries have offered a better field for enterprise.[3]

---

[1] *British Industries*, p. 141.

[2] Chart, *Econ. Hist. of Ireland*, p. 127 ; Riordan, op. cit., table on p. 111.

[3] On this subject see Dr. J. H. Clapham's *Econ. Development of France and Germany*, pp. 255–6, 289–92. In 1882 hand-looms were in a great majority in Germany. In France, as late as 1913, 20,000 of the 42,000 looms for linen and hempen goods were hand-looms. Dr. Clapham attributed the decline in France ' to a backward technique, which made earnings in linen less than those for corresponding work in cotton ; to the absence of special climatic advantages, such as those which have favoured Ireland ; and to the competition of a neighbouring population with a lower standard of life, a less exacting factory code, and a greater acquired capacity for certain processes of the industry—the Belgians '. He also mentions that a low standard of

One difficulty which might have checked progress in Ireland was avoided by a happy coincidence. The power loom could be worked by women—in fact from the beginning one woman regularly worked two looms. Already the spinning mills employed a great preponderance of women, but the men had been able to find abundant work as weavers. That field was now closed to them, and there would have been serious dislocation, or possibly disaster, if it had not been for the shipbuilding industry, which grew at an extraordinary rate after the middle of the century, and ever since that time has absorbed a large body of labour in Belfast.[1] Thus linen manufacture and shipbuilding, with its allied industries, were able to work together in a most fortunate manner, and continue as the main occupations in the city.

Technical and commercial improvements, together with the indirect help given by shipbuilding and other trades, have enabled the linen trade of Ulster to hold its position in the world's textile markets. But they have done no more. There has been no conspicuous progress or revolutionary change during the last sixty years—nothing so far-reaching as the rise of bleachers or the introduction of steam power. The headway actually made has been chiefly in the weaving, finishing, and making-up branches. The output of yarn has not greatly increased, although Ulster has still nearly a third of the spindles in the world.

In recent years—apart from the temporary gains due to contracts for aeroplane cloth—the industry has met with many difficulties, more serious than those which impeded progress

life has been ' a condition of success not altogether absent from Ulster '. The question of industrial remuneration is, in fact, one of the main problems confronting the trade in Ireland. It has received much attention in recent years, and the prosperity of the industry in the near future is closely bound up with its satisfactory solution.

[1] Cf. *British Industries*, pp. 144–5. An interesting account of the growth of shipbuilding in Belfast was contributed to Smiles's *Invention and Industry* (chap. xi) by E. F. Harland, founder of the great shipyard on Queen's Island. See also Owen, *History of Belfast*, pp. 301 sqq. ; Riordan, op. cit., chap. ii ; and Professor C. H. Oldham's *History of Belfast Shipbuilding*.

As Sir R. L. Patterson pointed out, the more highly paid workers in the shipyard do not as a rule send their daughters into linen mills. But this exception does not apply to other shipyard employees or to those engaged in the numerous trades which have sprung up by the side of the two staple industries.

during and after the Napoleonic War.[1] The crisis, however,
has served rather to stimulate than to depress enterprise. At
the present time there is great activity in invention, research,
and organization ; and it is reasonable to expect that new
methods, devised in a period of stress, will lead, as they did a
hundred years ago, to a fresh era of development and prosperity.

[1] e. g. the price of the best foreign flax was for some time about £1,000
a ton, and it reached £1,400—nearly ten times as much as the highest price
of Russian flax during the Napoleonic War. The system of Government
control kept Irish flax to a maximum of £360 a ton ; but home-grown flax
was far from supplying all the needs of the industry. Sir R. L. Patterson
said that the highest price he had ever paid for flax was £120 a ton, and that
the average price between 1860 and 1900 was £58 (*British Industries*, p. 132).

APPENDIX I

TABLE OF MARKETS FOR BROWN LINEN

THIS table serves to show the relative importance of the various markets indicated on the map. When small markets disappeared they would often be replaced, as they had been preceded, by sales at fairs. About a dozen markets, in cos. Tyrone, Donegal, Fermanagh, and Cavan, lay outside the area included in the map. But as only two of these markets—those at Strabane and Omagh, co. Tyrone—were of any importance, the map may be taken as showing practically the whole of the industrial districts.

The markets at Ballygawley, Fintona, Ballymoney, Portglenone, and Enniskillen were held fortnightly; and those at Moneymore, Maghera, Magherafelt, and Kilrea were held monthly. In these cases the figures have been reduced to a weekly average.

The remarkable fall in the figures for 1820 is discussed in Chapter XIV. It is suggested there that the slump was confined to the best qualities of cloth, so that the total *quantity* sold in 1820 was probably not far short of the total for 1816.

The special case of the markets in co. Down is also dealt with in Chapter XIV. It is worth while to notice here that the returns for Banbridge, Newry, and Downpatrick actually show an increase in 1820; consequently they do not support the explanation given above of the trading depression in that year. Since these markets were used largely for the sale of fine linens we should expect a great fall instead of a rise. As a matter of fact it is not unlikely that there was a fall, and that the figures, supplied to Corry by the inspector for south Down, were inaccurate. It is scarcely possible that the fine trade should flourish in these three markets, when only a few miles away there was less than half the normal demand. Moreover, the returns in some cases are inconsistent. For instance, the average price of cloth in Downpatrick was given in 1820 as 1s. 8d.; whereas the statistics for 1821, when the fine trade was improving, show an average of only 1s. 5½d. It would be well, therefore, not to base any assumptions on the figures for south Down. The inspector, finding trade in one or two of his markets at a low ebb, and private sales rapidly increasing, would be tempted to magnify the importance of the markets that remained.

A striking feature of the tables for 1820 and 1821 is the enormous increase of trade in the market of Armagh. This increase was almost entirely in the sale of very coarse webs : in 1821, out of a total of £6,932, there was a turnover of £4,000 a week for cloth valued at 5*d.* to 7½*d.* a yard. Many of the cheap cloths sold at this time in Armagh, Down, and Antrim were really unions (see Chap. XIII, note ii).

The figures for 1821 show a gradual recovery of trade, particularly the trade in fine cloth.

Course of Trade in Open Markets.

County.	Market.	Approximate weekly sales.			
		1784 (Greer).	*1816* (Corry).	*1820* (Corry).	*1821* (Corry).
		£	£	£	£
ANTRIM	Ahoghill . .	—	350	260	337
	Antrim . .	50	—	—	—
	Ballycastle .	—	—	5	4
	Ballymena [1] .	1,000	2,500	1,068	1,612
	Ballymoney [1] .	625	1,100	423	599
	Belfast . .	1,000	4,000	1,583	1,787
	Dervock . .	—	—	34	71
	Larne . . .	25	—	—	—
	Lisburn . .	2,000	5,000	1,630	1,868
	Portglenone .	150	600	133	217
	Randalstown .	300	—	123	157
	Total .	5,150	13,550	5,259	6,652
ARMAGH	Armagh [1] . .	1,800	3,800	6,887	6,932
	Keady . .	150	—	—	—
	Lurgan [1] . .	2,500	1,850	2,690	2,935
	Portadown .	—	150	—	—
	Richhill . .	600	—	—	—
	Tanderagee .	500	1,000	1,080	1,001
	Total .	5,550	6,800	10,657	10,868
CAVAN	Arvagh . .	—	400	230	318
	Ballynagh .	—	500	310	396
	Cootehill [2] .	1,000	1,000	1,070	1,179
	Killeshandra .	300	400	290	350
	Total .	1,300	2,300	1,900	2,243

County.	Market.	Approximate weekly sales.			
		1794 (Greer).	*1816* (Corry).	*1820* (Corry).	*1821* (Corry).
		£	£	£	£
DONEGAL	Ballybofey .	—	—	34	44
	Ballyshannon .	—	—	38	37
	Letterkenny .	120	160	133	199
	Rathmelton .	150	227	326	255
	Stranorlar. .	—	130	90	110
	Total .	270	517	621	645
DOWN	Ballynahinch .	300	17	26	16
	Banbridge. .	500	1,038	1,205	1,176
	Castlewellan .	80	—	—	—
	Downpatrick .	300	750	865 *	947
	Hillsborough .	350	8	—	—
	Kilkeel . .	200	400	317	341
	Kircubbin. .	—	150	87	43
	Newry . .	1,000	922	1,355	1,297
	Portaferry. .	50	—	—	—
	Rathfriland .	100	66	303	303
	Total .	2,880	3,351	4,158	4,123
FERMANAGH	Brookeborough	75	—	—	—
	Enniskillen .	—	225	390	399
	Irvinestown .	—	—	77	51
	Total .	75	225	467	450
LONDONDERRY	Coleraine [2] .	75	850	792	1,425
	Dungiven . .	60	—	26	12
	Kilrea . .	—	230	276	340
	Limavady. .	300	—	44	156
	Londonderry .	1,000	1,130	1,820	1,514
	Maghera . .	125	230	—	—
	Moneymore [2] .	250	625	369	515
	Magherafelt [2] .	150	370	366	484
	Total .	1,960	3,235	3,693	4,446
MONAGHAN	Ballybay . .	500	1,200	885	945
	Castleblayney .	200	850	505	448
	Clones . .	600	650	260	307
	Glaslough . .	—	240	195	199
	Monaghan. .	700	1,000	750	870
	Total .	2,000	3,940	2,595	2,749

* The annual sales in Downpatrick were given as only £4,500. But the statement that 21,600 pieces were sold at an average price of 1s. 8d. a yard, shows that the amount intended was £45,000, giving a weekly average of £865.

| County. | Market. | Approximate weekly sales. | | | |
		1794 (Greer).	1816 (Corry).	1820 (Corry).	1821 (Corry).
		£	£	£	£
TYRONE	Aughnacloy .	500	—	90	184
	Ballygawley .	—	325	125	138
	Caledon . .	—	—	95	127
	Cookstown [1] .	120	1,300	840	842
	Dungannon .	1,500	4,000	1,560	1,682
	Fintona . .	—	800	650	751
	Fivemiletown .	—	—	17	19
	Moy . . .	175	—	—	—
	Newtown Stewart	600	400	620	617
	Omagh . .	—	920	990	974
	Stewartstown .	800	630	515	628
	Strabane . .	700	2,380	1,490	1,650
	Total .	4,395	10,755	6,992	7,612
Total weekly sales in Ulster . .		23,580	44,673	36,082	39,788

[1] Markets existing in 1855, but not mentioned in 1862.
[2] Markets existing in 1862.

APPENDIX II

TABLES AND DIAGRAMS OF EXPORTS

THE tables given below are taken from the Appendix to Corry's Report of 1822. Corry quoted the statistics for the period 1711–80 from various parts of the Commons Journals. He took the account of exports of linen, yarn, and flax from 1781 to 1820 from the Dublin Custom House Books. These tables, together with Corry's account of the import of flax-seed 1780–1820, are reprinted in Horner's *Linen Trade of Europe*.

In Diagram I the figures are reduced to five-yearly averages, in order to give a more concise view, with the short-period fluctuations more or less cancelled out. The diagram shows how trade increased steadily and with little interruption for three-quarters of the eighteenth century. The set-back of 1773, which gave rise to a parliamentary inquiry, was plainly a passing and unimportant affair—less important certainly in Ireland than in Great Britain. The American War had a more serious effect. But the most striking features of the diagram are the very sharp rise between the American and French wars (corresponding closely to the general increase of exports from Great Britain); the rapid falling off and more gradual recovery

during the Napoleonic War ; and the further increase in the
next five years.   In regard to the export of yarn, which is treated
in the same way, there is a similar increase up to 1770.   The
crisis of 1773 had a much greater effect because it meant a large

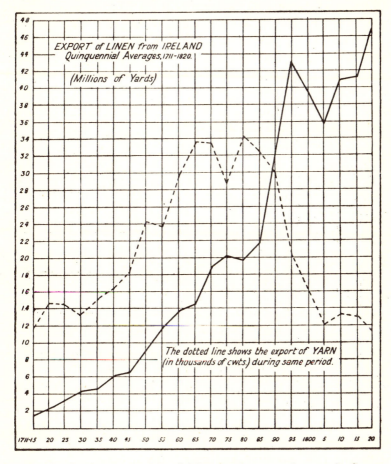

reduction in the demand for Irish yarn for manufacture in Great
Britain.   After 1780 there came a prodigious fall, caused partly
by the increased use of cotton goods, and in particular by the
substitution of cotton warp for linen in the calico manufacture.[1]
Since 1774 calico made of pure cotton had paid only half the

[1] G. W. Daniels, op. cit., pp. 80, 93, 117.

previous duty (i. e., 3*d*. a yard instead of 6*d*.) ; and cotton warp could be twisted cheaply and in abundance by means of the water-frame. Further, from 1787 onwards there was a rapid growth of machine spinning of flax in England and Scotland, consequently a smaller demand for Irish hand-spun yarn, at any rate for yarn of coarse quality. After 1800 there was a slight revival, because of the difficulty of getting either yarn or flax from the Continent. But, as the third column of the table shows clearly, it was flax rather than yarn that was wanted in Great Britain. Even when Russian supplies were available

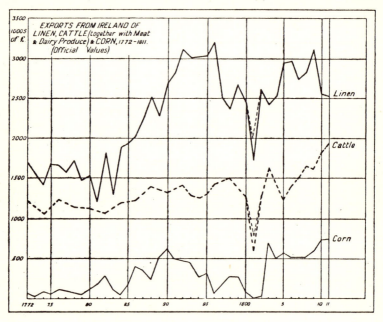

again, and the demand for yarn once more fell away, the export of flax remained as high as the export of yarn had been between 1750 and 1780, and was sometimes much higher.

Diagram II is chiefly interesting as showing the predominant · importance of linen in the overseas trade from Ireland. It emphasizes the difficulty of making up mixed cargoes for foreign and colonial trade ; for exports of other goods than the three classes shown here were very small indeed. The sensational drop in 1801 was partly due to the fact that the figures referred only to the period from 25 March 1800 to 5 January 1801. The dotted lines show approximately how the graphs would have appeared for a full year's trade. But there would still have been a serious fall, mainly on account of a general failure of crops in 1800. An absolute famine followed, and measures of relief, such as the importation of maize, had to be organized. John Richardson and John Hancock, of Lisburn, had a large share in this work (McCall, p. 68). The diagram is based on detailed tables given by Wakefield (vol. ii, pp. 46–53).

Year ending 25 March			Linen (yds.).	Yarn (cwt.).	Flax (cwt.).
1712	.	.	.	1,376,122	7,916	
1713	.	.	.	1,819,816	11,803	
1714	.	.	.	2,188,272	15,079	
1715	.	.	.	2,153,120	13,931	
1716	.	.	.	2,188,105	10,747	
1717	.	.	.	2,437,265	18,053	
1718	.	.	.	2,247,375	14,051	
1719	.	.	.	2,359,352	15,070	
1720	.	.	.	2,437,984	15,722	
1721	.	.	.	2,520,701	14,696	
1722	.	.	.	3,419,994	14,754	
1723	.	.	.	4,378,545	15,673	
1724	.	.	.	3,879,170	14,594	
1725	.	.	.	3,864,987	13,701	
1726	.	.	.	4,368,395	17,507	
1727	.	.	.	4,768,889	17,288	
1728	.	.	.	4,692,764	11,450	
1729	.	.	.	3,927,918	11,855	
1730	.	.	.	4,136,203	10,088	
1731	.	.	.	3,775,830	13,746	
1732	.	.	.	3,792,551	15,344	
1733	.	.	.	4,777,076	13,358	
1734	.	.	.	5,451,758	18,122	
1735	.	.	.	6,821,439	15,901	
1736	.	.	.	6,508,151	14,744	
1737	.	.	.	6,138,785	14,696	
1738	.	.	.	5,175,744	15,946	
1739	.	.	.	5,962,316	18,200	
1740	.	.	.	6,627,771	18,543	
1741	.	.	.	7,207,741	21,657	
1742	.	.	.	7,074,168	16,331	
1743	.	.	.	6,058,041	14,169	
1744	.	.	.	6,124,892	18,011	
1745	.	.	.	7,171,963	22,066	
1746	.	.	.	6,836,667	27,742	
1747	.	.	.	9,633,884	28,911	
1748	.	.	.	8,692,671	19,418	
1749	.	.	.	9,504,339	21,694	
1750	.	.	.	11,200,460	23,373	
1751	.	.	.	12,891,318	23,743	
1752	.	.	.	10,656,003	23,407	
1753	.	.	.	10,411,747	23,238	
1754	.	.	.	12,090,903	22,594	
1755	.	.	.	13,379,733	27,949	
1756	.	.	.	11,944,328	26,997	
1757	.	.	.	15,508,709	31,079	

Year ending 25 March.				Linen (yds.).	Yarn (cwt.).	Flax (cwt.).
1758	.	.	.	14,982,557	31,995	
1759	.	.	.	14,093,431	27,571	
1760	.	.	.	13,375,456	31,042	
1761	.	.	.	12,084,881	39,700	
1762	.	.	.	15,559,676	35,950	
1763	.	.	.	16,013,105	34,468	
1764	.	.	.	15,201,081	31,715	
1765	.	.	.	14,355,205	26,127	
1766	.	.	.	17,892,102	35,018	
1767	.	.	.	20,148,170	30,275	
1768	.	.	.	18,490,019	32,590	
1769	.	.	.	17,790,705	37,037	
1770	.	.	.	20,560,754	33,417	
1771	.	.	.	25,376,808	34,166	
1772	.	.	.	20,599,178	32,442	
1773	.	.	.	18,450,700	18,079	
1774	.	.	.	16,916,674	29,194	
1775	.	.	.	20,205,087	30,599	
1776	.	.	.	20,502,587	36,153	
1777	.	.	.	19,714,638	29,698	
1778	.	.	.	21,945,729	28,109	
1779	.	.	.	18,836,042	35,673	
1780	.	.	.	18,746,902	42,370	
1781	.	.	.	14,947,265	37,202	
1782	.	.	.	24,970,303	28,188	
1783	.	.	.	16,039,705	35,813	
1784	.	.	.	24,961,898	33,014	
1785	.	.	.	26,677,647	28,842	
1786	.	.	.	28,168,666	31,062	
1787	.	.	.	30,728,728	31,049	26
1788	.	.	.	35,487,691	27,275	65
1789	.	.	.	29,344,633	28,742	25
1790	.	.	.	37,322,125	31,573	26
1791	.	.	.	39,718,706	27,000	109
1792	.	.	.	45,581,667	17,191	61
1793	.	.	.	43,312,057	16,645	40
1794	.	.	.	43,257,764	19,056	58
1795	.	.	.	42,780,840	22,731	15
1796	.	.	.	46,705,319	20,601	343
1797	.	.	.	36,559,746	12,865	6
1798	.	.	.	33,497,171	20,331	188
1799	.	.	.	38,466,289	16,851	27
1800	.	.	.	35,676,908	12,201	12

(To 5 January.)				Linen (yds.).	Yarn (cwt.).	Flax (cwt.).
1801	.	.	.	25,041,516	11,135	4
1802	.	.	.	37,767,077	23,492	1,669
1803	.	.	.	35,491,131	9,315	173
1804	.	.	.	37,432,365	7,847	2,811
1805	.	.	.	42,988,621	8,967	2,453
1806	.	.	.	43,534,971	7,075	373
1807	.	.	.	30,049,727	8,705	299
1808	.	.	.	40,901,442	12,443	8,255
1809	.	.	.	43,904,382	25,392	4,888
1810	.	.	.	37,061,859	13,701	6,839

(To 5 January.)	Linen (yds.).	Yarn (cwt.).	Flax (cwt.).
1811 . . .	36,846,971	6,049	1,080
1812 . . .	31,392,845	9,282	14,343
1813 . . .	35,787,671	21,043	65,655
1814 . . .	38,994,381	19,123	69,225
1815 . . .	42,964,064	11,362	24,368
1816 . . .	43,383,732	11,934	29,910
1817 . . .	45,617,854	13,852	33,482
1818 . . .	55,770,636	14,009	44,269
1819 . . .	50,805,586	10,627	38,353
1820 . . .	37,464,279	5,553	32,149
1821 . . .	43,507,928	9,257	65,394

APPENDIX III

NOTES ON THE MAP

(i.) *The distribution of markets* shows how manufacture flourished largely in lowland districts, where communications were easy. The map also indicates that the Bann and Lagan Valleys were the most suitable districts for bleaching. The smaller group of bleach-greens near Coleraine and Limavady was needed to supply the Londonderry market.

(ii.) Dubourdieu wrote (*Antrim*, ii 474) in regard to *Bally-mena* : ' From whatever cause it proceeds, this is one of the most prosperous places in the county, though so far inland.' The map suggests the cause : Ballymena was a natural collecting point for a very wide district. If contours were shown in greater detail this fact would appear still more clearly. As there were many independent weavers in north Antrim, and as Ballymena was fairly remote from Belfast, there was much scope for drapers, even in the nineteenth century. Dubourdieu remarked on the large number of drapers dealing in Ballymena, and the consequent good provision of inns—' wherever the linen drapers regularly attend, decent accommodation at least may be expected.' One or two of the old inns, very handsome buildings, remain to-day.

(iii.) *The Antrim Coast* is cut off from Ballymena and other inland markets by a great mass of mountain and moorland ; therefore, although flax was abundant, there was little manu-facture. Even the small market in Larne disappeared when supplies of cotton became available. The excellent coast road, which now provides easy communication with Belfast, did not exist at the time with which we are dealing.

(iv.) *Carrickfergus*, although well placed for sea-going traffic, was similarly cut off from the markets of north Antrim, and was too remote from the southern centres of manufacture to secure their export trade. Belfast, on the other hand, after the opening of the Lagan Canal, and improvement of the harbour, was admirably fitted to be a focus of trade with England.

(v.) In the north and west of *co. Tyrone* there were some markets, such as those of Strabane and Omagh (beyond the range of this map), which were separated by the Sperrin Mts. and other masses of highlands from the trading connexions of east Tyrone. They had better communications with Londonderry, and sent a large part of their cloth there for distribution.

(vi.) *Machine Spinning.* It is interesting to notice where the first spinning mills were erected. They appeared on the Antrim coast (at Cushendall), in north Antrim, the centre of Down, south Armagh, and Tyrone. In all these districts, even high up in the hill-country, there is much flax cultivation to-day, and there would certainly be abundant supplies of raw material early in the nineteenth century. We may conclude that the combination of raw material and water-power decided the position of the early spinning mills.

(vii.) *Roads.* The roads shown in this map are those marked in the *Maps of the Roads of Ireland*, by Taylor and Skinner, published in 1778.

APPENDIX IV

BIBLIOGRAPHY

I. MANUSCRIPTS

(a) *In the Public Record Office, Dublin.*

Proceedings of the Board of Trustees of the Linen Manufacture in Ireland, 1711–1828. The years from 1711–37 are adequately covered by the printed *Precedents and Abstracts* (q. v.). From 1784 onwards the *Proceedings* were printed. But the records of the intervening years are only to be found in manuscript volumes in the Public Record Office, Dublin.[1] The minutes reflect the irregular methods of the Trustees and their officials, but the volumes are well indexed.

Census Returns of 1821. Summaries of the census returns were printed, but the original, detailed statements made by enumerators for each parish, are far more valuable. The original summaries, from which copies were

---

[1] The present tense is retained here, but I fear that these documents are now destroyed.

printed, are in manuscript in the Irish Record Office. They only give genera-lized information, such as the numbers employed in each townland and parish in manufacture or agriculture, without distinguishing the trades. The original returns, on the other hand, give a remarkably vivid picture of the whole countryside. They show the whole of town and village society, the doctors, schoolmasters, clergy, and gentry, small shopkeepers, weavers, reed and shuttle makers, and sealmasters. They give the size of every farmstead and the occupation of every member of the household. In glancing over the pages one can see clearly how manufacture was still spread all over the country, and spinning or embroidery was carried on by nearly all women. Besides the important economic facts which can be deduced from the census, and are dealt with in the foregoing chapters, many vivid details of the daily life of the people are brought incidentally into the lists. A widow of seventy-four tries to support herself with spinning, while her son, who is blind, goes out as a wandering fiddler. Another widow has a son, nine years of age, who works as a chimney-sweep. A young wife, classed like all the rest as a spinner, has to maintain her husband, who is ' in a decline '. At times the record is brighter. It is said of one woman : ' To the best of my knowledge she is about eighteen stone weight.' Another woman is described, by a conscientious enumerator, as an idler. Often the word ' weaver ' is spelt phonetically as ' waver '. An enumerator sometimes breaks into descriptions of scenery : ' Here is a little lough in the shape of a pair of spectacles.' The census as a whole was admirably organized. The original MSS. are bound in thick quarto volumes—on an average one or two parishes to each volume.

Official Papers (1st series, 1760–89 ; 2nd series, 1790–1831). Miscellaneous documents in the Record Office and Dublin Castle, made up in bundles. In recent years manuscript catalogues have been made. The documents contain many incidental references to trade.

(b) In the Public Record Office, London.

> *Treasury :*   *Out-Letters,* T. 14, 24. Correspondence relating to Irish affairs, 1826–30.
> ,,   *Reports from Commissioners of Accounts* (Audit Office), A.O. 17, 428. Detailed annual statements of revenue and expenditure of the Linen Board, from 1816.
> *Home Office :* H.O. 100, 216. Correspondence relating to Ireland. The most useful documents are the collection dealing with distress in Ireland in 1826.

(c) Private. Ledgers and *Cash Book* of J. & J. Richardson. These books are described in Chapter XIII.

II. OFFICIAL AND SEMI-OFFICIAL PUBLICATIONS.

Statutes at large (Ireland), for full text of the acts relating to the Linen Trade. *Statutes at large* (Great Britain).

Irish Statutes, revised edition (W. F. Cullinan, ed. 1885), contains only a summary of most of the linen laws.

The statutes from 1703 to 1738 were reprinted in a convenient form in a small, black-letter volume, entitled *Linen Laws.*

An *Abstract of the Linen Laws* was issued in 1784 ; and in 1808 G. P. Bush, the Attorney to the Linen Board, made a *Digested Abridgement* for the Board's use. These works were arranged under subject headings, and are therefore less useful to historical students than the chronological collections.

Journals of the Irish House of Commons, give several reports on the linen trade, summaries of debates and petitions, etc. which contain many useful side-lights. The indexes are very full. In this work references are given, for all Parliamentary proceedings down to 1760, to the second edition, published in 1763. The later volumes, down to 1800, were issued at irregular intervals.

Journals of the Irish House of Lords, have a few special reports which were not communicated to the House of Commons.

Precedents and Abstracts, a selection from the *Proceedings* of the Linen Board, 1711-37, gives a very useful survey of the Board's work during the period when the trade was growing to prime importance, and the Board was making its chief constructive experiments. This volume is well indexed. It was published in 1784.

Proceedings of the Linen Board, annual volumes from 1784 to 1828, printed from the MS. volumes.

Reports of (English) Parliamentary Committees on the linen trade, 1744, 1751, and 1773 : *House of Commons Reports*, vols. ii and iii. The committees themselves were of little importance : they were summoned to deal with slumps in trade, and on each occasion the witnesses were chiefly concerned to persuade Parliament to prohibit foreign competition. But evidence was collected from all parts of the British Isles, and a good deal of it is of historical interest, though more so for English and Scottish than for Irish trade.

Reports of Inspectors to the Linen Board :

Robert Stephenson's *Considerations on the Present State of the Linen Manufacture*, 1754 ; *Journal of a Tour of Inspection* in the southern provinces, June to September, 1755 ; *Inquiry into the State and Progress of the Linen Manufacture of Ireland*, 1757 ; *Letter to the Trustees*, 1759 ; *Reports and Observations*, 1760-1, 1762-3. These papers are the best material for the middle years of the eighteenth century, containing the first-hand evidence of the most competent observer in Ireland. Stephenson published in later years, *Observations on the Present State of the Linen Trade of Ireland* (1784), and a second *Letter to the Trustees* (1789). John Greer, *Report on the State of the Linen Markets of Ulster*, 1784. A short but useful record. Greer was the first Inspector-General for Ulster, appointed under the terms of the Act of 1782. Peter Besnard, *Report of a Tour of Inspection* through Leinster, Munster, and Connaught, 1817. Fuller and more graphic. Besnard was an Inspector-General for the southern provinces. James Corry, Secretary to the Linen Board, *Report of a Tour of Inspection* through the Province of Ulster, 1817 ; *Reports on the Linen Markets of Ulster*, 1821, 1822 ; *Account of Flaxseed Imported and Sown*, 1824.

William Marshall (Inspector-General for Ulster), *Report of a Tour in Yorkshire and Scotland*, 1817.

These reports, taken together, form some of the best evidence of progress and organization between 1750 and 1825.

Statistical Surveys of counties, by various writers, published by the Royal Dublin Society between 1800 and 1820. They deal chiefly with agriculture, which was the Dublin Society's main interest, but there are many allusions to manufacture. These volumes are, and were meant to be, similar to the semi-official surveys made at the same time in England and Scotland. The most useful volumes for the study of the linen industry are :

Dubourdieu, Rev. J.	. .	*Antrim*, 2 vols., 1812.
,, ,,	. .	*Down*, 1802.
Coote, Sir Charles	. .	*Armagh*, 1804.
,, ,,	. .	*Monaghan*, 1801.
Sampson, G. V.	. .	*Londonderry*, 1802.

Some use has also been made of Coote's surveys of *King's County* (1801) and *Queen's County* (1801), Dutton's *Clare*, Tighe's *Kilkenny*, and Welde's *Roscommon* ; but these naturally contain few allusions to the linen trade. Twenty surveys in all were published at various times.

Bradshaw, T., *Belfast and Lisburn Directory*, 1819. Besides alphabetical and trade directories, contains a good deal of descriptive and historical matter.

Dublin Directories (Wilson's and Thom's).

III. Books and Pamphlets Published before 1825.

Temple, Sir Wm., *Essay upon the Advantages of Trade in Ireland*, 1673 (*Miscellanea*, Pt. i, pp. 97–145).

Crommelin, Louis, *Essay towards the Improving of the Hempen and Flaxen Manufactures of Ireland*, 1705.

Hall, Richard, *Observations on the Methods used in Holland in Cultivating or Raising of Hemp and Flax*, 1724.

Dobbs, Arthur, *Essay upon the Trade and Improvement of Ireland*, 1729.
(The references to Dobbs's essay given above are to the reprint in *Thom's Tracts*, vol. ii.)

Prior, Thomas, *List of Absentees of Ireland*, 1729.
Other editions 1769, 1783. References are given to the second edition.
Observations on the Trade of Ireland, 1749. (These two essays were also reprinted in *Thom's Tracts*.)

Carte, Thomas, *History of the Life of James, Duke of Ormond*, 2 vols., 1736.

Anon., *Thoughts on the Importance of the Linen Manufacture to Ireland*, 1739.

Harris, *The Ancient and Present State of the County of Down*, 1744.

Cox, Sir Richard, *Letter to Thomas Prior* showing a sure method to establish the Linen Manufacture, 1749.

Pamphlets on the dispute of 1762:

Reasons against the Brown Seals, 1762. (An imaginary dialogue in verse between drapers in the Dublin Linen Hall, written with a good deal of humour and ability, in the manner of 'Hudibras'.)

A Review of Evils that have prevailed in the Linen Manufacture of Ireland, 1762.

A Brief State of the Debate concerning the Sealing of Brown Linens, 1763.

Observations upon the Linen Trade, humbly submitted to . . . the Trustees of the Linen Manufacture, by the Drapers of Belfast, 1763.

Observations on Materials for a New Linen Bill . . . by the Weavers of Belfast and Lisburn, 1763. The 'Materials for a New Linen Bill' had been presented to the Trustees by Williamson & Bell in February, 1763 : I do not know of any extant copy.

Taylor & Skinner, *Maps of the Roads of Ireland*, 1778.

Hutchinson, J. Hely, *Commercial Restraints of Ireland considered*, 1779.

Young, Arthur, *Tour in Ireland*, 1780.

Nevill, John, *Seasonable Remarks* on the Linen Trade of Ireland, 1783.

Merchant, C. S., *Informations to the People of Ireland* concerning the linen trade of Spain, Portugal, and the Spanish West Indies, 1790.

Latocnaye, *A Frenchman's Walk through Ireland*, 1799 (translated by J. Stevenson, 1917).

Oddy, J. J., *European Commerce*, 1805.

Macpherson, D., *Annals of Commerce*, 4 vols., 1805.

Newenham, Thomas, *Statistical and Historical Inquiry* into . . . the Population of Ireland, 1805.
View of the Natural, Political and Commercial Circumstances of Ireland, 1809.

Stephenson, S. M. (Dr.), *Linen and Hempen Manufacture of Ulster* (in *Select Papers* of the Belfast Literary Society), 1808.

Wakefield, Edward, *Account of Ireland*, statistical and political, 2 vols., 1812.

Williams, W., *Correspondence with the Rt. Hon. Robert Peel*, 1820.

Belfast News Letter, Belfast Commercial Chronicle, Belfast Magazine, Newry Magazine.

IV. Modern Works on the Linen Trade.

McCall, Hugh, *Our Staple Manufactures*, 1855. A second edition, entitled *Ireland and Her Staple Manufactures*, 1865. References are given to the first edition. Contains a large amount of useful information, with hardly any attempt at arrangement.

Charley, W., *Flax and its Products in Ireland*, 1862. A short work, chiefly on the technique of flax production and manufacture, but with many allusions to methods and organization of trade.

Warden, A. J., *The Linen Trade, Ancient and Modern*, 1867. A standard work, written by a Scottish manufacturer. Includes all counties and periods, but only gives a slight chronological account of developments before the nineteenth century.

Horner, John, *The Linen Trade of Europe* during the Spinning-Wheel period, 1920. A very useful work, expanded from a guide to the magnificent collection of distaffs, wheels and other implements presented by the late Mr. Horner to the Belfast Museum. It consists largely of quotations and summaries taken from the chief writers of earlier times, and statistics from official sources, some of them, such as the figures of exports from Russia, by no means easy of access.

Lectures on Commerce and Industry given in Queen's University, Belfast, 1918. Contains five lectures on the Linen Trade, by various writers.

Moore, A. S., *Linen from the Raw Material to the Finished Product*, 1914. *Linen*, 1922. Interesting and well-informed works. The second is larger and more detailed.

V. Miscellaneous.

Ashley, Sir W. J., *British Industries*, 1903 (see Patterson).
Benn, G., *History of the Town of Belfast*, 1823 (second edition, 1877–80).
Blok, W., *History of the People of the Netherlands*, 1898, etc.
Bonn, M. J., *Die englische Kolonisation in Irland*, 2 vols., 1906.
Bradbury, F., *The Linen Industry*, in *Textiles* (ed. A. F. Barker), 1910.
Bremner, D., *The Industries of Scotland*, 1869.
Butler, W. F. T., *Confiscation in Irish History*, 1917.
Chart, D. A., *The Story of Dublin*, 1907.
 Ireland from the Union to Catholic Emancipation, 1910.
 Economic History of Ireland, 1920.
Clapham, J. H., *The Economic Development of France and Germany*, 1921.
Connolly, G., *Labour in Ireland*.
Daniels, G. W., *The Early English Cotton Industry*, 1920.
Dillon, M., *History and Development of Banking in Ireland*, 1889.
Dufferin and Ava, Marquis of, *Irish Emigration and the Tenure of Land*, 1867.
Froude, J. A., *The English in Ireland in the Eighteenth Century*, 3 vols., 1872–4.
Hager, K., *Flachs und Hanf, und ihre Verarbeitung im Bündner Oberland* (*Jahrbuch des Schweizer Alpenclubs*), 1918.
Hancock, J., *Letter to Sir M. Hicks Beach*, 1877.
Heaton, H., *Yorkshire Woollen and Worsted Industries*, 1920.
Hill, Rev. G., *An Historical Account of the Plantation in Ulster*, 1877.
Hume, A., *Spinning and Weaving, their Influence on Language and Literature, Historical Notices of Spinning and Weaving*. Both these essays were reprinted in 1876 from the *Ulster Journal of Archaeology* (nos. xviii and xix).
Kane, R., *Industrial Resources of Ireland*, 1844.
Lecky, W. E. H., *History of Ireland in the Eighteenth Century*, 5 vols., 1892.

Lewinski, J. S., *L'Évolution industrielle de la Belgique*, 1911.

Lewis, S., *Topographical Dictionary of Ireland*, 3 vols., 1837.

M'Skimin, S., *History and Antiquities of Carrickfergus*, third edition, revised by E. J. M'Crum, 1909.

Marmion, A., *Ancient and Modern History of the Maritime Ports of Ireland*, 1855.

Mavor, *Economic History of Russia*, 2 vols.

Montgomery, W. E., *Land Tenure in Ireland*, 1889.

Murphy, J. N., *Ireland, Industrial, Political and Social*, 1870.

Murray, A. E., *History of the Commercial and Financial Relations between Great Britain and Ireland*, 1903.

Nicholls, Sir G., *History of the Irish Poor Law*, 1856.

O'Brien, G., *Economic History of Ireland in the Seventeenth Century*.
Economic History of Ireland in the Eighteenth Century.

Oldham, C. H., *The Irish Woollen Industry*, 1909.

O'Reilly, S., *The Dublin Linen Hall, its Times and Neighbourhood*, 1914.

Owen, D. G., *History of the Port of Belfast*, 1918.
History of Belfast, 1921.

Patterson, Sir R. L., *British Flax and Linen Industry* (in Ashley's *British Industries*), 1903.

Pim, Jonathan, *Condition and Prospects of Ireland*, 1848.

Pirenne, H., *Histoire de Belgique*, 1900, etc.

Probyn, J. W. (ed.), *Land Systems of various Countries*, 1881. (See especially chapters on Ireland by Judge Longfield ; and Holland and Belgium by E. de Lavaleye.)

Posthumus, N. W. (ed.), *Bijdragen tot de economische Geschiedenis van Nederland*, vol. i, 1916.
(Essay by J. Goldberg, *Nederlandsche Textielindustrie*.)

Riordan, E. J., *Modern Irish Trade and Industry*, 1920.

Rowntree, B. S., *Life and Labour, Lessons from Belgium*, 1910.

Salmon, J., *Early Irish Bankers and Banking* (*New Ireland Review*, vol. xii, nos. 2 and 3, Oct. and Nov. 1899).

Scott, W. R., *History, Constitution, and Finance of Joint-Stock Companies*, 3 vols.

Smiles, S., *The Huguenots . . . in England and Ireland*, 1889.
Invention and Industry, 1884.

Smith, F. W., *Irish Linen Trade Handbook and Directory*, 1876.

Tarlé, E., *L'Industrie dans les Campagnes en France*, 1910.

Tooke, T., *History of Prices*, 6 vols., 1837, etc.

Watson, E., *Royal Mail to Ireland*, 1917.

Westerfield, R. B., *Middlemen in English Business*, 1915.

Young, R. M., *The Town Book of Belfast*, 1892.

Zimmermann, A., *Blüthe und Verfall des Leinengewerbes in Schlesien*, 1885.

INDEX

PRINTED IN GREAT BRITAIN
AT THE UNIVERSITY PRESS, OXFORD
BY VIVIAN RIDLER
PRINTER TO THE UNIVERSITY

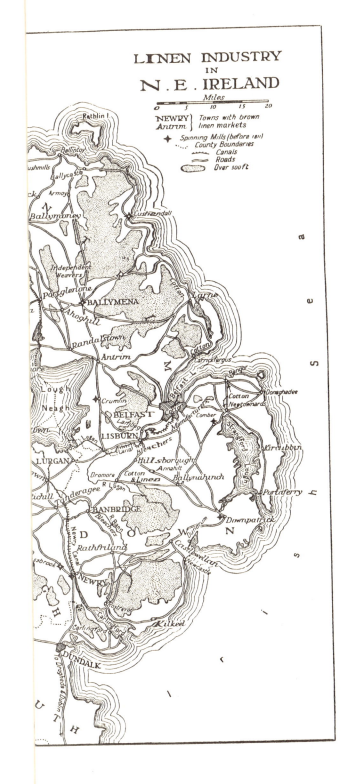